THE COLLECTED PLAYS
II
THE TRAGEDIES AND TRAGIC-COMEDIES

The Coole Edition
General Editors:
T. R. Henn, C.B.E., Litt.D.
Colin Smythe, M.A.

THE TRAGEDIES AND TRAGIC-COMEDIES OF LADY GREGORY, BEING THE SECOND VOLUME OF THE COLLECTED PLAYS

edited and with a foreword by
Ann Saddlemyer

COLIN SMYTHE
GERRARDS CROSS
1979

Copyright © 1971 The Lady Gregory Estate
Foreword Copyright © 1971 Colin Smythe Ltd.

First published in one volume on 1 March 1971
by Colin Smythe Ltd, Gerrards Cross, Buckinghamshire
as the sixth volume of the Coole Edition
ISBN 0–900675–30–6

First published in paperback format in 1979

British Library Cataloguing in Publication Data

Gregory, Isabella Augusta, *Lady*
    The collected plays
    2: The tragedies and tragicomedies of Lady
    Gregory – Coole ed.
    I. Title   II. Saddlemyer, Ann
    822′.9′12   PR4728.G5A19

    ISBN 0–86140–017–8

Printed in Great Britain

FOREWORD

"Those who serve Ireland take for their lot lasting battles—lasting quarrels. They are building, and ever building; and ever and always ruin comes upon them before the house is built."

(*Prologue to* Kincora, *1905*)

Nowhere does Lady Gregory's love of country show itself more clearly than in her tragedies and the closely related history plays. They begin with the keen, that formal lament celebrating a passion of grief that extends beyond the personal sorrow of the bereaved into the depths of the race itself. In the simple song of sorrow in the shadow of Galway gaol, as in the wailing of McDonough's pipes, can be heard Lady Gregory's plea for the return to Ireland of an ancient dignity. In the personal story of the idealist and his dream, frequently set within the facts and myths of the nation, can be felt as well the dramatist's own ambition for her art and for Ireland. "We are the music makers. And we are the dreamers of dreams . . .", she writes in her notes to *McDonough's Wife*; it is appropriate that she includes in her catalogue of image-makers the old piper of Roxborough, whose music had followed her from the great sheep-shearing festivals of her ancestral home to Coole for the celebration first of her wedding, later of her son's coming of age.

It is hardly surprising, given Ireland's own story, that tragedy and the history play should be so closely linked. But even so, as Lennox Robinson once observed, Lady Gregory's preference in history had always been for "the noble and, perhaps, fated." Apparently her favourites among her own plays were *The Gaol Gate* and *The Image*, and she has herself admitted that although she wrote comedies because they were needed, "tragedy is easier." In the tragic form, with the character of comedy deliberately left out, one could celebrate strength where "fate itself is the protagonist." "You may let your hero kick or struggle, but he is in the claws all the time." The same realism which forbade sentiment to prevail in comedy decrees that tragedy and failure stalk those who aspire to free their people or, less heroically, hold the "heart-secret" of the image-maker. The fate of Brian in *Kincora*, Sarsfield in *The White Cockade*, Moses/Parnell in *The Deliverer*, Grania, Don Quixote, as of Malachi Naughton and Peggy Mahon, the two cracked myth-makers of *The Image*, is to learn that inexorable truth, "the more ecstatic the vision the more impossible its realisation."

But although doomed to failure, there is excitement in the dream itself and exultation in the strength of the dreamer. Lady Gregory's note to the one published play she would not allow to be produced in her lifetime reveals more of the author herself than she would perhaps have cared to admit; it also indicates the precise point in her plays at which personal tragedy and public history intersect: "I think I turned to Grania because so many have written about sad, lovely Deirdre, who when overtaken by sorrow made no good battle at the last. Grania had more power of will, and for good or evil twice took the shaping of her life into her own hands." Similarly her dedications to the plays of this volume indicate a personal commitment not noticeable in her comedies: *The Image* to her nephews Hugh Lane and John Shawe-Taylor, "Image-Makers"; the first series of folk-history plays, "concerning strong people of the world", to Theodore Roosevelt, "one of the world's strong men"; the second series to yet another strong American, John Quinn, "best friend best helper." And haunting all her plays, openly admitted as hero of one, is her generation's greatest dreamer and most tragic figure, Ireland's dead King, Charles Stewart Parnell.

The Deliverer is the only bitter play Lady Gregory wrote. It may well be her sorrow at the failure of her own people to follow Parnell's star that led her to include it in the volume labelled "tragic-comedies," alongside the most farcical of all her history plays, *The White Cockade* and *The Canavans*, where the "non-heroes" are weaklings who refuse to accept either the rôle put upon them by the people or the consequences of their own actions. The only admirable character in either play is Patrick Sarsfield, the loyal young captain whose ambition to have his name "set in clean letters in the book of the people" results in only disappointment and shame.

It is, however, *Kincora*, the first of her folk-history plays and the one which caused her most difficulty in the writing, that expresses most clearly Lady Gregory's own evaluation of the fate of the image-maker. Gormleith, the queen whose restlessness plunged her country again and again into battle, remarks, "Ireland has been fighting these ten thousand years, and that custom to be changed, it is likely she would go to nothing," a sentiment the old Kiltartan Jew Malachi later echoes. Brian the High King speaks for all dreamers, "I will make an end of quarrels. I will make an end of this custom of death answering to death through the generations," but lives to see that dream mocked. And the prophecy of the old Beggarwoman is heard again in the words of mad Lady Dereen and The Travelling Man: "Those that hear that music will never be satisfied in any place where it is not found." Out of this tension between history and the dream, myth and destiny, Lady Gregory wove her interpretations of Ireland's story and prepared the way for her later wonder plays.

Dervorgilla is left alone to face "the swift, unflinching, terrible judgment of the young," and that play was written as protest against the hiring of an English stage-manager at the Abbey Theatre. It was to the young the author also addressed herself in these history plays, for, as she explains in *Our Irish Theatre*, she saw her work as part of a greater plan: ". . . I had had from the beginning a vision of historical plays being sent by us through all the counties of Ireland. For to have a real success and to come into the life of the country, one must touch a real and eternal emotion, and history comes only next to religion in our country. And although the realism of our young writers is taking the place of fantasy and romance in the cities, I still hope to see a little season given up every year to plays on history and in sequence at the Abbey, and I think schools and colleges may ask to have them sent and played in their halls, as a part of the day's lesson."

From the beginning, too, she exulted in the contribution their theatre made to the greater literary revolution in Ireland, "the discovery, the disclosure of the folk-learning, the folk-poetry, the folk-tradition." One cannot look therefore in these "folk-history plays" for fidelity to the commonly accepted textbook versions of the battles of Clontarf and the Boyne, the characters of King James and Queen Elizabeth, the feats of Finn, Brian, or Sarsfield; instead, as her notes indicate, she turned to "the book of the people". In fact the play which caused her so much trouble that she had to call on both Yeats and Synge for help was *Kincora*, of which she ruefully admits, "I think I kept too closely to history."

For this reason, in addition to the technical problems of a small stage and few players, she ignores "the middling class," which rarely exists in folk history, and concentrates only on servants and kings. Later she was proudly to report, "When my *White Cockade* was first produced I was pleased to hear that J. M. Synge had said my method had made the writing of historical drama again possible." The language also is of the people, faithfully following the "Kiltartan" adopted from the speech of her own district, where grammatical formulas and the transposition of Irish thoughts into

English idiom create a slightly archaic flavour well suited to her subject. Again, she could point with justifiable pride to Synge's acknowledgement of her use of the dialect which "he had been trying to master."

She was particularly fortunate, perhaps more so than her two colleagues, in her players. During the early years of the Abbey Theatre, success of *The Gaol Gate* and *Dervorgilla* especially can be traced directly to the golden voice of Sara Allgood. When Lady Gregory turned once again, therefore, to a patriotic subject, she thought of Sally, and wrote to her from Coole on 15 September 1923:

"I enclose the poem. It is strange that I began to make it up in Sept. '21, in the train, coming from Dublin on one of the first days of the Truce, and I made up the last lines, or the four beginning 'This is our Rosary of praise' in the train last Wednesday as I came home. I am sure you would make a fine thing of the recitation of them.

Have you one of the old Galway rosaries, with dark and silver beads? They are not to be had now, but I have one to give you. Don't give a copy of the lines to anyone, but if they would help peace, you may read them."[1]

In the last hours of 1923, Sara Allgood recited "The Old Woman Remembers" from the stage of Dublin's Abbey Theatre. Once again, private mythology and public history became one.

Ann Saddlemyer

1. This letter is in the possession of the Sligo County Library, by whose permission and that of Major Richard Gergory, it is here quoted. See Appendix for variant readings.

THE PLAYS OF LADY GREGORY
HISTORY OF FIRST PRODUCTIONS BY THE ABBEY
THEATRE COMPANY AND PUBLICATION DATES

Colman and Guaire [1901]. Not produced. Published under title *My First Play* (London: Elkin Mathews and Marrot, 1930).

A Losing Game. Not produced. Published only in *The Gael* (New York), December 1902.

Twenty-Five [*A Losing Game* revised]. Produced 14 March 1903. Never published.

The Poorhouse (with Douglas Hyde). Produced 3 April 1907. Published in *Samhain*, September 1903; with *Spreading the News* and *The Rising of the Moon* as Vol. IX of Abbey Theatre Series (First Series) (Dublin: Maunsel, 1906).

The Rising of the Moon. Produced 9 March 1907. Published in *Samhain*, December 1904; with *Spreading the News* and *The Poorhouse* as Vol. IX of Abbey Theatre Series (First Series) (Dublin: Maunsel, 1906); and included in *Seven Short Plays* (Dublin: Maunsel, 1909).

Spreading the News. Produced 27 December 1904. Published in *Samhain*, November 1905; with *The Rising of the Moon* and *The Poorhouse* as Vol. IX of Abbey Theatre Series (First Series) (Dublin: Maunsel, 1906); and included in *Seven Short Plays* (Dublin: Maunsel, 1909).

Kincora. First version produced 25 March 1905; revised version 11 February 1909. Published as Vol. II of Abbey Theatre Series (First Series) (Dublin: The Abbey Theatre, 1905); revised form in *Irish Folk-History Plays First Series* (New York and London: Putnam, 1912).

The White Cockade. Produced 9 December 1905. Published as Vol. VIII of Abbey Theatre Series (First Series) (Dublin:

Maunsel, 1906); included in *Irish Folk-History Plays Second Series* (New York and London: Putnam, 1912).

Hyacinth Halvey. Produced 19 February 1906. Published in *Samhain*, December 1906; and included in *Seven Short Plays* (Dublin: Maunsel, 1909).

The Doctor in Spite of Himself (from Molière). Produced 16 April 1906. Published in *The Kiltartan Molière* (Dublin: Maunsel, 1910).

The Gaol Gate. Produced 20 October 1906. Published in *Seven Short Plays* (Dublin: Maunsel, 1909).

The Canavans. Produced 8 December 1906; revised version produced 31 October 1907. Published in *Irish Folk-History Plays Second Series* (New York and London: Putnam, 1912).

The Jackdaw. Produced 23 February 1907. Published in *Seven Short Plays* (Dublin: Maunsel, 1909).

Dervorgilla. Produced 31 October 1907. Published in *Samhain*, November 1908; included in *Irish Folk-History Plays First Series* (New York and London: Putnam, 1912).

The Unicorn from the Stars (with W. B. Yeats [a re-working of *Where There is Nothing* written by Yeats in 1912 with the help of Lady Gregory and Douglas Hyde]. Produced 21 November 1907. Published in *The Unicorn from the Stars and Other Plays* (New York: Macmillan, 1908) and included in the Third Volume of *The Collected Works of William Butler Yeats* (Stratford-on-Avon: Shakespeare Head Press, 1908).

Teja (from Sudermann). Produced 19 March 1908. Never published.

The Rogueries of Scapin (from Molière). Produced 4 April 1908. Published in *The Kiltartan Molière* (Dublin: Maunsel, 1910).

The Workhouse Ward [*The Poorhouse* revised]. Produced 20 April 1908. Published in *Seven Short Plays* (Dublin: Maunsel, 1909).

The Travelling Man. Produced 2 March 1910. Published in *Seven Short Plays* (Dublin: Maunsel, 1909).

The Miser (from Molière). Produced 21 January 1909. Published in *The Kiltartan Molière* (Dublin: Maunsel, 1910).

The Image. Produced 11 November 1909. Published as Vol. I of Abbey Theatre Series (Second Series) Dublin: Maunsel, 1910).

Mirandolina (from Goldoni). Produced 24 February 1910. Published separately (London and New York: Putnam, 1924).

The Full Moon. Produced 10 November 1910. Published by the Author at the Abbey Theatre, 1911; included in *New Comedies* (New York and London: Putnam, 1913).

Coats. Produced 1 December 1910. Published in *New Comedies* (New York and London: Putnam, 1913).

The Deliverer. Produced 12 January 1911. Published in *Irish Folk-History Plays Second Series* (New York and London: Putnam, 1912).

Grania. Not produced. Published in *Irish Folk-History Plays First Series* (New York and London: Putnam, 1912).

McDonough's Wife. Produced 11 January 1912. Published in *New Comedies* (New York and London: Putnam, 1913).

The Bogie Men. Produced 4 July 1912 at the Court Theatre, London. Published in *New Comedies* (New York and London: Putnam, 1913). Later revised.

Damer's Gold. Produced 21 November 1912. Published in *New Comedies* (New York and London: Putnam, 1913).

The Wrens. Produced 1 June 1914 at the Court Theatre, London. Published in *The Image and Other Plays* (London: Putnam, 1922).

Shanwalla. Produced 8 April 1915. Published in *The Image and Other Plays* (London: Putnam, 1922). Later revised.

The Golden Apple. Produced 6 January 1920. Published separately (London: John Murray, 1916).

The Dragon. Produced 21 April 1919. Published separately (Dublin: Talbot Press, 1920); included in *Three Wonder Plays* (London: Putnam: 1923).

Hanrahan's Oath. Produced 29 January 1918. Published in *The Image and Other Plays* (London: Putnam, 1922).

The Jester. Not produced professionally. Published in *Three Wonder Plays* (London: Putnam, 1923).

Aristotle's Bellows. Produced 17 March 1921. Published in *Three Wonder Plays* (London: Putnam, 1923).

The Old Woman Remembers. Produced 31 December 1923. Published in *The Irish Statesman,* 22 March 1924; included in *A Little Anthology of Modern Irish Verse,* selected by Lennox Robinson (Dublin: Cuala Press, 1928).

The Story Brought By Brigit. Produced 15 April 1924. Published separately (London and New York: Putnam, 1924).

On the Racecourse [a re-writing of *Twenty-Five*]. Not produced. Published separately (London and New York: Putnam, 1926).

The Would-Be Gentleman (from Molière). Produced 4 January 1926. Published in *Three Last Plays* (London and New York: Putnam, 1928).

Sancho's Master. Produced 14 March 1927. Published in *Three Last Plays* (London and New York: Putnam, 1928).

Dave. Produced 9 May 1927. Published in *Three Last Plays* (London and New York: Putnam, 1928).

PLAYS UNPUBLISHED AND UNPRODUCED

Michelin
The Meadow Gate
The Dispensary
The Shoelace
The Lighted Window
Heads or Harps (with W. B. Yeats)

CONTENTS

DEDICATIONS

Lady Gregory grouped *Grania, Kincora* and *Dervorgilla* together for her dedication.

These three plays concerning strong people of the world I offer to Theodore Roosevelt one of the world's strong men.

The Canavans, The White Cockade and *The Deliverer* were dedicated to:

Dear John Quinn, best friend, best helper these half-score years on this side of the sea.

New York, February 1912.

Of *The Image*, Lady Gregory wrote:

When this play was first printed eleven years ago I dedicated it "to my nephews, Hugh Lane and John Shawe-Taylor, image-makers," as I now do to their dear memory.

1922.

The Tragedies

THE GAOL GATE

THE GAOL GATE

PERSONS
MARY CAHEL. *An old woman.*
MARY CUSHIN. *Her daughter-in-law.*
THE GATEKEEPER.

SCENE. *Outside the gate of Galway Gaol. Two countrywomen, one in a long dark cloak, the other with a shawl over her head, have just come in. It is just before dawn.*

MARY CAHEL. I am thinking we are come to our journey's end, and that this should be the gate of the gaol.

MARY CUSHIN. It is certain it could be no other place. There was surely never in the world such a terrible great height of a wall.

MARY CAHEL. He that was used to the mountain to be closed up inside of that! What call had he to go moonlighting or to bring himself into danger at all?

MARY CUSHIN. It is no wonder a man to grow faint-hearted and he shut away from the light. I never would wonder at all at any-thing he might be driven to say.

MARY CAHEL. There were good men were gaoled before him never gave in to anyone at all. It is what I am thinking, Mary, he might not have done what they say.

MARY CUSHIN. Sure you heard what the neighbours were calling the time their own boys were brought away. "It is Denis Cahel," they were saying, "that informed against them in the gaol."

MARY CAHEL. There is nothing that is bad or is wicked but a woman will put it out of her mouth, and she seeing them that belong to her brought away from her sight and her home.

MARY CUSHIN. Terry Fury's mother was saying it, and Pat Ruane's mother and his wife. They came out calling it after me, "It was Denis swore against them in the gaol!" The sergeant was boasting, they were telling me, the day he came searching Daire-caol, it was he himself got his confession with drink he had brought him in the gaol.

MARY CAHEL. They might have done that, the ruffians, and the

5

boy have no blame on him at all. Why should it be cast up against him, and his wits being out of him with drink?

MARY CUSHIN. If he did give their names up itself, there was maybe no wrong in it at all. Sure it's known to all the village it was Terry that fired the shot.

MARY CAHEL. Stop your mouth now and don't be talking. You haven't any sense worth while. Let the sergeant do his own business with no help from the neighbours at all.

MARY CUSHIN. It was Pat Ruane that tempted them on account of some vengeance of his own. Every creature knows my poor Denis never handled a gun in his life.

MARY CAHEL (taking from under her cloak a long blue envelope). I wish we could know what is in the letter they are after sending us through the post. Isn't it a great pity for the two of us to be without learning at all?

MARY CUSHIN. There are some of the neighbours have learning, and you bade me not bring it anear them. It would maybe have told us what way he is or what time he will be quitting the gaol.

MARY CAHEL. There is wonder on me, Mary Cushin, that you would not be content with what I say. It might be they put down in the letter that Denis informed on the rest.

MARY CUSHIN. I suppose it is all we have to do so, to stop here for the opening of the door. It's a terrible long road from Slieve Echtge we were travelling the whole of the night.

MARY CAHEL. There was no other thing for us to do but to come and to give him a warning. What way would he be facing the neighbours, and he to come back to Daire-caol?

MARY CUSHIN. It is likely they will let him go free, Mary, before many days will be out. What call have they to be keeping him? It is certain they promised him his life.

MARY CAHEL. If they promised him his life, Mary Cushin, he must live it in some other place. Let him never see Daire-caol again, or Daroda or Druimdarod.

MARY CUSHIN. O, Mary, what place will we bring him to, and we driven from the place that we know? What person that is sent among strangers can have one day's comfort on earth?

MARY CAHEL. It is only among strangers, I am thinking, he could be hiding his story at all. It is best for him to go to America, where the people are as thick as grass.

MARY CUSHIN. What way could he go to America and he having no means in his hand? There's himself and myself to make the voyage and the little one-een at home.

6

MARY CAHEL. I would sooner to sell the holding than to ask for the price paid for blood. There'll be money enough for the two of you to settle your debts and to go.

MARY CUSHIN. And what would yourself be doing and we to go over the sea? It is not among the neighbours you would wish to be ending your days.

MARY CAHEL. I am thinking there is no one would know me in the workhouse at Oughterard. I wonder could I go in there, and I not to give them my name?

MARY CUSHIN. Ah, don't be talking foolishness. What way could I bring the child? Sure he's hardly out of the cradle; he'd be lost out there in the States.

MARY CAHEL. I could bring him into the workhouse, I to give him some other name. You could send for him when you'd be settled or have some place of your own.

MARY CUSHIN. It is very cold at the dawn. It is time for them open the door. I wish I had brought a potato or a bit of a cake or of bread.

MARY CAHEL. I'm in dread of it being opened and not knowing what will we hear. The night that Denis was taken he had a great cold and a cough.

MARY CUSHIN. I think I hear some person coming. There's a sound like the rattling of keys. God and His Mother protect us! I'm in dread of being found here at all!

(*The gate is opened, and the* GATEKEEPER *is seen with a lantern in his hand.*)

GATEKEEPER. What are you doing here, women? It's no place to be spending the night time.

MARY CAHEL. It is to speak with my son I am asking, that is gaoled these eight weeks and a day.

GATEKEEPER. If you have no order to visit him it's as good for you to go away home.

MARY CAHEL. I got this letter ere yesterday. It might be it is giving me leave.

GATEKEEPER. If that's so he should be under the doctor, or in the hospital ward.

MARY CAHEL. It's no wonder if he's down with the hardship, for he had a great cough and a cold.

GATEKEEPER. Give me here the letter to read it. Sure it never was opened at all.

MARY CAHEL. Myself and this woman have no learning. We were loth to trust any other one.

7

GATEKEEPER. It was posted in Galway the twentieth, and this is the last of the month.

MARY CAHEL. We never thought to call at the post office. It was chance brought it to us in the end.

GATEKEEPER (*having read letter*). You poor unfortunate women, don't you know Denis Cahel is dead? You'd a right to come this time yesterday if you wished any last word at all.

MARY CAHEL (*kneeling down*). God and His Mother protect us and have mercy on Denis's soul!

MARY CUSHIN. What is the man after saying? Sure it cannot be Denis is dead?

GATEKEEPER. Dead since the dawn of yesterday, and another man now in his cell. I'll go see who has charge of his clothing if you're wanting to bring it away.

(*He goes in. The dawn has begun to break.*)

MARY CAHEL. There is lasting kindness in Heaven when no kindness is found upon earth. There will surely be mercy found for him, and not the hard judgment of men! But my boy that was best in the world, that never rose a hair of my head, to have died with his name under blemish, and left a great shame on his child! Better for him have killed the whole world than to give any witness at all! Have you no word to say, Mary Cushin? Am I left here to keen him alone?

MARY CUSHIN (*who has sunk on to the step before the door, rocking herself and keening*). Oh, Denis, my heart is broken you to have died with the hard word upon you! My grief you to be alone now that spent so many nights in company!

What way will I be going back through Gort and through Kilbecanty? The people will not be coming out keening you, they will say no prayer for the rest of your soul!

What way will I be the Sunday and I going up the hill to the Mass? Every woman with her own comrade, and Mary Cushin to be walking her lone!

What way will I be the Monday and the neighbours turning their heads from the house? The turf Denis cut lying on the bog, and no well-wisher to bring it to the hearth!

What way will I be in the night time, and none but the dog calling after you? Two women to be mixing a cake, and not a man in the house to break it!

What way will I sow the field, and no man to drive the furrow? The sheaf to be scattered before springtime that was brought together at the harvest!

I would not begrudge you, Denis, and you leaving praises after you. The neighbours keening along with me would be better to me than an estate.

But my grief your name to be blackened in the time of the blackening of the rushes! Your name never to rise up again in the growing time of the year! (*She ceases keening and turns towards the old woman.*) But tell me, Mary, do you think would they give us the body of Denis? I would lay him out with myself only; I would hire some man to dig the grave.

(THE GATEKEEPER *opens the gate and hands out some clothes.*)

GATEKEEPER. There now is all he brought in with him; the flannels and the shirt and the shoes. It is little they are worth altogether; those mountainy boys do be poor.

MARY CUSHIN. They had a right to give him time to ready himself the day they brought him to the magistrates. He to be wearing his Sunday coat, they would see he was a decent boy. Tell me where will they bury him, the way I can follow after him through the street? There is no other one to show respect to him but Mary Cahel, his mother, and myself.

GATEKEEPER. That is not to be done. He is buried since yesterday in the field that is belonging to the gaol.

MARY CUSHIN. It is a great hardship that to have been done, and not one of his own there to follow after him at all.

GATEKEEPER. Those that break the law must be made an example of. Why would they be laid out like a well behaved man? A long rope and a short burying, that is the order for a man that is hanged.

MARY CUSHIN. A man that was hanged! O Denis, was it they that made an end of you and not the great God at all? His curse and my own curse upon them that did not let you die on the pillow! The curse of God be fulfilled that was on them before they were born! My curse upon them that brought harm on you, and on Terry Fury that fired the shot!

MARY CAHEL (*standing up*). And the other boys, did they hang them along with him, Terry Fury and Pat Ruane that were brought from Daire-caol?

GATEKEEPER. They did not, but set them free twelve hours ago. It is likely you may have passed them in the night time.

MARY CUSHIN. Set free is it, and Denis made an end of? What justice is there in the world at all?

9

GATEKEEPER. He was taken near the house. They knew his foot-mark. There was no witness given against the rest worth while.

MARY CAHEL. Then the sergeant was lying and the people were lying when they said Denis Cahel had informed in the gaol?

GATEKEEPER. I have no time to be stopping here talking. The judge got no evidence and the law set them free.

(*He goes in and shuts gate after him.*)

MARY CAHEL (*holding out her hands*). Are there any people in the streets at all till I call on them to come hither? Did they ever hear in Galway such a thing to be done, a man to die for his neighbour?

Tell it out in the streets for the people to hear, Denis Cahel from Slieve Echtge is dead. It was Denis Cahel from Daire-caol that died in the place of his neighbour!

It is he was young and comely and strong, the best reaper and the best hurler. It was not a little thing for him to die, and he protecting his neighbour!

Gather up, Mary Cushin, the clothes for your child; they'll be wanted by this one and that one. The boys crossing the sea in the springtime will be craving a thread for a memory.

One word to the judge and Denis was free, they offered him all sorts of riches. They brought him drink in the gaol, and gold, to swear away the life of his neighbour!

Pat Ruane was no good friend to him at all, but a foolish, wild companion; it was Terry Fury knocked a gap in the wall and sent in the calves to our meadow.

Denis would not speak, he shut his mouth, he would never be an informer. It is no lies he would have said at all giving witness against Terry Fury.

I will go through Gort and Kilbecanty and Druimdarod and Daroda; I will call to the people and the singers at the fairs to make a great praise for Denis!

The child he left in the house that is shook, it is great will be his boast in his father! All Ireland will have a welcome before him, and all the people in Boston.

I to stoop on a stick through half a hundred years, I will never be tired with praising! Come hither, Mary Cushin, till we'll shout it through the roads, Denis Cahel died for his neighbour!

(*She goes off to the left,* MARY CUSHIN *following her.*)

Curtain.

GRANIA

GRANIA

PERSONS
GRANIA.
FINN.
DIARMUID
TWO YOUNG MEN.

ACT I

SCENE. *The scene is laid at Almhuin in Ireland. Time, evening. Inside a richly decorated tent; a fire in brazier centre, a high candlestick on each side; a table with round loaves and wine. An opening at each side of tent.* FINN *is leading in* GRANIA; *she is wearing a golden dress and jewels. Music and joyous shouts are heard outside.*

FINN. My five hundred welcomes to you, Grania, coming into Almhuin.

GRANIA. I thank you, Finn.

FINN. Who would be welcome if it was not the King of Ireland's daughter, that will be my wife to-morrow?

GRANIA. Your people that were outside and on the road lighted all the district with fires as I came.

FINN. We would have been better prepared if your coming was not so sudden at the last. You did not come too soon, that is a thing that could not happen. But the big house of Almhuin will not be set out fit for you till to-morrow, and it is in the tents of our captains you and your company must be sheltered to-night.

GRANIA. It was my father, before going to Lochlann, said he must leave me in a husband's care.

FINN. Who would protect you if I would not?

GRANIA. I am sure of that. Are you not the best of all the world's big men?

FINN. They told me you could have made great marriages, not coming to me?

GRANIA. My father was for the King of Foreign, but I said I would take my own road.

FINN. He has great riches and a great name.

GRANIA. I would have been afraid going to him, hearing talk of him as so dark and wild looking, and his shield tusked with the tusks of a boar.

FINN. You were not in dread coming to me, and you so delicate and so cherished?

GRANIA. I had an old veneration for you, hearing all my lifetime that you are so gentle to women and to dogs and to little children, and you wrestling with the powers of the world and being so hard in war.

FINN. It would be strange any person not to be gentle with you.

GRANIA. And another thing. I had no wish to go travelling forth and hither to strange countries and by strange seas. I have no mind for going through crosses. I would sooner pass my life at Almhuin, where I ever and always heard there are wide white halls and long tables, and poets and fine company.

FINN. Your father has a good house.

GRANIA. There was little to listen to but my father planning the wars in Lochlann. There was no pleasant stir in it, unless what there might be in myself.

FINN. It may be you will tire of Almhuin itself after a while.

GRANIA. There will be good company. I have heard talk of the men and the captains of the Fenians, of Oisin and Osgar and Goll, that came to meet me a while ago.

FINN. The man you will think most of is not with them to-day, that is my own kinsman, Diarmuid.

GRANIA. I heard of him often. They say him to be the best lover of women in the whole world, and the most daring in the war.

FINN. He has a good name from gentle and simple, from the big man and from the poor. Those even that have no call to him, cannot but love him.

GRANIA. It was he fought seven days and seven nights with the terrible wild ox upon the mountains.

FINN. Any time I am tired or fretted, all he could do for me he would not think it enough.

GRANIA. Where is he at this time, that he did not come to meet me with the rest?

FINN. I sent him to a far lonesome hill where I have a secret store of treasures and of jewels. It is right there should be a good man to guard them upon the road. It is for you he is bringing them, he will be here within a short while.

GRANIA. It is likely it is a man of that sort a woman would find it easy to love.

14

FINN. Did you ever give a thought to any man in the way of love?

GRANIA. I did—at least I think I did—but that was a long time ago.

FINN. Who was he? Did he belong to your own place?

GRANIA. I do not know. I never heard his name—but I saw him.

FINN. Did you speak to him?

GRANIA. No, he was but as if a shadow, that came for a moment and was gone.

FINN. Tell me all the story.

GRANIA. They had been hunting—there were a great many strangers. I was bade keep away from the hall. I was looking from a high window—then there was a great outcry in the yard—the hounds were fighting, the hounds the strange men had brought with them. One of them made as if to attack a little dog I owned at the time—I screamed out at the hounds. Then a young man ran out and beat them away, and he held up my little dog to me, laughing, and his cap fell off from his head.

FINN. Did they not tell you his name?

GRANIA. I was shy to ask them, and I never saw him again. But my thoughts went with him for a good while, and sometimes he came through my dreams.—Is that now what you would call love?

FINN. Indeed, I think it is little at all you know of it.

GRANIA. I heard often in the stories of people that were in pain and under locks through love. But I think they are but foolishness. There was one of a lover was made go through a fire for his sweetheart's sake, and came out shivering. And one that climbed to his darling's window by one golden thread of her hair.

FINN. There are many such tales and there are more in the making, for it is likely the tearing and vexing of love will be known so long as men are hot-blooded and women have a coaxing way.

GRANIA. I asked the old people what love was, and they gave me no good news of it at all. Three sharp blasts of the wind they said it was, a white blast of delight and a grey blast of discontent and a third blast of jealousy that is red.

FINN. That red blast is the wickedest of the three.

GRANIA. I would never think jealousy to be so bad a smart.

FINN. It is a bad thing for whoever knows it. If love is to lie down on a bed of stinging nettles, jealousy is to waken upon a wasp's nest.

GRANIA. But the old people say more again about love. They say there is no good thing to be gained without hardship and pain, such as a child to be born, or a long day's battle won. And I think it might be a pleasing thing to have a lover that would go through fire for your sake.

FINN. I knew enough of the heat of love in my time, and I am very glad to have done with it now, and to be safe from its torments and its whip and its scourge.

GRANIA. It being so bad a thing, why, I wonder, do so many go under its sway? That should be a good master that has so many servants and is so well obeyed.

FINN. We do not take it up of ourselves but it sweeps us away before it, and asks no leave. When that blast comes upon us, we are but feathers whirled before it with the dust.

GRANIA. It is a good thing surely, that I will never know an unhappy, unquiet love, but only love for you that will be by my side for ever. (*A loud peal of laughter is heard outside.*) What is that laughter? There is in it some mocking sound.

FINN (*going to the door*). It is not laughter now—it is a merry outcry as if around some very welcome friend. It is Diarmuid that is come back.

(DIARMUID *comes in.* GRANIA *shrinks back from him.*)

DIARMUID. I am here, Finn, my master.

FINN. What way are you, Diarmuid? There is some wound upon your arm.

DIARMUID. It is a wound I was given on the road. But all you sent me for is safe.

FINN. I knew you would mind them well. But was that hurt cared and eased?

DIARMUID. It is nothing to signify. I drove the robbers off. All is safe. They are bringing the bags in here.

(*Two fair-haired young men come in two or three times laying bags on the floor during the next sentences.*)

I will stop here and mind them through the night time. I would sooner keep charge until you will open them for the wedding on the morrow. I will sit there by the hearth. They are jewels would be coveted by the witches of the lakes, or the sea-women sporting among the golden ribs and the wreckage of the ships of Greece.

FINN. It is to a woman worthy of them they are to be given.

DIARMUID. I am sure of that, indeed, and she being worthy to wed with you.

FINN. Come here, Grania, until I make you acquainted with the branch and the blossom of our young men.

GRANIA (*coming forward*). It is—who is it?

16

(*She gives a little cry and goes back a step as* DIARMUID *takes off his cap.*)

FINN. What is it ails you, Grania, that you are turned to be so wild and so shy?

GRANIA. It is that—that—he is wounded.

FINN. You have lost your talk on the road, Diarmuid, you, that were always so ready to string words and praises for comely young women.

DIARMUID. I had no time to wash away the dust and the sweat. I did not know Grania was in the place. You should have fore-warned me.

FINN. He thinks you are vexed because he is not settled out in handsome clothes.

GRANIA. It is strange—it is all strange to me—I will get used to meeting strangers. Another time—in a very short while—my voice will be more steady—my heart will leave starting.

FINN. You will get courage knowing you are a queen. Where, Diarmuid, is the crown I bade you bring? It is not the high crown of pearls from the far Indies I want, but the thin golden crown shaped like the rising sun, that I thought of late would be never used, and that I had been keeping till I met with my own queen and my bride.

DIARMUID. It is wrapped about with tanned marten skins and bound with purple thongs.

FINN (*unwrapping it*). Come to me, Grania. (*He puts the crown on her head.*) Courage will come into your heart now, with this sign and token of your estate.

GRANIA. I am tired. It is weighty on my head—it is time for me to be with myself only. I have seen too much company since morning.

FINN. That is so, and I am much to blame, not taking better thought for you. Come to your women, they will bring you to your tent that is close at hand. You have travelled a long strange road, and to-morrow is your wedding day.

GRANIA. To-morrow? Could it not be put off for a while? This is but May, and no great luck in the moon. There is more luck in the last moon of July—or the first new moon after it. Put it off until that time.

FINN. That cannot be. Your father looked to me to put you in your right place without delay. You must be my wife to-morrow.

GRANIA. Must it be to-morrow?

FINN. All the armies are gathered together for that, and the feasts are ready. You yourself will be ready when you have taken your sleep through the night time.

GRANIA. Sleep—sleep—yes, I will go sleep if I can.

FINN. Diarmuid is tired as well as you.

DIARMUID. I have no desire to sleep. I will sit and watch here till the dawn.

(*He sits down by the hearth, pulling cloak over his head.* GRANIA *turns back to look at him from the door as* FINN *takes her out. After a moment* FINN *comes back and sits near fire.*)

FINN. Tell me, Diarmuid, is it right that a man past the mering of age should give any thought to love?

DIARMUID. It is right for a man with a great burden of care upon him to have a place of his own where he can let it fall from him. And what is a home or a house without a wife and companion at the hearth?

FINN. That is so, and that is what I had in mind at the time this marriage was settled and pressed on, for the good of Ireland and my own good. But as to love, that is another thing.

DIARMUID. It is another thing, sure enough.

FINN. I thought myself on the far side of it and of its trouble and its joy. But now this young girl has come to me, so fearless, so mannerly, so plain and simple in her talk, it seems to me I would wed with her, and she not a king's daughter but a poor girl carrying the bag. (DIARMUID *nods, but is silent.*) It is not the one way with you and me, Diarmuid, for many women have offered you their beauty and themselves; but as for myself, there is no one I ever gave my heart to but was swept from me in some hard way. And this is come like good wine to the mouth that was filled for a long while with grey mist and rain. And indeed, indeed my heart leaps up with her. Is not that natural, Diarmuid, and she so well reared and so young?

DIARMUID. It is natural, indeed.

FINN. Would you not say her to be well shaped and of good blood and wise?

DIARMUID. She is all that, indeed.

FINN. It is not often I have known you to be so begrudging of praise.

DIARMUID. What call have I to be praising her? I could tell you no more than you knew before, through your own heart and through your eyes.

18

FINN. But, tell me this, now. Is she that is so airy and beautiful any sort of a fitting wife for me?

DIARMUID. You are brave and she will put her pride in you. You are the best of all, and she is a woman would only join with the best.

FINN. With all that, I would be well pleased if I could change my years for yours, Diarmuid. I would give you in their place all the riches I have ever won.

DIARMUID. Such a woman will be a right head for Almhuin. She is used to a king's house, she will be open-handed, and open-hearted along with that.

FINN. I think, indeed, she will be a right wife for me, and loyal. And it is well that is so, for if ever any man should come between her thoughts and mine I would not leave him living, but would give him the sorrow of death.

DIARMUID. There is no good lover in Ireland but would do the same, and his wife or his sweetheart failing him.

FINN. Yet, in the end there are but few do it; for the thought of men that have passed their midday is mixed with caution and with wisdom and the work they have in hand, or weakness is gaining on their limbs. And as for youngsters, they do not know how to love, because there is always some to-morrow's love possible in the shadow of the love of to-day. It is only the old it goes through and through entirely, because they know all the last honey of the summer time has come to its ferment in their cup, and that there is no new summer coming to meet them for ever. And so (*he gets up and stirs fire*) they think to carry that cup through life and death and even beyond the grave. But can I bring this young girl to be satisfied with that one love?

DIARMUID. There is no one among the men of Ireland can stand against your will. It should be easy for you to keep a woman faithful.

FINN. Yet the story-tellers make out that love is the disturber; that where it is on the road it is hard to be sure of any woman at all or any friend.

DIARMUID. It is I can give you out an answer to that. My master, you are sure of me.

FINN. I am sure of you, indeed, and it is many a time you put your life in danger for my sake.

DIARMUID (*standing up*). I am your son and your servant always, and your friend. And now, at this marriage time, I will ask one asking.

FINN. Who would get his desire and you not to get it?

DIARMUID. I am tired of courts and of sports and of wars where we gain the day always. I want some hard service to put my hand to. There are the dark men of Foreign, their King has laid it down he will come and master Ireland. Let me go out now and put him down in his own country.

FINN. I will give you leave, but not till after the wedding moon.

DIARMUID. No, but let me go now, this very night, at the brink of dawn.

FINN. No, but stop near me. You are more to me than any of my comrades or my friends.

DIARMUID. It is a strange thing, the first asking I have made, you have refused me.

FINN. Go then and take your own way, and my blessing go with you.

DIARMUID. I thank you for that leave.

FINN. But you will be tired out before morning. You have been on the road these three days, you got no sleep last night.

DIARMUID. I am drowsy enough and tired, but I will go.

FINN. Lie down over there upon the otter skins. I will sit here by the fire and keep a watch in your place.

DIARMUID. Make a promise then, to wake me at the first whitening of the dawn.

FINN. I will do that.

(DIARMUID *lies down on skins and sleeps.* FINN *looks at him a moment and covers him, then puts out candles and sits down where* DIARMUID *had been sitting, pulling his cloak over his head. Silence a moment,* GRANIA *comes in.*)

GRANIA (*in a low voice*). Diarmuid! (*No answer.*) Diarmuid! (*She comes nearer to* FINN *and speaks a little louder.*) Diarmuid, help me! (FINN *slightly moves.*) Give me your help now. I cannot wed with Finn. I cannot go to him as his wife. I do not know what has happened—half an hour ago I was content to go to him. You came in—I knew you—it was you I saw that day at Tara—my heart started like a deer a while ago. There is something gone astray —the thought of Finn is different. What way could I live beside him and my heart, as I am thinking, gone from him? What name might I be calling out in my sleep? (*She goes close to* FINN *and puts her hand on his shoulder.*) Have you no way to help me, Diarmuid? It would be a terrible thing, a wedded woman not to be loyal—to call out another man's name in her sleep. (FINN *gets up and goes back into shadow.*) Oh, do not turn away from me! Do not leave me to the marriage I am in dread of. You will not help me? Is it you, Diarmuid, are failing me, you that came to my help that other time. Is it to fail me you will now? And is it my fault if this strange thing has come upon me, and that there is as if no one in all the world but you? You are angry with me and vexed, and it is a bad day, the day I came into this place. But I am not ashamed. Was it my fault at all? I will light now this candle, I will dare to show you my face. You will see in that I am not come to you as a light woman that turns this way and that way, but that I have given you the love I never gave to any man and never will give to any other! (*She lights candle and holds it up.*)

FINN (*sternly*). Grania!

GRANIA. Oh! It is Finn! And where then is Diarmuid?

FINN. There he is before you. It is the boy lying down and rising with me has betrayed me.

DIARMUID (*moving and starting up*). What is it? What has happened? Is that Grania?

FINN. You were looking for her to come. She was ready and willing. You are well fitted to rear traitors to one another.

DIARMUID. You are out of your wits. I had no thought she was coming here. What brought her?

FINN. Did she come giving you her love unasked? I thought she was a king's daughter.

DIARMUID. She is, and well worthy!

FINN. What was her mother then? Was she some woman of the camp? (*Pushes her from him.*)

DIARMUID (*putting his arm round her*). I will not let any man say that. (*Half draws sword.*)

FINN. My life is a little thing beside what you have taken!

DIARMUID. You are talking folly. You never found a lie after me in any sort of way. But the time courage was put in your heart there was madness furrowed in your brain!

FINN. Was it every whole minute of your life you were false to me?

DIARMUID. You would not have said that, the day I freed you from the three Kings of the Island of the Floods.

FINN. It is quickly you have been changed by a false woman's flattering words!

GRANIA. It is not his fault! It is mine! It is on me the blame is entirely! It is best for me to go out a shamed woman. But I will not go knocking at my father's door! I will find some quick way to quiet my heart for ever. Forgive me, Finn, and I have more cause yet to ask you to forgive me, Diarmuid. And if there were hundreds brought together this day for my wedding, it is likely there will be at my burying but the plover and the hares of the bog! (*Goes towards door.*)

DIARMUID (*seizing her*). I will not let you go out this way. I will not fail you!

FINN. There is all your talk of faith to me gone down the wind!

DIARMUID. I will not forsake her, but I will keep my faith with you. I give my word that if I bring her out of this, it is as your queen I will bring her and show respect to her, till such time as your anger will have cooled and that you will let her go her own road. It is not as a wife I will bring her, but I will keep my word to you, Finn.

FINN. Do you give me your oath to that?

DIARMUID. I do give it.

FINN. It is the woman will make you break that swearing. There pitiful hag with the hair matted wild to her knees.

DIARMUID. It will not be broken. Let my own heart break and be torn by wild dogs before that promise will be broken at all.

FINN. The moon is coming now to the full, and before its lessening you will have lied to me.

DIARMUID (*taking up a loaf*). Look at this cake of bread. I will send you its like, white and round and unbroken at every moon of the year, full moon and harvest moon, while I am along with her, as a sign my own oath is in the same way clean and whole and unbroken.

FINN. It is the women will make you break that swearing. There will be another telling bye and bye.

DIARMUID (*taking* GRANIA'S *hands*). There is this league between us, Grania. I will bring you with me and I will keep you safe from every danger. But understand well, it is not as a wife I will bring you, but I will keep my faith with Finn.

GRANIA. Do as is pleasing to you. I have made an end of askings.

DIARMUID. Come out with me now, till I put you in some place of safety.

FINN. You will find no safety in any place or in any Connacht corner north or west. And out in the big world itself, there is no one will give my enemy so much as shelter from the rain.

DIARMUID. I know well I have earned enemies in the big world because I fought with all its best men for your sake.

GRANIA. Oh, take me, take me away out of this! For it is hard treatment is falling upon me!

DIARMUID. And I tell you, Grania, but that I am bound to Finn by my word I have given him, and by kindnesses past counting and out of measure, it would be better to me than the riches of the whole world, you to have given me your love!

GRANIA. I have given it to you indeed. (*She puts up her face to be kissed.*)

DIARMUID (*kissing her forehead*). That is the first kiss and it will be the last.

FINN. You will give up your life as the charge for that kiss!

GRANIA. Come out! Come out! The very blood of my heart is rising against him!

FINN. I will not let you go! Let our wedding be here and now, and I will call in as my witnesses to that word Goll and Oisin and Osgar and the captains of the armies of the Fenians!

(FINN *goes to door, blows horn, then turns towards* GRANIA *as if to seize her, sways and falls.*)

GRANIA. Oh, is it death!

DIARMUID. It is but a weakness that took hold of him, with the scorching of his jealousy and its flame.

GRANIA. Come away before he will rise up and follow us. My father's horses are in the field outside.

DIARMUID. Come out then to the hunting—for it is a long hunting it will be, and it is little comfort we will have from this out. For that is a man driven by anger, and that will not fail from our track so long as the three of us are in the living world.

(*The sound of many horns and shouts is heard at Right.* DIARMUID *opens door at Left.* GRANIA *goes out quickly. He follows with bowed head.*)

Curtain.

23

ACT II

[Seven Years After]

SCENE. *Interior of a rough tent. The door opens on a wood out-side. A bed strewn with rushes.* DIARMUID *lying on it asleep.* GRANIA *is moving about and singing.*

GRANIA. Sleep a little, a little little;
      Green the wild rushes under my dear.
      Sleep here quiet, easy and quiet,
      Safe in the wild wood, nothing to fear.
  (She stirs fire and puts some round cakes she has been making,
    to bake over it. Then comes to DIARMUID *and puts her*
    hand on him as she sings :)
      Waken darling, darling waken!
      Wild ducks are flying, daylight is kind;
      Whirr of wild wings high in the branches.
      Hazel the hound stands snuffing the wind!
DIARMUID (*awaking and taking her hand*). There is a new light in your eyes—there is a new blush in your cheeks—there is a new pride stirring in your thoughts. The white sun of Heaven should be well pleased shining on you. Are you well content, Grania, my wife?
GRANIA. I am well content indeed with my comrade and my man.
DIARMUID. And did you love me ever and always, Grania?
GRANIA. Did I not tell you long ago, my heart went down to you the day I looked from the high window, and I in my young youth at Tara.
DIARMUID. It was a long waiting we had for our marriage time.
GRANIA. It was a long waiting, surely.
DIARMUID. Let us put it out of mind and not be remembering it at all. This last moon has made up for all those seven years.
GRANIA. It was a troublesome time indeed and a very trouble-some life. In all that time we never stopped in any place so long as in the shades and the shelters of this wood.
DIARMUID. It seems to me only one day we have been in it. I

24

would not be sorry in this place, there to be the length of a year in the day.

GRANIA. The young leaves on the beach trees have unfolded since we came.

DIARMUID. I did not take notice of their growth. Oh, my dear, you are as beautiful as the blossoming of the wild furze on the hill.

GRANIA. It was not love that brought you to wed me in the end.

DIARMUID. It was, surely, and no other thing. What is there but love can twist a man's life, as sally rods are twisted for a gad?

GRANIA. No, it was jealousy, jealousy of the King of Foreign, that wild dark man, that broke the hedge between us and levelled the wall.

DIARMUID (*starting up*). Do not bring him back to mind! It was rage that cracked me, when I saw him put his arms about you as if to bring you away.

GRANIA. Was it my fault? I was but gathering a sheaf of rushes for our two beds, and I saw him coming alongside of the stream to the pool. I knew him by the tusks on his shield and the bristled boar-skin cloak.

DIARMUID. What was it ailed you not to call to me?

GRANIA. You were far away—you would not have heard me—it is he himself would have heard my call. And I was no way afraid —I hid myself up in the branches of the big red sally by the pool.

DIARMUID. That was a foolish place to go hiding.

GRANIA. I thought myself safe and well hidden on the branch that goes over the stream. What way could I know he would stop at that very place, to wash the otter blood from his spear, and the blood from his hands, and the sweat?

DIARMUID. If I had been near, it is his own blood would have splashed away in the pool.

GRANIA. He stopped then to throw the water on his face—it was my own face he saw in the pool. He looked up of a sudden—he gave a great delighted laugh.

DIARMUID. My lasting grief that I was not there, and my hand gripping his throat.

GRANIA. He bent the branch—he lifted me from it—he not to have caught me in his arms I would have fallen in the stream.

DIARMUID. That itself might have been better than his hand to have rested on you at all!

GRANIA. Then you were there—within one minute. You should likely have heard the great shout he gave out and the laugh?

DIARMUID. I lifted my hand to strike at him, and it was as if struck down. It is grief to my heart that he escaped me! I would have crushed him and destroyed him and broken his carcase against the rocks.

GRANIA. It was I myself struck your hand down. I was well pleased seeing you in that rage of anger.

DIARMUID. If I had known that, it is likely I would have killed you in his place.

GRANIA. But you did not kill me.

DIARMUID. What was it happened? I was as if blind—you were in my arms not his,—my lips were on the lips he had nearly touched, that I myself had never touched in all those seven years.

GRANIA. It was a long, long kiss.

DIARMUID. That moment was like the whole of life in a single day, and yet it was but a second of time. And when I looked around he was gone, and there was no trace of him and he had made away and I could not kill him.

GRANIA. What matter? You should forgive him, seeing it was he brought us together at the last. You should help him to win another kingdom for that good deed. There is nothing will come between us now. You are entirely my own.

DIARMUID. I am belonging to you, indeed, now and for ever. I will bring you away from this rambling life, to a place will be all our own. We will do away with this trade of wandering, we will go on to that bare shore between Burren and the big sea. There will be no trace of our footsteps on the hard flagstones.

GRANIA. We were in that craggy place before and we were forced to quit it. To live on the wind and on the air you cannot. The wind is not able to support anybody.

DIARMUID. We will get a currach this time. We will go out over the waves to an island. The sea and the strand are wholesome. We shall sleep well, and the tide beating its watch around us.

GRANIA. Even out in those far Aran Islands we would be threatened and driven as happened in the time past.

DIARMUID. But beyond Aran, far out in the west, there is another island that is seen but once in every seven years.

GRANIA. Is that a real place at all? Or is it only in the nurses' tales?

DIARMUID. Who knows? There is no good lover but has seen it at some time through his sleep. It is hid under a light mist, away from the track of traders and kings and robbers. The harbour is well fenced to keep out loud creaking ships. Some fisherman to break through the mist at some time, he will bring back news of a place where there is better love and a better life than in any lovely corner of the world that is known. (*She turns away.*) And will you come there with me, Grania?

GRANIA. I am willing to go from this. We cannot stop always in the darkness of the woods—but I am thinking it should be very strange there and very lonesome.

DIARMUID. The sea-women will rise up giving out news of the Country-under-Wave, and the birds will have talk as in the old days. And maybe some that are beyond the world will come to keep us company, seeing we are fitted to be among them by our unchanging love.

GRANIA. We are going a long time without seeing any of the people of the world, unless it might be herds and fowlers, and robbers that are hiding in the wood.

DIARMUID. It is enough for us having one another. I would sooner be talking with you than the world wide.

GRANIA. It is likely some day you will be craving to be back with the Fenians.

DIARMUID. I was fretting after them for a while. But now they are slipping out of mind. It would seem as if some soul-brother of my own were calling to me from outside the world. It may be they have need of my strength to help them in their hurling and their wars.

GRANIA. I have not had the full of my life yet, for it is scared and hiding I have spent the best of my years that are past. And no one coming to give us news or knowledge, and no friendly thing at all at hand, unless it might be Hazel the hound, or that I might throw out a handful of meal to the birds to bring me company. I would wish to bring you back now to some busy peopled place.

DIARMUID. You never asked to be brought to such a place in all our time upon the road. And are you not better pleased now than when we dragged lonely-hearted and sore-footed through the days?

GRANIA. I am better pleased, surely—and it is by reason of that I would wish my happiness to be seen, and not to be hidden under the branches and twigs of trees.

DIARMUID. If I am content here, why would not you be content?

GRANIA. It is time for you to have attendance again, and good company about you. We are the same here as if settled in the clay, clogged with the body and providing for its hunger and its needs, and the readying of the dinner of to-day and the providing of the dinner for to-morrow. It is at the head of long tables we should be, listening to the old men with their jokes and flatteries, and the young men making their plans that will change the entire world.

DIARMUID. That is all over for me now, and cast away like the husk from the nut.

GRANIA. They will be forgetting us altogether.

DIARMUID. No, but they will put us into songs, till the world will wonder at the luck of those two lovers that carried love entire and unbroken out beyond the rim of sight.

GRANIA. That may be. And some night at the supper the men will turn their heads hearing that song and will say, "Is Diarmuid living yet?" or "Grania must be withered now and a great trouble to those that are about her." And they will turn to the women that are smiling beside them, and that have delicate hands, and little blushes in their cheeks, and that are maybe but my own age all the same, but have kept their young looks, being merry and well cared. And Grania and Diarmuid will be no more than a memory and a name.

DIARMUID (*taking her hand*). These white hands were always willing hands, and where, I wonder, was this discontent born? A little while ago it was the woods you wanted, and now it is the palaces you want.

GRANIA. It is not my mind that changes, it is life that changes about me. If I was content to be in hiding a while ago, now I am proud and have a right to be proud. And it is hard to nourish pride in a house having two in it only.

DIARMUID. I take pride in you here, the same as I would in any other place.

GRANIA. Listen to me. You are driving me to excuses and to words that are not entirely true. But here, now, is truth for you. All the years we were with ourselves only, you kept apart from me as if I was a shadow-shape or a hag of the valley. And it was not till you saw another man craving my love, that the like love was born in yourself. And I will go no more wearing out my time in lonely places, where the martens and hares and badgers run from my path, but it is to thronged places I will go, where it is not through the eyes of wild startled beasts you will be looking at me, but through the eyes of kings' sons that will be saying: "It is no wonder Diarmuid to have gone through his crosses for such a wife!" And I will overhear their sweethearts saying: "I would give the riches of the world, Diarmuid to be my own comrade." And our love will be kept kindled for ever, that would be spent and consumed in desolate places, like the rushlight in a cabin by the bog. For it is certain it is by the respect of others we partly judge even those we know through and through.

DIARMUID (*getting up and speaking gravely*). There is no going back for us, Grania, and you know that well yourself.

GRANIA. We will go to my father's house—he is grown old, he will not refuse me—we will call to your people and to my people— we will bring together an army of our own.

DIARMUID. That is enough of arguing. There is no sense or no reason in what you are saying.

GRANIA. It is a bad time you have chosen to give up your mannerly ways. You did not speak that way the day you found me in the hand of the King of Foreign. You would maybe be better pleased if I had gone with him at that time.

DIARMUID. You are but saying that to vex and to annoy me. You are talking like an innocent or a fool.

GRANIA. He made me great promises. A great place and power and great riches.

DIARMUID. I can win you riches in plenty if that is what you are coveting in your mind.

GRANIA. I cared little for his talk of riches—but—when he put his arms about me and kissed me——

DIARMUID. You let him leave a kiss upon your mouth?

GRANIA. It as if frightened me—it seemed strange to me—there came as if a trembling in my limbs. I said: "I am this long time going with the third best man of the Fenians, and he never came as near as that to me."

DIARMUID (*flinging her from him*). Go then your own way, and I would be well pleased never to have met you, and I was no better than a fool, thinking any woman at all could give love would last longer than the froth upon the stream!

(*The sound of a rattle is heard outside.*)

GRANIA. What is that? Who is it?

(FINN *disguised as a beggar is seen at door.*)

DIARMUID. It is but a beggar or a leper.

FINN. Is this a house is sheltering a handsome young woman and a lathy tall young man, that are not belonging to this district, and having no follower but a hound?

DIARMUID. Who are you? Keep back from the door!

FINN. I am no leper if I am a beggar. And my name is well earned that is Half-Man—for there is left to me but one arm by the wolves, and one side of my face by the crows that came picking at me on the ridge where I was left for dead. And beyond that again, one of the feet rotted from me, where I got it hurted one time through a wound was given me by treachery in the heel.

DIARMUID. Take off that mask till I see your face.

FINN. I will and welcome, if you have a mind to see it, but it is not right a lovely young lady to get a view of a bare gnawed skull, and that is what this caul covers. It is by reason of that I go sounding the rattle, to scare children from the path before me, and women carrying child.

DIARMUID. If it is alms you are seeking it is a bare place to come, for we carry neither gold or silver, there being no market in the woods.

FINN. Not at all, not at all—I am asking nothing at all. Believe me, the man that sent me is a good payer of wages.

DIARMUID. What call had he to send you here? We own nothing for any man to covet.

FINN. With a message he sent me, a message. You to be the man and the young woman I am searching after, I have to give a message and get a message. That is all the business I have to do. I will get fair play, never fear, from the man that sent me.

DIARMUID. Tell me who is that man, till I know is he enemy or friend.

FINN. You to see him you would not forget him. A man he is, giving out gold from his hand the same as withered leaves, and having on his shield the likeness of the rising sun.

GRANIA. That can surely be no other than Finn. What did he want sending you?

FINN. I will tell you that, and it is little I know why would he want it. You would not say him to be a man would be in need of bread.

GRANIA. Tell out now what you have to tell.

FINN. Wouldn't you say it to be a strange thing, a man having that much gold in his hand, and the sun in gold on his shield, to be as hungry after bread as a strayed cur dog would have nothing to eat or to fall back on, and would be yelping after his meal.

DIARMUID. Give out the message.

FINN. It is what he bade me say: "Tell that young woman," he said, "and that youngster with her," he said, "that on every first night of the round moon these seven years, there used to be a round cake of bread laid upon my road. And the moon was at her strength yesterday," he said, "and it has failed me to find on any path that cake of bread."

DIARMUID. It is Finn that sent him! It is Finn is calling me to account because I have forgotten my promise to him, and my faith.

GRANIA. He has come upon our track. We must go our road again. It is often we escaped him before this. I am no way afraid.

DIARMUID. It is not fear that is on me, it is shame. Shame because Finn thought me a man would hold to my word, and I have not held to it. I am as if torn and broken with the thought and the memory of Finn.

GRANIA. It is time to put away that memory. It is long enough you gave in to his orders.

DIARMUID. I did that with my own consent. Nothing he put upon me was hard. He trusted me and he could trust me, and now he will never put trust in me again.

GRANIA. It may not be Finn will be getting his commands done, and our friends gathering to our help. Let him learn that time, not to thrust his hand between the wedges and the splint.

FINN (*who has been sitting crouched over fire*). Have you the message ready and the bread I was bade bring back to the champion that met me on the path?

GRANIA (*taking up one of the cakes*). It is best send it to him and gain the time to make our escape.

DIARMUID. No, no more lying. I will tell no more lies to my master and my friend!

(DIARMUID *takes cake from* GRANIA *and flings it down, then throws himself on the bed and covers his face with his hands.* GRANIA *takes up cake, breaks it again and again, and gives it to* FINN.)

GRANIA. That is the answer to his message. Say to him that as that bread is broken and torn, so is the promise given by the man that did right in breaking it. Tell Finn, the time you meet him, it was the woman herself gave that to you, and bade you leave it in his hand as a message and as a sign!

FINN. Take care now. Is that a right message you are sending, and one that you will not repent?

GRANIA. It is a right message for that man to get. And give heed to what I say now. If you have one eye is blind, let it be turned to the place where we are, and that he might ask news of. And if you have one seeing eye, cast it upon me, and tell Finn you saw a woman no way sad or afraid, but as airy and high-minded as a mountain filly would be challenging the winds of March!

FINN. I can tell him that, surely, and you not giving it out to me at all.

GRANIA. And another thing. Tell him there is no woman but

would be proud, and that oath being broken for her sake. And tell him she is better pleased than if she was a queen of the queens of the world, that she, a travelling woman going out under the weather, can turn her back on him this day as she did in the time that is past. Go now, and give that message if you dare to give it, and keep those words red scorched in your mind.

FINN. I will bring that message, sure enough, and there will be no fear on me giving it out. For all the world knows Finn never took revenge on a fool, or a messenger, or a hound. But it would be well for them that send it to bear in mind that he is a hard man— a hard man—a hard man, surely. As hard as a barren stepmother's slap, or a highway ganders' gob.

GRANIA. Go, go on your road. Or will you take food and drink before you go?

FINN. Not at all, I will eat in no man's house or in any place at all, unless in the bats' feeding time and the owls', the way the terror of my face will not be seen. I will be going now, going my road. But, let you mind yourself. Finn does be very wicked the time he does be mad vexed. And he is a man well used to get the mastery, and any that think to go daring him, or to go against him, he will make split marrow of their bones.

DIARMUID (*looking up*). There might kindness grow in him yet. It is not big men, the like of him, keep up enmity and a grudge for ever.

FINN. Who can know, who can know? Finn has a long memory. There is Grania he doted down on, and that was robbed from him, and he never threw an eye on any woman since and never will, but going as if crazed, and ransacking the whole country after her. As restless as the moon of Heaven he is, and at some times as wasted and as pale.

GRANIA. It is time for him to leave thinking about her.

FINN. A great memory he has and great patience, and a strong fit of the jealous, that is the worst thing ever came from the skies. How well he never forgave and never will forgive Diarmuid O'Duibhne, that he reared on his knee and nourished with every marrow-bone, and that stole away his wife from him, and is dead.

GRANIA. That is no true story. Diarmuid is not dead, but living!

FINN. That's my hearing of the thing. And if he is on the earth yet, what is he doing? Would you call that living? Screening himself behind bushes, running before the rustling of a wren on the nest. In dread to face his master or the old companions that he had.

GRANIA. There is no man but must go through trouble at some

time; and many a good man has been a stranger and an exile through a great share of his lifetime.

FINN. I am no friend to Diarmuid O'Duibhne. But he to be my friend, I would think it a great slur upon him it being said a man that had so great a name was satisfied and content, killing hares and conies for the supper, casting at cranes for sport, or for feathers to stuff a pillow for his sweetheart's head, the time there is an army of the men of Foreign in Ireland.

GRANIA. I can tell you it will not be long till he will be seen going out against them, and going against some that are not foreign, and he having an army of his own.

FINN. It is best for him make no delay so, where they are doing every whole thing to drag the country down.

DIARMUID (standing up). I will go out and fight. I will delay no minute.

GRANIA. No, but do as I tell you. Gather your friends till you can make your own stand. Where is the use of one man only, however good he may be?

FINN. A queer thing indeed, no queerer. Diarmuid, that was the third best man of the whole of the armies of the Fenians, to be plucking and sorting pigeon's feathers to settle out a pillow and a bed.

DIARMUID. I will go as I am, by myself. There is no man living would let his name lie under reproach as my name is under it.

GRANIA (to FINN). Go quick—you have brought messages—bring another message for me, now, to the High King's house at Tara.

DIARMUID. I will wait for no man's help. I will go.

GRANIA. Is it that you will leave me? It is certain Finn has tracked us—we have stopped too long in the one place. If Finn is there his strength will be there. Do not leave me here alone to the power and the treachery of Finn! It is in at this door he may be coming before the fall of night.

DIARMUID. I will stop here. I will not leave you under Finn's power for any satisfaction to myself. (To FINN) Go, as you are bidden, and bring help from the King at Tara.

FINN. Very good, very good. That now is the message of a wise housekeeping husband.

DIARMUID. I give my word it needs more courage at some times to be careful than to be forward and daring, and that is the way with me now.

FINN. Maybe so, maybe so. And there is no wonder at all a common man to be tame and timid, when Diarmuid, grandson of Duibhne has a faint miserable heart.

DIARMUID. That is the wicked lie of some old enemy.

FINN (*going to door*). Very likely, very likely; but maybe it would be better for Grania I was speaking of, to have stopped with the old man that made much of her, in place of going with the young man that belittles her.

GRANIA. That is a slander and no true word.

FINN (*at door*). Ha! Ha! Ha! It is a story makes great sport among gentle and simple in every place. It is great laughing is given out when the story is heard, that the King of Foreign put his arms about Grania's neck that is as white as a hound's tooth, and that Diarmuid saw him do it—and that the King of Foreign is living yet, and goes boasting on his road! (*Goes out.*)

DIARMUID (*fastening on sword*). Give that to me. (*Points to spear.*)

GRANIA (*throwing it from her*). Oh, stop with me, my darling, and my love, do not go from me now or forsake me! And to stay in the lonely woods for ever or in any far desolate place, you will never hear a cross word or an angry word from me again. And it is for you I will wear my jewels and my golden dress. For you are my share of life, and you are the east and the west to me, and all the long ago and all that is before me! And there is nothing will come between us or part us, and there will be no name but yours upon my lips, and no name but my own spoken by your lips, and the two of us well contented for ever!

FINN (*comes back and looks in at door*). It is what they were saying a while ago, the King of Foreign is grunting and sighing, grunting and sighing, around and about the big red sally tree beside the stream! (*He disappears.* DIARMUID *rushes out.*)

Curtain.

Act III

[Afternoon of the same day]

SCENE. *In the same tent.* GRANIA *has put on her golden dress and jewels, and is plaiting gold into her hair. Horns and music suddenly heard, not very near. She goes startled to door, and falls back as* FINN *comes in. He is dressed as if for war and has his banner in his hand. He looks older and more worn than in the First Act.*

FINN. I have overtaken you at last, Grania.

GRANIA. Finn! It is Finn! (*She goes a step back and takes up a spear.*)

FINN. It would be no great load upon you to bid me welcome.

GRANIA. What is it has brought you here?

FINN. Foolishness brought me here, and nature.

GRANIA. It is foolishness for a man not to stop and mind his own estate.

FINN. A wild bird of a hawk I had, that went out of my hand. I am entitled to it by honest law.

GRANIA. I know your meaning well. But hearken now and put yourself in a better mind. It is a heavy punishment you put upon us these many years, and it is short till we'll all be in the grave, and it is as good for you leave us to go our own road.

FINN. A queer long way I would have walked for no profit. Diarmuid is gone out from you. There is nothing to hinder me from bringing you away.

GRANIA. There is such a thing.

FINN. Is it your own weak hand on that spear?

GRANIA (*throwing it down*). No, but your own pride, if it has not gone from you and left you snapping and angry, like any moon-crazed dog.

FINN. If there is madness within me, it is you yourself have a right to answer for it. But for all that, it is truth you are speaking, and I will not bring you away, without you will come with me of your own will.

GRANIA. That will be when the rivers run backward.

35

FINN. No, but when the tide is at the turn. I tell you, my love that was allotted and foreshadowed before the making of the world will drag you in spite of yourself, as the moon above drags the waves, and they grumbling through the pebbles as they come, and making their own little moaning of discontent.

GRANIA. You have failed up to this to drag or to lead me to you.

FINN. There is great space for rememberings and regrettings in the days and the nights of seven years.

GRANIA. I and Diarmuid stopped close to one another all that time, and being as we were without hearth or frolic, or welcome or the faces of friends.

FINN. Many a day goes by, and nothing has happened in it worth while. And then there comes a day that is as if the ring of life, and that holds all the joy and the pain of life between its two darknesses. And I am thinking that day has come, and that it will put you on the road to myself and Almhuin.

GRANIA. You think I will give in to you because I am poor in the world. But there is grief in my heart I not to have strength to drive that spear through you, and be quit of your talk forever.

FINN. Would you think better of me if I had been satisfied to put this crown on some other woman's head, and it having rested upon your own for one moment of time? (*Takes crown from under his cloak and holds it up.*)

GRANIA. It would have been best. I would be well pleased to see you do it yet.

FINN. But I would not do that to gain the whole world entirely. And I to have my youth seven times over, it is after you I would come searching those seven times. And I have my life spent and wasted following you, and I have kissed the sign of your foot in every place all through Ireland.

GRANIA. I have no forgiveness for you that have been a red enemy to my darling and my man. I have too long a memory of all the unkindness you have done.

FINN. It is your fault if I did them. Every time the thought of kindness came to me, the thought of you came with it, and put like a ring of iron around my heart.

GRANIA. It is turned to iron indeed. And listen to me now, Finn, and believe what I say. You to have hunted us through crags and bushes, and sent us out in the height of hailstones and of rain, I might overlook it and give you pardon. But it is the malice you showed, putting a hedge between myself and Diarmuid that I never will forgive, but will keep it against you for ever. For it is you left

36

my life barren, and it was you came between us two through all the years.

FINN. I did right doing that. There is no man but would keep the woman he is to wed for himself only.

GRANIA. It was your shadow was between us through all that time, and if I carry hatred towards you, I leave it on your own head. And it is little I would have thought of hardships, and we two being lovers and alone. But that is not the way it was. For the time he would come in, sweaty and sorefooted from the hunting, or would be dull and drowsy from the nights of watching at the door, I would be down-hearted and crabbed maybe; or if I was kind itself, it would be like a woman would be humouring a youngster, and her mind on some other track. But we to have a settled home and children to be fondling, that would not have been the way with us, and the day would have been short, and we showing them off to one another, and laying down there was no one worthy to have called them into the world but only our two selves.

FINN. You are saying what is not true, and what you have no right to say. But you know well and you cannot deny it, you are man and wife to one another this day.

GRANIA. And if we are, it is not the same as a marriage on that day we left Almhuin would have been. It was you put him under a promise and a bond that was against nature, and he was a fool to make it, and a worse fool to keep it. And what are any words at all put against the love of a young woman and a young man? It was you turned my life to weariness, and my heart to bitterness, and put me under the laughter and the scorn of all. For there was not a poor man's house where we lodged, but I could see wonder and mockery and pity in the eyes of the woman of the house, where she saw that poor as she was, and ugly maybe and ragged, a king's daughter was thought less of than herself. Because if Diarmuid never left his watch upon my threshold, he never came across it, or never gave me the joy and pride of a wife! And it was you did that on me, and I leave it on your own head; and if there is any hatred to be found in the world, and it to be squeezed into one cup only, it would not be so black and so bitter as my own hatred for you!

FINN. That hatred is as if crushed out of the great bulk of my love for you, that is heaped from the earth to the skies.

GRANIA. I am not asking it or in need of it. Why would I listen to a story I have heard often and too often.

FINN. But you will listen, and you will give heed to it. You came

37

of your own free will to Almhuin to be my wife. And my heart went out to you there and then, and I thought there would be the one house between us, and that it was my child I would see reared on your knee. And that was known to every one of my people and of my armies, and you were willing it should be known. And after that, was it a little thing that all Ireland could laugh at the story that I, Finn, was so spent, and withered, and loathsome in a woman's eyes, that she would not stop with me in a life that was full and easy, but ran out from me to travel the roads, the same as any beggar having seven bags. And I am not like a man of the mean people, that can hide his grief and his heart-break, bringing it to some district where he is not known, but I must live under that wrong and that insult in full sight of all, and among mockery and malicious whisperings in the mouth of those maybe that are shouting me!

GRANIA. I have a great wrong done to you, surely, but it brings me no nearer to you now. And our life is settled, and let us each go our own course.

FINN. Is it not a great wonder the candle you lighted not to have been quenched in all that time? But the light in your grey eyes is my desire for ever, and I am pulled here and there over hills and through hollows. For my life was as if cut in two halves on that night that put me to and fro; and the half that was full and flowing was put behind me, and it has been all on the ebb since then. But you and I together could have changed the world entirely, and put a curb upon the spring-tide, and bound the seven elements with our strength. And now, that is not the way I am, but dragging there and hither, my feet wounded with thorns, the tracks of tears down my cheeks; not taking rest on the brink of any thick wood, because you yourself might be in it, and not stopping on the near side of any lake or inver because you might be on the far side; as wakeful as a herd in lambing time, my companions stealing away from me, being tired with the one corn-crake cry upon my lips always, that is, Grania. And it is no wonder the people to hate you, and but for dread of me they would many a time have killed you.

GRANIA. If I did you wrong, did I do no wrong against Diarmuid? And all the time we were together he never cast it up against me that it was I brought him away from his comrades, or, as he could have done, that I asked him without waiting for his asking. He never put reproaches on me, as you are reproaching me, now that I am alone and without any friend at hand.

FINN. Diarmuid has no harm in his heart, and he would find it

38

hard to do anything was not mannerly, and befitting a man reared in king's houses, if he is no good lover itself.

GRANIA. Diarmuid that gave all up for love is the best lover of the whole world.

FINN. No, for his love is not worth a reed of straw beside mine.

GRANIA. His love knows no weakening at all. He would begrudge me to walk the road! Listen to this now. The King of Foreign had put his arms about me—he had left but one kiss on my mouth—and for that much Diarmuid is gone out at this time to take his life!

FINN. Diarmuid to be a good lover, it is my own life he would have shortened. If he had any great love for you, it is I myself he would not have left living.

GRANIA. You are belittling Diarmuid, and I will judge you by your own words. You boast that you are a better lover. Then why are you wasting talk here, and you having let him go out of your hand to-day?

FINN. He is not gone out of reach of my hand.

GRANIA. He is! He is safe and gone from you. Would I have been so daring in talk, and I not certain of that?

FINN. It is hard for any man to escape the thing was laid down for him, and that he has earned.

GRANIA. It is no friend of yours he went out fighting. It is that foreign king. He will be well able to put him down.

FINN. It is not a man weakened with love that goes out to win in a fight. It is a foreign hand will do judgment upon him, but it was I myself sent him out to that judgment.

GRANIA. That is not true! It is a boast and a bragging you are making to threaten me. You would never dare to do it. He is of your own blood.

FINN. You are beautiful and I am old and scarred. But if it was different, and I to be what I was, straight as a flag-flower, and yellow-haired, and you what the common people call out that hate you, wide and low-born, a hedgehog, an ugly thing, I would kill any man at all that would come between us, because you are my share of the world and because I love you.

GRANIA. You are speaking lies—I know it is a lie and that it was not you sent him out to that fight. It was not you, it was that sharp-tongued beggar, that spiteful crippled man.

FINN. There is no man only a lover, can be a beggar, and not ashamed.

GRANIA. It was not you—you were not that cripple.

FINN. This is the hand where you put the broken bread.

GRANIA. It was you sent Diarmuid out! It was you came between us! It was you parted us! It was your voice he obeyed and listened to, the time he had no ears for me! Are you between us always?—I will go out after him, I will call him back—I will tell him your treachery—he will make an end of it and of you. He will know you through and through this time. It will fail you to come between us again.

(*A heavy shout is heard.*)

FINN. Hush, and listen! (*Goes to the door.*)

GRANIA. What is it? Let me find Diarmuid——

FINN (*holding her back*). It is Diarmuid is coming in.

(DIARMUID'S *body is carried in by two fair-haired* YOUNG MEN. *They lay it on the bed and take off their caps.* FINN *looks at him, takes his hand, then lays it down and turns away.*)

Death and the judgment of death have overtaken him.

GRANIA (*bending over him*). Oh, Diarmuid, you are not dead! You cannot be dead! It is not in this hour you could die, and all well between us, and all done away with that had parted us!

FINN. He is dead indeed. Look at that wound in his neck. He is bleeding and destroyed with blood.

GRANIA. Come back to me, come back, my heart's darling, my one love of the men of the world! Come back, if but for one moment of time. Come back, and listen to all I have to tell. And it is well we have the world earned, and is it not a hard thing, a young man to die because of any woman at all casting an eye on him, and making him her choice, and bringing her own bad luck upon him, that was marked down for her maybe in the time before the world. And it is hunger I gave you through my love, and it is a pity it is around you it was cast, and it is a pity now, you to be loosed out of it. And it would have been better for you, some girl of the ducks and ashes, hard reared and rough, to have settled out your pillow, and not myself that brought ill-will upon you, and the readying of your grave!

FINN. Where is the use of calling to him and making an outcry? He can hear no word at all, or understand anything you say. And he has brought with him a good memory of happiness and of love; and some of the world's great men bringing with them but empty thoughts of a life that was blasted and barren.

GRANIA. Ochone, my grief! For all is at an end, and you are clean wheat ground and bruised and broken between two hard stones, the luckless love of a woman, and the love turned to anger of a friend.

FINN (*putting his hand on her arm*). That is enough. A red death is a clean death, and the thing that is done cannot be undone, and the story is ended, and there is no other word to say.

GRANIA (*pushing him away*). You stood between us long enough and he living, but you cannot come between us and he dead! And I own him from this time any way, and I am glad and could nearly laugh, knowing your power is spent and run out, and that it will fail you to come meddling any more between us that are lovers now to the end!

FINN. Your bitter words are no matter. There is no one to give heed to them.

GRANIA. It is well I will keen him, and I never will quit his grave till such time as the one flagstone will cover the two of us from the envious eyes of the women of Ireland and from your own. And a woman to lose her comrade, she loses with him her crown! And let you go to some other place, Finn, for you have nothing to say to him at all, and no other hand will be laid on him from this out but my own!

FINN (*bending over him*). He is not dead—his lips are stirring— there is a little blush in his face——

GRANIA (*stooping*). Oh, Diarmuid, are you come back to me? (*He moves.*) Speak to me now. Lift now your lips to my own— hush! He is going to speak. Oh, Diarmuid, my darling, give me one word!

DIARMUID (*turns his head slightly and looks at* FINN). Is that you, my master, Finn? I did not know you were dead along with me.

GRANIA. You are not dead, you are living—my arms are about you. This is my kiss upon your cheek. (*Kisses him.*)

DIARMUID (*not noticing her*). The King of Foreign is dead. I struck him down by the sally tree—as he was falling he struck at me, and the life went out of me. But what way did you meet with your death, my master Finn?

GRANIA. You are living I say—turn towards me. I am Grania, your wife.

DIARMUID (*still speaking to* FINN). It is a very friendly thing you to have met me here, and it is Ireland and the world should be lonesome after you this day!

GRANIA. Speak to him, Finn. Tell him he is astray. Tell him he is living. Bring the wits back to him.

FINN. Diarmuid, you are not dead, you are in the living world.

GRANIA. Come back, now, come back to life! Finn thought he had sent you to your death, but it failed him—he is treacherous—he is no friend to you. You will know that now. Come back, and leave thinking of him!!

DIARMUID (*still speaking to* FINN). There was some word I had to say meeting you—it is gone—I had it in my mind a while ago.

GRANIA. Do you not see me? It is I myself am here—Grania!

DIARMUID. Some wrong I did you, some thing past forgiving. Is it to forgive me you are waiting here for me, and to tell me you are keeping no anger against me after all?

FINN. Come back now, and put out your strength, and take a good grip of life, and I will give you full forgiveness for all you have done against me. And I will have done with anger, and with jealousy that has been my bedfellow this long time, and I will meddle with you no more, unless in the way of kindness.

DIARMUID. Kindness—you were always kind surely, and I a little lad at your knee. Who at all would be kind to me and you not being kind?

FINN. I will turn back altogether, I will leave you Grania your wife, and all that might come between us from this time.

DIARMUID. What could there be would come between us two? That would be a strange thing indeed.

FINN. I will go, for the madness is as if gone from me; and you are my son and my darling, and it is beyond the power of any woman to put us asunder, or to turn you against me any more.

DIARMUID. That would be a very foolish man would give up his dear master and his friend for any woman at all. (*He laughs.*)

GRANIA. He is laughing—the sense is maybe coming back to him.

DIARMUID. It would be a very foolish thing, any woman at all to have leave to come between yourself and myself. I cannot but laugh at that.

FINN. Rouse yourself up now, and show kindness to the wife that is there at your side.

DIARMUID. There is some noise of the stream where I died. It is in my ears yet—but I remember—I am remembering now—there was something I begrudged you, the time our bodies were heavy about us. Something I brought away from you, and kept from you. What wildness came upon me to make me begrudge it? What was it I brought away from you? Was not Hazel my own hound? (*He dies.*)

42

FINN. Lift up your head, open your eyes, do not die from me! Come back to me, Diarmuid, now!

GRANIA. He will say no word to either one of us again for ever. (*She goes to wall, leaning her head against it, her hands working.*)

FINN. Are you gone indeed, Diarmuid, that I myself sent to your death? And I would be well pleased it was I, Finn, was this day making clay, and you yourself holding up your head among the armies. It is a bad story for me you to be dead, and it is in your place I would be well satisfied to be this day; and you had not lived out your time. But as to me, I am tired of all around me, and all the weight of the years is come upon me, and there will be no more joy in anything happens from this day out forever. And it is as if all the friends ever I had went to nothing, losing you. (*After a moment's silence he turns to the* YOUNG MEN.) Bring him out now, slaves of Britain, to his comrades and his friends, and the armies that are gathering outside, till they will wake him and mourn him and give him burial, for it is a king is lost from them this day. And if you have no mind to keen him, let you raise a keen for the men of your own country he left dumb in the dust, and a foolish smile on their face. For he was a good man to put down his enemies and the enemies of Ireland, and it is living he would be this day if it was not for his great comeliness and the way he had, that sent every woman stammering after him and coveting him; and it was love of a woman brought him down in the end, and sent him astray in the world. And what at all is love, but lies on the lips and drunkenness, and a bad companion on the road?

(*The body is carried out. The bearers begin to keen. The keen is taken up by the armies outside.* FINN *sits down, his head bowed in his hand.* GRANIA *begins fastening up her hair and as if preparing for a journey.*)

FINN. You are doing well going out to keen after him.

GRANIA. It is not with him I am going. It is not with Diarmuid I am going out. It is an empty thing to be crying the loss of a comrade that banished me from his thoughts, for the sake of any friend at all. It it with you I will go to Almhuin. Diarmuid is no more to me than a sod that has been quenched with the rain.

FINN. I will meddle no more with what belongs to him. You are the dead man's wife.

GRANIA. All the wide earth to come between Diarmuid and myself, it would put us no farther away from one another than what we are. And as for the love I had for him, it is dead now, and turned to be as cold as the snow is out beyond the path of the sun.

43

FINN. It is the trouble of the day that is preying on you.

GRANIA. He had no love for me at any time. It is easy know it now. I knew it all the while, but I would not give in to believe it. His desire was all the time with you yourself and Almhuin. He let on to be taken up with me, and it was but letting on. Why would I fret after him that so soon forgot his wife, and left her in a wretched way?

FINN. You are not judging him right. You are distracted with the weight of your loss.

GRANIA. Does any man at all speak lies at the very brink of death, or hold any secret in his heart? It was at that time he had done with deceit, and he showed where his thought was, and had no word at all for me that had left the whole world for his sake, and that went wearing out my youth, pushing here and there as far as the course of the stars of Heaven. And my thousand curses upon death not to have taken him at daybreak, and I believing his words! It is then I would have waked him well, and would have cried my seven generations after him! And I have lost all on this side of the world, losing that trust and faith I had, and finding him to think of me no more than of a flock of stairs would cast their shadow on his path. And I to die with this scald upon my heart, it is hard thistles would spring up out of my grave.

FINN. Quiet yourself, for this is grief gone wild and that is beyond all measure.

GRANIA. I to have known that much yesterday I would have left him and would have gone with that King that clutched at me. And I would have said words to Diarmuid would have left a burn and a sting.

FINN. I will call in women to cry with you and to be comforting you.

GRANIA. You are craving to get rid of me now, and to put me away out of your thoughts, the same as Diarmuid did. But I will not go! I will hold you to your word, I will take my revenge on him! He will think to keep your mind filled with himself and to keep me from you,—he will be coming back showing himself as a ghost about Almhuin. He will think to come whispering to you, and you alone in the night time. But he will find me there before him! He will shrink away lonesome and baffled! I will have my turn that time. It is I will be between him and yourself, and will keep him outside of that lodging for ever!

FINN. I gave him my promise I would leave you to him from this out, and I will keep it to him dead, the same as if he was still living.

GRANIA. How well he kept his own promise to you! I will go to Almhuin in spite of you; you will be ashamed to turn me back in the sight of the people, and they having seen your feet grown hard in following and chasing me through the years. It is women are said to change, and they do not, but it is men that change and turn as often as the wheel of the moon. You filled all Ireland with your outcry wanting me, and now, when I am come into your hand, your love is rusted and worn out. It is a pity I that had two men, and three men, killing one another for me an hour ago, to be left as I am, and no one having any use for me at all!

FINN. It is the hardness of trouble is about my heart, and is bringing me down with its weight. And it seems to me to be left alone with December and the bareness of the boughs; and the fret will be on me to the end.

GRANIA. Is it not a strange thing, you, that saw the scores and the hundreds stretched dead, that at the sight of one young man only, you give in to the drowning of age. It is little I will give heed from this out to words or to coaxings, and I have no love to give to any man for ever. But Diarmuid that belittled me will not see me beating my hands beside his grave, showing off to the cranes in the willows, and twisting a mournful cry. It is the thing I will give him to take notice of, a woman that cared nothing at all for his treachery.

FINN. Wait till the months of mourning are at an end, and till your big passion is cold, and do then what you may think fit, and settle out your life, as it is likely there will be another thought in your mind that time. But I am putting no reproach on you, for it is on myself the great blame should be, and from this out I have no more to say to love or friendship or anything but the hard business of the day.

GRANIA. I will not wait. I will give my thoughts no leave to repent. I will give no time to those two slaves to tell out the way I was scorned!

FINN. The men of the armies will laugh and mock at you, seeing you settle out a new wedding in the shadow of your comrade's wake.

GRANIA. There is many a woman lost her lord, and took another, and won great praise in the latter end, and great honour. And why should I be always a widow that went so long a maid? Give me now the crown, till I go out before them, as you offered it often enough. (*She puts it on her head.*) I am going, I am going out now, to show myself before them all, and my hand linked in your own. It is well I brought my golden dress.

FINN. Wait till the darkness of the night, or the dusk of the evening itself.

GRANIA. No, no. Diarmuid might not see me at that time. He might be gone to some other place. He is surely here now, in this room where he parted from the body—he is lingering there by the hearth. Let him see now what I am doing, and that there is no fear on me, or no wavering of the mind. Open the door now for me!

(FINN *opens door and they go to the opening, she taking his hand. There is a mocking laugh heard. She falls back and crouches down.* FINN *tries to raise her.*)

FINN. I thought to leave you and to go from you, and I cannot do it. For we three have been these seven years as if alone in the world; and it was the cruelty and the malice of love made its sport with us, when we thought it was our own way we were taking, driving us here and there, knocking you in between us, like the ball between two goals, and the hurlers being out of sight and beyond the boundaries of the world. And all the three of us have been as if worsted in that play. And now there are but the two of us left, and whether we love or hate one another, it is certain I can never feel love or hatred for any other woman from this out, or you yourself for any other man. And so as to yourself and myself, Grania, we must battle it out to the end.

(FINN *raises her up. A louder peal of laughter is heard.*)

GRANIA (*going towards the door*). It is but the armies that are laughing! I thought I heard Diarmuid's laugh.

FINN. It is his friends in the armies gave out that mocking laugh.

GRANIA. And is it not a poor thing, strong men of the sort to be mocking at a woman has gone through sharp anguish, and the breaking of love, on this day? Open the door again for me. I am no way daunted or afraid. Let them laugh their fill and welcome, and laugh you, Finn, along with them if you have a mind. And what way would it serve me, their praise and their affection to be mine? For there is not since an hour ago any sound would matter at all, or be more to me than the squeaking of bats in the rafters, or the screaming of wild geese overhead!

(*She opens the door herself.* FINN *puts his arm about her. There is another great peal of laughter, but it stops suddenly as she goes out.*)

Curtain.

46

KINCORA

KINCORA

PERSONS

MALACHI. *High King of Ireland.*
MAELMORA. *King of Leinster, brother to Gormleith.*
BRENNAIN. *Brian's servant.*
RURY. *Malachi's servant.*
PHELAN. *Maelmora's servant.*
BRIAN. *King of Munster, afterwards High King.*
MURROUGH. *His son.*
GORMLEITH. *His wife, formerly Malachi's wife.*
SITRIC. *Her son by Olaf of the Danes.*
A BEGGAR GIRL.

ACT I

SCENE. *A room in* BRIAN'S *palace at Kincora.* MALACHI *and* MAELMORA *at a table.*

MALACHI. Brian may be a great man, Maelmora, and he may have earned a great name. But he hadn't a stim of sense, no more than I myself, when it came to the choosing of a wife.

MAELMORA. Let you keep in mind now when you speak of Brian's wife, it is of my own sister you are speaking.

MALACHI. It is hard to keep that in mind and very hard. It is as if something went crossways in the making of the two of you, the way you turned out peaceable, and she that is a woman to be giddy and full of stir. I give you my word you would have as much ease being in the one house with her, as to be lodging in a nest of wild bees.

MAELMORA. You took her on the wrong side always, crossing and criticising her, and tormenting her to attend to the needle and to the business of the house. Brian will make a better hand of his marriage, letting her go her own way, and believing as he does there are not her three equals in the world wide.

MALACHI. I gave her a good house and good means and a good name the day I made her the High King's wife. Was not that enough to satisfy any woman within the ring of Ireland? And when

49

she turned her hand to meddling with my own business, and with things she had no call to at all, I said good-morrow to her and made a good provision for her; and the Pope of Rome gave her, or did not give her, leave to go suit herself better in a man.

MAELMORA. She is getting a good man, getting Brian.

MALACHI. That it may come happy! I had enough of that tongue of hers that has the grey scrape of the Spring. I did not begrudge her to Brian the time she came to him, herself, her coach, and her bridesmaids. It is well if we get through the business that brought us here without her. Brian is a hard man, and very hard, at making his own bargain, without having her at his back.

MAELMORA. It would be more answerable to us getting time to see our own advisers at home. What chance have we against him, and he in his own place at Kincora?

MALACHI. What chance had we against him since the time he brought his fleet of boats up the Shannon? You know well he threatened myself in my own strong place in Meath. It is little chance you yourself had, the time he went following you into Leinster. It is well for you he joined with your sister, or you would have been swept before this.

MAELMORA. Hard as they are, he said he would not move from these terms. But it is likely he might come around to give in a little here or there.

MALACHI. Every man has a right to do that, and not to push things too far. It would be a queer rope that would not be slackened at one time or another.

MAELMORA. He lays down that I myself must be under him, outside such things as concern my own district, and make no league or bargain on my account with any king in or outside of Ireland. But I have made out a new agreement here. Let him leave me to go my own way until there will be some time of need, and then I will come of my free will, and bring all the choice men of Leinster to his help.

MALACHI. He wrote in my own agreement that he must have entire authority in Munster and in the whole of the South. He goes so far as to say he can call for judgments to be given here in his own place. I now am not inclined to give in to that. So long as I am High King, I must have every law and every decree given out in Tara.

MAELMORA. He is entirely too hard on Sitric. If he is head of the Danes itself, he is my own sister's son, and I must see that he will get fair play. His people should get better treatment, and not be set labouring in the fields and dragging the same as four-footed beasts.

> (BRENNAIN, RURY, *and* PHELAN *come in.* BRENNAIN *pulls forward his master's chair.* BRIAN *comes in and sits down.*)

MALACHI. I myself and the King of Leinster are ready for you now, Brian.

BRIAN. Is Sitric here, or is there any sign of him coming?

MAELMORA. He cannot be far off. There was news he will be here within the hour.

BRIAN. But you yourselves have put your names to the agreements we made out. Give me yours here, Maelmora.

MAELMORA. I did not put my name to it yet. I made some changes. I was thinking you are too hard on me in this.

BRIAN. You did not think that way the time my army was visiting you in Leinster. Your memory is gone from you in its track. You came asking and calling to me to quit your province, saying you would give in to anything I might lay down. No, there is no cause for that flush on your face. It was only some little forgetfulness. We could find a cure for it quick enough, if I should come again upon the plains of Kildare.

MAELMORA. Give it here, I will put my name to what you wrote. (*Signs.*)

BRIAN. And what about Sitric? You will remember you went bail for him?

MAELMORA. If I did I will hold to it. What have we to do? It is you yourself have the power. It is as well to be under you, and to get your protection for ourselves.

BRIAN. You see how the High King is not slow or unwilling putting his name to his own agreement. No, he has not written it. Brennain, go seek a better pen for the High King's use. It is the pen that has failed, and not his own word. Malachi is like myself, he always holds to his word.

MALACHI (*signing*). Well, Brian, you are a hard man. But you are doing what I suppose I myself might be doing, and I being in your place. I sounded the pipes yesterday, you are sounding them to-day. There you have an equal share of Ireland with myself.

BRIAN. That is right now. Yourself and myself between us can sweep the whole country, and turn it all to peace.

MALACHI. You are a terrible wicked man, Brian, to go out fighting with for peace.

BRIAN. It is nothing less than that I have been fighting for, through the most of my lifetime, up to now.

MAELMORA. I cannot make out at all why so hardy and so dreaded a man should have his mind set on doing away with war.

BRIAN. It is because I have had my fill of it. Through all the generations my race was for fighting, my father, and my old father, and all that went before. Lugaidh son of Aengus, Cathal son of Aedh, Corc son of Anluan, Lorcan son of Lochta, Cennedigh son of Lorcan; there was no one of them all was reared to any other trade. What way did I myself pass my early time? Watching and attacking, through long winter nights and long summer days, striving to drive out altogether the enemies of Ireland and of Munster. It is well I have earned the right by this to turn from wicked to kind.

MALACHI. If there is any man at all can turn peaceable and keep his name up, it is yourself should be able to do it, for there is no one can say it was through any slackness you are doing it, or any fear, for that is a thing never came into the one house with you.

BRIAN. In troth it is a scarce thing among us. To go into danger shouting, the feet as if rising off the ground with the stir put in them by the pipes, the heart airy in the same way, there is no common man of our armies but will feel that much, the time the troops of his enemies are coming at him, with their attacks and with their cries.

MALACHI. That is an easy courage enough. It is a harder thing to hold to what is won, and to keep out meddlers, and to force respect for the law. To work that out, and to sweat it out, watching and foreseeing through the day, the heart starting and uneasy in the night time, that is a heavy load for any man to be carrying through the weeks and the months and the years.

BRIAN. There is no one in this country hardy enough to face it out but the two, or maybe the three, of us in this room. And as to myself, it is long ago I might have run from it, but for respect for the Man that laid the charge on me, that is God.

MALACHI. It is often I thought there was a good saint spoiled in you, Brian, and you taking to the straight sword and not to the Bishop's crook.

MURROUGH. It might have been better for yourself, Malachi, if my father had never meddled with a sword.

MALACHI. Hearken to the crowing of the young cock! We are done with all that now, Murrough. The sparrows are nesting to-day that were scolding at one another yesterday.

BRIAN (*getting up and looking out*). It is a pity Sitric is not come to make an entire end of this business.

MAELMORA. I tell you I am answerable for my nephew Sitric. He is giving in altogether.

MALACHI. He had nothing to do but to give in, the time you took away the help of Leinster from him.

MAELMORA. I will go out by the Hill of the Grey Rock to meet him. It is likely he may be coming by Lough Graney. I promised him a good welcome from you, Brian.

BRIAN. You did well promising that. Go you, Murrough, with Maelmora. I myself will go towards the weir. He might chance to come from the south.

MALACHI. I will go along with you, Brian. We can be pricing the colts in the river meadows as we go.

BRIAN (*To Brennain*). Make the table ready, Brennain. When Sitric comes all we have to do is to see his name put to the agreement, and to sit down to dinner.

(*The Kings all go out. The servants come forward.*)

PHELAN. This peace is a great celebration now of Brian's wedding with Queen Gormleith. Malachi the High King owning the whole of the North. Brian King of the whole of the South! Maelmora safe in his own place in Leinster. Meddling with one another no more than the white and the yolk of an egg! Peace as round and as sound as the eggshell itself. Peace forever in Ireland and Leinster and in Kincora!

BRENNAIN. Ah, what signifies talking about eggs and about agreements? The one is as perishable as the other. Believe me there is some mother of mischief does be always at roost overhead in Ireland, to claw and to shatter pacifications or any well disposed thing at all. Peaces and treaties! I would make no treaty with the Gall but to strike their head off!

PHELAN. You are always ready, Brennain, to put ridicule upon anything I will lay down. But I know well, whatever may have happened at any other time, this peace will never be broken. Who is there to frustrate it? It is not the Danes will do that and they being the way they are, not daring to let a squeal out of them, no more than a hunted otter would have gone hiding in a stream.

RURY. Whoever may break that peace it will not be my master Malachi. Too wide he is and too fleshy, and too easy, to be craving more of the cares and the hardships of the world. It is quiet he is asking now, to get some comfort and to train his four-year-olds, and to be sleeping his sound sleep through the night time.

PHELAN. Whoever might break the peace it will not be my own

master Maelmora. Now that the Danes are beat, he has no mind to be beat along with them, and in my opinion he is right.

BRENNAIN. There is no one but must say that Brian has done his best for peace, and he going so far as to bring home a wife, as a notice and as a sign that the country should be tranquillised. It is not out of Kincora that any provocation will be rising up. Sure our teeth are clogged yet with the leavings of the wedding feast.

RURY. There is no chance I suppose, my hero, that the newly married Queen might bring the pot to the boil?

BRENNAIN. Ah, not at all! What call would she have to be meddling in things of the sort? A very pleasant plain lady, kind and nice and lucky; it's as easy talk to her as a child.

PHELAN. I was wondering not to see her to-day and the kings having that big work in hand. That is not the way she used to be in her early time in Leinster.

BRENNAIN. Spearing eels she went, up in the shallows of the river. A good housekeeper she is. She is not one would take her ease and leave the Friday without provision. And there are many not having as much as her, wouldn't walk the road with pride.

RURY. You are a very clever man surely Brennain and a good judge of the Queens of the world and their ways.

BENNAIN. Sure we had a Queen in it previously. Murrough's mother that was a girl of the Hynes out of Connacht. A very nice biddable woman, rocking the cradle with Murrough, and thanking God for her own good luck through the Sundays and holidays of the year. And what Brian got at the first offer, it is not likely it will fail him secondly, and he being high up in the world, and getting sense and experience through up to near three-score years.

PHELAN. Stop your mouth now. Here she is herself coming up the path from the river side. Stepping on the tops of the grass she is, as if she never felt the weight of her crosses; and she a widow-woman before Malachi joined with her itself.

(GORMLEITH *comes to threshold and stands looking in. All the servants fall back and bow obsequiously.*)

BRENNAIN. A welcome before you, Queen, and that you may keep your luck ever and always; and what you have not to-day, that you may have ten times more this day twenty years!

GORMLEITH (*giving him her eel-spear and net*). Who are these that are come to the house? Is that not Phelan of the King of Leinster's people? You are Rury, King Malachi's serving man. But the High King is not here yet?

RURY. The High King is here these three hours, Queen; he took notice of you in the boat, and you going up the river.

GORMLEITH. It is likely he is taking some rest, according to his custom.

RURY. He is not, Queen, but he is after doing the business he had taken in hand.

GORMLEITH (*coming to* MAELMORA'S *chair, putting her hand on the back of it*). What put that hurry on him? He used not to be so eager, but slack.

RURY. Troth he made no delay this time, but sent word to Brian it was best to make a start and to finish the work out of face. Himself and Maelmora sat down after that, and never quitted arguing and sounding out the writings they had put down, till such time as they had their agreement made out with Brian.

GORMLEITH (*to* PHELAN). Did my brother agree to this new bargain?

PHELAN. He did agree where he had to agree to it, and Malachi that had him led to make a stand against Brian, giving in and agreeing on his own side.

GORMLEITH. He had a right to have come to me for advice. Maelmora is as simple and as innocent as a child.

PHELAN. What now has Malachi himself got out of this? Did the High Kingship slip from him yet?

RURY. Malachi is High King now and always, and with the help of God he will be King in Tara to the end.

GORMLEITH. What part have the Danes now in the new agreement? Is Sitric given any share in the country?

PHELAN. Sitric is to be forced to quit the country before the quarter, and his troop of Danes along with him, or to be under the jurisdiction of Malachi and of Brian.

GORMLEITH. I was never told that. Did Sitric agree to be banished, or to take orders from Malachi?

PHELAN. It is what I heard them saying, he will give in to stop here under orders. Maelmora, that went security, said he would write his name to that treaty of pacification, between this and the fall of night.

GORMLEITH. They did not forewarn me he was coming. I thought the business would not be pressed on in this way.

PHELAN. It is for himself they are waiting at this time. They are gone out to hurry him, and they are right doing that. He to make any more delay, it will not be answerable to the dinner.

GORMLEITH. They will be wanting their dinner after such great

55

work. I am greatly in your way, Brennain. You had best make ready the tables.

BRENNAIN. All is ready and waiting, Queen. We have but to set the chairs, and to bring in the dishes that are dressed.

GORMLEITH. I do not see you stirring yourself, Rury. Is there no help you can give?

RURY. I can be putting the chair ready for the High King. (*Pulls a chair forward.*)

GORMLEITH. Do not put that chair for him, that is King Brian's chair.

RURY. It is the custom to give the best chair to the High King of Ireland.

GORMLEITH. It was the custom. But remember the High King is not above King Brian now. He is but his equal. They are the Kings of the North and the South.

RURY. I would never give in to put Malachi below any other man at all.

PHELAN. Where can I put the King of Leinster's chair?

BRENNAIN. Put it there—by Malachi's left hand. That is it. A little farther down.

GORMLEITH. You are putting it too close, Phelan. King Malachi is so high over all, there must be the length of a sword left between him and any other King of a Province.

PHELAN. My master is good enough to sit close up to any one of the kings of the world.

GORMLEITH (*to Rury*). You should put these forgetful men in mind that your master is master over them.

RURY. So he is, so he is! It is Tara is the capital of Ireland.

BRENNAIN. It is not, but Kincora that is the capital.

PHELAN (*at window*). There is Sitric coming; himself and the King of Leinster are on the brow of the hill.

BRENNAIN. It is best for us to be putting the meat on the table so. (*Goes to the door, and brings back dishes one by one from outside.*) Sitric will sign his name with the less delay the time he will see the fat of the mutton hardening.

GORMLEITH (*who has gone to the window, turning from it*). They are a long way off. I will go meet them. You have time enough. I will leave you an advice. Be sure that the best dish is set before the greatest of the Kings. (*Goes out.*)

BRENNAIN. Here is the best dish, the salted round of the beef. I will set it here before King Brian.

56

RURY. It is before Malachi it has a right to be put. The best dish should be put before the High King.

BRENNAIN. You heard what Queen Gormleith is after saying, that Brian is every bit as good now as Malachi.

RURY. He is not as good as the King of Tara; and he never will be as good. Put the beef here.

BRENNAIN. Here is a dish is as good, a roasted quarter of a boar.

RURY. We have plenty of pigs in the North. A pig is no great dish for a King. The beef is the more honourable dish.

BRENNAIN. If it is, it is to the more honourable man it is going.

RURY. How do you make that out? The High King is the most honourable man.

BRENNAIN. The High King is it? Where would he be this day but for Brian?

RURY. What is that you are saying?

BRENNAIN. I tell you if it was not for Brian taking the Danes in hand the way he did, it is hares of the wilderness Malachi might be looking for milk from to-morrow morning, instead of from cows!

RURY. Brian is it? Where was Brian the day Malachi took the golden collar from the big Dane? Answer me that!

BRENNAIN. That Malachi may be choked with that same collar before the size of my nail of this beef will go down his gullet until he has asked it first of Brian!

RURY. Asked it of Brian!

BRENNAIN. Asked it and begged it, the same as a queen's lapdog begs at the table.

PHELAN. And what share of the meat is the King of Leinster to get? It is another round of the beef should be put before him!

BRENNAIN. The next time the King of Leinster comes here he will find his fill of beef before him— his own cattle that will be coming from now to then, as tribute from the traitors of Leinster!

PHELAN. Holy Saint Brigit! Listen to what they are saying of your own province!

RURY. Brennain is right that time. Tripe and cow-heels and pigs' crubeens are good enough for that troop, and too good!

PHELAN. Oh, let me out of this! Tripe and crubeens, and all that plenty in the house. I will call upon all the poets of Leinster to put the curse of scarcity on Kincora!

BRENNAIN. My grief I have not the time to sharpen this knife. No matter. It is on your own bones I will sharpen it. (*All seize knives and threaten each other.* MAELMORA, MURROUGH, SITRIC, *and* GORMLEITH *come in.*)

57

MURROUGH. Have the dogs been let loose from the kennels? Brennain, what is the meaning of these noises?

BRENNAIN. It is those ones that made an attack on me. For quiet I myself am, and for getting ready the table.

PHELAN. Taking the best of the beef he was, and leaving my master to the culls.

BRENNAIN. It was Rury that was asking the best of the chairs for Malachi.

RURY. Let you keep your chair so! Malachi will be master in whatever chair he may sit.

MURROUGH. Malachi master here! That is a new thing for us to know.

PHELAN. Some say he is uppermost, and some say Brian, but the King of Leinster is put in the lowest place of all.

MAELMORA (to MURROUGH). Am I thought to be so greatly below Brian, on the head of agreeing to a settlement with him?

MURROUGH. You agreed to pay rent for your province. It is not the one is uppermost that sends in a rent.

MAELMORA. If Brian had spoken in that way I would not have given in to send it. I have a mind to keep it back even now.

MURROUGH. If we send our men looking for it, there will be maybe more profit with us than with yourself.

MAELMORA. I am well able to hold my province against the men of Kincora. Let them fish and shiver like cranes in moonlight, before they will see so much as one staggering bullock coming from Leinster.

SITRIC (to MAELMORA). You made out it was for peacemaking you brought me here. It seems to me more like the making of a battle.

GORMLEITH. If that is so, it might happen as lucky. You are in your early days, it might chance you to make a better fight for yourself.

SITRIC. It is a great pity I came to Kincora without bringing a good back of my own men.

MURROUGH. If you had come bringing your fleet of Danes, it is likely you might have got a welcome would have kept you here until the brink of Judgment!

SITRIC. It would have been right to have smoked out this den in the winter nights that are past.

MURROUGH. That smoke would have brought us out to do what was done on you at Sulcoit.

GORMLEITH (to MAELMORA). It was your advice that brought

Sitric here. Are you satisfied he is getting good treatment and a friend's welcome?

MAELMORA. Keep your tongue quiet, Murrough. It is hardly Sitric will bear from you, what he might bear from Brian.

SITRIC. I will take no scolding salute from Brian or from any other man, whatever you yourself may be in the habit of taking.

MAELMORA. I have no such habit. I will not let any man say that.

SITRIC. You have taken his orders, you are dragging me into his service the same as yourself.

MAELMORA. If I joined in his league it might happen to me to break away from it yet. It might be less troublesome after, even if it should bring me to my death.

MURROUGH. There is many a man met with a woeful death through setting himself up against King Brian.

BRENNAIN. That is good talk, Murrough! It is Brian has the sway in every place! It is Murrough, my darling, and Brian, are the two hawks of battle of the Gael!

PHELAN. It is myself and Maelmora will turn you to jackdaws! It is ourselves will change your note for you!

RURY. Malachi and the Hill of Tara!

BRENNAIN. Kincora and the River Shannon!

PHELAN. No rent to Brian! We'll hold the cattle!

RURY. Hi for Tara!

BRENNAIN. Out with the Meath graziers!

PHELAN. Down with Kincora!

BRENNAIN. No, but down with Leinster! (MURROUGH, SITRIC, and MAELMORA *are striking at one another with their swords*.)

RURY. The Kings! (MURROUGH, MAELMORA, *and* SITRIC *draw back as* BRIAN *and* MALACHI *come in. The servants fall back*.)

BRIAN (*sternly*). Murrough, what ails you? Are these mannerly ways?

MURROUGH (*suddenly taking hand from sword*). It is you they were faulting, and Kincora. They gregged me with their threats and their jibes. They said they were as great as you. They said—I forget now what they said.

BRIAN. Shut your ears, Murrough, to stiff words said under your own roof. It is best not to hear what you have no leave to answer. (*To* SITRIC *and* MALACHI.) I ask your pardon— I am sorry such a thing has happened.

(*He goes aside with them.* MALACHI *and* GORMLEITH *meet.*)

MALACHI (*to* GORMLEITH). I got no chance before this to salute the Queen of Munster.

GORMLEITH. She is very thankful to King Malachi for the God-speed that was said to her in Tara.

MALACHI. It would seem that you have found in Kincora the stir it failed you to find in my own house.

GORMLEITH. It is likely I would have found stir if I had stopped with you for another while, and yourself and myself facing one another on the hearthside, through the dark evenings of the year.

MALACHI. It would be no wonder, in my opinion, if the Queen herself had put the kindling to his crackling wisp?

GORMLEITH. I would not put a lie on the High King, whatever opinion he might be giving out.

MALACHI. Mind now, Queen, what I am going to say. I am not joking or funning. You are come into a good man's house. Give heed to your flighty headstrong ways, or it may happen you some day to put kindling to no less a thing than the roof that gave shelter to you.

BRIAN (*coming over to them*). I am sorry, Queen, you have seen such disorder in this place, and you being in it so short a while. You will bring order into it now. I had to straighten out my own home, or it would fail me to shape the whole country to the one pattern. A house without a good woman over it is no better than a busy hillside, where men are shouting, and hounds are snapping at their prey, and mannerly ways are out of mind.

GORMLEITH. Indeed I have no complaint to make of all that I have found before me.

BRIAN. It is seldom a woman's voice was heard here through the years past, unless it might be in the keening, when the dead of our race are brought home.

GORMLEITH. It is no sleepy place I am come to, or a place where slackness would be in fashion. I am satisfied and well satisfied with the roof that has given me shelter.

MALACHI. Let us not be wasting time now, and the day going. Sitric is here with us. Let him put his name to the agreement, and the dinner will turn the whole company to better humour. Good meat and good drink are maybe the best peacemakers.

BRIAN. There is the agreement, Sitric. Maelmora, your uncle, put down the terms you had settled between you. You have but to put your name. The securities will be written with it to-morrow (SITRIC is silent.) Will you cast an eye on it? Or are you satisfied with whatever Maelmora has written?

MALACHI. We put down in the writing that you and your army

would agree to quit Ireland or to live in quiet, without arms, in the service of myself and of Brian.

SITRIC. I will not write my name to it.

BRIAN. You came here promising to do it.

MALACHI. It was of your own free will you sent in your submission. Why would you draw back from it now?

SITRIC. Words have been said to me that I am not used to put up with.

BRIAN. This is Murrough's foolishness. I have asked your pardon for it, and he will ask your pardon.

SITRIC. I will not agree to obey or give in to any one of you at all.

MALACHI. What is that you are saying?

SITRIC. I will not give in to yourself or to Brian. I will not give in to be a stranger and an exile. I will not bid my people to give up their arms. I will bid them to go on fighting to the last.

BRIAN. You know well you could not stand against us alone, through the length of a winter day.

MAELMORA. He will not be alone. I give up my share in this league. I would sooner be with the Danes, than under Brian of the Tributes.

MALACHI. How quick you youngsters are at taking offence! A couple of foolish words said, and all our trouble gone to loss. When you are as long on the road as we are you will take things easy. In my opinion Brian was too soft with the two of you up to this. It would have been better to have banished you, and gained some comfort for the both of us. (*To* BRIAN.) Maybe we can make them some offer. Let them have their own way with Leinster so long as they will not meddle with ourselves. A new war would be a weighty business. You were saying awhile ago the country was in great need of peace.

BRIAN. Entire peace is what is badly wanting, but a half peace is no better worth the winning than the half of the living child was brought to the Judgment of Solomon.

MALACHI. In my opinion you will not see entire peace or the end of quarrels in Ireland, till such time as the grass stops growing or talk comes to the thrush.

BRIAN. I tell you I will make no settlement that will leave any one of the five Provinces a breeding ground for the enemies and the ill-wishers of Ireland. When Charlemagne of the French took his work in hand he left no such a nest of mischief; or Harold in Norway, or Alfred of the burned cakes, that is in the histories. This tossed tormented country has to be put in order, and to be kept in order, and travel whatever road God laid out for it, without arguing and backbiting and the quarrelling of cranky bigoted men. Sitric must put his name to this or make himself ready for a battle and a check.

SITRIC (*takes parchment, looks at it a moment, then cuts it through with his sword and throws it down violently*). There is an end of your agreement!

BRIAN (*taking out sword*). This edge is sharp yet. God knows I am telling no lie saying I would sooner see it rusted than raddled.

MALACHI. War is a troublesome business. There is maybe no one of us will be the better of it in the end.

BRIAN (*unbuckling sheath*). But as to this cover it may rust and rot, for I will make no use of it from this out so long as there is so much as a whisper of rebellion or of treachery in any province or barony or parish, east or west, north or south! (*Throws it down.*)

SITRIC. Let my own stay with it till I come to bring it away! (*Throws down sheath.*)

MAELMORA. And there is mine along with it! (*He and* SITRIC *turn to go.*)

GORMLEITH (*to* MALACHI). That is the way we strike the board till we see the cards coming to us! The trump will be in our hands yet! Are you loth, Malachi, to trust your luck to the cards? Do not be daunted, Brian is on your side this time! But believe me, the world will wonder yet, at the luck you let go from you to Brian!

Curtain.

ACT II

[AFTER GLENMAMA]

SCENE: *Same room at Kincora. Heap of spoils on floor.* BRENNAIN *has just come in holding* PHELAN, *who is bound. Music outside and shouting.* RURY *is looking at spoils on floor.*

BRENNAIN. Those are terrible great shouts the people are letting out of them to welcome King Brian, that has beat the whole fleet of traitors at Glenmama, and has them ground as fine as meal!

RURY. And to welcome King Malachi that beat them along with him, and that will be here within the hour.

BRENNAIN. And maybe to welcome myself! What now do you say to me taking this prisoner in the battle! Drove him before me I did the whole of the way from Glenmama. Believe me it's the Leinster men can run well!

RURY. Is it my brave Phelan is in it, that went out such a hero to the war?

BRENNAIN (*pushing* PHELAN *before him*). Come on here! Is it that you said we were jackdaws? Give me a wisp of lighted straw, till I'll make him shout for King Brian!

RURY. That's the chat! That's the chat! Put terror on him now, till he'll let out a shout for the High King!

BRENNAIN. That's the way we drag traitors back, that went boasting and barging out of Kincora.

PHELAN. If I did boast, you need not be putting the blame on myself. The dog to get a bone, the dog's tail must wag. I do but wag as my master pleases.

BRENNAIN (*looking at heap of spoils*). It is ourselves are nourished with the bone presently! Satin stuffs, gold rings, jewels would buy out the entire world! Coming in since morning they are! You would not meet a car or a Christian on the road but is charged with them! Robbed by the Danes they were from every strong place in Ireland and from the hidden houses of the Sidhe!

RURY. I am best pleased my own mind to be dwelling on the prisoners. Sitric to be taken with his army of Danes. The King of Leinster to be brought here (*turns to* PHELAN) spancelled in a gad, the same as his own serving man.

BRENNAIN. It was Murrough took him, my darling boy! Concealed he was in a yew tree. It was Murrough dragged him out of it, the same as a wren's nest.

PHELAN. It is very unmannerly you are, to be casting up that yew tree against the King of Leinster. Sure he not to go hide in it, he might not be at this time in the living world.

RURY. What now will Queen Gormleith have to say, her son and her brother the same as judged and executed, and the whole of their means made our prey.

PHELAN. That is a thing will not happen. I tell you, that is a lady is well able to bring a man from the foot of the gallows. She is not one would leave it to God to rule the world, the time she herself has a hand to put to the work.

BRENNAIN. Brian that was turning to be kind will not show kind-

63

ness this time. He took it very bad, Maelmora and Sitric to stand up to him the way they did, and he after binding them by an act of peace. It is not consanguinity will save Queen Gormleith's brother, or get off her lad of a son.

PHELAN. She will gain safety for him, and for the two of them, through some enticement or some strategy of her own. It is easy seen, Brennain, that you were never joined with a wife.

BRENNAIN. If I was itself, there is no woman or no score of women, cranky or civil, coaxer or cross, would ever put me from my opinion, I once to have laid it down.

PHELAN. It is likely Brian will give in to the asking of the woman he will have beside him through the length of the four quarters of the year. Whinging and whining, she will come to him; making threats she will go perish on their grave. I tell you there are women in it, would coax the entire world.

RURY. And what way would it profit her, striving to influence Brian? Sure there is no one has power to judge and to chastise these prisoners at all, but only the High King, that is Malachi.

BRENNAIN. It is a bad chastisement he will be apt to be giving them. Brian would be severe on no person if there was anything at all to be said for him. But as to a wind from the North, it will never be civil or kind.

RURY. It will no way serve her to come purring around Malachi. She knows that well herself. It is more likely a taste she will give him of the sharpness of her claws.

PHELAN. The Lord be with Malachi she to set herself against him, in earnest! She would have him out of the High Kingship between this and the roosting of the hens.

RURY. It is not likely Brian would be asking to earn the name of a grabber, snapping up the High Kingship for himself.

BRENNAIN. If he did grab it, he would turn it to better profit than what Malachi is doing. What signifies a High King that is satisfied with such things as may come into his hand, without any sort of big thoughts and of lofty plans? Brian now would stand at his own hall door and cast an eye over the whole of the domains of the world and Tir-nan-oge along with them. To get this country pacified, the way he could work out all that he had in his mind, that is what set him cracked and craving after peace. I never knew him to be disconcerted but the day that last treaty was tore. "Give me twenty year, or ten year itself, of quiet," says he to the Queen, "and the world will bow down to the name of Ireland." "Give us the High Kingship," says I

64

to myself with myself, "and we will find something more to do with it, than to go racing garrans in Meath."

RURY. No fear of you getting it. It was sealed and witnessed in the bond, Malachi to preserve it for his lifetime.

BRENNAIN. Brian to get it, he would make Ireland the leader of the universe! The men of arts from every part coming to learn their own trade; coming by shoals they would be, like mackerel on the spring tide! Every smith of a forge shaping golden bracelets! Every scholar in a school speaking the seven languages! Every village of cabins a city with towers and with walls! Towers am I saying, no but rounded steeples would penetrate the thunder in the clouds.

RURY. Well you are great old warriors for giving out boasting talk in Kincora.

BRENNAIN. It is Brian will put his orders on the ocean, on the narrow seas and the wide! His ships will go searching out every harbour! Every strange sail will moult and wither, getting a sight of his lime-white sail. He will put his rent on the kings of the world, they will pay him a heavy rent!

RURY. Pride grew in you, as rank as cabbage of the young moon, since you chancing on a straggler of your own!

BRENNAIN. Rents they will send, and tributes they will send! Sea-horses having blue eyes, barrels broke and bursting with the weight of rendered gold! Elephants' teeth, hairy men, and peacocks, the same as to Solomon of the Jews.

PHELAN. It was a woman's wit baffled King Solomon at the end, the time he thought to drive her from his house. What is Queen Gormleith apt to be at all that time? Do you think will she be satisfied to be sitting quiet, and her thoughts near as flighty as your own?

BRENNAIN. She will be satisfied and tethered and clogged, with the sight of the grandeur all around! There is no woman at all but would be subjugated, and all the nations to be blowing the horn before her man.

RURY (looks out of window. A shout outside). There is King Brian himself at the door, and the people going cracked after him. Malachi should be on the road yet. I see no sign of him coming. It is best for me to go ask news of him, and be getting a shout for him by the time he will come in view. (Goes out.)

(BRENNAIN pushes PHELAN off through door. BRIAN comes in, goes slowly to his chair.)

BRENNAIN. The Branch to King Brian! All the people are gone

wild for you! The poets are starting a poem about the great victory of Glenmama! A song with as many verses as my fingers and toes, and a great deed in every verse.

BRIAN. That it may be a good one, for if I get my own way I will give them no cause to make songs from this out, on the head of battles or of slaughter.

BRENNAIN. Good is it? The words are coming fast as the running of the Danes before us! Making for the sea they were the same as gulls; they are putting the screaming of gulls in the poem.

BRIAN. Let them twang it a long way off! I have had enough of noises. (*Sits down and takes off sword.*)

BRENNAIN. What will we do with the treasures we brought away? The whole place is choked up with them.

BRIAN. Make three shares of them. A share for the High King, and a share for the learned men, and a share for Kincora.

BRENNAIN. I will, I will keep the best share for ourselves.

BRIAN. The best must go to the High King.

BRENNAIN. It is you yourself have a right to be High King, Brian, after this great victory. I tell you all Ireland is thirsting for it.

BRIAN. I know, I know, they were sounding it out on the roads. They are calling out against two kings being in the one saddle. But they may deafen themselves with shouting before they will make me break my peace with Malachi.

BRENNAIN. They'd sooner you. It is not Malachi will master the five provinces, tearing and spitting at one another the way they are. Five wild cats struggling in a bag, and four times five claws on every one of them.

BEGGAR (*at door*). In the name of Brigit is beside me with her cloak,
   In the name of Michael is before me with his power,
   MacDuagh, MacDara, and Columcille of my love,
   I put this house under the power of the Man having the candle!

BRIAN. Who is that?

BRENNAIN. Some travelling woman carrying the bag—the heavy sweat running down beside her—she should have been running on her road. (*Beggar comes in.*) What is it brings you here? What call have you coming here, you that are used to ditches and to haggards, to be standing on the royal threshold of the King?

BRIAN. It is sometimes those that go sleeping on the straw of a haggard have their own view of angels of heaven. You would seem not to have got any long sleep in any place. Where was it you spent the night-time?

BEGGAR. Last night at the feet of the poor,
  To-morrow at the feet of the Son of God.
  I ran fast, and very fast, to come as far as yourself, Brian.

BRIAN. What is it makes you so uneasy?

BEGGAR. Looking I am for the hidden key. Go search it out yourself, King Brian, in this day of your great victory.
  For all you have won of silver and of store,
  And the people raising you in their arms,
  Let you be remembering bye and bye,
  Let you do your ploughing for the harvest in heaven!

BRIAN. God knows I have ears for that call if the hurry of the times did not hold me.

BEGGAR. Come searching for the key of heaven. It is in some hidden vessel.
  Come out before your candle will be spent,
  At the asking of the Man beyond, the King of Sunday.
  Make yourself ready for the day of the Mountain,
  Before your lease will be out and your summons written!

BRIAN. It is the wanderers of the world should be happy, being freed as they are to run that road. I myself am a labouring man under orders, having the weight of this (*holding up sword*) in my hands through the days and the hours and the months and the years.

BEGGAR. Any labouring man at all would be free to throw down the scythe at the end of the day, and the bell ringing.

BRIAN. In my contract, the Saturday night is all one with the Monday morning. It is the King of the Angels gave this to me. It is with it I am striving to cut the name of Ireland in clean letters among the nations. It is with this I have to do my work, until such time as the poor class, the people that are very sorry, will get some ease and some comfort and some wealth.

BEGGAR. You are out of it! You are out of it! Bruise the ground and that will be done for you. Put that weighty thing out of your hand. Take in place of it nine drops of the water of wisdom—bring down Adam's paradise till we have it about us on every side; teach all the people to be telling the hours, till they have their eyes clear to see the angels walking Ireland in plenty!

BRIAN. I will surely turn to no other work, the time I will have freed the whole of the country from all keening and mischief and treachery. It is to bring that time I have stooped my back till now from the rising of the sun.

BEGGAR. That that time may come soon and come happy!

BRIAN. Look now at that ring. It is worth great riches. Take it and give me your prayers. Bring me word that a lone woman can walk Ireland carrying a ring like that, and no one troubling her, and I will take it as a sign I am given leave to sit down at the table of the angels.

BEGGAR. I will do that, I will do that for you. I will run and run till I will loosen your mind from its cares. My grief that I am not a salmon to go leaping through the streams of Ireland to bring news there is no blemish on its peace, or a crane to go flying in the same way. My grief that I have but these two bare feet. (*Takes ring and turns to go.*)

Brigit of victories, put your cloak around me,

Come, Michael Oge, and take me by the hand,

O bush of shelter, O well reared archangel,

Come travel beside me over ridges, over bogs!

GORMLEITH (*coming in*). Brennain, take away this poor woman from the place she has no right to be, let her sit with the other beggars at the gate or give her a charity and let her go. Leave me here with the King. (BRENNAIN *and beggar go out*.)

BRIAN. Ah, my Queen, I had sent for you. Have you no welcome before me?

GORMLEITH. A welcome and a great welcome to you, Brian.

BRIAN. It is in your words—but your face gives no good welcome. You are not looking flowery, but pale.

GORMLEITH. There has heavy news reached to me, that has put me to and fro.

BRIAN. No wonder in that, my poor Gormleith. I your own comrade on the one side, and your own blood and kindred on the other side, there must trouble fall upon you, whatever side is uppermost.

GORMLEITH. The trouble is gone from me. You are back here with me, and you are not looking vexed but kind.

BRIAN. My dear, you are nearer to me than my heart.

GORMLEITH. I knew there would be no fear, you being in the one house with me again.

BRIAN. There will be nothing to call us from one another from this out. We have a great work to do for this country together. Our best time is coming, and our shining time.

GORMLEITH. And you will not refuse me my first request?

BRIAN. You had no request to make up to this, because I gave all before your asking. Tell me what is it you are wanting from me now?

68

GORMLEITH. You will put no hard punishment on Maelmora and on Sitric? You will not banish them out of Ireland? You will forgive them? You will let them go free?

BRIAN. As for myself, the time of hardness is behind me. But you are forgetting it is not by me they must be judged.

GORMLEITH. Ah, but whisper now, you will do it this time, you will make some way to bring it about? You would not see me fretting, fretting, after my son that is my darling—and my brother?

BRIAN. It is the High King has to be judge.

GORMLEITH. Malachi? Then they are the same as lost! What chance will they have facing him? He will be bitter against them on my account.

BRIAN. You are not right saying that. It is given in to Malachi that he is a fair man and an honest man.

GORMLEITH. It is not my son will get fair play from him. Judge him yourself, Brian, and give him the punishment you think right, and whatever it is I will make no complaint.

BRIAN. I would be glad and very glad to comfort you, but that is a thing cannot be done.

GORMLEITH. You are a great man and a great king. You can do everything. Give in to this now, and it is not to-day or to-morrow I will serve you, but every day.

BRIAN. What I can give I have given, without any interest or any bargain.

GORMLEITH. Why would you give in to Malachi? Through this while past he is lessening, you are strengthening, there is no one but will say you are the strongest.

BRIAN. The law is stronger again. It is the law that the High King must judge kings and makings of kings.

GORMLEITH. That is a crooked law. Break away from it, Brian.

BRIAN. Give heed to me now, I agreed to the laws and swore to them, and I will not be the one to turn and to renage. You would have no good opinion of me yourself, Gormleith, I doing that.

GORMLEITH. Then it is certain they will be sent to their death.

BRIAN. They took the chance of that, and they going into the war. There are many have lost life and all through their work.

GORMLEITH. He will put me down, putting them down. That will not satisfy him. He will accuse me along with them, he will say I stirred them up. It is best for me to take my place beside them. Let the three of us be judged together.

BRIAN. That will not happen. The High King himself would not dare to meddle with my wife.

GORMLEITH. It will be best. It is not to banishment they will be sent. I will go meet my own death with them, with Sitric and with Maelmora. I will not go on living after them. My heart will break in me, and I will die! It is soon we all will be in the ground together.

BRIAN. I thought the woman I married had more courage in her.

GORMLEITH. Ah, it is hard to keep courage when trouble comes scalding the heart.

BRIAN. If they had been killed in any of their battles, you would have keened them, and put a high stone over them, and raised your head again and not given in to grief.

GORMLEITH. That would have been a good death. But what are they going to now but a poor shameful lonely death? Oh, Maelmora! Oh, Sitric! Oh, dear black head! Oh, my child that I have never wronged! But God be with all the mothers of the world!

BRIAN. You were brought up in a king's house, you knew the rules of every quarrel and of every game. And you were married into kings' houses, and you should know, whatever hand the cards come into, the game must be played out fair. And those laws and these rules will not be broken, even if they should break a queen's heart, or it might be a king's in its track.

MURROUGH (coming in). Here now is the High King.

BRIAN. Bring in the prisoners before him. (MURROUGH goes out. GORMLEITH goes back into corner where she is not seen.)

MALACHI (comes in and sits down at table). I was delayed on the way. Your Munster roads are good inn-keepers, they would not let the wheels of my chariot go from them.

(MURROUGH comes in with SITRIC and MAELMORA bound, followed by BRENNAIN, RURY, and PHELAN.)

BRIAN. The prisoners are here before you.

MALACHI. There is no cause for delay. Their judgment will be a quick one.

BRIAN. Let it be a merciful one as well as just.

MALACHI. It is sometimes what is the hardest to one or to two, is the punishment kindest at the last to the scores and the hundreds.

BRIAN. Have they any excuse to make for themselves?

MURROUGH. They have made none to me.

MALACHI. There is no excuse for them to make.

BRIAN. What have you to say in your own defence?

MURROUGH. You hear, Maelmora and Sitric, what my father is asking.

70

MAELMORA. I will say no word. I went out fighting, and the fight turned against me.

SITRIC. Where is the use of talking? Nothing I could say would turn your mind from whatever you may have planned.

BRIAN. What do you say, High King?

MALACHI. There is nothing to be said, but the story we all know before. These men were bound to peace, they had promised peace. I had need of quiet, Brian was calling for quiet, the whole country was in need of it. The whole of Ireland was a raddled fleece, a flock torn by wild dogs. We that were as if herding, were tired out with keeping them off. I agreed to give up a great deal to Brian for the sake of a settlement, and I held to my word, and they broke their word. There is no one can put trust in them from this out. That is the whole story. Is there a lie in what I have said, Brian?

BRIAN. There is no lie in it. All you have said is true.

MALACHI. You know well what way the law would condemn them; and these have no more right to law than a dog or a fox from the woods.

BRIAN. That would mean death.

MALACHI. The wild dog that is hanged will worry no sheep. The fox that is dead will devour no lambs.

MURROUGH. They can make no complaint. They did not spare their own prisoners, or their rebels.

GORMLEITH (coming forward). Malachi!

MALACHI (sternly and rising). This is not a right place for you, or a fitting place.

GORMLEITH. Malachi, the time you and I myself parted one from another, there was many a thing to forgive between us. Whatever you may have working in your mind against myself, I beg and pray you not to let it work against these.

MALACHI. God knows, that is above us, there is nothing in my heart against them, but the thing all this country that they have wronged must have against them, the attack made by them upon the peace of Ireland, and the great slaughter done by their means at Glenmama.

GORMLEITH. I will ask no other thing of you for ever, Malachi, but to stretch out now and to forgive them.

MALACHI. I would wish any other in the whole world to have made that request, till I would show it is no grudge or no malice is making me refuse it, but the great necessity of this country.

GORMLEITH. Put it from your mind there is any woman before

you, but only King Brian's wife. It is a good man's wife is making this asking.

MALACHI. It is his own good name I am serving. I am not willing for the people to say, and the generations that are rising, that King Brian came meddling with the laws that are for their protection and their safety. It is not Brian would wish it to be said among the people, it was a woman came around us and misled us.

GORMLEITH. Ah, if it is to the people you are calling to bear witness, I can tell you what is it the people are saying. They say it is you yourself have the sway, and that it is under your sway all they own has been turned to wrack and to ruin. Yes, Brian, I know what I am saying (BRIAN *has tried to interrupt her*). In his early days there was no one to beat him, he was wary, he was hardy, he was great. But look now the way things are in his province, and in every place that is under him! No one travelling your highways, but it is in the byroads men must creep, your wheat fields all headland, the children treading on the hungry grass. They are cursing you for that. Oh, I have heard them. They say they would as soon be under the wicked Danes as under Malachi that is turned careless and turned weak. That is why you will not let off these enemies that are beaten! You are afraid to show kindness, you are in dread of those poor hungry people, you are in dread they would say, "Take his place away from him, we were right; Malachi has turned to be weak."

MALACHI. You have said one true word, Gormleith, saying that I am in dread. I am that. I am afraid to show kindness. And I do not say but that these two left alone would be apt to give in, and to carry out their bargain straight and fair. But they would not do it, and they would not be let do it. It was I myself brought you back from the Danes, thinking to turn you to be loyal as a queen should. And it failed me to do it, and it will fail Brian, and it has failed him!

BRIAN. Take heed what you are saying! You are coming near to danger saying that.

MALACHI. Danger, yes, there is danger wherever this woman comes, and I have one question to put to her. The cause of this last war to be searched out, who is it would be found at the root of it?

GORMLEITH. I told you, Brian, he would draw down this on me, I forewarned you. It is best for me to take my place between my two. I will take my chance along with them. (*She goes between* MAELMORA *and* SITRIC.) If the fault was mine, let me pay the penalty. An unkind word to be thrown at a woman, it is little till it brings down her name altogether. The tree to begin to fade, what is there would bring it around? Malachi, I am willing to take you as my judge. You have accused me, give out the decree against me. Judge me here now on this floor.

MALACHI. I have no mind to judge any one at all, in this place. I made a great mistake giving in to come into it at all.

BRIAN. It was laid down between us, this work was to be done in Kincora.

MALACHI. I had no business coming here to be checked and dogged on every side. Tara is the place for judgments, and not the house of a king of a province.

BRIAN. This is a house that had the name of an honest house, and of a house for fair play to the high-up and to the poor.

MALACHI. There is too much meddling in it, meddling that will lead to confusion and the breaking of laws. I lay it on you, Brian, to keep order in the first place in your own home. As to these kinsmen of yours, I will bring them as I had a right to have done at the first, to Tara and before the Council of Tara.

GORMLEITH. You have very big pride in Tara, Malachi. But all Ireland knows, and you know, this man could put you out of it to-day if he would but lift his hand up and give the sign. It is only his kindness and his goodwill have left you up to this the name of being High King.

MALACHI. Is that your own opinion, Brian, or is it but the giddy talk of a woman that is vexed? If you think yourself equal to me, say it out, and the two of us will settle the case together.

BRIAN. I do say it. I say the time is come when there can be but one master in Ireland.

MALACHI. I agree to that. But whoever has Tara is master.

BRIAN. Wherever the greatest strength is, the Hill of Tara is. My strength has dragged Tara westward.

MALACHI. I will not give in to that. It is only in Tara I will give from this out any decree or any judgment.

BRIAN. Then I will give out my own judgment. I draw down on Maelmora, King of Leinster, that he has broken from the league made with me and the High King of Ireland, and turned his hand against us. I draw down on Sitric, the Dane, the great oppression he and his people have done upon Ireland.

MURROUGH. I will tell our men outside they have your orders to come in and to bring them to their death.

BRIAN. They have earned death and well earned it. They have nothing to urge against it. But stop! Let no one meddle with them! I will leave them their liberty and their life.

MALACHI. If Brian had not said that, I would say a fool had said it.

BRIAN. I am strong enough to show kindness, I have done with killing, I will have no more of it.

MALACHI. If you let them go, there will be quarrels again and killing.

BRIAN. I think not. They have learned their lesson, they know their master.

MURROUGH. If you let them go, it is hardly our own army will let them.

BRIAN. Is it with the threat of an army you are thinking to force me, boy?

MURROUGH. It is as if you yourself are forcing a peace.

BRIAN. That is what I am doing and what I have the right to do. I will make an end of quarrels. I will make an end of this custom of death answering to death through the generations, like the clerks answering to one another at the Mass. I will force a peace. Murrough, cut these cords. (MURROUGH *does so slowly*.)

MALACHI. It is against my will you are doing it.

BRIAN. Are they freed? Give back their arms to these kings.

MALACHI. They are no kings now, but traitors that have been worsted.

BRIAN. I say they are kings. Maelmora, I give you back your own kingdom of Leinster. Sitric, I give you your old town of Dublin to keep and to mind, for Ireland and for me.

MALACHI (*rising*). This is war then and the breaking of peace.

BRIAN. It is not, but the beginning of peace.

MALACHI. I will raise Connacht against you. I will call to my kinsmen in the north.

GORMLEITH. You know well you will get no help from the north, or from any other place, against King Brian.

MALACHI. That will be known soon and very soon.

BRIAN. If you think you can keep the High Kingship by force, I will give you the length of a month or of a quarter to bring your men together.

MALACHI. A month will be enough. I will lose no minute. The north and the west will be against you. (*He goes out followed by* RURY.)

BRIAN. War upon us again. Well, it was laid down—and I am ready.

GORMLEITH. He will get no help, Brian. No one at all will come out against you. His own messenger has said that in a song. He

74

went east and west, north and south, and he found the one story in every place. There was not a man in all Ireland that would raise a hand against King Brian.

BRIAN. His own messenger has said that? Then the sap of power has turned from him to me. The Man beyond is giving Ireland into my charge! His right hand is stretched over the north, his left to the south towards the sun, his face is towards the west. His angels have set their ladder upon Usnach, Victor, angel of Patrick, Axal, angel of Columcille, Michael, leader of armies! It is a great thing they are doing for me giving me the help of their hands. (*Rises.*) Ireland, Ireland, I see you free and high and wealthy; wheat in every tilled field, beautiful vessels in the houses of kings, beautiful children well nourished in every house. No meddling of strangers within our merings, no outcry of Gael against Gael! It is not so, Malachi will get help. Why am I taking the words of a woman, of a song? I have not done with war.   (MALACHI *comes back.*)

MURROUGH. He has come back to ask more time.

BRIAN. If he is in need of more time, I will give him up to a year.

MALACHI. I have a hard thing to say. I will not bring destruction on my people. I take back my big words. The luck has turned against me. The people have turned from me. I have no help to get. Queen Gormleith was speaking truth.

BRIAN. You are saying you will not bring out your men against us?

MALACHI. I will keep them ready, but it will be against the Gall.

BRIAN. You will give up all you are claiming. You will give up that crown?

MALACHI. I will not, but I must. (*Takes it off.*)

BRIAN. God has given me the power, it is to God I have to answer, it is for the peace of Ireland I have taken it.

MALACHI (*giving it*). Take it and the weight of it. Yet it was in the prophecy that I would be king after you in Tara.

BRIAN. I lift it in my hand that is stronger than your hand. I will send out the name of this kingdom through the entire world. I will bring all Ireland under the one strong rule.

GORMLEITH. Long life and a good life to Brian, High King of Ireland!

ALL (*but* MALACHI). Long life to the High King.

MALACHI. It is not you, yourself, Brian, have done this. It may seem to you this queen has brought you luck doing it. She has turned my luck backwards. Who is the next she will turn her hand against?

GORMLEITH (*going on her knees*). Do not listen to him, Brian. I would walk the world for you, and you having showed kindness to my darlings! You are my master, he never mastered me! In the time to come whoever may fail you, I myself will never fail or disappoint you!

BRIAN (*lifting her and turning to* BRENNAIN). Brennain, you need not share these riches. They are little enough altogether to offer to the Queen of Tara. (*They all turn to look at the spoils.*)

RURY (*at door*). The coach is ready master. The horses are fed and rested. (*He goes out.*)

MALACHI (*at threshold*). I will go. I have been long enough in this little place. A little place, a narrow place for so much buying and selling. Great gains, great losses. The crown of Ireland for Brian, the High Kingship for Brian, the treasures of Glenmama for Gormleith. Who has the worst of it? Brian has that Crow of Battle!

(*Goes out.*)

Curtain.

ACT III

[*Before Clontarf*]

SCENE. *Same room at Kincora.* GORMLEITH *sitting in a chair gloomily, her head in her hands.* SITRIC *asleep at back.* MAELMORA *comes in.*

MAELMORA. Are you so much up in the world at this time, Gormleith, that you will not give me a welcome?

GORMLEITH (*getting up to greet him*). I did not know you were come. They never told me. Speak easy. Do not waken Sitric, he is only here a short while. He was travelling through the night time from Dublin.

MAELMORA. They told me you were here. They said you did not like to be troubled with messengers.

GORMLEITH. I do not like the messages they bring me, that is all. "Will the Queen come to hear the reading of holy writings?" "Will

76

the Queen come to make ready for saints and bishops?" "Will the Queen come and kneel to wash the muddy feet of the poor?"

MAELMORA. Brian is surely getting a great name of piety to put along with his name of riches and of power; having, as he has, his head in the skies, and his hand in every good work.

GORMLEITH. Where is the use of gaining power if you go turn from it after to shadows? Heaven may be there as they say, but it is on earth we are living yet. We cannot stop the work of the day to go blinking after dreams of the night. And that is the thing Brian is doing at this time.

MAELMORA. If he does, it is that age is coming upon him as it must come upon us all. What ails you not to let him travel his own way?

GORMLEITH. There is no other way to rouse him. It is laid on me to keep him to the strength and the power of a king. It is I myself made him call the whole army together on this day, to do its exercises that you were bidden to come and see.

MAELMORA. I took notice a long way off of the tents and the flags and great troops of men. But what occasion is there for gathering them at this time more than any other time?

GORMLEITH. When Brian will see his men that helped him in his fighting time, it may stir his mind with the thought of those days, and turn it to do some great hardy thing.

MAELMORA. You had best have left the army to its rest. There is no peacock can have his tail spread out ever and always. And mind what I say, it is a woman's trade to be making all easy for her comrade the time he has a mind to live easy. To go rising early, hunting, or fighting, he is well content to do it, if it is of himself he does it. But a woman to be rousing him at the calling of the pigeons to the dawn, and to be drawing down on him the work he has to do, he will think her the worst in the world.

GORMLEITH. I am wishful indeed to be pleasant to him. He was very good to me. The world never saw a better man.

MAELMORA. Give in to him now and humour him. If it pleases him to make much of learned men, let you yourself make more again of them. If it pleases him to be praying, let you be at hand to say out the Amen; and believe me you will put a net about him that will never give way.

GORMLEITH. Indeed I have striven these many years to be helpful to him. He used to be uneasy, not having me at his hand. I lived in his looks and he in mine.

MAELMORA. That is the way it should be. Let you keep on that road and you will never go astray.

GORMLEITH. But now it seems like as if my hold on him is going from me. His mind is as if slipping away to some place I cannot reach to, that I do not know.

MAELMORA. He is near spun out, and it is right for him to be attending to his soul. Do not be grudging him his own comfort in fasting and in psalms. To be worrying yourself starts wrinkles. Keep the flowery look in your face and do not be managing more than your share. Did you learn yet to put thread in a needle? The clasp is gone from this cloak. Have you e'er a one to give me before I will wear it again?

(SITRIC *moves and leans on elbow listening.*)

GORMLEITH. I will put my own clasp on it and welcome. When was the old one lost?

MAELMORA. It was in the journey this morning. My people and the people of the Desii were bringing the fir trees Brian had sent asking for, and a dispute arose who should take the lead. I was not willing there should be any delay, and I put my own shoulder under one of the trees.

GORMLEITH. You, my brother, put your shoulder under a load?

MAELMORA. There was no dispute after that who was to take the lead. But the branch of a tree caught in the clasp and dragged it, and it was lost.

GORMLEITH. You, the King of Leinster, carried a load of timber into Kincora! I will sew no clasp upon the cloak.

MAELMORA. I saw no shame doing that much for Brian that gave me my liberty and my life.

GORMLEITH. But I myself see great shame in it. I see you growing soft and gentle, like an old man that would be nearing his end.

MAELMORA. Quiet yourself, Gormleith. You were always wild in your young youth, dragging me there and hither from the nurses. You have had the tormenting of three husbands since that time. Leave your brother alone.

GORMLEITH. I will not give in to it! It is Brian is bringing you to it with the doing away of war. No marching and running and wrestling, but attending on the preaching of the friars. There is not a hound belonging to you dares so much as to follow a hare across the merings, without leave from the judges or the law. You are getting no fair play, closed in here and there, having no liberty in the way you used, to go out fighting for your own profit. I tell you, the time Brian will die from you, he will leave you weak and groping and blind, your hands without strength or readiness, by reason of having slackened from the work. Drowsy you are growing the same as old spent men. The priest sounds the bell, and Brian follows it, and the rest of you follow after Brian.

MAELMORA. My poor Queen, I give you up altogether. You were surely born on a Friday, and the briars breaking through the green sod. Give me my cloak and I will go where the chess players are. Murrough called to me from there a while ago.

GORMLEITH. I will sew no clasp upon the cloak, or let you put it on you at all. It is no up-reared man it is fit for, but a serving man. Let the fire burn it to ashes, the fire is its fitting place.

(*She throws it in the fire and* MAELMORA *goes out.* SITRIC *rises up and comes forward.*)

SITRIC. That was good talk you were giving out to Maelmora. It is a queer thing a brother of your own to be some way sleepy and easy to satisfy.

GORMLEITH. I am no way to be blamed for my brother; but it would be right to put blame on me, my son to turn sluggish in the same way. And that is not a likely thing to happen. It is not my son that is without sap running in him. It is not a king's son of the Danes will content himself using meat, or stretched in sleep like a rich man, or calling out his sins like an old man, or a man on his last sick bed.

SITRIC. I knew well you would give your countenance to the work I have taken in hand.

GORMLEITH. What work is that?

SITRIC. I am come from joining with my own people. There was a ship of their ships came to Dublin, bringing presents for Brian, as was said. The whole of their ships are on their way. It is given out they are to make an attack upon Wales. It is not to Wales that they are going. When the Danes were driven out from here, there was no one of them gave up the claim to his land and its ownership. It is to get back their estates they are coming with their army at this time.

GORMLEITH. The Danes coming against us?

SITRIC. Brian will be left his own estate and his domain. Never fear, there will no harm happen him. He will be left with the most thing he cares for, with his churches and with his bells.

GORMLEITH. The Danes coming back to Ireland! That is a thing that must not happen! I will not let it be done! They must be driven back if they make any attempt to land.

SITRIC. It is at Clontarf they are coming to land. I myself am giving them my help, and I am expecting your own help.

GORMLEITH. You are out of your wits thinking that. You know well I will give you no help. What are you thinking to do is no less than treachery.

SITRIC. What way were you scolding at Maelmora this very minute, casting up against him that he was soft and peaceable, clogged with ease, doing nothing for his own hand? You were jibing at him because he gave in to Brian's law. I have my mind made up to break away from it, and you are no better content with myself. You know well you were calling out this good while, that nothing would serve the country but some war.

GORMLEITH. I tell you I will not let treachery be used by any one that is belonging to me. If I called for war, I did not call to you to bring it, but to leave it to the chances of the times.

SITRIC. If you had not led me to make sure of your help, why would I have promised to Sigurd Earl of Orkney and to Brodar of the Isle of Man?

GORMLEITH. You promised them that?

SITRIC. They asked a promise. Sigurd would not come join us without your call, he wrote his asking in this letter. Brodar wrote an asking of his own—there are the letters, you have to put your name to them. We have not so good a chance without having Brodar and Sigurd at our back.

GORMLEITH (reading letters). What daring they have, writing that! What sort are they thinking me to be? I will send them no answer at all. I will go and tell out the whole case to Brian. Let Brian himself send the answer.

SITRIC. Do so, and make ready a sheet for my burying. It is known I have been speaking with the messengers of the Danes. I am surely dead, or as good as dead, you making Brian uneasy and questioning.

GORMLEITH. Hurry, hurry then, go away out of this! I will not tell him until such time as you are safe. Make no delay! I must give the warning. He must lead his army to protect Clontarf. Go, hurry, make yourself safe.

SITRIC. Where would I go to? In what place would I be safe? Is it in Brian's country, hunted as an outlaw? Or with the Danes, telling them I had broken my promise and my word? I have no mind to go wandering, hiding in bushes and under rocks.

GORMLEITH. I will send you word if Brian goes against you—I will not let any harm fall on you. Go, now go.

SITRIC. I will not quit this place, until such time as your name is put to this letter and to that.

GORMLEITH. You are talking madness. That would be a treason out of measure! I am bound to Brian. I will be faithful to Brian. I am well pleased I turned against Malachi. I will never fail Brian or disappoint him.

BRENNAIN (*at door*). The High King is coming here, Queen, to take a view of the army from the door.

SITRIC. You have leave to give me up to him. I am well rewarded for taking heed to a woman's words. It is only a fool would pay attention to big words from any woman at all. Queen or no queen she will turn timorous, and run and fail you at the last.

BRIAN (*coming in*). You are welcome here, Sitric. Did you bring any strange news from Dublin? They were telling me you had calling on you some messengers of the Danes.

SITRIC. A ship that called to me with payments. They have sent back at your order the golden vessels and the painted books that were stolen from the churches in the time gone by. There are here a couple of the books. The vessels are weighty, they are at the door below. (*Shows books.*)

BRIAN. I am well pleased to get them. I would not wish those holy vessels to be left in any heathen hands. Go, Sitric, give them into the hands of the priests to be put in the chapel before the vespers will ring. I will call to the Bishops to consecrate them, coming back to the service of Christ.

SITRIC. The ship having left them, sailed away. (*Goes.*)

BRIAN. Take notice, Queen, that the men of the army have been gathered together according to your desire.

GORMLEITH (*at window*). I was looking at them a while ago. The hillsides are speckled with the troops of them.

BRIAN (*sitting down*). It is a comfortable thought it is only for show and for pleasure they are come. We have nothing to go out fighting for any more.

BRENNAIN. That is so, that is so, what need is there for fighting? Men of all learning struggling at the door, seven kings' messengers asking our friendship, a hundred cooks dressing the dinner, a tun of wine offered us for every day in the year. We will have to widen the whole world to hold Ireland, and to widen Ireland itself to hold Kincora!

GORMLEITH (*turning to* BRIAN). Come and look from the window. You can see a great throng of your men.

BRIAN. I think the time is come when I can let them all scatter to their own districts.

GORMLEITH. We have work for them to do together yet.

BRIAN. Their best work would be to put a thatch to their houses, and to turn all the wild scrub to barley gardens. What did the wandering woman say? To bring down Adam's Paradise again. I had some dream in the night time, it has gone from me—some dream of a place where war was not remembered.

GORMLEITH. It is best to keep our men to the work they are trained for, that is fighting.

BRIAN. I have made Ireland safe. I have put her name up among the nations. I have put on her the three crowns, the crown of wheat for strength, the crown of apples for pleasantness, the crown of lasting peace. I will break up the army for a year and a day. I will leave every man time to forgive his enemies, and to make his own settlement with God.

GORMLEITH (coming to BRIAN). You would make a great mistake doing that. I give you a strong advice to keep the army at its full strength. Believe me I am not without reason saying that.

BRIAN. Has there any news come to you of danger?

GORMLEITH. News, news, it is nothing new I am saying. Ireland has been fighting ten thousand years, and that custom to be changed, it is likely she would go to nothing. Peace, the priests have their tongues framed to it, peace, peace, peace. Is it certain it is so good a thing? Some that know all might not say that. It is in the sluggish time the little men grow to be many, and the great men give up living, and the trader has the sway. It is not you yourself would be satisfied, seeing that time to come.

BRIAN. I will be satisfied and well satisfied the time I will have shaped everything that is under me to the will of God. There is no fighting in that good place the Almighty has of his own.

GORMLEITH. This is the world and you cannot change the world's old custom. There must be fighting so long as there is anything at all worth fighting for. If there was not war in the world it would be right to make a war, to search out something to hate. Yes, I know all the talk of love and charity, but it is not of malice I am talking, but of the fury of a blast of wind against a heap of rotten dust. Keep your army ready to your hand now. Have you never a mind to go forcing the Cross on the nations of the East? Armenia, where the Holy Tree was put up, is owned now by heathens that deny it. Other uses to fail, that would be a great thing and a grand thing for your army to do.

BRIAN. If I had a score less of years upon me, that would be a good thing to do. But the time fails me, and I have no leave to do but the one thing. I have leave in my own narrow kingdom to begin the thousand years of peace.

GORMLEITH. Maybe some danger may rise up. We are never done with danger. Suppose now the Danes should come attacking, striving to win back what they have lost.

BRIAN. That is a thing will not happen.

GROMLEITH. They are coveting to get back their old estates—they will not give up what they owned so readily as you may think. They might send out a fleet of ships—they might make it out to be going to some other place—they might gather other leaders to their help. When all would seem safe and quiet, just as it does this day, they might come to land suddenly—giving no warning. Let you keep your men ready for that.

BRIAN. Sitric has but just come from seeing their messengers and speaking with them. He has the whole strand in his charge, he would know if there was any thought of an attack. There is no fear of the Danes.

GORMLEITH. Yes, yes, Sitric would know—then they cannot be coming. But the provinces? You said you would not take your hand from the work till you had made all quiet in the provinces. There is a stir in them. They are starting up against you here and there. They are going back to their lawless ways. There is a king of Burren wanting to force a rent on Galway. There are uproars and robberies in the north.

BRIAN. That is bad news, but it may not be true, it may have grown in the telling. Are you very certain it is true?

GORMLEITH. I am certain.

BRIAN. I am sorry indeed to hear that. I thought the very day had come when I could free myself from this (*touches sword*) altogether. But that hope was a deceit and a flattery.

GORMLEITH. Come out now and consult with the captains. Bid them make themselves ready to go and put down all these troubles.

BRIAN. If there is trouble to be put down I myself will go and do it. I will not slacken my hand so long as there is work to be done. But my heart is tired out with waiting for the keening and the treachery to be at an end.

GORMLEITH. Come out, come out before the door. They will give you a great welcome there.

(*They are going to door when* BRENNAIN *appears in it.*)

BRENNAIN. There is some one here that is asking to see the King.

GORMLEITH. The King cannot see any person at all at this time.

BRIAN. Who is it is wanting me?

BRENNAIN. The travelling woman was here a long time ago—she has the appearance of one that would be wasted and worn with the length of the road.

BRIAN. Bid her to come in. (BRENNAIN *turns and lifts hand,* BEGGAR *comes in.*)

BEGGAR. It is many long days since I saw you before, King Brian.

BRIAN. What have you been going through in all that time?

BEGGAR. Going on my two feet, tramping fro and hither, looking for the news would free you to sit down at the table of the angels.

BRIAN. Christ knows well I would hurry to that supper, and I being free to attend it. But I am hindered here and there. At this time the trouble and the disturbance is in the provinces of Ireland.

BEGGAR. There is no disturbance and no trouble.

BRIAN. What way can you know that?

BEGGAR (*holding up ring*). Are you remembering the ring you gave me? There it is before you. I had to hide it for a good while, the time of quiet was not come. But at the last I have walked the whole country, and I lifting it up in my hand.

BRIAN. Did you go with yourself only, without company?

BEGGAR. Through the five provinces I went, from this to Toraigh in the north and from that again to Cliona's Wave in the south, with no one but myself and the goodness of the Lord.

BRIAN. Did no one meddle with you?

BEGGAR. When I was passing through Connacht there were young men riding horses, and they came as if at me. But then they said: "We will leave her free seeing we ourselves are free and all Ireland is free."

BRENNAIN. That is good, that is good. If Connacht is quiet all Ireland is quiet.

BEGGAR. When I went down into the north I took notice of a troop of rough men and one of them said: "It is no harm to rob this girl that is of the province of Munster." But another man of them said: "Do not, for it is not to the north or the south we belong now, but to the whole of Ireland." And for the peace of the whole country, King Brian, they thank God and you.

BRIAN. That is a lucky journey you have made, and a great story you have brought me. Many a woman has sat beside a king through her lifetime, and has done less than that to be remembered by.

BEGGAR. You can put away your sword this time, and turn your face entirely towards Heaven.

GROMLEITH. The King has work to do yet. His life has not run to its end.

BEGGAR. You are out of it, Queen, his life is near its beginning—the beginning of the lasting life of Heaven.

GORMLEITH. You do well preaching quiet, and your own heart so uneasy. You run here and run there, changing and vanishing like the moon.

BEGGAR. I run towards my home that is in the place beyond. I will take my rest when I have reached my home. Now I will go, I have given my message to the King.

BRIAN. It is a great message you have carried. It is from beyond the world it is come. This great new peace was made for me beyond the world. I saw it in a vision of the night. It is your voice is calling it back to me.

BEGGAR. It is likely it was the one message sent by some other messenger.

BRIAN. I saw in my dream a woman coming to me, many coloured, changing, that was Aoibhell the friend of my race. She came and she called to me and swept the darkness away, and showed me the whole country, shining and beautiful, an image of the face of God in the smooth sea. All bad things had gone from it like plover to the north at the strengthening of the sun. The rowan berries on Slieve Echtge were the lasting fruits of Heaven. The Gael had grown to be fitting comrades for the white angels. I could hear the joyful singing of the birds of the Land of Promise.

BEGGAR. That was a good vision and a very good dream. Those that hear that music will never be satisfied in any place where it is not found.

BRIAN. It went from me then, and I cried out after it, but Aoibhell said: "It is only at Clontarf you will come again to that vision and that perfect peace."

BEGGAR. Why did she say Clontarf? I wonder what meaning she had in that.

BRIAN. It is often dreams have not a straight meaning, or waking breaks it. It is here at Kincora I have had a witness to the perfect peace and not at Clontarf. Now, now at last I can put away my sword!

BEGGAR. Give it here to me. Give me that sword, I will hang it here upon the wall. (*He gives it and she hangs it up.*).

GORMLEITH. Has the army that is outside gone from your mind?

BRIAN. I am going out to it now, it is the last time I will have need of it. I will set every man of them free after the supper, that will be the feast of God's peace.

GORMLEITH. I ask of you, Brian, and I beg and I pray you to give in to what I say. I came here to put your name up, to bring you luck. I turned every stone for you, you will lose your name, you will lose me, oh, what can I say to turn you?

BRIAN. Have I and time not quieted this whirling heart? Go get yourself ready for the supper. Put on your silks and your jewels to do honour to it, your eyes are shining, they will shine out at the feast.

BEGGAR. Come, Brian, to the supper of the angels. To the Garden of Paradise and the branchy Tree of Life.

GORMLEITH. Go away, woman, out of this! He would listen to what would save him, and you not meddling! You are putting spells of weakness on him with your hymns. Do not let her entice you, Brian! Do not listen to that travelling woman of the roads, that tattered moon-mad beggar.

BRIAN. It is not her voice is calling to me but the voices from the place beyond.

BEGGAR (*at door*)

    Gabriel, the Virgin's messenger, is come,
    Michael, the rider of the speckled horse, is come.
    Axal, the good steerer, Rafael of our love
    Giving out the blessing for the supper of the King.

GORMLEITH. Go then, go, go to your destruction, drag the King to his destruction, let him go his own way! I do not begrudge it to him or to you. I tried to save him. He would not listen. He has made his choice, I am not in fault! The curse of Ireland be upon all beggars and their meddlings!

BRIAN (*turning back in doorway*). Go, Gormleith, to the church and pray, bend your knees, pray and repent, pray and repent, till the wildness has gone from your eyes and the pride from your heart, and the darkness from your vexed unhappy mind. (*He goes out.*)

GORMLEITH. Go then, go, I have done all I can do. I have done. I have no place and no part in you! I have not, I have not, I am done with Kincora. (*She throws herself in chair tearing her handkerchief in her rage.* MAELMORA *and* SITRIC *come in.*)

MAELMORA. We thought Brian was with you.

GORMLEITH. What brings you back here? Have you no more loads to carry? Why are you not carrying firing for the priests that have mastered your High King?

MAELMORA. This is a good welcome I am getting this day. Insults from you and insults from Murrough.

GORMLEITH. What did you do to anger your master's son?

SITRIC. He was watching Murrough at the chess and he gave an advice, and Murrough followed it and lost the game. Murrough was angry then.

MAELMORA. I would not stop to listen to him. He has no right to put insults on me.

GORMLEITH. He had a right to do it. You give in to a master that gives in to monks and beggars. It is certain you and Ireland were never under disgrace till now.

SITRIC. You will sign these letters now, I think, that you would not sign a while ago.

GORMLEITH. I will—I will! Give them to me quickly. He made little of me. He will be sorry. He bid me go and pray, he bid me repent. I will not, it is he himself will be made repent!

(*Takes up pen.*)

MAELMORA. What is it you are doing?

GORMLEITH. I am breaking away from Brian, I am breaking Brian's peace.

MAELMORA. You, his wife?

GORMLEITH. It was to a great king I came as a wife, not to a monkish man serving heaven on his knees.

MAELMORA (*holding her hand*). You must not go against him.— He that gave you all.

GORMLEITH. He has taken all away that was worth having.

SITRIC. Let her sign.

MAELMORA. This is no less than treachery.

GORMLEITH. Go and call your king, so, and give me up to him. (*She signs.*) Send the letters, Sitric, I am ready to go. (*Gets up.*)

MAELMORA. Where are you going?

GORMLEITH. To welcome the foreign armies that are on the sea now coming to Ireland.

MAELMORA. You must not do it! I will not let you be a traitor in this house.

GORMLEITH. Be a king again, Maelmora; join with us and fight in the old way. You yourself and Sitric could keep Ireland against all the world.

MAELMORA. I will call out to Brian.

GORMLEITH. You need not call to him. Here is Murrough his son, give us up to him, humble us before him. Humble yourself before him, and let the son of the Connacht woman put bonds upon me and on my son.

(MURROUGH *comes in.* SITRIC *goes out quickly, hiding the letters.*)

MURROUGH. Are you giving advice to the Queen, Maelmora, as you gave it to me a while ago? I am ashamed that you vexed me then, but she seems twenty times more vexed.

MAELMORA. It is the Queen that is giving advice to me. It may be better for you if I do not take it.

MURROUGH. I am no good at guessing riddles. But if there is some threat in your voice I will answer it.

MAELMORA. Have a care now. You may thank the four bones of your father I did not answer you a while ago.

GORMLEITH. What was it he said to vex you?

MURROUGH. I said the King of Leinster was well able to give advice. I said it was good advice he gave his comrades, the Danes, the day they ran from us like scared sheep at Glenmama.

MAELMORA. It may happen us yet to meet in another battle, where it is not my men but your own men that will run like scattered sheep.

MURROUGH. When that battle is at hand, King, see that there is a good yew-tree near by, a tree where you can hide while your men are running as you hid yourself at Glenmama.

MAELMORA (*half drawing sword*). I will not lay a hand on you in this house; my answer will be in some place of battle.

MURROUGH. That answering will not be sooner than I wish it.

GORMLEITH. Its day will come sooner than you think.

MURROUGH. No, our ill-wishers do not come out against us now, they only plot and plan.

GORMLEITH. They are coming out now. They are coming to make their attack on you.

MURROUGH. I do not think so; they are afraid.

GORMLEITH. No, they are not afraid; you will not stand against them this time. They will sweep you and your race out of Ireland.

MURROUGH. Where are these great men coming from? Will the grass stalks turn to be an army?

GORMLEITH. I am giving you a last warning. They are on the sea now. The north wind is bringing them to Clontarf.

MURROUGH. That is the foolish talk of women in a parlour. Sitric would bring his men out from Dublin, they would have a rough landing at Clontarf. Where is Sitric? He has stolen away. Where is he gone?

GORMLEITH. Sitric is young, he is hardy; he would not sit down and count his beads through his life. The old have worn out their time, from this out is it for you and Sitric to strike the ball.

MAELMORA. This is no place for us now. Come away, Gormleith, out of this.

MURROUGH (*standing at the door*). No one must leave this till the King comes. (*Calls out*) Here, men, call in the King—hurry, there is trouble before him—tell him to make no delay.

GORMLEITH. I would not have crept out of the house secretly. I will tell him myself what I have done.

MURROUGH. You will not tell him of your treachery, and I that am not your friend will not tell him. I have no mind to scald my father's heart.

BRIAN (*coming in*). What is this call of trouble?

MURROUGH. The armies of the Gall are on their way to Ireland.

BRIAN. Are you sure of what you say?

MURROUGH. I have it from those that know. It is certain.

BRIAN. The army is ready, we are well prepared. Call in our advisers; I will see what is best to do. Come here to me, Gormleith, it is your hour now, you are very wary in giving advice and very brave in danger. Stay here beside me now while we make our plans.

GORMLEITH. I cannot—I do not know what to say—you made me angry. You must not trust me.

BRIAN. My heart has trusted you since we were linked in marriage, many long days ago. Sit here as you used—take that pen and mark down the orders for our troops. (*Takes pen and gives it to her.*)

GORMLEITH (*throwing it from her*). I cannot—oh, it must be stopped—they must be turned back—it is not too late—help me, Maelmora, Sitric must do as I bid him. Call him back—go after him, he must obey me—no, I will go myself. I will drag him back. Yes, Brian, you may trust me—I will stop him, everything will turn out well. (*She is going to the door when* MALACHI *appears in it.*) Who is that? Malachi!

MALACHI (*putting up his hand*). Stop where you are. I have a thing to say to the High King.

GORMLEITH. Oh, are you come for my destruction at the last?

MALACHI. I have heavy news for you, Brian. There is danger on its way towards us.

BRIAN. I got news of it on the minute. You are in time to help us. We are on the one side, we have had such dangers before this.

89

MALACHI. Are you very sure there are no traitors here to make our enemies welcome?

BRIAN. There should surely be some weighty reason urging you to give out such a word.

MALACHI. I would sooner some other one would ask, is there treachery within the very lintel of this door?

BRIAN. Maelmora, have you any answer to give to that?

MAELMORA. The time Murrough called to you, it was to tell what I was after telling him.

BRIAN. Murrough would not screen any traitor at all, whoever it might happen to be.

MURROUGH. Maelmora is in it—and——

BRIAN. And what other one?

MURROUGH. I am loth to say it. It is best for you to question her yourself.

BRIAN. Question her? Who is there to question? There is no woman here but the Queen.

GORMLEITH. Make an end of it, Murrough. Tell out what he is asking you to tell.

MURROUGH. Queen Gormleith is giving her own welcome to the Danes.

BRIAN. That is not possible, that is some great mistake. Tell him, Gormleith, it is a mistake and a lie.

GORMLEITH. He has told you no lie. The thing he has said is true.

BRIAN. It is not true. You are taking this thing on your own head with some thought of saving your son.

GORMLEITH. Ask King Malachi. He knows me, he made prophecies, he will tell you. I would sooner you to know the truth, and the end to have come and the finish. Tell it out, Malachi, I make no defence, and tell him along with that what wages are my due.

MALACHI. I am done with giving judgments this long time. It is God is the rightful judge.

GORMLEITH. I did it and I did not do it, Brian—I was not entirely to blame. I thought myself to be wise, to drag things here and there, to do some great thing, moving men with big words. Oh, I have pulled down the rafters of the roof that sheltered me! (*She is putting out her hand to* BRIAN *but* MALACHI *goes between.*)

BRIAN. Let her go, let no one lay a hand on her. And may God have mercy on every woman's vain changing heart!

GORMLEITH. Do not say that, Brian, do not think it, it was not my heart that changed, it was anger and jealousy made me crazy at the time.

(BRIAN'S *head has sunk in his hands.* MALACHI *gently leads her towards the door.*)

MALACHI. Go now as he has given you leave. Go free, if freedom can profit you, a broken woman, a spoiled queen, travelling the roads of the world. God is the judge. You were maybe misled, made use of, others putting it on you that you yourself were doing all.

GORMLEITH. No, Malachi, I did my own part, I have no mind to deny or to hide my own share in it at all. You promised Brian I would turn my hand against him, and I thought that a thing was not possible, and I did it against him in the end. Listen now to this. Brodar of Manannan's Island would not give his aid to the Danes unless I promised him myself, and I promised it. I put my own hand to that. Sigurd, Earl of Orkney, asked the same promise, and I gave it. I did not leave any lie on you at all—your words have come around. There will be fighting for me yet! Fighting for me and about me. Are you satisfied now, Malachi of the foretellings?

MALACHI. Look at the work you have done. (*He points to* BRIAN.) Go out and hang your head for shame. The man that was steady and strong is broken. It is hardly he will reach to the battle.

GORMLEITH. No fear, no fear, Brian will reach to the battle. There is no fear at all of him not doing that. It is not Brian would wish to die the death of a man that is lessening and stiffening, the time he grows attentive to his bed, but of a winner that is merry and shouting, the time his enemies are put down. I was maybe a right wife for him. A right wife, a lucky wife, in spite of all! (*Goes out.*)

MALACHI (*going to* BRIAN *and putting hand on his shoulder*). Lift up your head, Brian.

BRIAN. The blame is on me. It is I myself have betrayed my people. War, war, keening and treachery, Ireland red again, red and stained through and through—trouble and treachery and war.

MALACHI. Make ready your orders for the army.

BRIAN. Is all ready for the Queen's journey? Give her the horses from Connacht.

MALACHI. Listen to what I say, we must send messengers.

BRIAN. The speckled horses, she liked them best, and the carved chariot from the north.

MALACHI. Attend to what I am saying.

BRIAN. But who was it, who was it, that called in the Gall?

MALACHI. I cannot rouse him. It is no wonder. That treachery was too hard a blow.

(MURROUGH *comes in with standard in hand and stands on threshold. Spears and banners appear at window. War march is played.*)

BRIAN (*standing up*). But what did the dream mean? What did Aoibhell mean? She promised me lasting peace, lasting peace; she told it to me in my dream. (*He walks towards door.*) What did she mean? Is there no truth? Is every one treacherous? (*He comes face to face with* MURROUGH *and stands still.*)

MURROUGH. The army is ready, we must lead it to meet the Danes at Clontarf.

BRIAN (*standing very strong and straight*). Clontarf? Now I know what Aoibhell meant. She said it was at Clontarf I would find peace. That is well. My place is ready among the generations; Cathal, son of Aedh, Corc, son of Anluan, Lorcan, son of Luchta, Mahon, son of Cennedigh, all the race of Lugaidh reigned in this place, and went out of this door for the last time; and the traitors that betrayed them, and the women they loved. Give me my sword. (MALACHI *takes it down and gives it to him.*) It has another battle to win.

Curtain.

DERVORGILLA

DERVORGILLA

PERSONS

DERVORGILLA. *Once Queen of Breffny.*
FLANN. *An old servant.*
MONA. *His wife.*
OWEN. *A young man.*
OTHER YOUNG MEN.
MAMIE. *A girl.*
OTHER GIRLS.
A WANDERING SONGMAKER.

TIME—1193. Scene, outside the Abbey of Mellifont, near Drogheda.

SCENE. *A green lawn outside a garden wall.* FLANN *is arranging a chair with cloaks and cushions.* MONA *standing beside him.*

MONA. Put a cloak there on the ground, Flann. It would not serve the lady, the damp of the earth to be rising up about her feet.

FLANN. What ails her coming abroad at all, and the length of time she never asked to come outside the walls?

MONA. The young lads wanting to get prizes and to show off at their sports, it is that enticed her entirely. More sports there will be in it to-day than the most of them saw in their lifetime.

FLANN. Fighting and killings and robbery, that is the sport they were brought up to, and that is all the sport that was in it for the last twoscore years.

MONA. The Lord be with the good old times, when a woman suckling her child would be safe crossing Ireland from sea to sea! No wonder our own poor lady to be vexed and torn in the night-time. It seemed to me she had a very shook appearance this morning.

FLANN. There is no occasion for her to be fretting or lonesome, and the way her name is up through the whole of the province.

MONA. Why wouldn't it be up, after the way she fed old and young through the bad times, giving means and cattle to those the English had robbed.

FLANN. It is royal she is in giving as in race. Look at all the weight of gold the Abbey got from her, and the golden vessels upon the high altar.

MONA. No wonder the people to be saying she will surely get the name of a saint; the darling queen-woman of the Abbey of Mellifont.

FLANN. God grant it, God grant it. We have her secret well kept so far as this. It would be a queer thing if it would not be kept to the end. (*Shouts are heard.*)

MONA. It is the lads shouting for their own champions that are after beating the men of Assaroe.

(OWEN *and other lads come in.*)

OWEN. Is the lady herself coming out, Flann? Has she got good prizes in her hand?

FLANN. Good and too good. The lady is too much bothered with the whole of you, stretching out her hand to you the way she does.

ANOTHER LAD. Show us the prizes.

ANOTHER LAD. Are they there in the basket, Flann? Give them over here to me.

FLANN. Let you behave yourselves now and have manners, or you will get nothing at all.

OWEN. It is little we would get if you had the giving of it, Flann! Here, Mamie, come and see the grand things Flann is keeping under his cloak!

(*They all hustle* FLANN. MAMIE *runs in.*)

MAMIE. Do you see what is there beyond? Beyond upon the hill?

OWEN. A troop of men on horses. I suppose it is to race the horses they are come.

MAMIE. It is not, it is not; but a troop of English soldiers they are. Bows they have and swords. I am in dread of them. I went hiding in the scrub as they passed. Is there any fear, Flann, they will be coming to this place?

FLANN. Sure the lady herself is coming outside the gate. Would I let her do that, there to be danger in it? I tell you the place she is, is as safe as a burrow under rocks.

MONA. Let you stop your chat. Here she is now, coming to the gate.

MAMIE. I would never be in dread where she is. There are some say she has power from beyond the world, for there is no one knows her name or her race.

FLANN. Whisht, the whole of ye!

(*They stand back and* DERVORGILLA *comes in leaning upon her stick.* FLANN *and* MONA *lead her to her chair and she stands for a moment.*)

DERVORGILLA. God save you, children.

ALL. God save you, lady.

DERVORGILLA. His blessing be upon you, and my blessing, and the blessing of the summer time. Let me see that the doings of the great men are not forgotten, and that you can be as good runners, and as good hurlers, and as good at hitting the mark, as your old fathers were.

ALL. We will, we will.

OWEN. You will be proud, lady, to see what the men of Ulster can do against the men of Leinster and of Meath.

DERVORGILLA. That is so, I will be proud. For though I am an old woman given to praying, I can take pride yet in strength of body and readiness of hand; for I saw such things long ago in kings' houses.

OWEN. There is no fear of us at all! We will not be put down; we will gain the day! Come on, lads, some of the sports might be over. Come along, Mamie, and be looking at us from the bank of the embroiderers. (*They go out.*)

DERVORGILLA. It is many years since we had a day like this of sport and of mirth-making. It seems as if those were wrong who said the English would always bring trouble on us; there may be a good end to the story after all.

FLANN. There will be a good end, to be sure. A bad behaved race the people of this country are. It is the strong hand of the English is the best thing to be over them.

DERVORGILLA. England is a rich, powerful country to be joined to.

FLANN. We should surely grow rich ourselves joined with her, the same as a girl of the ducks and the ashes that would be married to a great lord's son.

DERVORGILLA. I can go in peace if I know I have left peace after me, and content, but sometimes I am afraid. I had a dream last night, a troublesome dream—What is that? I hear a cry.

(MAMIE *runs in with a dead bird.*)

MAMIE. Oh, look, lady, it is a crane. It is dead, they have shot it!

DERVORGILLA. The fowlers should have spared all life on a day of mirth like this.

MAMIE. It was one of the English bowmen; he shot it in the air. It fell at my feet. It died there at my feet.

DERVORGILLA. It vexes me, that to have happened on such a day as this.

FLANN. Get out of that now, Mamie. You should have more sense than to be bringing in a thing of the kind. Look now, there has blood dropped upon the lady's cloak. Bring it out of this and throw it in some place where it will be in no one's way. I wonder at you annoying the lady, and the way she is spending her means upon you all. (MAMIE *goes out.*)

DERVORGILLA (*looking at cloak which* MONA *is wiping*). It has brought to my mind other blood that was spilled, and that I, myself, have to answer for.

FLANN. You think entirely too much of it, lady, taking on yourself the weight of the bringing in of the English. It was the quarrelling of the provinces with one another brought them in.

DERVORGILLA. No, no. It was I brought them in for good or for evil, by my own sin and the wars that were stirred up for my sake.

FLANN. No, but it was in the prophecies that they would come. Didn't Blessed Caillen see them coming over the sea, and he at the brink of death waiting for the angels of God? There is no use at all trying to go against the prophecies.

DERVORGILLA. You are always trying to flatter and to comfort me, but surely I brought trouble upon Ireland, as well as on all I had to do with. Diarmuid, King of Leinster, that was my lover, perished like a beast fallen by the roadside, without sacrament, without repentance. It was I brought that curse upon him.

FLANN (*mutters*). It was he himself earned that curse; God knows he earned it well.

DERVORGILLA. Was it not I brought the curse upon O'Rourke, King of Breffny, the husband I left and betrayed? The head I made bow with shame was struck off and sent to the English King. The body I forsook was hung on the walls shamefully, by the feet, like a calf after slaughter. It is certain there is a curse on all that have to do with me. What I have done can never be undone. How can I be certain of the forgiveness of God?

MONA. Be easy now. Who would be forgiven if you would not be forgiven? Sure the Lord has seen your prayers and your crying, and your great giving and your holy life.

DERVORGILLA. Four years I have lived and fourscore, and for half my life I ran my own way, and through the other half of my life I have paid the penalty. For every day or night of pride or of pleasure, I have spent a day and a night of prayer and of pain. Will not that bring forgiveness? Is not that paying the penalty?

MONA. Indeed and surely you have made it up with God. Surely you are forgiven and well forgiven! It is God Himself will open to you the gate of heaven!

DERVORGILLA. But the people, the people; will they ever forgive what I have done!

MONA. They have enough to do to be minding themselves. What call would they have to go draw it down upon you at all?

DERVORGILLA. I dreamt last night that the people knew me, that they knew my story and my sin; that they knew it was for my sake the wars were stirred up and the Gall brought into Ireland. They seemed to curse and to threaten me. They stooped like this, to take up stones to throw at me, knowing me at last to be Dervorgilla!

(*A voice is heard singing.*)

MONA. Whist! Listen.

DERVORGILLA. What is that? Who is that coming?

FLANN. A beggar—some wandering lad. He has a great appearance of poverty. Will I go get something for him? There is no comfort at all comforts you like giving to the poor. Look now the way his shoes are broken!

DERVORGILLA. I can help the poor still. God gives me leave to do that. Thank God I have leave yet to be a giver of gifts. Go bring me shoes for him, and a cloak, and some silver money.

FLANN. Where is the use spoiling him with silver? Shoes are enough, shoes are enough. What call has a lad of his age to go begging; that is a trade of life should be left to give employment to the old.

(*He goes out. A ragged lad comes in. He is carrying a sort of rough fiddle.*)

DERVORGILLA. Where do you come from, boy?

SONGMAKER. From the province of Connacht I am come. Connacht yesterday, Armagh to-morrow. To-day it is Mellifont has got hold of me. (*Sings*)—

> Yesterday travelling Connacht,
> Drogheda has me to-day;
> My back to the empty pockets,
> My face to the place will pay!

DERVORGILLA. You are young to be wandering.

SONGMAKER. Where would I be stopping? This day five year the thatch I was reared under was burned by the Gall, and all I had of kindred scattered. I rambled Ireland since that time, just roving around. (*Sings*)—

99

Just roving around
    To my grief and my sorrow,
Under a rock to-day,
    Under a bush to-morrow.

It will be a long time till the Pope of Rome will get a hearth tax on my account, from the tax-gatherers of the King of England.

DERVORGILLA. Have you no trade that you can follow?

SONGMAKER. The best, the best. I have in me the makings of a poet—and a good poet—according to the treatment I would be given—one day sweet, another day sour. (*Sings*)—

Syrupy sweet to-day,
    Sour as sloes to-morrow;
Sweet to the lads that pay,
    Sour to the lads that borrow!

It is a sweet poem I would wish to be making in this grand place.

DERVORGILLA. You have no right to the name of a poet; you have not learned in the schools.

SONGMAKER. I did learn it well. Wasn't my grandfather a poet, and I reared up by him on the brink of a running stream? I know the rules well. Believe me, the mensuration of verses is a very ticklish thing.

DERVORGILLA. The old poets had knowledge from the well of wisdom. They could tell and foretell many things.

SONGMAKER. It is often the people far and near would draw to my grandfather to question him. Let them come to him, sick or sour, he had an answer for all of them, or a cure.

DERVORGILLA. Did you ever hear him say to any one that asked him, if a sin once committed could be forgiven?

SONGMAKER. It wants no poet's knowledge to know that. Can a sin be forgiven, is it? Why not, or who would people heaven?

DERVORGILLA. But—did you ever hear him say if it can be undone? Can a wrong once done ever be undone? Suppose there was some person who had done a great wrong, had brought, maybe, a bad neighbour into the house, or a hard stranger in among kindred —it might be a race, an army into a country. Could that person ever gain forgiveness, praying and sorrowing?

SONGMAKER. Well, God is good. But to bring in a bad neighbour is a hard thing to get over. It was a bad neighbour in the next house, drove St. Patrick back from Rome to Ireland.

DERVORGILLA. But if that neighbour, that stranger, that race, should turn kind and honest, or could be sent back, and all be as before, would not forgiveness be gained by that?

SONGMAKER. Wait, now, till I think. There was something my grandfather, God rest his soul, used to be saying. He had great wisdom, I tell you, being silly-like, and blind. Wait, now, till I see can I sound it out right. Talking, the neighbours were, about St. Martin's mitten. It was St. Martin made a throw of his mitten at the mice one time they had him annoyed, nibbling at the oatenmeal in the mill; and, in the throwing, it turned to be a cat, and scattered them. That was the first cat that ever was in Ireland.

MONA. To be sure; to be sure; so it was. St. Martin's mitten was the first cat. Everybody knows that.

SONGMAKER. But it is what my grandfather said, that if all the saints in Ireland had wished it, and if St. Martin himself had wished it along with them, it would fail them to have turned that cat to be a mitten again, or the English to be quiet neighbours again, furry and innocent, and having no claws!

FLANN (*bringing cloak and shoes*). Give thanks now to the lady that is giving you more than you deserve. (*Hands him the things and some money.*)

SONGMAKER. My blessing down upon you, lady, whoever you are. Faith, you have a strong pocket! The house you are in is no empty house, or any bad house at all. (*He sits down on the ground and begins to lace on shoes, singing:*)

> I am after being given two grand steppers,
>   Matching one another like two swallows on the wind,
> Made from the skin of the Brown Bull of Cuailgne.
>   Or the cow Argus minded, he that was not blind.
>
> It's the roads of the world will be proud to see them,
>   It's a great ornament they will be, far and near;
> She that gave them never learned to be a niggard,
>   Though the Gall are among us this four and twenty year!

(OWEN, MAMIE, *and the rest run in.*)

OWEN. I have the prize won! I was best over the leaps. I have taken the sway!

MAMIE. My worked border was the best! Every one gave in to that!

ANOTHER LAD. I leaped very high; I leaped as high as that!

ANOTHER. It was I won at the hurley! I took the goal from the men of Meath!

DERVORGILLA. You have all done well. I am proud of you, children. I can give you all prizes. Flann, give me the prizes. (*He hands them to her and she gives them one by one.*) Here, Mamie, is a necklace from the Eastern world. You have earned it well by your worked border. Make the borders of your house beautiful. Keep within its borders all God has given you in charge. (*To* OWEN.) Here is a silver cup. (*To another.*) Here is a cloak with a brooch. (*To another.*) Here, you are the youngest, you must have a prize. Take this hurl, this silver ball. Practice with them well and you will be first yet. (*They all stoop and kiss her hand as she gives the presents.*)

FLANN. Give a good shout now for the lady. (*They all shout, the singer joins.*)

OWEN. Who is that? A stranger? He has not the look of our own people. Is he come to make sport for us?

DERVORGILLA. He is a maker of songs. He has the sweet voice of Connacht men. They have the soft sea mist in their mouths.

OWEN. Give out a song now, till we'll hear what you can do.

SONGMAKER. Give me the key so. There can be no singing without a key.

OWEN. What do you call a key?

SONGMAKER. Three keys there are; you should know that. It is only love or drink or friendship can unlock a song.

DERVORGILLA. Give him a cup of wine.

FLANN. Will nothing do him but wine? Wine that is too good and too strong. (*Gives him a cup,* SONGMAKER *drinks.*)

SONGMAKER. What will you have now for a song? Destructions, cattle preys, courtships, feats of battle?

OWEN. No, no; we are tired of those.

SONGMAKER. Well, I'll rhyme you out a verse about Finn and the Danish wedding.

OWEN. Those old songs of Finn and his men are only for winter nights, and the feet among the sods. Give us out a new song.

SONGMAKER. It is best keep to the old ones. The old ones are merry, but the new ones are sorrowful.

OWEN. The sorrowful songs are sometimes the best. They tell of the death of the big men and of the quarrelling of kings.

SONGMAKER. Well, if it is a sorrowful song you want, it is easy to find it, for there was not made these forty years any song or any story in Ireland that was not sorrowful. And if it is the quarrellings of kings you want, I will tell you of a quarrelling brought such trouble into Ireland, that if a grain of it could be blown through a pipe in amongst the angels of heaven, it would bring a dark mist over their faces. (*Rocks himself.*) I tell you, that if the half of all the tears, shed through that quarrelling, could be sent through a pipe into hell, the flames would be put out, and the hearth of it black-flooded with otters!

OWEN. That must be the story of the coming of the Gall into Ireland.

FLANN. That trouble is surely lessening. There are no more killings. It is best to put away old griefs out of mind. Think now of some other thing. Something happened in Spain or in France.

DERVORGILLA. Do not meddle with him, Flann. It is not the telling of the story makes the story. Let me hear what is the common voice.

(SONGMAKER *sings:*)

It is pitiful and sharp to-day are the wounds of Ireland,
From Galway of white flaggy stones to Cork of the white
    strand;
The branches that were full of leaves and honey on the leaves
Are torn and stripped and shortened by the stranger to our
    grief.

It is long, O Royal Ireland, you were mannerly and kind.
A nursing mother to your sons, fair, hospitable, wise;
Now you are wine spilled from a cup beneath the strangers'
    feet.
The English-speaking troop to-day have trodden down our
    wheat.

The wild white fawn has lost the shape was comely in the
    wood,
Since the foreign crow came nesting in the yewtree overhead,
Since the red East wind brought to our hurt the troop of
    foreign rogues,
We are drifted like the wretched fur of a cat upon a bog!

FLANN. Where is the use of yelping and yowling like a hound that has lost the pack? Get out of this, if that screeching of a banshee is all that you can do.

DERVORGILLA. I have given him leave to sing his songs. Let him travel his own road. Let him take his own way.

SONGMAKER. It is hard for me to tell my story and that one not giving me leave to tell it. There must be a preparation for everything and a beginning. Wouldn't you hear the wind making its cry about the house before you would hear the hammering of the rain upon the stones? Give me time now, and I will give out the story of a man that has left a name will never be forgotten here, and that is Diarmuid MacMurrough, King of Leinster, that first called the English into Ireland. (*Sings:*)

> Through Diarmuid's bad sway we are wasted to-day,
> It was he brought away the Queen of Breffny;
> And when O'Rourke raised Connacht against him,
> Gave the English pay to come to Ireland.

> It were better for all that are under the Gall,
> If death made a call and he in the cradle;
> Bind him down very strong and bruise him long,
> The way he can wrong us no more for ever.

> His great body is down under the stone
> Chased by the hounds were before the world;
> It was Peter's own frown closed the door before him,
> It is Diarmuid is bound in cold Hell for ever!

DERVORGILLA. That is enough, that is enough! Why should you heap up blame upon one that is dead? King Diarmuid's lips are closed now with clay. It is a shameful thing, a cowardly thing, to make attacks upon a man that cannot answer. Are you not satisfied to let God be the judge?

SONGMAKER. I had no intention to give offence. To dispraise Diarmuid and the English; I thought that would give satisfaction in this place, the same as it does in Connacht.

DERVORGILLA. Those that have a good heart and a high nature try to find excuses for the dead.

SONGMAKER. So they would, so they would. It is finding excuses we should be for the dead. There is an excuse for every one; the Blessed Mother knows that, and she sitting every Saturday as the attorney for poor souls. Making out a case for them she does be.

DERVORGILLA. There is no one who might not be freed from blame, if his case and what led to his wrongdoing were put down.

SONGMAKER. I'll make out a case for him. I can tell out what led King Diarmuid into his sin and his treachery; and that is the thing brings mostly all mischief into the world, the changeable wagging nature of a woman. (*Sings:*)

He cares little for life, puts trust in a wife,
It is long it is known they go with the wind;
A queer thing a woman was joined with O'Rourke
To show herself kind to a pet from Leinster.

The rat in the larder, the fire in the thatch,
The guest to be fattening, the children famished;
If't was Diarmuid's call that brought in the Gall,
Let the weight of it fall upon Dervorgilla!

(DERVORGILLA *tries to rise and cannot.* MONA *supports her,*
FLANN *offers her wine. She lies back as if faint. They attend
to her, their backs to the rest. The singer crosses to the
young men, who give him money.*)

MAMIE. I often heard of Dervorgilla that left the King of Breffny
for Diarmuid, and started the war, but I never heard what happened to her after.

OWEN. There is no one knows that. Some say King Roderick put
her under locks in a cell at Clonmacnoise.

SONGMAKER. More likely she hanged herself, after setting the
whole of the country in an uproar.

OWEN. If she did they had a right to bury her with a hound on
her false heart, the same as Diarmuid himself was buried.

SONGMAKER. No, but Diarmuid's father was buried with the
hound. Excuse or no excuse, a bad race they are, a bad race.

FLANN (*to* SONGMAKER). Quit off now out of this place before I
will make you quit it. Take yourself and your rags and your venomous tongue out of this.

SONGMAKER. Let you leave me alone. Is that the way you are laying hands upon a poet?

DERVORGILLA. Leave him go, Flann. You are judging him now.
God is the Judge; let him go.

SONGMAKER. Look at the way you have me tore! It is where I'll
go on to that troop of English on the hill beyond. I'll sound my
songs for them. I will get better treatment from them itself, than I
am getting from you. If it wasn't for respect for the lady, it's a great
overthrow I'd make of you. I'll go on to the English. (*He goes off,
singing as he goes.*)

Since the Gall have the sway, it's for them I will play
There's none would lay blame on a boy that's a beggar,
But a queer thing a woman was joined to O'Rourke,
To show herself kind to a fox from Leinster!

OWEN. The English look to be friendly enough. They are drinking beer from the barrels. They are cheering the horses that go over the bank. Come along, boys, and see the big leaps.

MAMIE. Take care now, it would not be safe to go near the bowmen. Didn't you see the way they made an end of that crane a while ago?

OWEN. Flann said they would do no harm. I would like well to get a near view of the big bows. Come along, Mamie.

MAMIE. I will not. I will go into the garden of the Abbey.

(*She goes in through gate,* OWEN *and young men go out.*)

DERVORGILLA (*raising herself up*). Oh, my sin, my sin has come upon my head! Why did I come out from the Abbey walls? A cell is the only fitting place for me! I should never have come out into the light of the day!

FLANN. Ah, what does it signify? What is it all but a vagabond's song that was born in a minute, and will vanish away like a wisp of smoke.

DERVORGILLA. The dream of the night was true. It is coming true. My sin is remembered—I shall be known—I saw it all—they stooped to pick up stones—there was no forgiveness when they knew me to be Dervorgilla!

FLANN. That is a thing they will never know and that they have no way to know. Sure in the Abbey itself there is no one knows it outside the Order.

DERVORGILLA. It will be discovered, some one will see me.

FLANN. Ah, there are few living in any place that ever saw you in the old days. And if they should see you now itself, how would they know those holy withered cheeks to belong to the lovely lady that set kings fighting in her bloom? And many happenings have happened since then, and it is likely the Queen of Breffny is forgotten. Sure you heard them saying that Dervorgilla is dead.

DERVORGILLA. I will go in. Bring me back into the shelter of the walls.

FLANN. It might be best. There will be no drunken poets and schemers of the sort going in there to annoy you. It is too openhanded you are to them all, that is what makes them so stubborn and so high-minded. Gather up the pillows, Mona, till we'll bring the lady in.

MONA. It's best, it's best. Ah, don't be fretting, dear. There is no one on earth knows your secret and your name but myself, that was reared with you, and this man that is my own comrade. And you know well, and I swear to you, the both of us would be dragged

106

through briars, and ground under millstones, before we would consent to say out your name to any person at all. I would sooner my tongue to be turned to a stone here and now, than you to be uneasy the way you are.

DERVORGILLA. There is no hiding it, no hiding it. Dreams come true. Who was there to-day to tell it, and that beggar told the story. He will be singing it from troop to troop. The English will hear it, the runners will hear it, it will be blazed before night through the provinces, it will set them thinking of me, and talking.

FLANN. The devil skelp him! It would be no harm at all to come from behind and give him a tip of a hurl on the head to quiet his impudence and his talk. There is strength in my hand yet, and weight in my stick.

DERVORGILLA. No, no, I will not have any one hurt for my sake. I will have no other blood upon my head. But follow him, Flann. Go after him and put him under bonds to go away, to leave the province, to give up his singing. Give him money, all this money, that he may live in some far-away place, without singing and wandering.

FLANN (taking the purse). I will do that. Wait three minutes and I'll be coming back to bring you within the walls. I'll put him under heavy oaths to quit this, to go do his croaking with the crows of Scotland. That they may make an end of him with their beaks, and be pecking the eyes out of him, and lining their nests with every hair of his head! (He goes off.)

DERVORGILLA. It is of no use, dreams cannot lie, my punishment must come. I knew it all the time, even within the walls. I tried to make it up with good works. It was of no use, my name is in men's mouths.

MONA. What signifies one beggar's song? It is not on you the blame should be laid. It was not you went to Diarmuid MacMurrough. It was not you followed after him to Leinster. It was he came and brought you away. There are many say it was by force. There are many that are saying that. That is the way it will be written in the histories.

DERVORGILLA. If Diarmuid MacMurrough had taken me by force, do you think I would have lived with him for one day only? My hands were strong then. I had my courage then. I was free to make an end of myself or of him. Will the generations think better of me, thinking me to have been taken as a prey, like the Connacht hag's basket, or the Munster hag's speckled cow? Does the marten that is torn from the woods lull itself in its master's arms?

MONA. Maybe so, maybe so. I used to be better pleased myself hearing them say it, than putting the blame on yourself of leaving O'Rourke.

DERVORGILLA. O'Rourke was a good man, and a brave man, and a kinder man than Diarmuid, but it was with Diarmuid my heart was. It is to him I was promised before ever I saw O'Rourke, and I loved him better than ever my own lord, and he me also, and this was long! I loved him, I loved him! Why did they promise me to him and break the promise? Why was every one against him then and always, every one against Diarmuid? Why must they be throwing and ever-throwing sharp reproaches upon his name? Had a man loved by a king's daughter nothing in him to love? A man great of body, hardy in fight, hoarse with shouts of battle. He had liefer be dreaded than loved! It was he cast down the great, it was the dumb poor he served! Every proud man against him and he against every proud man. Oh, Diarmuid, I did not dread you. It was I myself led you astray! Let the curse and the vengeance fall upon me and me only, for the great wrong and the treachery done by both of us to Ireland!

(*A loud cry is heard. Both look towards where it comes from.*)

MONA. Listen, listen!

DERVORGILLA. What is it? What is that cry?

MONA. It is like the heavy shout does be given out over a man that has been struck down by his enemies. (*The shout is heard nearer.*)

DERVORGILLA. What is it!

MONA (*looking out*). The young men are coming back. Their heads are drooping.

DERVORGILLA. God grant no trouble may have fallen upon them.

MONA. There is trouble, and heavy trouble upon them, sure enough.

(MAMIE *comes in from garden, young men come in.*)

DERVORGILLA. What is it, my children? What has happened?

OWEN. The truce has been broken. The wasp we thought drowsy has found its sting. The hand of the Gall has again been reddened.

MONA. Tell it out, tell it out, what is it has happened at all?

OWEN. Get ready for the burying of Flann of Breffny, the lady's steward and distributor, and your good comrade.

MONA. Ah! that is foolishness. It cannot be true. He was here but a minute ago, standing in this spot.

OWEN. It is true.

DERVORGILLA. How did he die? Tell me all.

OWEN. He came where that Connachtman was doing his tricks

for the English troop. They asked a song of him; he was going to
give it out. Flann tried to bring him away. The bowmen had mugs
of beer in their hands; they were laughing at the tricks; they wanted
the song. They called out to Flann to leave him to make fun for
them, but Flann tried to bring him away. He spoke in his ear; he
put his hand over his mouth. They were rightly vexed then, and
one of them called out: "There, spoil-sport, is a spoiling of all
sport for you," and he drew his bow and sent an arrow through
Flann's body, that he fell like a stone, without a word. Then they
turned their horses, and one of them said it was a pity, but another
said their dinners would be spoiling in Drogheda. And so they rode
away in a hurry.

DERVORGILLA. Another. Death has come upon another. (*Holds
out her hands.*) Come to me, my poor Mona, my friend.

MONA. Is it Flann is dead? Flann, my husband? He had a year
less than I myself had. It was not his time to die. Who is there to
close my own eyes now? He always said he would close my eyes.

DERVORGILLA. Your trouble is no greater than my trouble. It was
for my sake and in following my bidding he died.

MONA. It was the Gall killed his two brothers and destroyed the
house and trampled down the field of oats. What did they want
killing him? Wasn't it enough to have destroyed his oats?

DERVORGILLA. Come into the Abbey and prepare for him there.

MONA. So near to the chapel, and not a priest to overtake him before he died. That was no death for a Christian man.

DERVORGILLA. Candles will be lighted, and many Masses said
for his soul.

MONA. And if it was with the sword itself he was killed, that's
natural. His brothers were killed with the sword. But an arrow!
Not one of the family was killed with that before. That is not a
thing you would be hearing in the ballads.

OWEN. Will you go where the body is? There are some that are
laying it out?

MONA. I will, I will. Bring me to my decent comrade; and bring
me to that singer was here. I will lay it upon him to make a great
cursing to put upon the Gall, a great heavy curse upon all that had
to do with the Gall. (*She is going off, but turns back to* DERVOR-
GILLA.) But it is not on your self I will let them put a curse, or lay
on you any blame at all. You know well I never put blame on you,
or said a sharp word of you, the time you were in Breffny with
O'Rourke, or the time you were in Leinster with Diarmuid Mac-

Murrough, and I myself following you from place to place. You know well, and the man that is stretched cold and dumb knows, I never said a hard word or an unkind word or a bad word of you yourself, Dervorgilla. (*She goes out babbling.*) Oh, no, no; I would never do such a thing as that!

OWEN (*to the others*). Dervorgilla! Oh, did you hear her say it is Dervorgilla?

DERVORGILLA (*stands up with difficulty*). Since you were born and before you were born I have been here, kneeling and praying, kneeling and praying, fasting and asking forgiveness of God. I think my father God has forgiven me. They tell me my mother the Church has forgiven me. That old man had forgiven me, and he had suffered by the Gall. The old—the old—that old woman, even in her grief, she called out no word against me. You are young. You will surely forgive me, for you are young. (*They are all silent. Then* OWEN *comes over and lays down his cup at her feet, then turns and walks slowly away.*) It is not your hand has done this, but the righteous hand of God that has moved your hand. (*Other lads lay down their gifts.*) I take this shame for the shame in the west I put on O'Rourke of Breffny, and the death I brought upon him by the hand of the Gall. (*The youngest boy, who has hesitated, comes and lays down his hurl and silver ball, and goes away, his head drooping.*) I take this reproach for the reproach in the east I brought upon Diarmuid, King of Leinster, thrusting upon him wars and attacks and battles, till for his defence and to defend Leinster, he called in the strangers that have devoured Ireland. (*The young men have all gone.* MAMIE *comes as if to lay down her gift, but draws back.* DERVORGILLA *turns to her.*) Do not be afraid to give back my gifts, do not separate yourself from your companions for my sake. For there is little of my life but is spent, and there has come upon me this day all the pain of the world and its anguish, seeing and knowing that a deed once done has no undoing, and the lasting trouble my unfaithfulness has brought upon you and your children for ever. (MAMIE *lays down her necklace and goes away sadly.*) There is kindness in your unkindness, not leaving me to go and face Michael and the Scales of Judgment wrapped in comfortable words, and the praises of the poor, and the lulling of psalms, but from the swift, unflinching, terrible judgment of the young! (*She sinks slowly to the ground holding to the chair. The stage begins to darken; the voice of the* SONGMAKER *is heard coming nearer, singing:*)

DERVORGILLA

The rat in the cupboard, the fire in the lap;
The guest to be fattening, the children fretting;
My curse upon all that brought in the Gall,
Upon Diarmuid's call, and on Dervorgilla!

Curtain.

McDONOUGH'S WIFE

McDONOUGH'S WIFE

PERSONS
McDONOUGH, *a piper.*
FIRST HAG.
SECOND HAG.

SCENE: *A very poor room in Galway with outer and inner door. Noises of a fair outside. A Hag sitting by the fire. Another standing by outer door.*

FIRST HAG. Is there e'er a sign of McDonough to be coming?

SECOND HAG. There is not. There were two or three asking for him, wanting him to bring the pipes to some spree-house at the time the fair will be at an end.

FIRST HAG. A great wonder he not to have come, and this the fair day of Galway.

SECOND HAG. He not to come ere evening, the woman that is dead must go to her burying without one to follow her, or any friend at all to flatten the green scraws above her head.

FIRST HAG. Is there no neighbour at all will do that much, and she being gone out of the world?

SECOND HAG. There is not. You said to ask Pat Marlborough, and I asked him, and he said there were plenty of decent women and of well-reared women in Galway he would follow and welcome the day they would die, without paying that respect to one not belonging to the district, or that the town got no good account of the time she came.

FIRST HAG. Did you do as I bade you, asking Cross Ford to send in a couple of the boys she has?

SECOND HAG. What a fool I'd be asking her! I laid down to her the way it was. McDonough's wife to be dead, and he far out in the country, and no one belonging to her to so much as lift the coffin over the threshold of the door.

FIRST HAG. What did she say hearing that?

SECOND HAG. She put a big laugh out of her, and it is what she said: "May the devil die with her, and it is well pleased the street will be getting quit of her, and it is hard to say on what mountain she might be grazing now."

FIRST HAG. There will no help come burying her so.

SECOND HAG. It is too lofty McDonough was, and too high-minded, bringing in a woman was maybe no lawful wife, or no honest child itself, but it might be a bychild or a tinker's brat, and he giving out no account of her generations or of her name.

FIRST HAG. Whether or no, she was a little giddy. But that is the way with McDonough. He is sometimes an unruly lad, but he would near knock you with his pride.

SECOND HAG. Indeed he is no way humble, but looking for attendance on her, as if she was the youngest and the greatest in the world.

FIRST HAG. It is not to humour her the Union men will, and they carrying her to where they will sink her into the ground, unless it might be McDonough would come back, and he having money in his hand, to bring in some keeners and some hired men.

SECOND HAG. He to come back at this time it is certain he will bring a fist-full of money.

FIRST HAG. What makes you say that to be certain?

SECOND HAG. A troop of sheep-shearers that are on the west side of the fair, looking for hire from the grass farmers. I heard them laying down they met with McDonough at the big shearing at Cregroostha.

FIRST HAG. What day was that?

SECOND HAG. This day week for the world.

FIRST HAG. He has time and plenty to be back in Galway ere this.

SECOND HAG. Great dancing they had and a great supper at the time the shearing was at an end and the fleeces lodged in the big sacks. It is McDonough played his music through the night-time. It is what I heard them saying, "He went out of that place weightier than he went in."

FIRST HAG. He is a great one to squeeze the pipes surely. There is no place ever he went into but he brought the whip out of it.

SECOND HAG. His father was better again, they do be saying. It was from the other side he got the gift.

FIRST HAG. He did, and from beyond the world, where he befriended some in the forths of the Danes. It was they taught him their trade. I heard tell, he to throw the pipes up on top of the rafters, they would go sounding out tunes of themselves.

SECOND HAG. He could do no more with them than what McDonough himself can do—may ill luck attend him! It is inhuman tunes he does be making; unnatural they are.

116

FIRST HAG. He is a great musician surely.

SECOND HAG. There is no person can be safe from him the time he will put his "come hither" upon them. I give you my word he set myself dancing reels one time in the street, and I making an attack on him for keeping the little lads miching from school. That was a great scandal to put upon a decent woman.

FIRST HAG. He to be in the fair to-day and to take the fancy, you would hear the nailed boots of the frieze-coated man footing steps on the sidewalk.

SECOND HAG. You would, and it's likely he'd play a notion into the skulls of the pampootied boys from Aran, they to be kings of France or of Germany, till they'd go lift their head to the clouds and go knocking all before them. And the police it is likely laughing with themselves, as if listening to the talk of the blackbird would be perched upon a blessed bush.

FIRST HAG. I wonder he did not come. Could it be he might be made away with for the riches he brought from Cregroostha? It would be a strange thing now, he to be lying and his head broke, at the butt of a wall, and the woman he thought the whole world of to be getting her burial from the workhouse.

(*A sound of pipes.*)

SECOND HAG. Whist, I tell you! It's the sound of the pipes. It is McDonough, it is no other one.

FIRST HAG (*getting up*). I'm in dread of him coming in the house. He is a hasty man and wicked, and he vexed. What at all will he say and she being dead before him? Whether or no, it will be a sharp grief to him, she to scatter and to go. He might give me a back-stroke and drive me out from the door.

SECOND HAG. Let you make an attack upon himself before he will have time to make his own attack.

MCDONOUGH (*coming in*). Catherine! Where is she! Where is Catherine?

FIRST HAG. Is it readying the dinner before you, or wringing out a shirt for the Sunday like any good slave of a wife, you are used to find your woman, McDonough?

MCDONOUGH. What call would she have stopping in the house with the withered like of yourself? It is not to the crabbed talk of a peevish hag a handsome young woman would wish to be listening and sport and funning being in the fair outside.

FIRST HAG. Go look for her in the fair so, if it is gadding up and down is her habit, and you being gone out from her sight.

MCDONOUGH (*shaking her*). Tell me out, where is she?

FIRST HAG. Tell out what harbour were you yourself in from the day you left Cregroostha?

McDONOUGH. Is it that she got word?—or that she was tired waiting for me?

FIRST HAG. She is gone away from you, McDonough.

McDONOUGH. That is a lie, a black lie.

FIRST HAG. Throwing a lie in a decent woman's face will not bring you to the truth.

McDONOUGH. Is it what you are laying down that she went away with some other man? Say that out if you have courage, and I'll wring your yellow windpipe.

FIRST HAG. Leave your hand off me and open the room door, and you will see am I telling you any lie.

McDONOUGH (*goes to door, then stops*). She is not in it. She would have come out before me, and she hearing the sound of the pipes.

FIRST HAG. It is not the sound of the pipes will rouse her, or any sound made in this world at all.

McDONOUGH (*trembling*). What is it?

FIRST HAG. She is gone and she is not living.

McDONOUGH. Is it to die she did? (*Clutches her.*)

FIRST HAG. Yesterday, and the bells ringing, she turned her face to the south and died away. It was at the hour of noon I knew and was aware she was gone. A great loss it to be at the time of the fair, and all the lodgers that would have come into the house.

McDONOUGH. It is not truth. What would ail her to die?

FIRST HAG. The makings of a child that came before its time, God save the mark! She made a bad battle at the last.

McDONOUGH. What way did it fail you to send me out messengers seeking me when you knew her to be done and dying?

FIRST HAG. I thought she would drag another while. There was no time for the priest itself to overtake her, or to put the little dress of the Virgin in her hand at the last gasp of death.

(McDONOUGH *goes into the room. He comes out as if affrighted, leans his head against the wall, and breaks into a prayer in Irish:* "An Athair tha in Naomh, dean trocaire orainn! A Dia Righ an Domhain, dean trocraire orainn! A Mhuire Mathair Dia, dean trocaire orainn!")

SECOND HAG (*venturing near*). Do not go fret after her, McDonough. She could not go through the world forever, and travelling the world. It might be that trouble went with her.

McDONOUGH. Get out of that, you hags, you witches you! You

croaking birds of ill luck! It is much if I will leave you in the living world, and you not to have held back death from her!

SECOND HAG. That you may never be cross till you will meet with your own death! What way could any person do that?

MCDONOUGH. Get out the door and it will be best for you!

SECOND HAG. You are talking fool's talk and giving out words that are foolishness! There is no one at all can put away from his road the bones and the thinness of death.

MCDONOUGH. I to have been in it he would not have come under the lintel! Ugly as he is and strong, I would be able for him and would wrestle with him and drag him asunder and put him down! Before I would let him lay his sharp touch on her I would break and would crush his naked ribs, and would burn them to lime and scatter them!

FIRST HAG. Where is the use raving? It is best for you to turn your hand to the thing has to be done.

MCDONOUGH. You to have stood in his path he might have brought you away in her place! That much would be no great thing to ask, and your life being dead and in ashes.

FIRST HAG. Quieten yourself now where it was the will of God. She herself made no outcry and no ravings. I did my best for her, laying her out and putting a middling white sheet around her. I went so far as to smoothen her hair on the two sides of her face.

MCDONOUGH (*turning to inner door*). Is it that you are gone from me, Catherine, you that were the blossom of the branch!

(*Old woman moans.*)

It is a bad case you to have gone and to have left me as lonesome after you as that no one ever saw the like!

(*The old woman moans after each sentence.*)

I to bring you travelling you were the best traveller, and the best stepper, and the best that ever faced the western blast, and the waves of it blowing from you the shawl! I to be sore in the heart with walking you would make a smile of a laugh. I would not feel the road having your company; I would walk every whole step of Ireland.

I to bring you to the dance-house you would dance till you had them all tired, the same in the late of the day as in the commencement! Your steps following quick on one another the same as hard rain on a flagstone! They could not find your equal in all Ireland or in the whole ring of Connemara!

What way did it fail me to see the withering of the branches on every bush, as it is certain they withered the time laughter died with your laugh? The cold of winter has settled on the hearth. My heart is closed up with trouble!

FIRST HAG. It is best for us shut the door and to keep out the noises of the fair.

McDONOUGH. Ah, what sort at all are the people of the fair, to be doing their bargaining and clutching after their luckpenny, and she being stark and quiet!

FIRST HAG. She has to be buried ere evening. There was a messenger of a clerk came laying that down.

McDONOUGH. May ill luck attend him! Is it that he thinks she that is gone has no person belonging to her to wake her through the night-time?

FIRST HAG. He sent his men to coffin her. She will be brought away in the heel of the day.

McDONOUGH. It is a great wake I will give her. It would not be for honour she to go without that much. Cakes and candles and drink and tobacco! The table of this house is too narrow. It is from the neighbours we should borrow tables.

FIRST HAG. That cannot be. It is what the man said, "This is a common lodging-house. It is right to banish the dead from the living." He has the law with him, and custom. There is no use you thinking to go outside of that.

McDONOUGH. My lasting grief it will be I not to get leave to show her that respect!

FIRST HAG. "There will a car be sent," he said, "and two boys from the Union for to bear her out from the house."

McDONOUGH. Men from the Union, are you saying? I would not give leave to one of them to put a hand anigh or anear her! It is not their car will bring her to the grave. That would be the most pity in the world!

FIRST HAG. You have no other way to bring her on her road. It is best for you give in to their say.

McDONOUGH. Where are the friends and the neighbours that they would not put a hand under her?

FIRST HAG. They are after making their refusal. She was not well liked in Galway. There is no one will come to her help.

McDONOUGH. Is that the truth, or is it lies you have made up for my tormenting?

FIRST HAG. It is no lie at all. It is as sure as the winter's frost. You have no one to draw to but yourself.

McDONOUGH. It is mad jealous the women of Galway were and wild with anger, and she coming among them, that was seventeen times better than their best! My bitter grief I ever to have come next or near them, or to have made music for the lugs or for the feet of wide crooked hags! That they may dance to their death to the devil's pipes and be the disgrace of the world! It is a great slur on Ireland and a great scandal they to have made that refusing! That the Corrib River may leave its merings and rise up out of its banks till the waves will rise like mountains over the town and smother it, with all that is left of its tribes!

FIRST HAG. Be whist now, or they will be angered and they hearing you outside in the fair.

MCDONOUGH. Let their day not thrive with the buyers and the sellers in the fair! The curse of mildew on the tillage men, that every grain of seed they have sowed may be rotten in the ridges, and the grass corn blasted from the east before the latter end of harvest! The curse of the dead on the herds driving cattle and following after markets and fairs! My own curse on the big far-mers slapping and spitting in their deal! That a blood murrain may fall upon their bullocks! That rot may fall upon their flocks and maggots make them their pasture and their prey between this and the great feast of Christmas! It is my grief every hand in the fair not to be set shaking and be crookened, where they were not stretched out in friendship to the fair-haired woman that is left her lone within boards!

SECOND HAG (*at door*). Is it a niggard you are grown to be, McDonough, and you with riches in your hand? Is it against a new wedding you are keeping your pocket stiff, or to buy a house and an estate, that it fails you to call in hired women to make a right keen-ing, and a few decent boys to lift her through the streets?

MCDONOUGH. I to have money or means in my hand, I would ask no help or be beholden to any one at all.

SECOND HAG. If you had means, is it? I heard by true telling that you have money and means. "At the sheep-shearers' dance a high lady held the plate for the piper; a sovereign she put in it out of her hand, and there was no one of the big gentry but followed her. There never was seen so much riches in any hall or home." Where now is the fifty gold sovereigns you brought away from Gregroostha?

MCDONOUGH. Where is it?

SECOND HAG. Is it that you would begrudge it to the woman is inside?

MCDONOUGH. You know well I would not begrudge it.

FIRST HAG. A queer thing you to speak so stiff and to be running down all around you, and your own pocket being bulky the while.

MCDONOUGH (*turning out pocket*). It is as slack and as empty as when I went out from this.

SECOND HAG. You could not have run through that much.

MCDONOUGH. Not a red halfpenny left, or so much as the image of a farthing.

FIRST HAG. Is it robbed and plundered you were, and you walking the road?

MCDONOUGH (*sitting down and rocking himself*). I wish to my God it was some robber stripped and left me bare! Robbed and plundered! I was that, and by the worst man and the unkindest that ever was joined to a woman or lost a woman, and that is myself.

FIRST HAG. Is it to lose it unknownst you did?

MCDONOUGH. What way did I lose it, is it? I lost it knowingly and of my own will. Thrown on counters, thrown on the drink-house floor, given for spirits, given for porter, thrown for drink for friends and acquaintances, for strangers and strollers and vagabonds. Scattered in the parish of Ardrahan and at Labane cross. Tramps and schemers lying drunk and dead drunk at the butt of every wall. (*Buries head in his hands.*)

FIRST HAG. That is what happened the gold yourself and the pipes had won? You made no delay doing that much. You have a great wrong done to the woman inside, where you left her burying bare.

SECOND HAG. She to be without a farthing dip for her corpse, and you after lavishing gold.

FIRST HAG. You have a right to bruise your knees making repentance, you that lay on the one pillow with her. You to be putting curses upon others and making attacks on them! I would make no complaint, you to be naked at your own burying and at the very hour of death, and the rain falling down on your head.

MCDONOUGH. Little I mind what happens me. There is no word you can put out of your mouth can do me any injury at all. Oh, Catherine, it is best for me go hang myself out of a tree, and my carcass to be torn by savage dogs that went famished through a great length of time, and my bones left without a token or a flag or a headstone, and my name that was up at one time to be forgotten out of mind! (*He bursts out sobbing.*)

FIRST HAG. The shadows should be lengthening in the street. Look out would you see the car to be coming.

SECOND HAG. It was a while ago at the far corner of the fair. They were but waiting for the throng to lessen.

FIRST HAG. They are making too much delay.

SECOND HAG. I see a hint of the livery of the poorhouse coming through the crowd.

FIRST HAG. The men of the Union are coming to bring her away, McDonough. There is nothing more to be done. She will get her burial from the rates.

MCDONOUGH. Oh, Catherine, Catherine! Is it I myself have brought you to that shame and that disgrace!

SECOND HAG. You are making too much of it. Little it will signify, and we to be making clay, who was it dug a hole through the nettles or lifted down the sods over our head.

FIRST HAG. That is so. What signifies she to be followed or to be going her lone, and her eyes being shut to the world?

MCDONOUGH. Is that the thought ye have within ye, ye Galway hags? It is easy known it is in a trader's town you were bred, and in a street among dealers.

FIRST HAG. I was but saying it does not signify.

MCDONOUGH. But I say it does signify! I will tell that out to you and the world! That might be the thought of a townsman or a trader, or a rich merchant itself that had his estate gained by trafficking, for that is a sort does be thinking more of what they can make out of the living than of keeping a good memory of the dead!

FIRST HAG. There are worthier men than yourself, maybe, in storehouses and in shops.

MCDONOUGH. But I am of the generations of Orpheus, and have in me the breed of his master! And of Raftery and Carolan and O'Daly and all that made sounds of music from this back to the foundations of the earth! And as to the rich of the world, I would not humble my head to them. Let them have their serving men and their labourers and messengers will do their bidding. But the servant I myself command is the pipes that draws its breath from the four winds, and from a wind is beyond them again, and at the back of the winds of the air. She was a wedded woman and a woman having my own gold ring on her hand, and my own name put down with hers in the book. But she to have been a shameless woman as ye make her out to be, and sold from tinker to tinker on the road it is all one! I will show Galway and the world that it does signify; that it is not fitting McDonough's wife to travel without company and good hands under her and good following on the road. Play now, pipes, if you never played before! Call to the keeners to follow her with screams and beating of the hands and calling out! Set them crying now with your sound and with your notes, as it is often you brought them to the dance-house! (*Goes out and plays a lament outside.*)

FIRST HAG (*looking out*). It is queer and wild he is, cutting his teeth and the hair standing on him.

SECOND HAG. Some high notion he has, calling them to show honour to her as if she was the Queen of the Angels.

FIRST HAG. To draw to silence the whole fair did. Every person is moving towards this house.

(*A murmur as of people.* MCDONOUGH *comes in, stands at door, looking out.*)

MCDONOUGH. I squeeze the pipes as a challenge to the whole of the fair, gentle noble and simple, the poor and the high up. Come hither and cry Catherine McDonough, give a hand to carry her to the grave! Come to her aid, tribes of Galway, Lynches and Blakes and Frenches! McDonough's pipes give you that command, that have learned the lamentation of the Danes.

Come follow her on the road, trades of Galway, the fishermen, and the carpenters, and the weavers! It is by no short road we will carry her that never will walk any road from this out! By Williams-gate, beside Lynch's gallows, beside the gaol of the hangings, the salmon will make their leap as we pass!

MEN AT DOOR. We will. We will follow her, McDonough.

OTHERS. Give us the first place.

OTHERS. We ourselves will carry her!

MCDONOUGH. Faith, Catherine, you have your share and your choice this day of fine men, asking to carry you and to lend you their strength.

I will give no leave to traffickers to put their shoulder under you, or to any that made a refusal, or any seaside man at all.

I will give leave to no one but the sheep-shearers from Eserkelly, from Moneen and Cahirlinny and the whole stretch of Cregroostha. It is they have friendship for music, it is they have a wish for my four bones.

(SHEEP-SHEARERS *come in. They are dressed in white flannel. Each has a pair of shears at his side. The first carries a crook.*)

FIRST SHEEP-SHEARER. Is it within there she is, McDonough?

FIRST HAG. Go in through the door. The boards are around her and a clean quilt over them. Have a care not to leave down your hands on it, and they maybe being soiled with the fair.

(*They take off their hats and go in.*)

McDONOUGH (*turning to her door*). If you got no great honour from your birth up, and went barefoot through the first of your youth, you will get great respect now and will be remembered in the times to come.

There is many a lady dragging silk skirts through the lawns and the flower knots of Connacht, will get no such grand gathering of people at the last as you are getting on this day.

It is the story of the burying of McDonough's wife will be written in the book of the people!

(SHEEP-SHEARERS *appear at inner door.* McDONOUGH *goes out, squeezing the pipes. Triumphant music is heard from outside.*)

Curtain.

The Tragic-Comedies

THE IMAGE

THE IMAGE

PERSONS

THOMAS COPPINGER. *A stonecutter.*
MARY COPPINGER. *His wife.*
MALACHI NAUGHTON. *A mountainy man.*
BRIAN HOSTY. *A small farmer.*
DARBY COSTELLO. *A seaweed hawker.*
PEGGY MAHON. *An old midwife.*
PETER MANNION. *A carrier.*

ACT I

SCENE. *A village street with a thatched house on either side, both whitewashed, one very poor. Grey sea and grey hills seen beyond a wall of loose stones. Some headstones are propped against the wall, one inscribed* "ERECTED FOR THOMAS COPPINGER AND POSTERITY." COPPINGER *is looking at it.* MRS. COPPINGER, *with her back to him, is looking out over wall.*

MRS. COPPINGER (*putting out clothes to dry on the wall*). If we heard noises in the night time I heard a great silence now. I was looking out to see what was it ailed the place. What has happened all the neighbours I wonder?

COPPINGER. I was wondering that myself. I don't see Brian Hosty or Darby Costello in any place, or anyone at all only Malachi Naughton, the crazy mountainy man, is coming hither from the strand.

(*He sits down and chips at headstone.*)

MRS. COPPINGER. It is a queer thing you to be content, Thomas Coppinger, and you knocking out a living among the dead. It is no way content I myself would be, and to be following a trade that is all for gloom.

COPPINGER. It is not, but in the world wide there is not so lively or so pleasant a trade. Wait now till I'll sound that out to you. A man to be a herd now, and to be sent back out of the fair with beasts, the very time the sport would begin, or to be landing fish from a hooker and to be made take the tide at the very minute

131

maybe the crowds would be gathering for a race, or an assizes, or a thing of the kind, it is downhearted you would be coming into your own little place, and all the stir left after you. But to be turning back from a burying, and you living, and all that company lying dumb, and the rain coming down through the clay over their heads, and their friends crying them, that is the time your own little cabin would shine out as good as a wake house, in the time a wake house was all one with a dance house.

MRS. COPPINGER. That is not so in this place. No playing or funning or springing, but to be talking they do be, stupid talk about themselves and to be smoking tobacco.

COPPINGER. And another thing. It is very answerable to the soul to be always letting your mind dwell on them that are gone to dust and to ashes, and to be thinking how short they were in the world, and to be striving to put yourself in terror of eternity. "Vanity of vanities," said King Solomon, and he owning all his riches and his own seven hundred wives.

MRS. COPPINGER. It's time for you give in to my asking, and to bring me away to the States, and the work all wore away from you, the way you have no earthly thing to put your hand to but that headstone of your own. There doesn't be so many wakes as there were, or so many buryings, or the half of the people in the world that there used to be.

COPPINGER. The headland is a very wholesome place, without killing or murdering, and the youngsters all go foreign, and in my opinion the dead are nearly all dead—unless it might be old Peggy Mahon within in the house beyond.

MRS. COPPINGER. With all the children she brought home to the world, and all the women she saved from being brought away, she is near spun out herself. There are some would give the world to be gone altogether with the state she is in. And it's time for her to go anyway. Cross she is and peevish, and in troth she'd be no great loss.

COPPINGER. Let you not be talking that way. It never was a habit of my habits to wish any harm to a neighbour, or to call down misfortune on them at all.

MRS. COPPINGER. It's a poor job to be lettering out your own name and for no profit. And you should be near done by this anyway. "In memory of Thomas Coppinger and Posterity." What is there to put to that but the day of your death, that it would fail you to have foreknowledge of, and the day it's likely you have no remembrance of, that you made your own start on the plains of this world.

COPPINGER. That is not enough. That is what has to be put on the slab of many a common man, where he did no big thing, or never stretched a hand to the poor.

MRS. COPPINGER. And what will there be to write on your own slab, more than that you lived and died on the Munster side of the headland of Druim-na-Cuan, and knocked out a poor way of living, hammering at hard stones?

COPPINGER. No fear of me being left that way. Some thing will come to pass. Some great man might come wanting a monument that would put up my name for ever. Some man so great his death would put away laughter in Ireland.

MRS. COPPINGER. Ah! If it is waiting you are for such a one to die, sure you don't know is he born at all yet, or his father or his grandfather, or at what time he might be born through the next two thousand years. You are talking as wild as a dream might fall upon you in the night time.

COPPINGER. There is dreams and dreams. And at every thousand years some great thing is apt to happen, such as the Deluge or the coming of the Milesians into Ireland—I tell you there is dreams and dreams. (*Turns and chips away at headstone.*)

(MALACHI *comes in slowly left and blinks at them.*)

MRS. COPPINGER. Well. Malachi Naughton, God bless your health, and what's the best news with you? You have the appearance of getting bad nourishment. They were telling me your hens were all ate with the fox. I wonder now you wouldn't quit the mountain side, and come make your dwelling in some place there would be company.

MALACHI. The towns do be in uproar and do be crowded, and the roads do be wet and wide; and as to the villages, there is spies in them, and traitors, and people you wouldn't like to be talking with. Too venomous they are and too corrupted with drink. I'd like to keep my own company, and I to have no way of living but the berries of the bush.

MRS. COPPINGER. There is no crowd in this place to-day, and no person at all to be heard or to be seen.

MALACHI. That wasn't so a while ago. (*Turning to* COPPINGER.) Tell me, Thomas Coppinger, did you hear e'er a noise in the night time?

COPPINGER. What way wouldn't I hear it? Thunder it's likely it was that was breaking from the clouds and from the skies, the same as it did ere yesterday, the time the Kerry men's hooker was destroyed out from Galway. It's likely the weather will cheer up now, the thunder having brought away the venom out of the air.

MALACHI. The clouds of the air had no hand in it at all. Thunder is natural. I tell you it is more than thunder came visiting this place last night.

MRS. COPPINGER. I was thinking myself it was no thunder. It was more like the roaring of calves, or the drowning of hundreds, or all the first cousins coming racing with their cars to a wedding after dark.

COPPINGER (*rises and looks over wall*). Have it your own way so. I'll go meet Brian and Darby, and they'll tell you was it thunder. I see Brian coming hither over the ridge is above the cliffs. Have you my boots cleaned, Mary, till I'll put them on to my feet?

(*He goes into house.*)

MALACHI. It was no thunder was in it, but the night that was full of signs and of wonders.

MRS. COPPINGER. What is it makes you say that? I didn't see any wonder you'd call a wonder. It's likely it is in your own head the wonders were.

MALACHI. A little bird of a cock I have, that started crowing in the dark hour of the night, the same as if the dawn had come and put him in mind of Denmark.

MRS. COPPINGER. A cock to crow out of season is no great wonder, and he to be perched on the rafters, and you maybe to be turning yourself on your palliase, that would be creaking with the nature of the straw.

MALACHI. Great noises I heard after that, as if of tearing and splashing and roaring through the tide.

MRS. COPPINGER. I heard them myself as good as you. I was in dread it might be the day of judgment. To put my head in under the quilt I did, till such time as it had passed away.

MALACHI. It was not quieted till after the whitening of the dawn in the skies. I went out at that time thinking to see the goat that was up to her kidding time, and she had the rope broke, and the stone thrust away that was in the door of the little pen I had made, and there was no sight or mind of her.

MRS. COPPINGER. Is it searching after her yet you are, or did you find her gone astray among the rocks?

MALACHI. Down by the brink of the sea I found her, a place she never was apt to go, and two young kids beside her, she that never had but the one before; and more than that again——

134

MRS. COPPINGER. You'll be in Heaven, she to have kidded, the way you'll have a drop of milk with your tea.

MALACHI. Two young kids beside her on the salt edge of the tide, and she chewing neither dulse, or carrageen, or seaweed, but lying in full content, and as if browsing upon a little bit of a board.

MRS. COPPINGER. Goats will eat all. There was a neighbour's goat mounted up on my own dresser one time, and made as if to devour the blessed palm was on the wall.

MALACHI. Did ever you hear up to this, Mrs. Coppinger, a beast to have got nourishment from a board?

MRS. COPPINGER. I did to be sure. Isn't it the way the body of Blessed Columcille was tracked the time it was sent back across the sea to Ireland for its burying? To sculpture directions on a stick they did, and it was a cow went licking it the time it was come to land. It is likely you heard that yourself?

MALACHI (*going to her and drawing a board from under his ragged shirt*). You that can read writing, ma'am, sound out to me now the testimony is on that board.

MRS. COPPINGER. So there is a name on it in painted printing—H, H, u, g, h—Hugh—Hugh O'Lorrha.

MALACHI. Hugh O'Lorrha—I was thinking, and I was near certain, the time I saw the letters it was the name of some person was in it, that had sent some message into my hand. Tell me now, ma'am, have you any account at all, or did ever you hear it told who was Hugh O'Lorrha?

MRS. COPPINGER. It seems to me to have heard such a name, but I can put no face to it or no account. There's many things I forgot that I heard in my lifetime. I only recollect things in the broad. (*Shades her eyes and looks out over wall.*)

MALACHI. There should be some meaning in it and some message. No doubt about it at all, it was a night full of wonders—Down in the tide there to be the noise as of hundreds, the bird in the rafters making its own outcry, and its call—the goat to be bringing me to that bit of a board—Hugh O'Lorrha, that should be a very high sounding name. What it is at all he is calling to me, and bidding me for to do?

(BRIAN HOSTY *comes in.*)

MRS. COPPINGER (*turning to door*). Come out here, Thomas. Here is Brian Hosty before you.

COPPINGER (*coming out*). There is no need for me go seek him so. Well, now, Brian, didn't you go abroad very early this morning?

HOSTY. It's easy rise up and go abroad early the time there does disturbance come, that will put away the sleep from your eyes.

COPPINGER. You heard the noises so?

HOSTY. What would ail me not to hear them? You would hear that roaring three mile off, as well as you would hear it a mile.

MRS. COPPINGER. Was it a fleet of seals maybe was coming in against the rough weather does be prophesied in the skies?

HOSTS. Did any one ever hear a fleet of seals to be giving out a sound like eight eights crying together, or like the seven banshees of Lisheen Crannagh? You to have seen those two beasts fighting through the tide, you would know them not to be seals. Tearing and battling they were. At the time they commenced roaring I went out, and Darby Costello rose up and put the crowbar to his own door, in dread they might be coming into the house.

MRS. COPPINGER. Beasts is it? Tell me now what were they at all.

HOSTY. Whales they were—two of them—they never quitted fighting one another till they came up upon the strand, and the salt water went and left them, that you would be sorry to hear them crying and moaning.

COPPINGER. And is it on the strand they are presently?

HOSTY. They are, and it is on the Connacht side of the headland they took their station, as was right.

COPPINGER. Take care but the tide might steal up on them. But I suppose they are dead by this?

HOSTY. What would hinder them from being dead? I am after going where they are, myself and Darby Costello. To cut a bit off of one of them I did. The flesh of it was like the dribbled snow, the same as a pig you would kill and would be after cleaning out for hanging, as clean and as white as that. And as for size, you to go up on them, you could see the whole of Galway.

MRS. COPPINGER. Would you say there to be oil in them? I heard in some place the oil would be rendered out of a whale would carry a big price.

HOSTY. Oil is it? I took a wisp of straw and lighted it at the side of one of them, and the oil of it went out into the sea, and never mixing with the salt water at all. The whole of the lakes of Ireland and the wide Shannon along with them, there is enough of oil in those two whales to make a scum and a covering over the whole of their brim.

MRS. COPPINGER. That now is maybe the luck, Thomas, you were thinking would be drawing towards you. Gather now all the vessels in the place till we'll see what we can bring away of oil. Here now is the tub, and the big pot, and the kettle.

HOSTY. I heard one time there was a doctor back in Connemara gave a pound a gallon for the oil was rendered out of a whale. To cure ulcers and cancers I suppose it did, the same as king's blood used to cure the evil.

MRS. COPPINGER. That's a whip of money! Let me see can I empty the milk out of the churn.

(MR. *and* MRS. COPPINGER *go into house.*)

MALACHI (*coming near*). Whales? Did you say it was whales came visiting this strand in the night time?

HOSTY. Amn't I after saying that it was?

MALACHI. What was it now brought those beasts to be travelling to this headland more than to any other place, and to find their own track to it across the wide ocean?

HOSTY. What would bring them but chance, or ignorance or the blindness that came on them with the strokes they were striking and hitting at one another under the waves.

MALACHI. It was those beasts so, brought that name and that board of timber. Who now in the wide earthly world will tell me who was Hugh O'Lorrha? (*Goes off.*)

HOSTY (*to* MRS. COPPINGER, *who has come to door*). What at all is Malachi raving about, Mrs. Coppinger, with his cracked talk and his questioning?

MRS. COPPINGER. Ah, that is the way he is, and something gone queer in his head. There is nothing left to him in life but high flighty thoughts.

HOSTY (*looking at vessels*). Well, Mrs. Coppinger, it's a share of the good things of the world you will be getting this time surely. It's to quit stone-cutting you will bring Thomas Coppinger that time.

COPPINGER (*leaning out over door*). No fear of me, Brian. Did ever you find east or west any place at all I broke my word? And isn't it long I promised you to print your own headstone and to dress it for you, the time your end would be drawing near?

HOSTY. I'm very thankful to you, Thomas. I am thinking it is a good while you are putting off making an end and a finish of your own slab.

COPPINGER. There is reason in that, I am thinking I might get a name yet would look bigger and handsomer on my tomb.

HOSTY. Whatever way you may write out your name or raise it, it will be but Thomas Coppinger in the end.

MRS. COPPINGER. It might not. Look at all that voted for the Parliament going from College Green to England, and that went to bed nothing and rose up lords in the morning! I would like well Thomas to be a lord, with two hundred acres of land.

HOSTY. Well, it's the people of Munster are taken up in themselves with pride and with conceit! My joy that I was not reared among them, but in the bright beautiful province of Connacht!

MRS. COPPINGER. Let you keep your great praises of Connacht and your talk for them are the other side of the earth and cannot see into it, as I myself can see it over the mering wall, and the fields that are all a flag, and the thistles as hardy as our own and as bold. It is not here I myself would wish to stop, in a narrow barren place, where you never would get your fill of the world's joy. It's out to America I would go, and a fair wind blowing!

HOSTY. I know well what it is you are dreaming to find before you in the States—beer from Denmark, honey out of Greece; rings and brooches and such things as are dear to women; high blood and grandeur and ringing of bells; a silver cushion having four edges, and you sitting on it through the day time the same as the Queen of Pride, and talking of the ways of the world and the war! But remember now I was in America one time myself!

MRS. COPPINGER. Why wouldn't there be grandeurs and good houses in Boston or in New York where many a bright pound was spent upon them?

HOSTY. All the grandeurs I saw was never the face of a fire but only a black stove, and not a chimney in the house but only a crooked pipe, and never a spring well but rotten water brought from the Lord knows where, and no way for going out unless you would take a stroll in a street car. And if there was quality food I didn't see it, or a bit of butter that was sweet!

COPPINGER (leaning in the half door). Let you leave challenging one another, and look at Darby Costello is running like a heifer had got a pick of a fly, or a rat there would be strong cats following.

MRS. COPPINGER (jumps up). Ask him what will he do with his share of the oil, and see will he be able to make a choice, besides putting insults on his next-door neighbour!

(COSTELLO runs in breathless.)

HOSTY. Tell me now what will be your own choice thing out of the spending and the profit of the oil?

MRS. COPPINGER. Let you chose some big thing will set you free from drawing seaweed till the day of judgment!

COSTELLO. I am striving to tell you that the whales——

138

MRS. COPPINGER. Tell us out quick now, what is your desire and your choice.

COSTELLO. Ah, now, what is my desire but peace and patience and to give no offence, or have any one annoying me, but there to be no law but love—and if I have another thing to ask it is leave to make my voice heard for one minute only, till you'll hear what I'm striving to tell——

COPPINGER. A pound a gallon we are to get out of the oil! It's the whole of us will get our chance!

COSTELLO. Ah, quit talking till I'll tell you—— It is little profit you will be getting for yourselves, where the whole country entirely is gathered at this time about the whales. In boats they are come from every side. Drawing lots for strips of them they are, the same as if they were seaweed on the sand.

HOSTY. They have no call to them at all! It is we ourselves were the first to find them and to put our mark upon their skin. Did you stand up to them telling them that?

COSTELLO. It isn't easy stand up to a throng of them. From Oranmore they are come I tell you and from Finevara and Duras and Balindereen. The Kerry men were wrecked in the hooker were in it along with them, very wicked looking they were.

HOSTY. They have no claim at all to be coming to our headland and to be bringing away our prey.

COSTELLO. I was striving to say that much to them, fair and civil; and the face they put on themselves was not the face of a friend would be drinking porter with you, but of an enemy would be coming at you with a gun. To fire a stone at me a one of them did, and they wouldn't leave me till now in the living world if I didn't run. There were rocks threw after me all the length of the road.

(MRS. COPPINGER *goes into house.*)

HOSTY. Give me a hold of a reaping hook till I'll go sweep them before me from where they are, and drive them under the sway of the living fishes of the sea!

COPPINGER (*picking up tools*). It is with my own hammer and my chisel I will tackle them! Leave your hand on a fork, Darby, or a spade, or so much as a big wattle of a stick; and let one of ye be humming Lord Byron's march, and he going out to war!

HOSTY. We'll put terror on them! We'll banish them!

COSTELLO (*sitting down*). Devil a fear of me! I had my enough, thinking as I did that I had not three minutes to live. There is

139

nothing is worse than your own life, and what call have you to go losing it?

COPPINGER. I never would go back before any enemy at all so long as my life would last! I tell you I never felt so merry in my life, and no bad bones about me. I wouldn't be afraid of the worst thing you could meet, a bee coming to sting you, or whatever it might be!

COSTELLO. I wouldn't face them again, I to get all the whales of the big ocean. I tell you they are hardy lads. There's few of the police would like to grabble with them.

COPPINGER. It is crippled and crappled you are with age, Darby, the way you do be failing in your walk!

COSTELLO. I am up to no such great age, but my feet that are sore with all they sweated. But it's you yourself is getting very slack in your work and very attentive to your bed.

COPPINGER. Is it that you are saying I am an old spent man? I'm not so old at all! I'm not as old as the hills of Gowra, whatever age that is! I'm not up to the age of Brian Hosty that has not hardly a blade of hair on his head, and has lost the whole of his teeth.

HOSTY. Leave your finger in my mouth till you'll see did I lose my teeth!

(PETER MANNION *comes in.*)

MRS. COPPINGER. Is it for commands you are come, Peter Mannion, and you going with your car to the town?

MANNION. The priest and the waterguard are after going where there is a gathering of strange lads around and about the two dead fishes on the strand.

COPPINGER. Sure it's to sweep the whole troop of them into the sea we are going out at this minute.

MANNION. The priest and the waterguard has them banished back to their own parish and their own district. To give them great abuse his reverence did, and the waterguard threatened them with the law.

COPPINGER. Is it to drive them away clear and clean they did?

MANNION. Every whole one of them, big and little.

COPPINGER. It's the priest is well able to break a gap before him and to put justice and profit into the hands of his own congregation!

HOSTY. To respect the first that came to the whales he will.

MANNION. It is what I was bid say, there is none of ye at all will get any hold of the whales.

COPPINGER. What's that you're saying? And a miracle after coming for to bring me my chance?

MANNION. The priest and the waterguard has laid down that the whole of the gain and the riches within in those two beasts of the sea, is not to be made over to this one or to that one, or to be made any man's profit and his prize, but to be laid out for the good and for the benefit of the whole of the headland, and of this point.

HOSTY. It is to the Connacht side they landed. It wouldn't be right giving the Munster side any share.

MRS. COPPINGER. We should give in, so, I suppose and to put up with the loss. It's best not vex a priest or to rub against him at all.

MANNION. Which now of ye is the oldest?

HOSTY. What meaning have you asking that?

MANNION. It is what I was bid say, there must some plan be made up without delay, for the spending of whatever will come from the whales. "It is the oldest inhabitant," says the priest, "should be best able to give out judgment as to that,"—and then the waterguard——

HOSTY. To make out a plan for the spending is it? That should be a great lift to any person.

MRS. COPPINGER (*taking* COPPINGER'S *arm and pushing him forward*). Rise up now, Thomas Coppinger, and make your claim. You should be the most ageable person in the place, you are far before seventy years.

MANNION. The waterguard that said then——

HOSTY (*pushing him away*). He is not the most ageable, but I that am older than himself. Look at the way he is fresh and flushy in the features, and no way racked looking the same as myself.

(MANNION *sits down and lights pipe*.)

MRS. COPPINGER. No, but tossed hair you are putting on yourself, and a cross face, the way you would look to be old. You to be minding and cleaning yourself you'd keep your youth yet. Tell them out now, Thomas, your age.

COPPINGER. What way could I say what age I am? When you are up to seventy year you wouldn't feel the years passing. I'm telling no lie saying that, no more than if I was on my knees to the priest.

HOSTY. I to have said you were passed your three score a half hour ago, it's likely you'd fly in my eye; but you have the tune changed now as quick as any piper.

COPPINGER. It's likely I have sixty years, and seventy years and another seventy along with them if it was counted right. But you yourself are but upon the bruff of age. Look at you as straight as a ribbon!

HOSTY. If I am straight, it is because there is more spirit in the Connacht men than in the Munster tribe, and more of a name for decency! I can remember when you'd walk out as far as the strand to catch soles and turbots and every quality fish, before the trawlers had them all destroyed.

COSTELLO. No, but my mother that remembered my brother falling on me in the cradle, and hiding in the bushes all the day in dread of her. And he was seventy-three when he died.

HOSTY. Ah, you weren't any age much that time at all. It is suppler you are than the whole of us. But I myself was six months the time of the big storm, and *that* can tell no lie.

COSTELLO. My dearest life! Sure I remember the big wind myself and all that went before it, if it wasn't I was so neglectful and so heedless in my early time.

COPPINGER. My mother, God rest her soul, that I heard saying I had a year more than Brian Hosty. And *she* remembered the landing of the French at Killala.

HOSTY. She did, and the Danes being driven out from Ireland I suppose, and the band playing Brian Boru's march!

(PEGGY MAHON *appears at her cabin door.*)

MRS. COPPINGER. There now is Peggy Mahon can settle the case. There is no person has knowledge of years only herself, where the dates are away and astray, she being such an old resident and drawing to a hundred years. Come out here to us now, Peggy Mahon, and at the fall of night I won't leave you without a drop of milk for your tea.

COPPINGER. Ah, she is shook this long time. Where's the use making any appeal to her, and she having but old stories and vanities.

HOSTY. Look at here now, ma'am. Didn't you give aid to my own three sons coming into the world, that are at this time buried in Minnesota? And my daughter that is looking at her children's children in Australia? And at that time I was up in age.

COSTELLO (*pulling* HOSTY *away from* PEGGY). Look, ma'am, isn't it three score years since you coming to the house the time my first young son was born? And it is what you said, that he was a present from God.

PEGGY. So he was, so he was. Every baby is a present from God, it is for God we should attend it. It is God puts you into the world and brings you out of it, and beyond that there is a woman in the stars does all.

COPPINGER. It is not well in the mind she is, and not remembering.

PEGGY. I remember, I remember. Lonesome after the old times I am. I am always remembering bye and bye.

COPPINGER. Cast back your mind so, to how many score years is it since you came attending the first wife I had, before I joined with herself secondly in marriage.

PEGGY. There is no second marriage, there is but the one marriage. He that was the best comrade, of a hasty man, God Almighty ever put a hand to, was brought away from me with little provocation twenty and half a hundred years ago. Brought away through death he was from this white world, and I myself left after him, a bird alone.

MRS. COPPINGER (to COSTELLO). The talk she does be always making about Patrick Mahon, you would say, listening to her, he was mostly the pride of the headland. And he but a poor-looking little creature they were telling me, and having an impediment in his speech.

COSTELLO. Old she is, and it's all in her brain the things she does be talking of.

COPPINGER. And what way now will a judgment be made, and a decree, which of us should be leader?

MANNION (getting up). It's time for you hearken to my news. The priest said the oldest man, and the waterguard said the three oldest, and the two of them agreed that if ye would agree they themselves would agree to that. I'll be coming again, where I have to bring the plan ye will lay out, to put before the Board of Guardians that are sitting on this day, so soon as I'll put the tacklings on the horse. (Goes.)

COPPINGER. I might be going to get my chance in the heel. Wait now till I'll lay my mind to it for a while.

MRS. COPPINGER. And what is your own mind, Brian Hosty, you that are my near neighbour and my most enemy? Show us now what the intellect and the wit of the Connacht man can do.

HOSTY. I would not tell a lie for one or for two, and I declare now and nearly take my oath, that I to have my choice thing and the riches of Damer and Chandler, it is what I would wish, this little dry stone wall to be swept from this village where I live to my grief and my sorrow, and a ditch to be dug from the Shannon to the sea, would divide the two provinces, and would be wide enough and bulky enough to drown every chattering word of the cranky women of Munster, and let me hear nothing but the sweet-voiced women of Connacht, from now to the womb of judgment.

COSTELLO. Oh, now, Brian Hosty, that is a very unneighbourly way to be saying such unruly words, that wouldn't be said hardly by the poorest person would be walking the road.

HOSTY. Tell out your own request so, and see will it give satisfaction, since you are so crabbed to be correcting myself.

COSTELLO. I wouldn't like to be going against any person at all. I would sooner to leave it to a committee.

HOSTY. So you would too, and you being every man's man. And it's time for Coppinger to speak his mind, if his wife will but give him leave.

COPPINGER. Every man to his trade—and I would like well to keep to my own trade—It is on stones my mind is dwelling and on rocks.

MRS. COPPINGER. Let you break up so and make an end of the rocks in the harbour where the Kerry men's hooker was broke up. To come against one of them it did, and never left it but in little sticks. A danger to ships they would be, and any ships to be coming in to the pier. They to be out of it, what would hinder ships coming in the way you could set out from this street to go to America or around the world? You wanting some big thing to do, there you have it to your hand—The harbour of New York there beyond, and the harbour of Druim-na-Cuan to be here and the one ocean to be serving the two of them!

HOSTY (laughing). You have a great notion, Mrs. Coppinger, what sort the harbour of New York is, and you thinking to make the like of it in this place, with sails and steamers drawing in from the world entirely, and the Statue of Liberty standing up high before you.

(MALACHI comes in and sits down at PEGGY'S door.)

MRS. COPPINGER. Why wouldn't there be a statue? A statue is a thing does be put in many a place. Sure you can see one to Saint Joseph, Protector of the souls in Purgatory, all the same as life across the bay.

HOSTY. And Thomas Coppinger that is thinking to shape it out I suppose with his hammer, according as his fancy tells him what way it should be worked?

MRS. COPPINGER. Why wouldn't he shape it and he having a mind to shape it, and being well used as he is to handle every sort of stone?

HOSTY. It is not of stone statues do be made, but of iron would

144

be rendered into a mould, the same as sheep's tallow you would be rendering for candles.

COPPINGER. I would never say iron to be as natural as stone, or as kind.

COSTELLO. Plaster now would be very tasty and very suitable, and a shelter to be put over it. It would be no way so costly as iron.

HOSTY. It is iron is more serviceable, and as to cost, the first expense would be the cheapest, the way it would be a good job, and not to turn against you after.

COSTELLO. What would you say now to cement, and a good stand being under it?

HOSTY. If it was a statue was to be made, it's an iron statue it should be.

COPPINGER. And what way would you hoist it to its place? It would have the weight in it of the devil's forge.

HOSTY. And what do you say to the weight of stone? Look at that slab of your own that has a hole wore through the street, and it but two year or so leaning towards the wall.

COPPINGER. It has not a hole made, but to settle itself it did, against such time as it would be called for and be wanting.

HOSTY. I to have an estate I would bet it, you would not be able to lift it or to stir it from the place it is standing at this minute.

COPPINGER. I'll engage I would, and to throw it over the collar beam of the barn I would, the same as a sack of oats——

(*They gather round headstone.* MANNION *comes in.*)

MANNION. Did you make up your mind yet to say out what thing it is ye have settled, for me to bring word to the Board Room in the town?

HOSTY. What way can we make our mind up till such time as we have a finish made of this argument?

COPPINGER. Did you ever hear it said in any place, Peter Mannion, iron to be more answerable for an image than stone?

COSTELLO. Wouldn't you say now, Peter, there is very lasting wear in cement?

MANNION. It is best for ye make your mind up. There are other old men in the district, and they getting older every minute.

COPPINGER. Give me but the time to bring proof to Brian Hosty that there is no weight to signify in a slab of stone. (*Tries to lift it, and* HOSTY *and* COSTELLO *encourage him, with sarcastic applause.*)

COSTELLO. All the strength you have wouldn't lift that flag.

HOSTY. Lift it is it? If you were as strong as Finn MacCumhail you wouldn't lift it.

MRS. COPPINGER (*dragging* DARBY *away*). You are a friendly man, Darby Costello, and always very liberal to do as I bid you, not like Brian that is stubborn—Let you settle an image to be made and be put up, and give the contract to Thomas—he is that greedy for work—and it would be a great thing for him rise out of headstones, and to get a decent job——

COSTELLO. I'd be in dread of Brian Hosty going against me. He is always someway contrary, that you couldn't teach him manners.

MRS. COPPINGER. It would be handsome work for him, and who is nearer than a neighbour? It might put life in him that he would bring me away to America yet. But that to fail us we might as well close the door—You to give your vote for it, and Thomas to give it, that would be two against one.

MANNION (*turning from* HOSTY *and* COPPINGER *to* MRS. COPPINGER). Will you tell me what at all is it they are arguing about?

(COSTELLO *escapes and goes off.*)

MRS. COPPINGER. It is that they cannot agree what is the right material for to put in a statue.

MANNION. And is it a statue so, they have laid down as their choice thing and their plan?

MRS. COPPINGER. Darby Costello will tell you if it is. Where is he? Well, he has but a bad heart of courage. Why would they be making so much talk about it, they not to have made it their plan?

MANNION. I would say it to be a queer thing for them to lay their thoughts to, and a very queer thing—Let me keep now the messages in mind—Candles for the shop—Paraffin oil for the priest—a pair of boots for the clerk—the Board of Guardians to be told there is a statue to be put up with the profit of the oil of the whales —(*Goes off as* COPPINGER *with a great effort upsets the stone, which falls with a crash.*)

HOSTY. Do you call it lifting it to throw it down?

COPPINGER. Wait a minute now till I'll strive secondly! ——

MRS. COPPINGER. Thomas! It's time bring the mash to the cow —run Brian Hosty, there's a sheep of your sheep—unless it might be a stone—is lying on its back near its death—— (BRIAN *jumps over wall.*)

COPPINGER. But sure we made no settlement yet.

MRS. COPPINGER (*shoving him into the house*). It's well for you to have some one to mind you and to take care of you—Believe me, Thomas Coppinger, you are going to get your chance!

Curtain.

146

ACT II

SCENE. *Same, but night time. Moonlight. Candle and firelight shining from the open half-door of* COPPINGER'S *house.* MRS. COPPINGER *heard singing within.*

MALACHI (*coming down street*). The fall of night is come and I didn't find him yet. East and west I'll go searching for him, east and west—he to be in the hollow I'll be on the hill, he to be on the hill I'll be in the hollow!

PEGGY (*coming from her cabin with milk jug*). What is on you, Malachi Naughton, that you are running there and hither, as if there was one dead belonging to you?

MALACHI (*stops short*). It is long you are in this world, Peggy Mahon, and you knew a power of people from birth to age, and heard many histories. Tell me, now, did ever you know or did ever you hear tell of one Hugh O'Lorrha?

PEGGY. What would ail me not to hear of him? Hugh O'Lorrha —Hugh Beg O'Lorrha.

MALACHI. That is it, ma'am, you have it—I knew well you should have that knowledge, and with all the generations that passed before you in your time.

PEGGY (*sits down near* MRS. COPPINGER'S *door*). I'd tell you out his story if I didn't think it too long to be keeping you on the soles of your feet while you'd be hearing it.

MALACHI. Tell it out, tell it out! You to be telling his story through the length of seven year, I wouldn't be tired listening to it.

PEGGY. Ah, it's near gone from me. All such things are gone from me, with the dint of fretting after them that flew away.

MALACHI. You cannot but tell it. It is through miracles his name was brought to this place. I tell you it was not brought without wonders.

PEGGY. To leave his mother's house he did——

MALACHI. So he would too. What would happen to the world the like of him to have stopped at home? He wasn't one would be sitting through the week the same as the police, having his feet in the ashes.

PEGGY. Out fighting on the road he went——

147

MALACHI. There were always good fighters in Ireland till this present time. The people have no fight in them now worth while, so lagging they are grown to be and so liary.

PEGGY. Fighting, fighting. To get into some trouble he did—it is hardly he escaped from the Naked Hangman——

MALACHI. It is the Sassanach twisted the rope for him so. Terrible wicked they were, and God save us, I believe they are every bit as wicked yet. Go on, ma'am, sound it out. Well, it was the one hand sent the whales steering over the tide, and brought me here to yourself gathering newses.

PEGGY (crossly). Where is the milk, Mrs. Coppinger has me promised? I'll tell no more. There's too many striving to knock talk out of me, and the red tea stewing on the coals, and I myself weary and waiting for the drop of new milk. Is it coming out you are, Mrs. Coppinger?

MRS. COPPINGER (from inside). I'll have it now for you within one minute.

MALACHI. They will mind me now, they will surely mind me now, when I tell them that name has to be put up. It is to myself the message was brought, Peggy Mahon, to put up the name of Hugh O'Lorrha, and to sound it in the ears of the entire world. Oh, there will be no fear from this out it will ever be disremembered again, or wither away from the mind of any person at all.

PEGGY. Have you no one of your own to keep in mind, Malachi Naughton, that you should go battling for a name is no more to you than any other, and not to be content with your own dead?

MALACHI. It is more to me than any other name. It is a name I would go walking the world for, without a shoe to my foot! And why would I do that for any common person, would be maybe as ugly as the people I do be seeing every day, and as cross and as crabbed? What call would I have going through hardship for a man would be no better maybe, and no better looking, than myself.

PEGGY. What sort of a tribe are you sprung from, or of a poor mountainy race, that you would have no one of your own kindred or of your blood, would be worth remembering?

MRS. COPPINGER (who has been listening, coming to door). The doctor called death a shadow, and death called the doctor a shadow! Faith the two of ye put me in mind of the both of them, and you disputing and arguing, and neither of you owning a ha'porth worth arguing for, or a perch of land only the street, or so much as a stim of sense.

MALACHI. Putting me down the whole of ye do be, and saying

I know nothing; and I maybe as apt as the best of ye, and as wide awake. That one counting her own dead in the count with Hugh O'Lorrha. A man that robbed the apple from the hundreds! But his name will go up in spite of ye, if God has a hand in it!

MRS. COPPINGER. Leave arguing with him, Peggy, you might as well be talking with the wind. If you go fighting, can't you fight for things that are worth fighting for.

PEGGY. Why would any person go set their mind upon the hither side of the grave, and not upon the far side? I have seen them come and seen them go, the scores and the hundreds, the same as if they came on a visit to a neighbour's house, and went from it again the time their clothes would be wore out and tattered. And the skin to be wore into rags, the soul is the one thing always, for it was the breath of God put into Adam, and it is the possession of God ever since. I know well where my own man is living yet, and where I will come to him when the Lord will send for me.

MRS. COPPINGER. It is hard know that. Any man that goes to punishment doesn't come back to tell his story, and in Heaven I suppose they keep a fast hold of them too. This world's the best to keep your eye on. Who knows will we see them again, or will we care much about it if we do see them? It would be best for you have taken another comrade in your bloom, in place of always lamenting him that is gone, and you without one to close your eyes the time you'll die, or the help of a man in the house, and without a son or a daughter in all Ireland.

PEGGY. You never laid an eye on Patrick Mahon, or never lived next or near him, and you saying that. The parting of us two was the parting of the body with the soul. I tell you there never set his foot on the floor of the world, and never told his secret to a woman, so good a man. Where would I find, east or west, the like of him of a comrade? The time he wanted me, and some were again it, we gave one another a hard promise to let no person at all come between us or separate us. And after he going they had a match made for me with some man they were bringing into the house. But I said I never would rear a son to rubbish, and I drove them out. (*She rises.*) And if I was glad to get a dry potato at some times, and a bit of Indian meal itself in the scarce July, I have my promise kept. Why would I take a man, I said, and my comrade sleeping with no woman?

MRS. COPPINGER. That's not the way with me, but I would sooner have some one to care and to nourish, than to be looking after a shadow you would have no way to be serving, but maybe with an odd prayer or a Mass, and that never might be aware maybe were you thinking about him or remembering him at all.

PEGGY. It's likely he knows, though I never saw him since, and never had a sign or a vision from him, and it's often I went out looking for him at the fall of day. Never a sign or a vision, but often and often he came across me in my sleep. Waiting for him I do be till such time as I will come to him, where the Almighty has a very good place of His own. (*Goes towards her own door.*)

MRS. COPPINGER. You might come to him, maybe—but it is hard to be sure of it, and what way can you know?

PEGGY (*turning*). What way can I know is it? I can give you God's bail for it.

MRS. COPPINGER. There can be no bail better than that—But to get to our dead itself, it is not likely they would know us or recognise us, and the length of the years does be between us.

PEGGY. Don't be saying that! Don't be putting that word out of your mouth! How dare you be putting your own bad thoughts between myself and my decent comrade?

MRS. COPPINGER. I didn't think you would be so much vexed I to say that. Here now is the drop of milk is warm from the cow yet.

PEGGY (*throwing it out of her jug*). I will not take it or take anything at all from your hand, and you after striving to rob me of my hope. I tell you, that to be gone from me, my heart would break, that is wore to a silk thread. He not to know me is it? Oh, Patrick! Oh, my grief! and maybe it might be so. For what am I but a bent crooked hag, withering through the world, and you yourself being, as I think, one of the fair-haired boys of Heaven! (*Goes in and shuts door.*)

(MRS. COPPINGER *goes into her house.* COPPINGER *and* COS-
TELLO *come in.* COPPINGER *crosses to his own door.*)

COPPINGER. Well, now the hurry of the day is over, we can settle our minds to the choice we have to make for laying out the benefit of the whales. (*Sitting down and taking hat off.*)

COSTELLO (*sitting down*). We'll get more fair play making a plan, and Brian Hosty not being in it, to be running down and ridiculing every word at all we will say.

COPPINGER. Ah, that is but a way he has, and a habit of his habits, to be running down every Munster person, and to be drawing his own province upon us. He to be cross, it is that the generations were cross before him.

COSTELLO. I don't know are we any way fitted to be taking such a load upon our shoulders at all.

COPPINGER. Why wouldn't we be fitted? A man that has the gift, will get more out of his own brain than another man will by learning will get the better of a college bred man, and will have better luck too. It's a great plan we will be making and a great story and a great sound through the whole ring of Ireland.

(HOSTY *comes in, gloomily.*)

COSTELLO. We were just waiting for you, Brian Hosty, till we'd start talking in earnest about the spending of the profit of the whales.

(MRS. COPPINGER *comes and stands at window, listening.*)

HOSTY. It's a great deal of talk you are wishful to be making. I tell you, ye have done enough of talking.

COSTELLO. Ah, don't be so cross now! A person to be cross it would scare me.

HOSTY. It is the chat of the both of ye, and your talking, has caused the appearance of fools to be put upon us and upon the whole of the headland, with the plan ye made up, and that ye sent unknownst to myself to the Board Room.

COPPINGER. Sure we made no choice at all yet and no plan. We didn't begin hardly to argue the matter yet.

HOSTY. Who was it sent word to the Board of Guardians so, that the three best men of the point of Druim-na-cuan had their mind made up—for the benefit of the whole parish and its gain—to lay out the riches cast up by the sea into their hand, on no other thing than a—statue!

COSTELLO *and* COPPINGER (*standing up*). A statue!

COPPINGER. Sure we had no intention at all of putting up a statue. Only conversing about such articles we were.

COSTELLO (*seeing* MRS. COPPINGER *make a sign to him*). It is likely Peter Mannion took in earnest the little argument we were going on with, and that Brian Hosty himself was the first to start.

COPPINGER. So he was, with his mention of the Statue of Liberty that is up above the harbour of New York.

HOSTY. Let Peter Mannion, that is coming up the street, be put upon his oath, till he'll say out who was it was seeking a job for himself, making mention of an image that would be cut out of stone.

COPPINGER. I was not seeking a job! I said, supposing there to be a statue wanted, stone would answer it best. I only said, "supposing."

COSTELLO. Sure it is only supposing the whole of us were. We were not meaning anything at all.

MANNION (*coming in*). I am after coming back from the Board Room. The plan you have made for the benefit of the headland was put before the Guardians. To give consent to it they were asked, and a grant if the means would run short.

COPPINGER. And is it a fact now, it was said before the Board that the plan we had laid out was for a statue?

MANNION. Why wouldn't it, when that was what the three of ye had agreed?

HOSTY. The three of us! Glory be to God! And all the world knowing we are three men that never could agree!

COSTELLO. My dearest life! And what now did the Guardians say hearing that?

MANNIO. They said it was a very nice thought, no better, and a very good thing to do.

HOSTY. They said that, is it?

COSTELLO. The Lord protect and save us!

MANNION. Themselves or the Rural Council—I'm not rightly sure between them—will send a commission on next Friday, that is a holy-day, to take a view of the site, and to lay the foundation stone. Speeches there will be, they bringing a member of Parliament purposely, and a meeting with banners and with bands.

COPPINGER. And no one in the place fit to put up the monument but myself! Wouldn't that be enough of a story to put upon the headstone of any man at all? Didn't I know well it was a miracle brought the whales, the way I would get my chance!

MANNION. The Guardians are wishful to know the name is to be put upon the statue.

COPPINGER. The name is it?

MANNION. The name to be sure of the patriot it will be made in the similitude of, and the shape.

HOSTY. The patriot!

COSTELLO. It's a statue of Liberty Brian Hosty was talking about in the commencement.

MANNION. Ah, who the hell cares about liberty? It is what the Board made sure you had the name chosen of some good man. Word I have to send them by the post-car will be passing at break of day. (*Goes off up street.*)

HOSTY. And in what place in the wide world are we to go looking for the name of a good man?

MALACHI (*rises and comes to them*). Is it what ye are going to do, to put up the name of some big man?

COSTELLO. It is, and his image along with it.

152

MALACHI. You need not go far looking for that. It is I myself am able to give you a name is worth while. As if blown away on the wind it was, till it was brought back this day, with messengers were not common messengers, but strange. You may believe me telling you he is the fittest man.

COPPINGER. Who might he be so, and where is he presently?

MALACHI. He not to be out of the world what would he want with miracles? He to be in it at this time wouldn't he be well able to cut a way for himself and ask no help from anyone at all.

COPPINGER. Tell us out who was he so?

MALACHI. A man he was that left his mother's house where he was reared, and went out fighting on the roads of the world.

COPPINGER. There is many a one did that in the last seven hundred years. It was maybe following after Sarsfield he went, and the Limerick Treaty broken?

MALACHI. It was out against the English he went——

HOSTY. A '98 man maybe?

MALACHI. It is hardly he escaped from the Naked Hangman——

COSTELLO. No, but a '48 man. There was few that escaped in '98.

COPPINGER. It's often their story wasn't put down right by the illiterate people in the old time. Tell out his name now till we'll see what do we know about it.

MALACHI. A great name, a great name will go sounding through the world. It is I myself got the charge to bring it to mind. Though my clothes are poor my story is high! Did ever any of ye hear till to-day the name of Hugh O'Lorrha?

HOSTY. I never did. I think it is but foolish talk he is giving out, that we are fools ourselves listening to.

COSTELLO. I never heard it I think—or maybe I did hear it.

COPPINGER. It is not to a mountainy man it would be left to make that name known, and it being the name of any big man. And I myself never hearing it at all. (*Goes and sits at his own door.*)

HOSTY. It is down from the mountains the whole country is destroyed, so wild and so unruly as ye do be, and so ready to give an opinion on everything in the world wide. (*He sits down at* PEGGY'S *door.*)

COSTELLO (*to* HOSTY). Light in the head he does be, every time there is a twist in the moon. It's best for him go back to the hillside.

MRS. COPPINGER (*at door*). Innocent he always was, and where there is innocence there is ignorance. To speak to him at all would bother you, as much as it would bother himself.

153

HOSTY. Laying down to us he is, to put our statue up to one Hugh O'Lorrha.

MRS. COPPINGER. Ah sure, he has my arm blackened with the dint of the pinches he gave me a while ago, striving to drive that story into my head, and he cherishing a bit of a board, and it squz up to his chest.

COPPINGER. Tell me this, Mary, you that have that much songs a horse wouldn't carry the load of them, did you meet in ere a verse of them with the name of Hugh O'Lorrha?

MALACHI. She did not to be sure. His name to be in a song, what would he want with stones or with monuments? Wouldn't any man at all be well satisfied, his name to be going through the generations in a song. My grief that I haven't the wit to make a poem for him or a ballad, and it is a great pity I am not prone to versify!

HOSTY. Ah, that one would keep you talking till the clear light of day! Go leave us now, where we have business to be thinking of.

MALACHI (*going to corner*). It is laid down for him his name to be put up. It is *for* him I say. (*Sits upon a stone.*)

HOSTY. Come now and make our settlement with no more delay. There being a statue to be put up in this place, and the whole fleet of guardians and councillors and members of Parliament wanting to get knowledge of the name we will put on it, who now is the most man to be respected, and to be done honour to, of all that ever came out of Ireland? What is your opinion now, Darby Costello, if you have any opinion at all?

COSTELLO. Don't be laying it on me now. I'm in dread I wouldn't find a name would be pleasant to every person, and that would give no offence in any place. Let you ask Mrs. Coppinger, that it is given in to to be the best singer in this place, and that has the praise of every man ever got praises in her songs.

MRS. COPPINGER. It's easy say who is the best man.

COSTELLO (*with a sigh*). It is not easy, but hard.

MRS. COPPINGER (*sings*)—

"His life and liberty he risked both here and everywhere,
Both slander and prison he suffered his own share,
I'm sure he loved all Ireland, 'tis admitted near and far
He would have gained a fortune just at the Irish Bar!"

COSTELLO. Good woman!

HOSTY. Rise it, ma'am, rise it!

MRS. COPPINGER (*coming a step forward*)—

"The foes of Ireland, well 'tis known he often made them
  quail,
With eloquence like thunder he defended Granuaile,
You may talk of Wellington and the battles that he won,
But in all that he deserved was nothing to what O'Connell
  done!"

COSTELLO. Very good! That's the chat now! "But in all he deserved was nothing to what O'Connell done!"

COPPINGER. He had a gift of sweetness on the tongue. Whatever cause he took in hand it was as good as gained.

HOSTY. The best man within the walls of the world he was. He never led anyone astray.

MRS. COPPINGER. What wonder in that, he being as he was the gift of God. Wasn't Ennis the best town in the thirty-two counties of Ireland, sending him to Parliament the time his own place had him put out?

COSTELLO (sings). "In the year '47 we laid him in Glasnevin." —I'm no songster like Mrs. Coppinger.

MRS. COPPINGER. To throw out the poison from his cup he did, the time there was death lurking in it. The English that put it within in it, because he was a pious man. I seen his picture in a book one time. I give you my word I kissed it there and then.

COPPINGER. His picture! No, but I that saw himself one time in Galway. I couldn't get anear him, all the nations of the world were gathered there to see him.

COSTELLO. Sure I seen him myself, it was the greatest thing ever I saw. He drove through the streets very plain, and an oiled cap on him, and he having but the one horse.

HOSTY. No, but seven horses in his coach he had the day I saw him. They couldn't get in the eighth.

COPPINGER. Oh, it's a great image and a great monument I will shape out for him the dear man——

COSTELLO. So you will! And he having one hand resting on a post, and a paper having Repeal on it held up to his chest.

MRS. COPPINGER. No, but Emancipation that should be on the paper. There is no other man that could be put beside him at all.

COSTELLO. That is settled now and well settled. That is a great satisfaction, there to be no quarrelling or no argument. It is a very nice thing, Brian Hosty, you to be no way thorny or disagreeable, but content and satisfied to be putting up a monument to a Munster man.

MRS. COPPINGER. And what objection could he urge against a Munster man, and he being worthier and more honourable than any man of the other provinces of Ireland?

HOSTY. I am not giving in to that.

COSTELLO. You are giving in to it, as is right for you to do. Every person seeing the image put up will know that you were of the one mind and the one opinion with ourselves, and you giving your voice for our man.

HOSTY. I to be as wise then as I am now, I would not have given in to you, or given you occasion to be running down my province, and giving the branch to your own.

MRS. COPPINGER. And where would you find now any sort of a hero in Connacht would give satisfaction far and near, and have his name up as good as the men of Munster? Dan O'Connell, Smith O'Brien, Brian Boru, O'Sullivan Bere——

HOSTY. Ah, we heard enough of that old string of heroes in the time that is past. They are all done away with now, and what is left of the best of them but a little fistful of bones? It's the champions of Connacht are battling yet. Let the statue be put up to some living man and where is Munster?

COSTELLO. What way would you put up a monument to a living man, and some traitors maybe turning against him in the latter end, and running him down?

MRS. COPPINGER (*coming over to* COPPINGER). Do not put your hand, Thomas, to a likeness of any living man at all, and his neighbours to be coming and criticising it, saying it would not resemble his features or his face.

HOSTY. Dead or living I've no mind to give my voice for any man was bred in Munster. You're a proud piece, Mrs. Coppinger, and you think you have got the better of me, but if O'Connell himself did his work fair enough, there were *some* in your province didn't turn out too well the time Cromwell was on the road, and to the day of my death I will never put praises on one of their district.

(COPPINGER *jumps up angrily.*)

COSTELLO (*stopping him*). Wait now till we'll think of some person would answer the two of ye——There is one was not from the west or from the south, that was Parnell. There are some say he was the best man ever lived.

COPPINGER. He was not, but O'Connell was the best, that wore his hat in the House of Commons what no man but the King can do.

HOSTY. If Parnell didn't wear his hat in it, he fought a good fight in it.

COPPINGER. If it wasn't for O'Connell there would be no members in the English Parliament at all would be Catholics!

HOSTY. If there wouldn't, there'd be no Catholic judges on the Bench, calling out for coercion and to do away with juries!

COSTELLO. It's best for ye agree to Parnell. I'm told if he had held out and kept up, he would have got the second best match in England.

HOSTY. He did more than any other man I tell you, and he to have lived till now Ireland would be different to what it is.

MRS. COPPINGER. Let you not agree to him, Coppinger. Sure I had his picture on the wall and I took it down after, the priest thinking it did not look well to be hanging where it was.

COSTELLO. Ah, they have but the one thing against him, and how do we know but that was a thing appointed by God?

MALACHI (*suddenly coming between them*). Look now at the fighting and quarrelling and the slandering is sent among ye, the way ye will be made give in to my own choice man. If you didn't give in to him at the first, you'll be druv to give in to him secondly! A shining image of silver I will see put up, and the words will be on it worked with red gold.

HOSTY. The devil bother you, Malachi, a poor foolish creature the like of you, to be interrupting our talk.

COPPINGER. Let you go in from under that moon that does be making your mind take a flight, till the worst thing you'll be saying you'll think it to be the best.

MALACHI. Let you not be belittling me! I tell you I wouldn't give the weight of that little board in my hand, for all that's on the headland of Druim-na-cuan!

COPPINGER. Pup, pup, Malachi, we have manners and were brought up to manners, and you have none.

MALACHI. I tell you there's three quarters of the world is not good enough to be drowned!

COPPINGER. No, but there are some have a tongue as bad as Judas had a heart, and that is bad enough.

MALACHI. Keep your own tongue off me so! It is what you are a bully, and the captain of all the bullies!

MRS. COPPINGER. What is ailing you? Be mannerly in your anger anyway. Yourself and your Hugh O'Lorrha, that was maybe some sort of an idolator or a foreigner, that went breaking all the commandments!

MALACHI. Whatever he was I'd go to the north side of hell for seven year for him! The whole fleet of ye together are not worth the smallest rib of his hair!

HOSTY. In my opinion he was an innocent or a fool the same as yourself, or you would not be infatuated with him the way you are!

(*All laugh.*)

MALACHI. That will be a dear laugh to you! Is it defaming the character ye are of my darling man? But I'll put terror on ye! I'll give you a clout will knock your head as solid as any stone in the wall! (*Flourishes board.*)

COPPINGER. Lay down that stick, you miserable imp!

MALACHI. I'll strike a blow with it will split bits off a rock. You big turkey gobbler you! Come on till I'll make a great scatter of you! (*They close round him seizing board.*) Death and destruction, but I'm as strong as you! (*He falls in the scuffle.*)

MRS. COPPINGER. Is it to kill him you did?

COPPINGER. Not a kill in the world, but the senses that is knocked out of him.

HOSTY. If it wasn't that there is luck with a fool, he'd be done for.

MANNION (*coming in*). Let ye stand back now. What call had you to go charging at him, and bearing him to the ground?

COSTELLO. No, but himself that came rushing into handigrips with us, the same as horned cattle in a field.

MRS. COPPINGER. It is bleeding in the head he is, with the sharpness of the stone he fell on; there is not much happened him beyond that.

COPPINGER. It's best lay him in the hooker below is just making a start for Ballyvaughan. To leave him in the infirmary ere morning they can, till such time as he will come around. Try now can you rise up, Malachi.

(*He is helped up, and* MANNION *and* MRS. COPPINGER *lead him towards pier.*)

MALACHI (*calling out as he goes*). Time is a good story-teller! Ye will do the business for me yet, till his name will be sung through the seven kingdoms! What is allotted cannot be blotted. It is for him I say—it is for him. (*He is led off.*)

COSTELLO. It is a pity he to have made that disturbance, and we being so pleasant and so peaceable together.

COPPINGER. We have time enough yet to make another choice. We didn't go through the saints of Ireland yet, or the seventeen kings of Burren.

HOSTY. Where's the use of calling it a choice, and I having two contrary men against me. Any time I will strive to get the goal for my own man, the two of ye will join to put me down.

(MRS. COPPINGER *and* MANNION *come back.*)

COSTELLO. It is a pity neighbours to be going contrary to one another. "Let ye be at one," Biddy Early said, "and ye will rule the world." It would be right to bring the whole case to a closure, and not to be hitting and striking and calling "Hi" for one, or "Hi" for another, the same as if it was a disputed election was in it.

MRS. COPPINGER. I saw a very wicked election in Ennis one time, and I rising. That was before there came in the voting by ballot.

COSTELLO. You are a great woman for thoughts, Mrs. Coppinger, and that is a thought will settle all. What would ail us not to give our votes by ballot? There would be no room then for disputing, the choice being over and made, fair and quiet, and without favour or intimidation.

COPPINGER. And where will you get ballot boxes and voting papers, and a courthouse, and two men sitting in it with themselves, and the voters writing—if they can write—and shouting out if they cannot, the name of their own man?

COSTELLO. What signifies clerks and papers? What do you say now to Peter Mannion? It is what we'll do, to come up to him and tell him secretly the name we have our mind made up to; and he to tell out after who has the benefit of the votes.

MANNION (*coming forward*). Let ye all fall back so, and not to be putting ears on yourselves, but to draw anear me one by one.

COPPINGER. That's it, and you yourself to be standing stark and quiet, the same as the image will be standing there in the time to come, and we to go west as far as the rick of turf——

MANNION (*standing stiffly*). Whatever champion of the champions of Ireland ye think to be the most worthy and the most fitting to have his name put up, let ye tell it out here to me privately. And that being done, I will make my count, and tell out after who is it has gained the day.

COPPINGER. That's business now. And which now of the three of us is to be the first to give his own vote?

MRS. COPPINGER. It is Peter Mannion is well able to settle that, and he being used to society, and the meetings at the union.

MANNION. Let ye come so according to the letters of your name —A, B, C, C, Coppinger—or Costello—C o Coppinger C o Costello, it isn't easy say which of the two of ye has to go first.

COSTELLO. Let it be Thomas so. I'd be someway shy and delicate to be called in at the start. Thomas the first, and I myself will follow after.

(*They all go out of sight.* MRS. COPPINGER *goes into house.*)

MANNION. Come on, so, Thomas Coppinger, and give out your vote, according to your opinion and your conscience and your choice.

COPPINGER (*coming in and speaking to* MANNION *confidentially with hand to mouth*). It is what I am thinking, Peter Mannion, there is truth in what herself was saying a while ago. It is a hard thing to be asked to go make a likeness of a man, and his appearance to be known before. And the people to be criticising, now they have got to be so crafty and so enlightened. But a man not to have his appearance known, you would have leave to put on him any shape that might be pleasing to yourself, or that would come handy, according as the stone would be slippery or be kind. Now every person knows, by pictures, or by seeing them, or by history from one to another, the features of Parnell and of Daniel O'Connell——

MANNION. Hurry on now. It is not sitting hearing a sermon in the chapel I am, and in dread of the Missioners to go slip out of the door.

COPPINGER. Did ever you hear now any person to have seen a picture or a likeness of Malachi Naughton's man?

MANNION. I cannot bring to mind that ever I did.

COPPINGER. I give my voice and my vote so for Hugh O'Lorrha. (*Goes into his house.*)

MANNION. Come on now and draw near to me, Darby Costello.

COSTELLO (*coming close to* MANNION). It is often I was saying, Peter Mannion, unfriendliness among neighbours to be a very awkward thing. I never would be asking to rise a dispute, or to bring any person into one at all.

MANNION. Is it through the dark hours of the night you are wishful to keep me perishing in the air that is of the nature of frost and of sleet?

COSTELLO (*seizing his arm*). It's easy seen you are not living in this village, Peter Mannion, or within three fields of it. If I say Dan O'Connell, Brian Hosty will be making attacks on me, and if I say Parnell, Mrs. Coppinger will be picking at me and going on at me, and maybe putting up Thomas to be mis-spelling my name, and he printing it on the head-piece he has me promised at the last——

MANNION (*shaking him off.*) I give you my word I'll leave you here and now, to be giving out your reasoning to the seals and to the gulls of the air.

COSTELLO (*holding him*). It is impossible to say what men would be best, and good and bad being together in the whole of them. And all I would wish is the name of some man that never gave offence, and had ne'er an enemy worth while—and it's likely that would be the mountainy man's choice, Hugh O'Lorrha.

(*He goes off.*)

MANNION. Come on now, Brian Hosty, and let me go out of this.

HOSTY (*coming in*). There are some on this headland want to get the master hand—(*Points towards* COPPINGER'S *door*.) Himself and his fireball!

MANNION. Hurry on now.

HOSTY. To give them too much of a scope, and not to give them a check, it would be impossible to live anear them. It would be worse they to be in power than Martin Luther.

MANNION. Don't be delaying, but see can you agree with the two that are agreed at this time.

HOSTY. They to have agreed, it is some plan they have made to get the mastery over myself and over Connacht. I never told a lie but two or three, and you may believe me saying, that if there were two hundred Dan O'Connells, and twenty thousand Mr. Parnells, and a sovereign in the hands for every vote I'd vote, I'd give it to none of them, but to a man I'm sure and certain sure Darby or Thomas, or his wife, never gave out a challenge for, and never blew the horn for, and that is the fool's man, Hugh O'Lorrha!

MANNION (*beckoning the others in*). Let ye draw near to me now. Come up here Mrs. Coppinger, till I'll count out the returns. By the opinion, and the judgment, of the three fairest men, and the three choice men of Druim-na-cuan, and they voting together the same as children of one house, without deceit or trickery, the image is to be reared on this headland is to stand for the honour and the memory and for the great name and the fame of Hugh O'Lorrha!

ALL. Hugh O'Lorrha!

(*They raise their hands in astonishment, and look at one another.*

Curtain.

ACT III

SCENE: *same as before. Four days later, mid-day.* MRS. COP-PINGER *putting out chairs and a table and sweeping.* COSTELLO *looking on.*

COSTELLO. It is certain this will be a great meeting of people, and a grand white day for the headland of Druim-na-cuan. I would want a slate and a pencil to count all I saw coming the road.

MRS. COPPINGER. Isn't it a big hurry is on them, to ask to come laying the stone for the monument, and it never mentioned or thought of at all up to four days ago.

COSTELLO. Sure at that time the whales had the last puff hardly gone out of them.

MRS. COPPINGER. What way are the whales presently? I thought to go see them but it failed me, and the neighbours from all parts drawing in for talk every whole minute.

COSTELLO. It was the one way with myself, I didn't get the time to draw anear them. It is what Thomas was saying, next Monday maybe, with the help of God, we'll go start drawing off the oil.

MRS. COPPINGER (*dusting a chair*). That now is all the chairs they can get. Sure they could not all expect to be seated, and they coming in their hundreds. There is not a west of Ireland man will not be in it.

COSTELLO. Indeed, ma'am, you have accommodated them very well with everything. It's well for them get a place to stand itself. From all I hear, and they congregated, it would fail you to put a pin between any two and two or any twelve and a dozen. Pressing to hear the speeches they will be. They are saying the Chairman of the Board to be a very solid speaker.

MRS. COPPINGER. It's the member for North Munster is the best. Grand out and out he is, and has very tasteful drawn out talk. The reporters themselves couldn't follow it or put the half of it down.

COSTELLO (*looking out over the wall*). Tents and booths they are setting up upon the strand. Glory be to God, it's like a theatre to be looking at them arriving. They were waiting for the turn of the

162

spring-tide. You were craving sprees this long time, Mrs. Coppinger, and it is with pride you are apt to be spending this day.

(MALACHI *comes in from left, his head tied up, and his arm.*)

MRS. COPPINGER. And who now would be the first to come to the meeting but Malachi Naughton! And indeed it is much like a ghost he is looking, that would knock a start out of you, or a shadow would be wandering through the world.

MALACHI (*looking about on the ground*). It is there I left it down. I'm certain it is in that spot I left it out of my hand.

MRS. COPPINGER. What way did they do a cure on you in the Workhouse, Malachi? Bet up I was fearing you were, and that it's hardly you would be eating this world's bread again.

MALACHI. Just battled it out I did—just battled it out— Did ye see in any place my bit of a board I used to have?

MRS. COPPINGER. I did not see it, unless it might be thrust as kindling in under the turf on the hearth.

MALACHI. Isn't that a hard case now, my bit of a board to be robbed from me, and it after being brought to me over the ocean and all the dangers of the sea, and having on it the name you know. That to be swept away from me, I am penetrated and tossed.

MRS. COPPINGER. You to burn the house down it's not likely you would find it. But you may quit fretting and breaking your heart, for if it is the name of Hugh O'Lorrha you are craving to see, you will see it in a short while printed in clean letters beneath the soles of his feet, and his own image reared up in this spot all the same as life, in the shape will be put upon him by my own man, according to the pictures and the plan are to come to us from Dublin on this day.

MALACHI. I heard that, I heard that. I knew well his name would be put up in spite of ye. But it's for the whole world that will be, and they coming from the east and from the west to do honour to him; and he might take it bad of me, I to go lose that little bit of a board.

MRS. COPPINGER. You heard of all was doing so far away as the Workhouse Infirmary? Isn't it a great wonder now tidings to go out so speedy and so swift.

MALACHI. It was in every person's mouth ere last night, in the ward where I was screeching with the pain, and the doctors after taking the full of a bucket of badness out of my bones. As much blood nearly came away from me as would be in three men. But I rose up after hearing that news.

MRS. COPPINGER. I wonder they to have let you out and the

way you are, that you couldn't hardly put a rack through your hair.

MALACHI (*sits on chair beside the table*). I asked no leave. I slipped out in the half dark at the battling of the day with the night. The road to be seventeen times as long, I wouldn't feel it. I tell you I was that strong I could walk on water, my heart being light and airy the way it is with the thought of his name being put up and his image, that will be shining out as bright as stars on a frosty night, and all the whole country pressing to look at it.

MRS. COPPINGER. It isn't likely it is shining it will be, it would take marble would be rubbed for to shine, and the hardness of that would not serve Thomas's tools. And the colour of it wouldn't answer either, the spotted or the black. It is likely he was a man having a white front to his shirt—I wonder now is it swarthy he was or red-haired?

MALACHI. It is I myself could give you knowledge of that.

MRS. COPPINGER. What way could you have knowledge, and he being dead?

MALACHI. God be with the company that left me in the night time!

MRS. COPPINGER. Is it to see one belonging to him, or that had acquaintance with him you did?

MALACHI. I'd burst if I didn't tell it! A crosscut I was making that was eight strong miles across the mountain, and I was travelling down a little avenue of stones by the forth that was all shining with the brightness of the night—More people I saw in it than ever I saw at a hurling, and I'd ask no better sight than that in high Heaven.

MRS. COPPINGER. Where now did all that company come from?

MALACHI. More people than ever I saw in twenty fairs. And beyond that I saw twelve of the finest horses ever I saw, and riders on them racing around the forth. Many a race I saw since I lived in this world, but for tipping, and tugging, and welting the horses, never a race like that—and there was a rider of those riders without a twist in him—at the first there was like a fog about him——

MRS. COPPINGER. Ah, it is but visions of the night you are talking about; or your sight that spread on you. It was but the shadow of some soul you saw, or people that are out of this world. Or maybe it is dreaming you were, and you stepping out through your sleep.

MALACHI (*getting up*). Take care but it was no dream! Let you go out looking yourself so in the night time. And if you do go, it is likely you will see nothing but the flaggy rocks and the clefts, for it's not all are born to see things of the kind. I'll tell you no more, I wish I had told you nothing, and I wish I didn't lose my little bit of a board! (*Goes into* COPPINGER'S *house looking for it on the ground.*)

COPPINGER (*coming in*). Well, I have brought you tidings you will wonder at, and that will raise and comfort your heart!

MRS. COPPINGER. There is nothing would make me wonder after all happened in these days past. I to rise up in the morning under lofty rafters in Boston, I give you my word I'd take it as simple as a chicken would be hatched out of the shell!

COPPINGER (*sits on table*). Did ever you hear the name of a Hosty or a Costello or my own name, that is as good as their own through the father, besides any flight it might take with the mother, to be put up on the papers with praises around and about them?

MRS. COPPINGER. Why would they be put up on the papers with praises? I never heard of Brian or Darby no more than yourself, ever to have been brought before the magistrates, or to have put his head inside a goal.

COSTELLO. Who was telling you?

COPPINGER. The Dispensary Doctor that stopped his side-car on the road, and the driver of the mail car, and *he* would tell no lie, and Morrissey is herding for Cunningham, and that was bringing back a score of lambs from the market at Cloon.

MRS. COPPINGER. And what account were they giving of what was on the papers?

COPPINGER. Three honourable men, the papers said we were, that showed respect where respect should be showed. A pattern and an example for all Ireland they said we were, the nut of the bunch, the flower of Druim-na-cuan and the clean wheat of the Gael!

COSTELLO. Do you tell me so?

COPPINGER. And more than that again, the Board of Guardians gave out a great lacerating to all the rest of the Unions of the two provinces, where they had never stretched a hand to raise up the memory, or so much as to change the address on a street, to the great high up name of Hugh O'Lorrha!

MRS. COPPINGER. That is very good. Believe me, there is not a Board or a Board Room west of the Shannon, but will have a comrade cry sent out between this and the Feast of Pentecost.

COPPINGER. I ask you, Mary, and I ask the two of you, did you often hear me saying I would surely get my chance?

COSTELLO. I wonder now you to have courage to go think yourself fitted to make a figure of a champion all the world will be coming to see.

COPPINGER. I'm no way daunted or turning my back upon the work! I tell you if it was three statues was wanted, of the three sons of Usnach, or the three Manchester martyrs, or the three saints of Burren, MacDuagh, MacDara and Columcille, it's ready I'd be and greedy I'd be to set my hand to the work!

HOSTY (*coming in with rolls of paper, going to seat outside* PEGGY'S *door*). I got the pictures from the Clerk of the Union where he sent for them to Dublin. Two able lads that drew them he was telling me, that have laid their mind to sketching as their trade.

COPPINGER. They should be very apt and very handy, making so little delay in putting down a thing of the kind.

MRS. COPPINGER (*opening one roll*). Wait now till we'll take a view of them before the meeting will gather about them. (*Unrolls it and shows conventional design for statue of an orator.*)

COSTELLO. That is very nice now and very good.

COPPINGER (*feebly*). It wouldn't be an easy job now, any person to come around the like of that. Wait till we'll see the comrade, is it any way more simple and more plain.

MRS. COPPINGER (*opens it*). It is mostly the same as the other, but for having on it a cloak in place of a coat.

COPPINGER. It's a queer thing, now, not to get a picture laid down by some skilled person would be used to going through stone, and not to be leaving it to the fancies of young pups of boys rising up.

HOSTY. It would be hard to beat it. Grand out and out it is. But sure the both of them are great. They were very smart surely to make a picture of the sort, without a button left out or a ha'porth. But it's you yourself, I am thinking, that is in dread it will fail you to carry through the job.

COPPINGER. I give you my word the one of them would be as light to me as what the other would be. I am asking no reprieve from the work. But the ancient monuments that were the best, such as you'd see in the Abbey beyond, where the hero didn't ask to be put upon his two feet, but was content to lie stretched the way you might be lying on a bed, and you not seeking sleep.

HOSTY. Shove over that box, Darby, and hold up the one of them—(COSTELLO *hangs one back and front from his neck and gets up on box.*) That now is the way it will be—And it is not yourself, Thomas, will have the choice to make this time. It is the Board itself will keep that in their hands.

166

COSTELLO (*standing on box*). That is best, it would be a great load on us to have to do that part of the job. It is easy for themselves, that are used to be judging between contracts and tenders and the like.

HOSTY. It's not so easy as you think.

COSTELLO. I tell you they have good practice in their business, settling and pitching as they must between the choice and the cull.

HOSTY. One of the lads is nephew to the member for North Munster.

COSTELLO. Let them give him the proffer so.

HOSTY. By the two mothers, the second of the lads is first cousin to the Vice-Chairman of the Board.

COSTELLO. Let them choose the two of them so, and put them back to back—It might be settled into some sort of a groove that it could be shoved from side to side—(*Turns slowly round on box.*) It to revolve, there would be no aspersion.

MANNION (*coming in*). I was bid see is all ready for the big men are on the road, with their side-cars and with their band.

MRS. COPPINGER. Let them come now and welcome. We have all ready before them. The table, the chairs, the stone is to be made a hole for, and the pictures.

MANNION. It is what I was bid to ask, is the writing made out, is to be put at the butt of the statue?

COPPINGER. The writing is it?

MANNION. That's it. The name and the date of Hugh O'Lorrha's birth, and the place he was reared, and the length of his years, and the deeds he has done. Write me out a docket now having that put down upon it clear and plain.

HOSTY. Let Thomas Coppinger do that.

MRS. COPPINGER. Why wouldn't he do it, and you yourself being illiterate and not able to put down your mind on paper?

HOSTY. I am not illiterate, but as well aware of things as yourself. But he that is used to be putting such things over the bones of the whole of the district, the pen should be light in his hand as is natural, and should be kind.

COPPINGER. Not at all, but every man that comes to be buried that gives me the years and the names. I have enough to do after, bringing them within their scope on the slab. It isn't easy keep them from running around the edges. Let Brian Hosty put it down himself.

HOSTY. It never was my trade to be spilling out words on paper, the same as a poet or a clerk. It is Darby Costello has practice, where he was forced by the police to print his name and dwelling-place on the shaft of his ass-car, ere last year.

COSTELLO. Ah, let me alone, I'm in dread I might not do it in a way would satisfy all that are coming.

COPPINGER. Ah, what are you wanting to put down? His christened name we have, and the name of his family and his tribe, and that is more than was wrote down of some of the world's great men, such as Homer that spoke Greek and never wrote a lie.

MANNION. It is likely that will not be enough. Reporters that were asking in the town, what place was Hugh O'Lorrha born.

COPPINGER. You should know that, Brian Hosty, where your memory has no burdens on it like my own.

HOSTY. I forget it as good as yourself.

MANNION. Well, who is it has the whole account? Sure it must have been written down at some time, in a history or in a testament.

COSTELLO. Who would have it but Malachi Naughton? He'll remember us of it.

HOSTY. Come out here, Malachi, you're wanting.

MALACHI (coming out of house). What is it you are wanting of me?

COPPINGER. Give out now, Malachi, if you can give it, the deeds and the greatness of the man is to be set up on a stone in this spot.

MANNION. Ah, it is likely it is little he knows or can tell about him at all.

MALACHI. Why wouldn't I know about him, and I after seeing him with my two eyes?

COPPINGER. Is it to see him you are saying you did?

MALACHI. Clear and plain I saw him in the night time. If I didn't why would my heart leap up with him the way it does?

COPPINGER. Is it with yourself you were, seeing him?

MALACHI. I have no witnesses but the great God and myself. Crowds and crowds of people I saw. Men like jockeys that were racing—and one that was the leader of them, on a bayish horse—the sun and the moon never shone upon his like—eyes he had were more shining than our eyes, and as to comeliness, there was no more to be found. The champions of Greece, and to put all of them together, would not equal the flower of one drop of his strong blood.

COPPINGER. I'm thinking it is little satisfaction we will get questioning him, and his thoughts going as they do upon every queer track. Old he is, and it is all in his brain the things he does be talking of.

MALACHI. You have me tormented with your catechism, and you brought away my little bit of a board. Let you go ask Peggy Mahon, that knows all he went through better again than myself.

COPPINGER. Peggy Mahon to know him it is likely he was born in this district. She maybe got knowledge he would be some great man, picking it out of the stars.

MRS. COPPINGER. No, but go, Peter Mannion and ask a loan of the Register that has all the names of the parish set down for maybe four score years or a hundred years back.

MANNION. I won't be long getting it, supposing the clerk to be at hand. It isn't easy find him within. The dates not to be away and astray, it would be very handy to get some information from penmanship, besides dragging it as if from the depths and the bottom of a bog. (Goes.)

MALACHI. You would stand to look at him in a fair I say. Fair hair on him the colour of amber. Twelve handsome riders and he before them all——

COSTELLO. Sure we have the likeness of him here that was made to represent him the way he was thought to be, or that other great men of his sort would be in the habit of appearing. (Holds up picture.)

MALACHI (coming up eagerly close to picture, staring and falling back). The devil's welcome to you! Is it you is calling yourself Hugh O'Lorrha? My bitter curse upon you, how well you stole his name! (He backs away from it.)

COSTELLO. If you had intellect to understand things of the sort you would not be running it down. It is away in Dublin that was made, and they should know.

MALACHI. I'll shave you without soap or razor! It's a skelp of a stone I would be well pleased to be giving you, and you laying claim to his name! That God may perish you! Is it for the like of you the sea was filled with wonders and with signs?

COPPINGER. Indeed it is not much the way it is put down on paper, but cutting will be a great addition to it, the time it will be shaped in stone.

MALACHI. A man that had seven colours in his eyes! That was for beauty and for strength beyond a hundred! His name in lines of golden letters written on his own blue sword! A man could whip the world and that broke every gap! —Sure you have no action in you, no action at all, without liveliness, without a nod. The devil himself wouldn't take you or the like of you!

COSTELLO. Well now, Malachi, haven't you the terrible scissors of a tongue! He is well-looking enough if it wasn't he has some sort of a comical dress.

MALACHI (*threatening picture, but held back by* MRS. COP-PINGER). Be off out of that you unnatural creature, or it is I will twist your mouth round to your poll! I'll blacken the teeth of you and whiten the eyes of you! It is your brain I will be putting out through the windows of your head! If I had but a rod in my hand it's soon I would make you limber! It is powder I will make of your bones and will turn them to fine ashes! It is myself is well able to tear you to flitters and to part your limbs asunder! Be going now before I'll break you in thirty halves. (*Tries to rush at it, but stumbles over box.*) To be putting such an appearance and such an insult on my darling man! The devil skelp the whole of ye! My bitter curse upon the spot ye had planned out for to be putting up a thing the very spit of yourselves, and ugly out of measure. (*Kicks over box.*)

HOSTY (*picking up board, which has been hidden under it*). That is a bit of the Kerry men's green bordered boat, that was lost as was right, and they robbing our mackerel.

MRS. COPPINGER. I said that I heard the name of Hugh O'Lorrha in some place. It is what they were telling me, that was the name on the boat.

MALACHI (*snatching it*). Oh, my board, my little bit of a board! How well it failed them to hide from me what the waves of the sea could not keep from me!

COSTELLO. No wonder you to be comforting yourself, Malachi, the way you won't be fearing at any time your brave hero to be but a deceit and a mockery. Sure he must be some big man his name to be printed on a board.

MALACHI. A deceit is it? I to think that, why would I be wearing his livery? It is what I am thinking, Darby Costello, you are a very liary man. (*He puts board under his shirt.*) Oh, my heart-secret, wait till I'll hide you from them all, and they not able to understand a thing they are not fit to understand! There's a bad class of people in this place, are not worthy to see so much as your name! I don't want to be annoyed with them any more than I am. I'll keep my knowledge to myself, between myself and the bare stones. I'll go back to the beasts and the birds that pay respect to him!

HOSTY. Do so, and it might chance you to see him again, and the full moon working in your head.

MALACHI (*turning back for a moment as he goes*). So I will see him again! I'm well able to track him through fire and fair water.

And I'll know him when I will see him, and that is what you or the like of you will not do. And another thing. I tell you I'd sooner he not to be in it, than he to be in it, and to be what you are making him out to be! (*Goes.*)

(*Band heard in the distance.*)

MANNION (*coming in*). Here now, I chanced the clerk leaving the door. Here is the Register so far as it goes back, and that is but after the year of the Famine. To go astray the old ones did or some ignorant person that made an end of them. You will find the name you are looking for in this——

HOSTY. You will, the same time you will find a hundred goats without damage or roguery.

MRS. COPPINGER. Is it that the clerk said there was in it the name of Hugh O'Lorrha?

MANNION. He did, and he said beside that——

HOSTY. A name to be down in the register, it did not get there by itself. I was getting to be in dread he might be some sort of a Jack o' Lanthorn.

COPPINGER. What way could he be that, and the country entirely calling their leagues and their hurling clubs by his name? It is not to a Jack o' Lanthorn I myself would be working out a statue of stone.

MANNION. If you will but listen till I'll tell you what the clerk was saying——

HOSTY. Let you sound out now, Darby Costello, whatever may be written in the book.

COSTELLO (*giving it to* MRS. COPPINGER). No, but Mrs. Coppinger. It would take *her* to do that; she that can read out the paper the same as if God put it in her mind.

MRS. COPPINGER (*sitting down and opening first page*). Michael —Michael Morrissey—that's not it—where now was he born?— Ballyrabbitt—he should be father so to the Morrissey is herding for Cunningham.

HOSTY. Don't be going through the races and generations now, or you never will make out the name.

MRS. COPPINGER. Thomas Fahy, and after that Joseph Fahy and Peter Fahy—— well, they got enough of space in the book, that whole tribe of the Fahys. It is a book for themselves they have a right to be paying for, and not to be taking space that is for the whole of the parish.

HOSTY. Go on now, ma'am, go on.

MRS. COPPINGER. Would you believe now here is more of the

Fahys. Congregated on the page they are, the same as a flock of stairs.

HOSTY (*seizing book and turning over pages to the end*). Make now a second reading—it's best begin at the finish till you'll get shut of them. There's a good deal of the Fahys wore away since that time.

MRS. COPPINGER. It's hard to please you, Brian Hosty, and you so hasty as you are. Here now is the last name in the book if that will satisfy you. What is it? H. Hugh—What will you say now hearing, it is no less than Hugh O'Lorrha?

COSTELLO. The man we are looking for.

COPPINGER (*looking over* MRS. COPPINGER'S *shoulder*). So it is too. Sound out the year now, Mary, and the day, the way I will space them in my mind.

MRS. COPPINGER. May the tenth in this year—the day ere yesterday——no but yesterday——

HOSTY. It is the year you are reading wrong. What way would a man be getting a monument, and he to be baptized within the last past two days.

MRS. COPPINGER. Reckon it for yourself so, if ever you learned figures on a slate.

HOSTY (*taking book*). The year our own year—sure enough, unless there did clouds rise up in my head.

MANNION. It is what the clerk was saying, and you to give me leave to be telling it, there is a man of the Fahys——

MRS. COPPINGER. Have done with your Fahys! Is it that you are saying Hugh O'Lorrha's name was ever Englished into Fahy?

MANNION. A man of the Fahys that is living anear the forge gave his young son, that was baptized yesterday, the name of Hugh O'Lorrha, where he was hearing it belled out through the whole of the district.

MRS. COPPINGER. I'm no way obliged to you, Peter Mannion, for keeping that close the way you did, and all the trouble I am after going to in the search. And what call had he to go tracking after names outside of his own generations and his tribe?

MANNION. It is what the clerk was saying, a young weak little family he has, ten of them there are in it; and he has the names were in his family, or on the best of the Saints, mostly used previously.

HOSTY. And as to the real Hugh O'Lorrha, we are as wise as we were at the first.

COPPINGER. What are books and what are Registers put beside

any person's mind? Come out here now, Peggy Mahon, and tell us what you can tell us, and what we are craving to know.

HOSTY. You will get nothing at all out of that one, unless it might be cracked talk and foolishness.

(PEGGY *comes out and they all crowd around her. She has a cat in her arms, and sits down on the seat outside her door.*)

MRS. COPPINGER. Tell us out now, Peggy, all you can tell, about one Hugh O'Lorrha.

PEGGY. I am not in humour for talking and for foolishness. The cat that has my tea destroyed, that's all the newses I have. To put his paw in it he did, that I should throw it out of the door. There is no person would drink water or any mortal thing and a cat after touching it, for cats is queer, cats are the queerest things on the face of the globe.

COPPINGER. Come on now, Peggy, till I'll question you.

PEGGY. The day I wouldn't get my drop of tea I could keep nothing at all in my mind. What call had he to go meddle with it? There is something is not right in cats.

HOSTY. Where's the use of questioning her? Giddy she is with age, and it's impossible to keep a head on her.

MRS. COPPINGER. Wait a second and I'll have her coaxed, bringing her out a cup of tea. (*Goes into house.*)

COPPINGER. Tell us now, the same as you told Malachi Naughton, all that happened to Hugh O'Lorrha, and that gave him so great a name.

PEGGY. Hugh O'Lorrha—Hugh O'Lorrha that was all the name ever he had, and it will be his name ever and always. I heard that since I was remembering, since I had sense or head.

COPPINGER. I suppose now it could hardly be yourself, ma'am, befriended him, and he coming into the world?

PEGGY. Wasn't that a rogue of a cat now, to go dip his paw down into my tea?

MRS. COPPINGER (*coming out with cup of tea*). Here now, Peggy Mahon, drink a sup of this and it will give you nice courage for a while.

PEGGY (*turning her shoulder to her*). What call had you to go saying my own man would not recognise me and I dead? And all the world knows that Him that ordered lights for the day and for the night time, has given out orders for all He will send for, to come before Him in their bloom.

COPPINGER (*taking cup and offering it to her*). That is so surely. At thirty years of age and in their bloom. (PEGGY *drinks tea.*)

COSTELLO. She won't refuse after that to tell her story, and she knowing it to tell, about Hugh O'Lorrha.

PEGGY. I know it, and it's myself does know it. I have a grand little story about him.

COPPINGER. Out with it so, ma'am.

PEGGY. There was a widow-woman one time, and she is not in it now, and what signifies if she ever was in it at all——

MRS. COPPINGER. That has the sound nearly of the beginning of some ancient vanity.

COPPINGER. Have patience now, it is coming.

PEGGY. She had but one son only, and the name was on him was Hugh Beg O'Lorrha.

COSTELLO. My dearest life! I was thinking the same thing before. Sure that is a folk-tale my grandfather used to be telling in the years gone by.

MRS. COPPINGER. Can you tell us now at what time did he live?

PEGGY. How would I know? I suppose at the time of the giants. He came in one day to his mother. "Go boil a hen for me and bake a cake for me," says he, "till I'll travel as far as the Court and ask the King's daughter."

COSTELLO. I know it through and through. It is nothing at all but a story-teller's yarn.

COPPINGER. Is that truth you are saying?

COSTELLO. To the best of my belief I am speaking the truth. I can tell it through to the binding. To take the life he did of the Naked Hangman, that was hid in the egg of a duck.

MRS. COPPINGER. Why didn't you tell us before now, Darby Costello, that you knew Hugh O'Lorrha to be but a deception and an empty tale.

COSTELLO. I was someway shy and fearful to be going against the whole of ye. And sure when we had to believe it, we must believe it.

HOSTY. And is it only in the poets' stories he is, and nothing but a name upon the wind? What way did it fail you to know that, Thomas Coppinger, and that Malachi had put his own skin upon the story.

COPPINGER. I don't know from Adam's race, unless it was witchcraft and spells and oracles. How well it failed you to find it out yourself.

MRS. COPPINGER. Sure he must have lived in some place, or why would we be putting up a monument to him?

(*Band and cars heard nearer.*)

HOSTY. He lived in no other place but in the Munster poets' lies. It is great ridicule will be put on us now by all that are coming the road. To jibe at us they will, we to be spending our means upon a man that never was in it at all.

COPPINGER. The thing that was to give me my chance to have brought me ruination in the end! Since the Gael was sold at Aughrim there never was such a defeat!

COSTELLO. I'm in dread it's to do violence to us they might. There will always be contrary people in a crowd. It is up to my neck in the tide I would wish to go, the way no person could come near me, or be making attacks on me. (*All sit down disconsolately.*)

PEGGY (*standing up and giving a delighted laugh*). Ha, Ha! Ye are defeated, and ye earned defeat! Sure ye know nothing at all. This one running down the fool's man, saying he was made but out of thoughts and of fancies; and this one (*pointing to* MRS. COPPINGER) running down my own man, saying he was of no use and of no account, and that he was not better, but worse, than any other one.

MRS. COPPINGER. It was you told that to her, Darby Costello, for to make mischief between neighbours were at one.

COSTELLO. If I did it was to raise her heart and to pacify her, where she was fretting with the thought she would not come to him and she dead. But the time I'll go doing comfortable things again, it's within in my own mind I'll go do them, the way I won't suffer in my skin. Such abuse to be getting! I might as well be a renegade.

COPPINGER. Give no heed to them, Peggy, and I myself will carve a slab will do credit to your man, and will keep his name above ground for ever.

PEGGY. I will give you no leave to do that! I'll ask no headstone and his name upon it, and strangers maybe to be sounding it out with the queer crabbed talk they have, and the gibberish, and ridiculing it, and maybe making out my clean comrade, my comely Patrick, to be but a blemished little maneen, having a stuttering tongue. (*She goes into cabin and turns at door.*) A queer race ye are, a queer race. It is right Malachi was quitting you, and it was wise. Any person to own a heart secret, it is best for him hide it in the heart. Let the whole world draw near to question me, but I'll be wise this time. I'll say no word of Patrick Mahon, and no word of Hugh Beg O'Lorrha, that is maybe nearer to him than some that are walking this street. Oh yes, oh yes, I'll be wary this time and I'll be wise. I'll be as wise as the man that didn't tell his dream! (*She goes into her house and shuts door.*)

MANNION (*coming in*). Is it long now since any of ye went to the place the whales landed upon the strand?

HOSTY. It would be seventeen times better for themselves and ourselves, those beasts to have stopped browsing where they were, in their pen that is beneath the green ocean.

COPPINGER. Hadn't I enough to do planning out the figure and the foundation and the stone? I'd have the day lost visiting them. Monday morning with the help of God, I'll go take a view of them.

MANNION. All the view you are apt to get, is of the seals spits lying on the strand, and of the waves and the wrackage of the sea.

COPPINGER. What are you raving about?

MANNION. In the argument the whales went out from ye.

COPPINGER. They couldn't stir unknownst to us. What way could they walk, having no legs?

MANNION. The Connemara lads have the oil drawn from the one of them, and the other one was swept away with the spring tide.

COSTELLO. For pity's sake! That cannot be true!

MANNION. It is true, too true to be put in the ballads.

HOSTY. It is no mean blow to the place losing them; and to yourself, Thomas Coppinger, and your grand statue swept away along with them.

COSTELLO. Let you not fret, Thomas. There did no badness of misfortune ever come upon Ireland but someone was the better of it. You not to go shape the image, there is no person can say, it is to mis-shape it you did. Let you comfort yourself this time, for it is likely you would have failed doing the job.

COPPINGER. I was thinking that myself, Darby. I to begin I'd have to follow it up, and the deer knows where might it leave me.

MRS. COPPINGER. We'll not be scarce of talk for the rest of our years anyway. For some do be telling the story was always in it, but we will be telling the story never was in it before and never will be in it at all!

(*The band is heard quite close playing "O'Donell Abu!" MRS. COSTELLO rushes in at door, looks out. COPPINGER hides behind headstone. HOSTY leaps the wall into Connacht. COSTELLO hides at side of PEGGY'S house. Only PETER MANNION left in centre. Band quite close and shouts of Hi! for HUGH O'LORRHA!*)

Curtain.

THE CANAVANS

THE CANAVANS

PERSONS
  PETER CANAVAN. *A miller.*
  ANTONY CANAVAN. *His brother.*
  CAPTAIN HEADLEY. *His cousin.*
  WIDOW GREELY.
  WIDOW DEENY.
  TIME—Reign of Queen Elizabeth.

ACT I

SCENE. *Interior of a mill town at Scartana, in Munster. Rough table and chairs. Sacks in corner. Cake, glasses, and wine on table.*

WIDOW GREELY (*who is carrying a basket of clean linen, knocking at door as she enters*). Are you within, Miller Canavan?

WIDOW DEENY. He cannot be far off, and he after bidding us to come see him.

WIDOW GREELY. It cannot be only his shirts he is wanting, and Sunday three days from us yet. But it was as good bring them, and they starched and ready to put on. (*Puts down basket.*)

WIDOW DEENY. Cake and wine on the table, and it is not a feast day at all. It is not as starchers and ironers he is wanting our company to-day.

WIDOW GREELY. A very kind man indeed, and a good employer of labour.

WIDOW DEENY. He is kind, so long as it will do no harm to himself to be kind. But there is no doubt at all about it, he is a very timorous man.

WIDOW GREELY. That is the nature of the Canavans, since the great-grandfather killed a witch-hare.

WIDOW DEENY. The heart of the hare went into them. What call had he to go eating it, and it after squealing in the pot? All he did was to cut the head off it, and throw it out of the door.

WIDOW GREELY. It is harebrained the miller's brother was, leaving home for the army as he did.

WIDOW DEENY. There did a wise woman prophesy, Peter would

179

be hare-hearted always, but Antony would get the big name and the branch for bravery, before ever he would come to his death.

WIDOW GREELY. No wonder a wealthy man like the miller to be hare-hearted and the country tossed the way it is. The Queens' troops and Lord Essex havocking the whole of Munster.

WIDOW DEENY. The Lord be with our own men that are hiding in the woods! It is for them I would have more respect than for any Canavan at all.

CANAVAN (*coming from inner door*). Welcome, Widow Greely, welcome, Widow Deeny. It is very neighbourly of you coming when I sent asking you; but you are always neighbourly and kind.

WIDOW GREELY. Why wouldn't we come? And here is the wash I brought with me. I tell you the Captain at the Castle does not get his shirts made up like that.

CANAVAN. The youngster Lord Essex left in charge? I believe he is a kinsman of my own.

WIDOW DEENY. I heard them saying that. He Englished his name to Headley it seems, he being a genteel young man. Canavan, one head, Headley. They say he has shirts and laces for every day of the year.

CANAVAN (*sitting down and motioning them to do the same*). Well, it is the reason of me sending for you, I am wishful to ask for your advice.

WIDOW GREELY. Do so, and it is likely we will give it in a way that will be pleasing to yourself.

CANAVAN. Now, when there is a course of action put before any man, there is but the one question to put and the one to answer; and that question is: Is it safe?

WIDOW GREELY. You were always wary, and why wouldn't you be wary?

CANAVAN. Now, when Lord Essex came besieging the Castle above, where did he get his oats and his straw and his flour from but from myself? I treated him well, and he treated me middling well. I made no complaint about payment—I was chary of doing that—it was best let the townland think it was taken from me by force. Well, it was not forgotten to me, and what has come but a letter from the Lord Deputy making me an offer.

WIDOW GREELY. If it is a good one I would recommend you take it.

CANAVAN. It is what he tenders me in this letter, in return for my services and believing me to be loyal to the Queen, to make me Mayor of Scartana.

WIDOW DEENY. No less than Mayor!

CANAVAN. Now all I want is to be safe; to keep my life, my quietness, my commodity. It is with the strongest I must take service to do that. I have but one head only, and what I have to do is not to lose it. If now, I take office, will the Queen's Government be protecting me to the end of my lifetime?

WIDOW GREELY. You may be sure they will, so long as you are of use to them, and that they have the upper hand.

WIDOW DEENY. There would be safety in one thing anyway, that you having taken the oath to the Queen, no one would expect you to put yourself out at any time, striking a blow for Ireland.

CANAVAN. Now, as to taking the oath, I don't say but it might go against me in the eyes of the neighbours. I am the loathest man in Munster to give offence to any one. But who, unless a fool, would go hop against a hill? There is many a little thing a man will do for the sake of safety, that he would not do at any common time. To turn his vest and he led away by enchantment in a field, or to cross himself passing by a churchyard in the night time; to do these things or to take the oath, what are they but a little token of respect to something that might be a danger. There can be no harm at all in that.

WIDOW DEENY. The Queen might be a danger with her troops in the Castle above. That is true enough.

CANAVAN. Caution is no load upon any one. And it might be safer for the district to have me as Mayor than a *real* Queen's man. I always said I would like to do something for Ireland when the right time, and the safe time, would come. But it didn't come yet. I see danger around on every side.

WIDOW GREELY. I suppose so. If every one would look as far before them as they do behind, they would see plenty.

WIDOW DEENY. O'Connor is gaining the day in some parts, the same as O'Neill in the North.

CANAVAN. That is what I have in my mind. Our own people to get the upper hand, would they think bad of me taking office under the Queen? The mill is a lonesome place—the roof of it is but thatch—any attack at all to be made on it would be a great danger.

WIDOW DEENY. I wonder now you would not bring in some person to be conversing with you and heartening you in the long evenings.

CANAVAN. I am best without any person. I was well pleased when Antony, my brother, left the house. Some notion he would never die he had, made him go playing and fooling, playing and fooling, tricking with danger like a ball. Came dressed in straw with the wrenboys one Stephen's night he did, set my knees shaking through his knowledge and his mockeries, I taking him to be no *right* man. It was on the head of that, I drove him out of the door.

WIDOW DEENY. He brought down his name with his own comrades, the time he went taking the pay of the Queen.

CANAVAN. It was maybe best. He to be sworn to the Queen, I myself to be thought a trusty man in Scartana; that is the way for a family to keep itself safe on *every* side.

WIDOW DEENY. Is it alive at all he is, since he went abroad to England? I believe there was no word of him this time past.

CANAVAN. I would not like to be putting myself forward, sending asking news of him. Any harm to have happened him, it is likely I would be sent word. If I got at any time certain news of his death, I would not begrudge laying out a fair share in Masses for the benefit and the safety of his soul.

(*Enter* ANTONY *disguised as a pedlar.*)

ANTONY. Who wants ruffs for the neck, hoods for the hair, all the fashions that are in any Court at all!

CANAVAN (*getting up*). Who is that? A pedlar. I have no good opinion of pedlars. There was a pedlar did a murder one time in Cashel. To carry away the limbs he did one by one in his pack.

ANTONY. I have better than that in my pack! Buying from the old, working out the new. Ruffs for the neck, hoods for the hair, wearables and jewellery, combs and laces fit for the Queen of England!

WIDOW GREELY. Are they now? (*He opens pack and takes out a ruff.*) I never saw so sizeable a frill as that one, or so much like a turkey-cock's neck.

ANTONY. That is the right size, ma'am. That is the way the Queen herself wears them.

WIDOW DEENY. What way would she get her neck into that? Sure it is like a nut on a platter her head would be!

ANTONY. Not at all, ma'am. It would become yourself well if you but knew how to wear it. Look here now—there is a likeness of her in the pack. (*Takes one out and holds it up.*) This is the way she is —a hood on her head—two bunches of hair at the sides of her face —the ruff around it like spokes around the hub of a wheel. (*Puts picture on wall.*) Look at that now for a ruff! It is quite easy if you know what way to wear it.

WIDOW DEENY. Isn't that great now. And it is like that she is?

Sure they say she has her hair dyed red like your own, since she came to the turn of her age.

WIDOW GREELY. Is that herself now! The woman that never took a husband, or fasted from a lover.

WIDOW DEENY. That she may be dancing quadrilles on a red hot floor this day twelve-month, along with her fitting father, Henry the Eighth!

CANAVAN. Get on now. We want none of your vanities. Get on out of this!

ANTONY. Oh, brother Peter, is that the way you are threatening a soldier of the big army!

CANAVAN. Antony!—Is it Antony it is! What is it brings you here?

ANTONY. You need not think of the safety of my soul yet, with many thanks to you, Peter.

CANAVAN. Are you after putting ears on yourself, and you outside the door?

ANTONY. I heard you say nothing but the thing I would expect you to say, and you the same as you were.

CANAVAN (to WIDOWS). What did he hear? What was I saying? It is as a spy from Lord Essex he is come!

ANTONY. It is not from Lord Essex I am come.

CANAVAN. He might be questioning you. Why did I open my mind at all? But I said no treasonable thing. Bear witness now I said no word at all against the Queen's Government!

ANTONY. I tell you I am no spy. You have leave to give me good treatment, and not harm yourself at all.

CANAVAN Well, now, as to stopping here—it is best be cautious —the neighbours might mislike it—they might bring it up against me, a Queen's man to be harboured in the house.

ANTONY. Oh, I am a quiet poor creature, will give no annoyance at all. I am not like a daring man would have his name rising up— first over the ditches in Friesland, spitting Spaniards like herrings on a pike—wounded in the gate at Antwerp—blowing up red hot guns with a match. If ever any one says it was I myself did those deeds, you may know he is an enemy of my own, and give no heed to him at all.

WIDOW GREELY. Little there'd be to boast of if you did do them. I'd think more of a push of a pike given for Munster, than of all your red hot guns!

WIDOW DEENY. After giving your strength to the enemy your

weakness is not much to bring home! It's the shell of the nut you are bringing us, and the husk of the winnowed corn.

ANTONY. That is right, that is right. That is the way I would like you to be talking.

WIDOW GREELY. A man to go against his own people for the sake of that lean upper crust! (*Points to picture.*)

ANTONY. Little at all I did of fighting, but to be sitting hatching in the camp. There is no great name on me at all!

WIDOW GREELY. It's a place for yourself you will hatch out. You will maybe be crier to the Mayor!

WIDOW DEENY. The miller has something to gain by it, but you to be a traitor and poor!

WIDOW GREELY. The rich of the world should get pity, because there is temptation at their side.

WIDOW DEENY. I would not blame their kinsman at the Castle that was reared to go following the Queen.

WIDOW GREELY. It is what I was often saying, the Canavans are not much of a race.

WIDOW DEENY. It is what I think, Miller Canavan, it is best for us be going home. We do not care much, with respects to you, for the company has come into your house. (*They go out.*)

CANAVAN. Now that those corn-crakes are gone, tell me what is it brings you home.

ANTONY. Didn't you hear me telling them I have left the Queen's army?

CANAVAN. What were you turned out for?

ANTONY. I was not turned out at all. I took my own leave. I was afeared to stop on in the army.

CANAVAN. I wouldn't wonder at that. The time fighting would be going on, the army is no good trade.

ANTONY. It is the way it was. It is in the prophecy I will not die until such time as my name is up. My name being down, I have no fear of death, but it is for ever I might live; and so whatever danger there is to face, I am safe facing it.

CANAVAN. My grief it was not for myself that prophecy was made!

ANTONY. But the time we were in Flanders, my name was going up in spite of myself, the same way it was going up and I a young lad, and that I enlisted to check it. And so it was to check it again that I deserted yesterday. I thought it no sin bringing that pack away with me in place of my pay. I thought to find a fortune in it, where it came by a Queen's messenger from London. But my curse be upon it, there is nothing at all but a suit of clothes and that picture, as a present for the Lord Deputy's lady!

CANAVAN. You made off without leave! That was a terrible dangerous thing to do! Hurry back now or they will say you are a deserter.

ANTONY. They will be doing no wrong saying that. It is a deserter I am.

CANAVAN. A deserter! What now would happen to me, it to be known you are a deserter! I will not abet you! Go back now before you will be missed! (*Tries to push him to door.*)

ANTONY. I will not. I tell you I am afeared. If I go fighting again my name will go up in spite of me. It is here in Scartana I will stop. A miller like yourself I will be. They know us here and they will not speak well of us. Sorting the grains I will be with you—keeping the hens from laying abroad.

CANAVAN (*rising*). A deserter from the army! And in this house! Get out of this, get out! Oh, why did I let you pass the threshold! A deserter! The thing there is no forgiveness for! Oh, this is a day of great misfortune!

ANTONY. You need not be so tender over me. They have not taken me yet.

CANAVAN. Tender over you! Is it of you I am thinking? I am thinking of myself. What black wind brought you here? (*Sits down and rocks himself.*) A deserter to come into my house! (*Walking up and down.*) Calling the whole army down upon me! A decoy duck in a pond! A wire rod in a thunder-storm! A squealing rabbit among weasels! A gabbling turkey poult among foxes! A running partridge to bring hawks! Was there ever any man put in such danger in his own house and in his own place since ever the world was a world!

ANTONY. Who would I look to to befriend and to cherish me, but my only brother?

CANAVAN. Why should a man be put in danger if he had forty thousand brothers? I will not be cumbered with you. I tell you I am going to be put in a very high station. Mayor of Scartana I am to be made. Look now, Antony, we were always fond of one other— just leave the place now, and go back for the sake of the name— don't endanger me.

ANTONY. Ah, you are a great coaxer. Will you wish me to go to the Castle above and to give myself up to be hanged?

CANAVAN. That won't do, that won't do, I'd be disgraced along with you. They might impeach me for consanguinity. You have no call to be twisting a rope for my neck along with your own. You must go into hiding, you must let no person see you at all!

ANTONY. I will hide, so, till nightfall, in the shed.

CANAVAN. No, no, one of the mill lads might get a sight of you!

ANTONY. Or in the loft?

CANAVAN. Not safe, not safe—there is not enough of straw to cover you. I would be well pleased the earth to open and to swallow you up out of sight!

ANTONY. I wouldn't wish the widows to know I deserted from the army. They would be putting big mouths on themselves among the neighbours, shouting me till a bonefire would be lit in my praise. Let no person know in Scartana I did anything worth praising at all.

(*Enter the* TWO WIDOWS.)

WIDOW GREELY. We have very tempestuous news, Miller!

WIDOW DEENY. Very strange news indeed, if we had but breath to bring it out.

WIDOW GREELY. The Queen's soldiers to be coming to this house!

WIDOW DEENY. You yourself that was going to be Mayor!

WIDOW GREELY. Indeed I would sooner it was any other one.

WIDOW DEENY. The soldiers had a very wicked look.

WIDOW GREELY. It is hard in these times to keep out of danger.

WIDOW DEENY. It is, where Miller Canavan has failed.

CANAVAN. What is that you are saying about danger?

WIDOW GREELY. It is much if you escape with your life!

WIDOW DEENY. It is harbouring rebels they say you are.

CANAVAN. Be off out of this, Antony Canavan, and don't be dragging me to my death.

ANTONY (*at door*). I must run—no, the troops are spreading themselves to surround the house.

WIDOW GREELY. Hide yourself here under the sacks—they might chance not to take notice of you. (*She points to a heap of sacks in the corner.*)

CANAVAN (*seizing* ANTONY). You will not hide under the sacks—it is myself they will be taking in your place!

WIDOW DEENY. It is likely indeed you will suffer, and a deserter to be found on your floor!

CANAVAN. I can make my defence! They cannot say I am a rebel —look now at all the things I might have done against the Queen and didn't do! All I ever did was to strive to keep my head safe. Is a man, I ask you, to go to his death for that?

WIDOW DEENY (*at door*). A great troop of them indeed—and

the young Captain leading them on. Go under the sacks I tell you, Antony, we will stand to the front of them ourselves.

CANAVAN (*dragging him from them*). No, no, every rib of my hair is rising! I am afeared, I am afeared, in the very cockles of my heart! It is I myself will go in under the sacks. Stop you here, take my coat—let you personate me—they will not harm you at all! (*Gives him coat and cap and creeps under sacks.*)

ANTONY (*putting on coat and cap and flouring himself*). There is no fear of my life. There is no big name on me yet. But you will die in a frenzy at the sight of them, the same as a mouse in a trap!

CANAVAN. Settle them over me, settle the sacks over me! If they rose off me the height of my finger I'd get the shivers.

(WIDOWS *cover him up.* ANTONY *sits at desk and takes up a paper.*)

ANTONY. Faith I'll make a handsome miller, I'll be picking fun out of the Captain. Four pecks one bushel, eight bushels one quarter, four bushels one coombe, thirty-six bushels one chaldron—five quarters one load.

(HEADLEY *appears at door and speaks to men outside.*)

HEADLEY. Stop there, Corporal, with your men. Watch all the doors. Let no one escape from the house—(*to* ANTONY) I am Captain Headley, on the Queen's business.

ANTONY. Welcome, welcome Captain. It is too great an honour you are doing me, and I but a poor trader, striving to knock out a living at the mill. I'm thinking the middle of the day is rising. We will have white meal from the wheat this year, for there's nothing so natural as the sun.

HEADLEY. A soldier has deserted from Lord Essex's troop. He has stolen Government property. He is said to be a relation of your own.

ANTONY. Ah, the mean villainous abominable rascal! To go bring disgrace upon my name!

HEADLEY. Has he come to this house?

ANTONY. That I may never sin if any person came in at this door to-day, but myself and the two widows with the wash.

HEADLEY. We have information that the print of his boots was found in the soft path above. (*Reads*) "One with two close runs of nails in the sole; one without a toe; one with a bit of another boot on it——"

ANTONY. The brazened backbiters! Sure that is the print of my own boots about the place! Look now, am I telling any lie? (*Holds up boot.*)

HEADLEY. We will search the house.

ANTONY. We will, we will, and welcome. It is I myself will go searching before you, the way you will not destroy your fine tasty suit. It is likely your honour may have heard I am to be made Mayor of Scartana?

HEADLEY. Even so, you might harbour a rebel of your own blood.

ANTONY. Is it of Canavan the miller you are saying that? Would you say, neighbours, is Peter Canavan a man to put himself in danger, to save the life of any person on earth?

WIDOW GREELY. He would sooner let the whole of the tribes of Munster go to their death.

HEADLEY. I believe if it were not for dread of our army you would all be rebels against our bright goddess, Elizabeth, the fairest princess beneath the skies.

ANTONY. Guide your eyes sideways. Look what is forenenst you on the wall—a picture of the Queens' majesty. Who would say now this is not a loyal place?

HEADLEY. Is that the Queen?

ANTONY. Herself indeed. (*Takes off cap.*) God bless the man that brought it here! Here now, Captain, is wine of Spain, you will not refuse to drink to her health.

HEADLEY. I will never refuse to drink to that glorious one. (*Drinks and falls on one knee.*) But what audacious man has tried to set down her portrait!

> "All were it Zeuxis or Praxiteles
>   His skilful hand would fail and greatly faint
>   Picturing her dainty beauty, Sacred Saint——"

Queen of Love! Paragon of Beauty! Prince of Peace! Crown of Lilies! Image of the Heavens! Mirror of Divine Majesty! Mirror of Grace! —oh, let me look nearer. (*Gets up.*) I suppose it is not a very exact portrait?

ANTONY. It is maybe a little too fleshy in the jaw—but she was much like that the last time I saw her.

HEADLEY (*drinking*). You saw the Queen?

ANTONY. I was mostly reared around this place, but I went one time to London—with samples of flour I went—they made use of some of it in the Court. But sure you must often have seen her yourself?

HEADLEY. Not exactly—I have not yet been in the royal presence. Of course I shall be whenever I go to England—but I didn't go there yet.

ANTONY. Not in England! I thought by you that you had never been reared in Ireland at all.

HEADLEY. What matter, it is all the one thing. I have English connections—I had always an English heart. Now I will call in the Corporal to search.

ANTONY (*stopping him*). Look here now, Captain, I am your well-wisher and I have a thing to put in your mind. Go over to the Court—make no delay—it will be a sure road to fortune.

HEADLEY. That has been said to me before.

ANTONY. I hope it is not a liberty, saying you are a high-up lovely young man.

HEADLEY. I am told there are some have called me the Apollo of the army.

ANTONY. I heard that—a very civil countenance—grand beautiful features—and believe me if I heard it, the Queen has not been without hearing it, for she has a great respect for comeliness.

HEADLEY. More than that again, I have been told that my name has come to the royal ear.

ANTONY. If she could but see you now; or maybe you poetise. They speak nothing at the Court but poetry.

HEADLEY. A sonnet maybe an odd time.

ANTONY. That is good. Write me out one now and I'll mix it in my flour. I'll take care she will get it in a cake of bread.

HEADLEY. I have not to go to those shifts. I have samples of my verse given to some who will lay it in the Queen's way.

ANTONY. And very good verse it is I'll engage.

HEADLEY. My comrades think well of it. (*Sings:*)

Ye traitors all that do devise
    To plague our Paragon,
And in your hearts in treacherous wise
    Let such vain thoughts run on.
Consider what your end will be
    Before you farther go;
The Crown of Lilies joyfully
    Will hang you in a row!

(*Waving handkerchief as he sings it falls among sacks; he takes another glass of wine.*) Essex keeps me here in this exile—there are some who say it is jealousy. I have not the chance to show myself off before Her Grace, even to write a report. But I go dine with him to-night to drink the Queen's health before he goes north.

ANTONY. Well, I won't delay you, Captain (*Leading him to the door*), I being proud to have showed you that likeness, and to be the same thing as dealer with the Court.

HEADLEY. Oh, yes, it was all a mistake; we must look in some other place for that rascally deserter. (*Turns back at door.*) Ah, I have dropped my handkerchief. (*Goes towards sacks, as* PETER, *who has looked out, puts down his head.*) There is some noise, a rustling——

ANTONY. It is but a mouse in the flour sacks.

HEADLEY. I thought I saw something shaking.

ANTONY. A mouse—nothing but a mouse. I know that mouse well.

WIDOW GREELY (*catching up clothes-basket and getting between* HEADLEY *and sacks.*) Your honour might want some starching done and crimping. This woman and myself are the best in the whole town.

WIDOW DEENY (*going beside her*). Great at frills we are and anything that is for show. Lace for the cuffs or the like.

HEADLEY. Go then to the Castle and see to my ruffles. They are not fit for me to wear at the dinner to-night. I suspect them of having been ironed with a rusty cannon-ball.

WIDOW GREELY. We will go up there on the minute. We will follow your honour and the troops.

HEADLEY. Very good. It's not easy to be too attentive to ruffles. (*Is going but turns again.*) But where is my laced handkerchief? (*Pushes past women.*) It must have dropped among the sacks. (*He pokes in sword. A loud shriek is heard and* CANAVAN *stands up.*)

CANAVAN. Spare me! Spare me! I hope I have not been thrust through with any sort of a poisoned dagger!

HEADLEY. You are the deserter I am looking for!

CANAVAN. Oh, such a thing to say! I, that never left the sound of the mill-wheel!

HEADLEY. As well as deserting, you stole this pack.

CANAVAN. Blessed if I ever saw it till within the last half hour!

HEADLEY. You have disguised yourself.

CANAVAN. Any one would do that for safety, and a wicked troop of men at his door!

HEADLEY. You were making your way to join the rebels.

CANAVAN. They would not take me if I would join them! I would make no fist at all of fighting. It would melt the marrow of O'Neill himself to hear the screams I would let out of me, and the first gun going off! They would as soon take me among them as they would weaken their drop of spirits with the shiver of the water from the mill-race! Speak up for me, Antony, and tell him who I am and what I am!

ANTONY. He is but a poor crazy hawker I befriend an odd time.

CANAVAN. I am not! I am the miller.

ANTONY. He has been drinking a drop too much—

CANAVAN. I was not. I am sober!

ANTONY. Light-headed he is—innocent—

CANAVAN. I am not innocent!

ANTONY. Wouldn't do any grain of harm—

CANAVAN. Let you not decry me!

ANTONY. As quiet as a child—

CANAVAN. Let you stop defaming me!

ANTONY. A simpleton—

CANAVAN. No more than yourself!

ANTONY. Ah, my poor Jack!

CANAVAN. That is not my name!

ANTONY. I thought you had forgotten it.

CANAVAN. It is you are miscalling me!

ANTONY (*tapping forehead*). It is easy known the moon is at the full.

CANAVAN. My curse upon the moon!

ANTONY. He is quiet at other times.

CANAVAN. I will not be quiet, I will tell—

ANTONY. Ah, tell tale, tell tale!

CANAVAN. I am the miller!

ANTONY. A fanciful fellow.

CANAVAN. I am Canavan the miller!

ANTONY (*sitting down on table*). I gave him shelter and clothed him, and now he says he is myself.

CANAVAN. Get out of this, you scheming juggler, you!

ANTONY. Go back to your sleep, my poor Jack, and I forgive you.

HEADLEY. Make an end of this clatter! One or other of you is a rogue.

CANAVAN. That's a true word! It is he is the rogue! I am honest! I am no rebel!

HEADLEY. It was guilt that made you hide among the sacks.

CANAVAN. It was he hid me, it was he disguised me. All I wanted was to keep myself safe! It is his own safety he was thinking of.

ANTONY. Oh, my poor wandering Jack!

CANAVAN. Wandering yourself! It is he is a stroller and a rambler and a deceiver and a bad character, and a mocker and a disturber and a rogue and a vagabond, and a deserter from the Queen's troops.

ANTONY. Look now, Captain, would you say that object to be the great miller, Canavan?

CANAVAN. Object yourself! I'll indict you for scandallation! Save me, save me! I am of your own blood—the province knows you are a Canavan the same as myself—Henry Canavan, that was reared in Waterford!

HEADLEY (*pushing him away*). Presumptuous trader! Audacious clown! You must be silenced! You are both rebels, a libeller of loyalists and a deserter from the Queen! I shall have something to write a report of at last, to lay before the royal feet! (*Turns to door.*) Here, men, come and seize these prisoners! (*To* ANTONY *and* CANAVAN.) To the Castle now to be warded for the night! You shall both be executed at dawn!

Curtain.

ACT II

SCENE: *A room at the Castle. A bed, a chair, a window, a heap of rubbish in corner and a large basket of turf. A lighted lantern hanging from wall. Antony asleep on the bed, his pack under his head.*

CANAVAN (*walking up and down and wringing his hands*). Rise up, Antony, and waken! Any one would think there was a sleeping-pin in your head!

ANTONY (*stretching himself*). Why are you wakening me? Is it time to rise up?

CANAVAN. Time! What way can you sleep at all, and go slugging through the night time? Do you remember we are mewed up as prisoners in the Castle, and locked and bolted and gaoled?

ANTONY. The waking is better than the dream I had. I was dreaming the people were shouting me.

CANAVAN. Is it nothing to you what you have brought me to, with your follies and your clowneries?

192

ANTONY. Brought yourself to, it seems to me, with your hiding and your crouching in the sacks.

CANAVAN. Would any one now think that a thing to hang a man for, to have striven to keep himself safe? Hiding is it? Why would nature teach the rabbits to hide, and the badgers to live in clefts, if there was harm in it and rebellion? And the otter to sink to the water's depths? I could have proved all that to the Captain, if you had but given me time to speak!

ANTONY. I spoke soft and blathered him; you would have been safe enough if you had but held your tongue.

CANAVAN. It was you put me in danger, making a mockery of me, and miscalling me and decrying me. He would have had respect for me if it wasn't for that.

ANTONY. He would not have seen you at all, if you had not gone stirring and shaking in the sacks.

CANAVAN. What way could I help it, and I panting and quivering the way I was? And that sword! What could any man do but call out and he getting a thrust of a sword? My chest was never in the same place since, with the start I got. Oh, tell me now, Antony, is it certain we are near our death?

ANTONY. The dawn is not far off. Cousin Headley said it was to be at dawn.

CANAVAN (*groaning*). To die! To die! Is it to die I am going! (*He walks up and down mopping forehead.*) Is it I myself am alive and hearing it, that I am going to my death?

ANTONY. That was what the Captain said, and his men that were locking the door.

CANAVAN. Death! Death! That is a thing I always had a great fear of. There are many things I was always in dread of, but I think that the most thing was death. I thought I had it kept a long way off from me—I never travelled by water, through the fear drowning would smother me, or on horseback through the fear of being knocked, or any way at all, if I could by any means stop in the house.

ANTONY. Where is the use of raving and crying? Death is not a mill-wheel you can stop at your will.

CANAVAN. Death! Death! I thought I was safe from any death but maybe death on the pillow. And I had myself barricaded against that itself. There was not a day hardly that I was without mint twigs tied around the wrist, or yarrow within the stocking, or an elder leaf for protection against the falling sickness! Drinking every night carrots to clear the blood, and knapweed to ease the

193

bones, and dandelion to strengthen the heart, and gentian to keep off fever; the nightmare charm, the toothache charm, the charm to quell a mad dog. And with everything a bit of camomile in my drink—for our grandmother lived to a hundred years with the dint of camomile!

ANTONY. Well, it is not yourself that will live to a hundred years. It is best for you give your mind now to what is on the other side of death.

CANAVAN. That is the worst! That is the worst! To be going maybe before this day is out, shivering and forlorn, into some strange giddy place—it might be with the body changing about you, and it might be getting giddy through the air—or maybe put into some strange new shape. There was a woman I heard of was put under the bridge beyond, working out her penance seven years —I would not like that, to be starved and consumed under a bridge.

ANTONY. Hearten yourself now, you might be put in the shape of a hare.

CANAVAN. I would not like to be put in the ugly shape of any beast, or to be spreading terror, rattling my chains in the night time.

ANTONY. Take courage. It is not likely you would be able to frighten any person at all.

CANAVAN. And all the rabble of the parish to be looking at me as I die! And not one I suppose will dare to coffin me, or to lay me in any grave worth while?

ANTONY. Never fear, if no other one does it, the crows will give you a safe burying.

CANAVAN. The widows might bury me in the night time; they had always a great respect for me. But tell me this, Antony, is it hanged we are to be, or is it beheaded we will be? Isn't it beheaded traitors do be? Is it not as traitors they are killing us, little as I deserve it myself?

ANTONY. Many a man would be proud of the honour of being beheaded.

CANAVAN. What way will it be with me, I wonder, and I after losing my head? And if it is in the night time the women lay my relics in the grave—is it the right head will be placed to the right body, or will I be mixed up with yourself? (*Rocking himself as he walks.*) Will I be going up to the Judgment with the sins of another man's body? Is it all your own sins I might have to answer for, and I making excuses for my own? It is little I ever did to harm any person in the world. I never drank nor beat any one. But how would I know what bad behaviour you may have had? It is likely you were breaking the law of God through every day of the year. I wouldn't wonder if you were drunken and quarrelsome, going after women—grasping and greedy—prone to gambling.

ANTONY. Cheating and stealing—

CANAVAN. Cursing and swearing.

ANTONY. Blaspheming and perjuring—

CANAVAN. A scoffer and mocker.

ANTONY. Working with witches, committing sacrilege, robbing the poor box, coining false money—what are you talking of? A hundred-murderer!

CANAVAN. Oh, do you tell me so! A murderer! A coiner! A blasphemer! Oh, you scum of the world! I that have one head only, to have a body of that sort joined on to it for eternity! I that didn't know the name hardly of that tribe of inhibited sins! I that kept myself out of every temptation! It is many a time I stopped in my loneliness that I might not have occasion to sin! My curse upon you, Antony Canavan, what brought you back into Ireland at all!

ANTONY. Quit roaring and crying, and let your last end be a credit to you. There can no harm happen, *your* name to go up. There is no occasion for *you* to shape yourself to be timorous, as there is for me.

CANAVAN. This is no time I tell you to be humbugging, and death beckoning at me the way it is!

ANTONY. Turn your mind from that, and give it to making your will. Stretch out now and write it in favour of myself. In my opinion I will not die, my name being down the way it is.

CANAVAN. Ah, don't be talking! How can I be thinking of wills and I so near my end? If I had a way to will my treasure, I would leave all to provide for the safety of my own soul!

ANTONY. I will lay out a share to do that much for you. Tell me where is it you have it hid.

CANAVAN. I will, I will! It is a great thing it should be a help to me at the last! The most of it is in—where now at all is it? In what corner or cleft have I it hid? I knew where it was and I coming here. But wherever it was, it is gone from my mind.

ANTONY. Hurry on now and remember.

CANAVAN. Amn't I trying to remember? But I cannot with the dint of the dread that is upon me.

ANTONY (*shaking him*). Search you mind and think of it.

CANAVAN. Amn't I ransacking my mind? Have I no care for my

own soul? But every time I try to make it out, I see nothing before me but a gallows and an axe.

ANTONY (*with another shake*). Summon your wits now.

CANAVAN. Don't be ill-using and abusing me! It is tossed and tattered my mind is. I give you my last solemn oath, my memory of the hiding place is gone. I would give the half of my treasure to anyone would tell me where it is!

ANTONY. Look at here now, I to find a way to get you out of this, what will you give me of your riches, to start me in some trade will keep my name down?

CANAVAN. All! All that I have! I swear it! I won't keep back so much as a miserable starvation farthing.

ANTONY. That is great. I will find a way of living will never let my name be heard but by my own customers and in my own street. There will be no fear of shouts and praises for me from this out.

CANAVAN. Make no delay! Save me! Oh, what way can you save me?

ANTONY. I will see what I can do with this. (*Takes a rope from rubbish in corner and knots another to it, twisting and tying in a piece of ribbon from his pack.*)

(*A knock at the door.*)

CANAVAN. There is some one knocking at the door! Oh, it is some new danger!

WIDOW GREELY (*looking through grating in door*). Are you living yet, Miller Canavan?

CANAVAN. I am—I think—but hardly—it is not until dawn we are to be made an end of.

WIDOW DEENY. We are till now settling out the Captain's shirts; he bade us make a clean job of them. We made our way up before going, to enquire after you.

WIDOW GREELY. We were thinking it might be comfortable to you to leave your last wishes with us; there will be no one else to pay respect to them, yourself and your cracked brother being dead.

WIDOW DEENY. It would be a pity the money you minded so well to be going into any wrong hands.

WIDOW GREELY. The Captain ought not to be getting it, letting on not to know his own race.

WIDOW DEENY. Those ruffians of soldiers might seize on it, and they setting fire to the mill, to fatten that red-haired battle-cock that is preying upon us all.

WIDOW GREELY. If you give us authority over it, we will not forget the repose of your soul.

196

CANAVAN. Be easy will you, my head is thrown to and fro! I wish I could leave it to be laid out for my soul! But to my grief and my misfortune it fails me to remember where I have it hid.

WIDOW GREELY. To the poor you could leave alms from it to open you the gates of Heaven.

CANAVAN (*taking his head in his hands*). Wait now—I put it supposing in the one place yesterday—and to-morrow I changed it to another. I can partly remember yesterday, but blindfold me if I can remember where it was to-morrow!

WIDOW DEENY. I am sure where it was twelve hours ago, the time that you were talking with ourselves, and that is under the second first board from the door.

WIDOW GREELY. The board you drew the sack over, and you after coming into the room.

WIDOW DEENY. The board you put your foot upon, and the pedlar coming into the house.

CANAVAN. What are you saying? You knew the places I kept my money?

WIDOW DEENY. The time you had it in the chimney, we could know it by the soot upon your cap.

WIDOW GREELY. The time it was hid in the stable, the bees made an attack on you through the smell.

CANAVAN. Oh, the spies! The peerers! The pryers! The magpies! The bloodhounds! The witches! Was ever a man in such danger and such peril of his life? To be watched and be nosed and be scented that way! To be tracked like a fox to his den! I not to be safe on my own floor, or by my own hearthstone! Is there no place, within or abroad, where a man can keep himself safe? The world never saw a greater wonder than I not being murdered for my gold!

ANTONY. It's a queer thing to be wasting time talking. Bid them look for the key, if you have a mind to escape.

CANAVAN. Where is the use of escaping out of this, and those ones having knowledge of the most lonesome thoughts of my heart!

WIDOW DEENY. Is it an answer you are giving us, Miller Canavan?

CANAVAN (*to widows*). What are you jabbering and jangling for? Can't you look? Do you see e'er a key?

WIDOW GREELY. It is very dark in the place where we are to search out a small thing like a key.

CANAVAN. Search in every place I tell you. I know every place a key can be hid. It might be in the pocket of a coat—or in the finger of a glove that would be lying on a shelf—or concealed under a cloth that would be hanging from the wall.

WIDOW DEENY. It should be in some place. It it was a dog, it would bite you. But I can find no trace of it at all.

CANAVAN. There are many good places to hide it in—I often hid a key of my own—in under the ashes of the hearth or put in a loaf of bread and a slice closing up the hole!

WIDOW GREELY. There is a fire alight on the hearth. I have myself scorched, and no key to be found.

WIDOW DEENY. I see no bread or anything to be eaten at all. And what is worse again, I hear horses coming into the yard. It is likely it is the Captain come home.

WIDOW GREELY. We had best not be here when he comes. I am sorry indeed we could do nothing. But we will be coming back again to see you hanged.

ANTONY. Look if it might be in the key-hole.

WIDOW DEENY. So it is in the lock all the while. I would have found it long ago if the miller had but left bothering me. Here it is. (*Throws it through grating.*) Little good it will do you, it is too late! It is much if we make our escape.

(*They go.*)

CANAVAN (*picking it up*). Oh, open the door. Oh, I can't get it into the hole. Oh, my hand is shaking—there they are in the room (*Laughter and voices heard*), it is too late. (*The* CAPTAIN'S *voice is heard singing rather tipsily.*)

ANTONY. We might make a dash through them.

CANAVAN. Oh, I cannot do that! I can hardly stand!

ANTONY. Try my plan then. I looked out there when we came in. (*Gets on chair and looks out of window and fastens rope to stanchion.*) There was a guard below, and we coming here—there is no one there now—this window is not far above a little sloping roof, we can drop on it with the help of this rope, and from that to another, and there's a buttress will help us to the ground. The night dark, the town and country to befriend. It's a good job the Captain has as good as no head at all. Here, Peter, go on first.

CANAVAN. Is it to get out of the window we must?

ANTONY. That is it, and to drop on to the roof. It is no great length of a drop.

CANAVAN. I cannot do it, I cannot do it. I am scared of going out into the clouds alone.

ANTONY. Well, let me go first, and I'll be a stay to you.

CANAVAN. You must not go. You might not wait for me at all.

ANTONY. Go through so yourself.

CANAVAN. I will not. How can I tell what danger there might be on the other side?

ANTONY. Get up on the chair and look out. It is nothing to be afraid of at all.

CANAVAN (*getting up and looking out*). I could not face it without I was a swallow or a thrush. I am certain I would fall. My head would go spinning like a wheel!

ANTONY. Go on. Why would I go to these rounds to break your neck, if I was craving to break it?

CANAVAN. If it was a level I might face it. But there is great danger of slipping on a roof.

ANTONY. There is the rope to hold to.

CANAVAN. It might give with me. It is no safe thing to hazard your life on the strength of a strand of rope. (*Gets down from chair.*)

ANTONY. Well, hang or climb or run out at the door. I myself will go this way. (*Gets on chair.*)

CANAVAN (*falling on knees and holding his feet*). Oh, don't go, Antony! Do not go and leave me in this case. Oh, listen to him, listen to him singing! Oh, I am in dread, I am in dread!

ANTONY (*shaking him off and getting down*). You miserable shaking-scraw! It's a charm you should carry against trembling, of the right hind leg of a hare. Is there any use in striving to save you at all? Though it might be no hard job to outwit Cousin Headley. If I had but a sheet, a ghost would do the job.

(HEADLEY *is heard singing close to the door.*)

ANTONY (*opening pack*). Crown of lilies! That's it. We'll allure him with Queen Elizabeth. (*Takes out dress and other things.*)

CANAVAN. Oh, he is coming in!

ANTONY. Clear the turf out of that basket—hurry.

CANAVAN. That basket—(*Throws out sods of turf.*) A good thought—it might cover me—the rods of it would not shiver the way the sack did. (*Sits down and pulls it over him.*) If I could get into the corner now—(*Begins crawling to corner with basket over him.*) I would be as hidden as a snail in its shell—if he does not think now of spitting me with that sword.

(ANTONY *meanwhile has slipped on the dress and arranged his hair with his fingers, and put on ruff and headdress. He bears a resemblance to the portrait of Queen Elizabeth. He takes up basket and rubs his face in miller's floury smock.*)

CANAVAN. Oh, oh, oh, is it the executioner! Oh, I feel the axe! It's as cold as amber! (*Rushes to the bed, kneels and hides his face in cloak, and remains there rocking and moaning.*)

(ANTONY *steps into basket spreading out skirt of dress over it as* HEADLEY *is heard close to door.*)

HEADLEY. Go to the guard room. I will have an hour's sleep before dawn. (*A trampling heard, footsteps die away.* HEADLEY *sings again.*)

(ANTONY *raps on floor with poker. He has a pair of slippers in hand, but having failed to put them on slips them into pocket.* HEADLEY *comes in singing. He suddenly catches sight of the figure in coif and silk dress.*)

ANTONY. Upon your knees!

HEADLEY. Who! Who!

ANTONY. Elizabeth, Regina Ingilterra, Francia, Hibernia, Deo gratia, Defendore Fides.

HEADLEY (*sinking on his knees*). The Queen! The excellent and glorious person of her Majesty!

ANTONY. You are before your sovereign.

HEADLEY. Oh, angelic face! Where the red rose has meddled with the white.

ANTONY. This is the man of whose beauty I have heard—who sent me sonnets.

HEADLEY. Oh, Queen, Queen!

ANTONY. I made a secret journey. I would know what Essex is doing. I turned aside. I would see the Apollo of my army.

HEADLEY. Oh, Phœbus blushes to find himself outshone!

ANTONY. This is your vaunted devotion. You have been absent. You have been swilling ale. No one to guard the gates. I came in unnoticed—no one heard the beat either of horsehoofs or my royal feet.

HEADLEY. Oh, the fourth of the Graces has read my sonnets!

ANTONY. That is prose. I expect a poet to talk poetry.

HEADLEY. Oh, that I had a pen—a pen—a pen.

ANTONY. Go on. Essex would do better than that.

HEADLEY. I'd say: God save the Queen—Amen, Amen—

ANTONY. That is getting on.

HEADLEY. Oh, Crown of Lilies, say that you forgive!

ANTONY. Do as I bid you and you yet may live.

HEADLEY. Lay orders, dearest dread, trust me again!

ANTONY. Then go at once and send away your men! —Look here, young Apollo, you must have the gates left clear for me to go out. There must be no blemish upon the name of Defendore Fides!

HEADLEY. I will go! But oh, let me kiss that royal foot!

ANTONY (*hastily*). No, no, the hem, the hem of my dress! (HEADLEY *kisses it. She gives him a slipper.*) There is my slipper; you may carry it away for a token.

CANAVAN (*who has but just looked from under his cloak, coming forward on his knees.*) Oh, your majesty! Oh, your Grace! Give me the other slipper! Let me have it for a sign, a sign to show the hangman!

ANTONY. Who is this floury fellow?

CANAVAN. Canavan the miller, your Grace, no traitor, your Grace—put up for harbouring traitors. I am innocent—it was all a mistake—I am no rebel and no deserter—it was a brother of mine —a vagabond, a trickster, a deserter, a very dangerous man!

ANTONY. Let him be beheaded in my name!

HEADLEY. It shall be done! His head shall make a footstool for this slipper!

ANTONY (*to* HEADLEY). Away, go, take your men. Go by the next wind to Whitehall. Who knows what preferment you may find. Wear that slipper round your neck; come to the Court wearing it.

CANAVAN. I will go to Whitehall! I take the oath of loyalty! I will take it as Mayor of Scartana. I swear on this slipper. (*Kisses it.*) I swear with every grain of my power, will, wit, and cunning, to be loyal and faithful to your Grace. God save the Queen!

ANTONY. Hush! Silence! Close your eyes! Close your ears!

CANAVAN. I will, I will! I will never open them again till such time as I will get commandment! (*Rushes back to bed and covers up his head.*)

ANTONY (*to* HEADLEY). Hasten, Poet, hasten, do not tarry—go through wind and weather—think of our meeting at Whitehall!

HEADLEY (*holding up slipper*).
      I flower, I flower that was a barren shoot
      I have a slipper from the royal foot!
      (*Rushes out.*)

ANTONY (*getting out of basket*). The window is quickest. Follow me, Peter, by the window or by the door. (*Looking at* CANAVAN.) He hears me no more than the dead! (*Gets up to window.*) Faith it's a short life I would have before me, my name to be as high as Queen Elizabeth's. (*Goes out of window.* CANAVAN *still kneels at bed, his head covered with his cloak.*)

Curtain.

ACT III

SCENE: *The Mill kitchen as before.* ANTONY *is pushing the dress, ruff, and coif up the chimney with tongs.*

ANTONY. There goes the last of her!

CANAVAN (*coming in at door*). What brought you running home from the Castle before me? What is it you are doing?

ANTONY. Hiding away things I am, that are best out of sight. Any one finds them now, will be full sure it was a witch went up the chimney.

CANAVAN. Well, this is a great night we went through, and a night full of wonders! The strongest! I know now who is the strongest! I am the Queen's man now. Oh, she is the strongest, a very fine woman!

ANTONY. What is it you are raving about?

CANAVAN. That Captain that has such power, an army at his command, on his knees she put him; trembling he was like oats in the breeze. If she daunted *him* that way what chance would there be for the like of us?

ANTONY. Pup, pup, pup, pup! Is it that you are thinking you saw the Queen?

CANAVAN. I did see her to be sure, and she gave me her own shoe.

ANTONY. Well, that was a great playgame! Wouldn't you think now it might be some one was letting on to be the Queen?

CANAVAN. She was not letting on. There was no letting on in it. Taller than any woman ever stood upon a floor she was! She stood up over me the same as an elephant! A great grand voice she had, pitched someway squeally like a woman's, but strong and high as if used to giving out orders.

ANTONY. A great beauty I suppose she was now?

CANAVAN. She was that. Like the picture she was. (*Points to it on wall.*) Long wisps of hair as bright as silver—eyes shining like sparks from the forge. I would sooner go creep through the keyhole than go face her or speak to her again.

ANTONY. Is it I that have that much beauty on me? Or is it the full moon is working in his eyes?

CANAVAN (*dragging out arm-chair*). Set this now to the rear of the table, the same as you would see it in a judge's court. I will tack up the picture on the back of it to simulate the royal arms. (*Puts picture on back of chair, hammering in tacks. Then puts on a long cloak and a chain he has fetched from inner room.*)

ANTONY. Leave those vanities now for a while. You promised me a share of your riches for to start me in a new way of life.

CANAVAN. What way is that?

ANTONY. Enter in some business I must, that will bring me no great credit and will never send my name up high. Clothier, cobbler, cutler, butcher, baker, skinner, tanner, grocer, barber, milkman, butterman, was there ever a shout given out on the heights for any one of that tribe, since ever grass grew on the fields of the earth or of the sea? Give me here now what will buy out some wealthy tradesman in the town of Scartana.

CANAVAN. Stop your blather. I made you no promise, or if I did, I didn't rightly know what was I saying with the terrification in my mind. Would you have a man bound by the thing he says when the wits are out of him with fright?

ANTONY. Fright or no fright, a promise is a promise.

CANAVAN. And so is a will a will, and if a man makes his will in a hurry, and he in the fear of death, has he no power to cancel it and he coming back from the grave?

ANTONY. You said you would give me all you had, I to save you from the gallows. I did save you, and now you go back on your word.

CANAVAN. You take credit that you saved me! You have a great opinion of yourself indeed. There was no one saved me but the Queen. A great woman!

ANTONY. Is it blind in the ears you are, the same as in the eyes? Don't you know, you crazed barley-grinder, it was I myself personated Queen Elizabeth?

CANAVAN. I do not know it indeed.

ANTONY. I tell you I did. Is it that you will misdoubt my word?

CANAVAN. I will misdoubt it. Didn't I hear you saying you were myself a while ago? "I am Canavan the miller," you said, "and that man in the sacks is Crazy Jack." It seems to me, Antony Canavan, that you are very full of lies!

ANTONY (*rises*). Will you give me nothing at all?

CANAVAN. I will not give you so much as the point of a rush, after the insult you are after putting on the Queen.

ANTONY (*goes to door*). I give up so. I will go join the boys that are fighting in the woods. My name to go up and my life to go down, it is you yourself have sent me out to that, and to come to my death in the fight.

CANAVAN. The fight? What fighting is that?

ANTONY. I must go join the boys that are fighting for to free Munster.

CANAVAN (*stopping* ANTONY *and shaking him*). Is it a rebel you are telling me you are? I am under orders as Mayor to prosecute and oppress with sword and fire any rebel at all, any one that would be prejudicial to Her Sacred Majesty. Sword and fire I will bring out against rebels. Are you giving heed to that?

ANTONY. Is it Protestant you turned in the night-time?

CANAVAN. No hurry, no hurry, till I will know is the new faith the safest in *both* worlds. I'm not one to say Her Majesty to be the *real* head of the Church. But it's greatly in her favour she being such a success. And no doubt at all about it she's a very fine woman, no doubt at all about that.

ANTONY. Heaven help your poor head! It was the terror of the night-time set it astray!

CANAVAN. At that time I had not understanding. I have taken office presently. I have settled myself to the service of the Queen. I must stick to my class. What now, I wonder, are all the other Mayors doing?

ANTONY. Give me the price of a horse and a suit itself.

CANAVAN. Would you suck and consume my treasure to nourish faction? Help you, is it? No, but hinder and impeach and plague and prosecute you. Amn't I a stay and a pillar of the Government and of the law?

ANTONY. Ah, sure, it would be more sociable like to be on the side of the neighbours. It's a very lonesome thing being with the law in Scartana.

CANAVAN. Not lonesome at all. It is happy and airy I am. Look at all the high comrades I will have, Marshals and Sheriffs and Aldermen, Sergeants at Arms, Constables, Coroners, Gaolers, Process Servers and Justices of the Peace. Grand times we will have together! Sharpening the degrees we will be! Shaping the laws to the people we will be—no, but the people to the laws. I'll give them plenty of goal according to their crimes! Oh, there is certain assurance of quiet and great good in settling yourself to the strongest. There is very great peace and immunity in surrendering our will to their commands.

ANTONY. Little good I got from commands, and I marching.

CANAVAN. There is good in them, if there is no other good but that they are commands. Would you be buzzing about at your own will the same as a heap of flies? I tell you thousands have been damned through no other thing than following their own will and fancy.

ANTONY. It is not long that the fear of the law would keep me from giving you a clout in the jaw, but that I think you an unfortunate creature that has madness put upon you by God.

CANAVAN (*taking up chair*). Ah, you savage rebel, you! You ragtail renegade! You stammering stroller, you! You pot-picker! You hangman's apron! You scabby clown! Would you strive and wrestle with your superior? Would you disparage the person of the law-giver? Would you deface the image of the Queen? I'll put the hue and cry after you! I'll hack and wrack and harry you! I'll give you up to stocks and rods, and the bitterness of martial law!

ANTONY. Well, now, the losing of your wits has put great spirit in you!

CANAVAN. Get out, out of that!

ANTONY (*at door*). Well, the Lord leave me the three faculties, wit, memory, and understanding! (*Goes out, but looks in again.*) Here are the widows now coming, thinking to see you hanged.

CANAVAN. I'll send you to the halter and the bough! The widows —it's well I have my clothes of credit put on, or they'd think nothing of me at all. (*Sits down in arm-chair and arranges himself.*)

WIDOW GREELY (*coming in*). On our way to the Castle to see the hanging we were, and Antony is after telling us there is no hanging at all. I wish I had got word sooner and I would not have put on my Sunday cloak.

WIDOW DEENY. I'm as disconcerted as to go to a wedding, and the bridegroom to have failed at the last. We that would have buried you and welcome, to go home without following you to the grave!

WIDOW GREELY. A great deception indeed. They say there is nothing so good for the soul as to see any person die hard.

CANAVAN. Well, you will not profit your soul seeing me hanged, now or at any other time. I have a strong back in the Queen from this out. I have a sure token of that.

WIDOW DEENY. Is it a ring or such like? They say Lord Essex has the Queen's ring, and that it will keep him safe for ever.

CANAVAN. What's in a ring? I daresay the Queen gives out a score of rings in the year. I have something from her own hand that is a surer pledge than the ring of day! Look here now at that! (*Holds up shoe.*)

WIDOW DEENY. A shoe! Nothing but a little red shoe!

WIDOW GREELY. You are not saying, I suppose, that this is the Queen's shoe?

CANAVAN. It is often you have said a thing that is farther from the truth than that.

WIDOW DEENY. Mind now what I am saying to you. Don't meddle with the Queen at all. Sure every man she ever had to deal with was sent to the block the next day.

WIDOW GREELY. They say there are chains rattling upon her that no one in this world can see.

CANAVAN. What do you know about kings and queens? Did you ever see one or ever speak with one?

WIDOW GREELY. You are growing light-minded, Peter Canavan, to think that you spoke with one yourself.

CANAVAN. Don't be calling me Peter! It's Your Worship I am to-day!

WIDOW DEENY. Is it Mayor you are now? It made you very consequential, you to have taken the oath!

CANAVAN. I'll have no traffic at all with traitors! I have the sacred commission to bring the country to loyal simplicity. Give me here the ledger. It's on that I will administer the oath.

WIDOW GREELY. Didn't you get very stiff with taking office? Or may be it is humbugging you are?

CANAVAN. You will see I am not humbugging. When I didn't spare my own brother, I will not spare yourselves or any rebel at all.

WIDOW GREELY. Was it some wind from the north made you turn about in a blast?

CANAVAN. Here now, don't be wilful, you yourselves will give an example to the whole district. You will swear on this book, the way I did on the shoe, with all your wit, will, and cunning, to support the authority of the Queen.

WIDOW GREELY (*turning her back to him*). The hearing is failing on me this while back by cause of cold I got through beetling the clothes.

WIDOW DEENY (*turning her back*). An oath is no thing to be taking, when you are likely not to keep it in the end. The beneficial of baptism you'd lose breaking it, and maybe you would never see God. (*They edge towards door.*)

CANAVAN (*getting between them and door*). Let you be humble now, and limber in your heart, and you'll find me to be kind. Sure it is through kindness I am wishful to bring you, the same as myself, under the strength of the Queen.

WIDOW GREELY. Her strength might not be as lasting as you think. Sure the Pope has his blessing promised to the generation that will bring her low.

CANAVAN. Ah, Job himself that got the heavens on the head of his patience, would grow surly having dealings with ye. The world would hear him yelling, and he to be arguing with a hag.

WIDOW DEENY. I wonder at you to be speaking such uncomely words! Our own old fathers were in this place before ever there was a Canavan in Scartana!

CANAVAN. Is that the way you are fleering at one in authority? Don't be turning me to be your enemy! Force you to take out a license for your clear starching I will! Using foreign importations you are, and paying no taxes to the Queen!

WIDOW GREELY. We are no clutch of pullets to be frighted by a cloud or a kite!

CANAVAN. I'll frame and fashion your manners for you! The next day you'll be late with the washing, I'll indict you for default of appearance! Tag and rag from the riverside to be correcting the Mayor on the bench!

WIDOW GREELY. I'd sooner be boiled, burned, baked, and roasted in that oven, and a hundred heating it, than give in to your orders at all!

CANAVAN. Quit now being sto stubborn and so disorderly! If you are deaf you are not dumb. You'd break the heart of any man, or any two men, in the house.

WIDOW DEENY. It is easy seen by your talk you were never of the blooded gentry! What right at all has the like of you to bereave us of our religion and our laws?

CANAVAN. Is it your strength you would try against me? It is little I pay heed to your threats! The time God made wicked cows, he gave them short horns.

WIDOW DEENY. We are well able to revenge ourselves. Whatever may be done in this district, it's the telling of the story is with us!

WIDOW GREELY. Have we no curses do you think? Let there be no path and no prosperity before you, from now to the womb of judgment!

WIDOW DEENY. A gapped shaving to you! And a Monday hair-cutting! And the blood of your body to be in the bosom of your shirt!

CANAVAN. I'll not let you quit this till I'll get you hunted with hounds! Don't be thinking to escape me now. Rebellion is all one with witchcraft, the ancient authors said that! (*Seizes and pushes them into corner.*)

WIDOW GREELY. Well now, Mayor Canavan, it is you has gained great courage and great strength!

CANAVAN. Why wouldn't I have courage? I am Mayor of Scartana, I am safe from this out. I am on the side of the strongest. I am Mayor in the Queen's service, and I have this shoe in my hand!

(*Enter* HEADLEY, *his shoe hanging round his neck. He has a gun in his hand, which he lays down.*)

HEADLEY. Where is that pedlar? I have searched the Castle, he is not there.

CANAVAN. He came here out of the Castle, and he is gone away out of this.

HEADLEY. He did not lose much time.

CANAVAN. It was I hastened him.

HEADLEY. You should have kept him.

CANAVAN. A worthless fellow!

HEADLEY. A prize—did you hear what *she* said? (*Taps shoe.*)

CANAVAN. I did, well. (*Taps other shoe.*)

HEADLEY. She said she would wish——

CANAVAN. The place left empty.

HEADLEY. The deserter's head.

CANAVAN. I forgot that.

HEADLEY. You told her he was a deserter.

CANAVAN. So he was, and a rebel.

HEADLEY. She asked for his head to put under her royal feet.

CANAVAN. So she would, too, and she being without her shoes.

HEADLEY. It would have been a love gift for me to proffer to her. I hurried back when I brought it to mind. I thought it would not take much time to whip off his head.

CANAVAN. I knew it was to be beheaded we were.

HEADLEY. I have wasted time, I have lost half an hour, I have come back looking for a gift for my sovereign and you have thrown it away. (*He strikes* CANAVAN *with shoe.*)

CANAVAN. Stop railing at me and attacking me! I have a shoe of my own! (*Threatens him with it.*) I am grown now to be as brave as a lion!

HEADLEY (*weeping*).

It had been worth a ballad or a sonnet

To lay that head where she could step upon it!

WIDOW DEENY. His own kinsman's head. But he knows well what sort of a present would the Queen like.

WIDOW GREELY. Ah, what signifies one head to her, unless it might belong to a bishop or a priest?

WIDOW DEENY. It is best for us to be going home; it is milking time—but we might pick up some little thing to bring along with us. There is a good ruff there on the hearth—I suppose it fell out of Antony's pack.

WIDOW GREELY. There are more of his wearables in the chimney (*She pulls down dress with tongs.*)—very grand gaudy stuff indeed. (*Feels it.*)

HEADLEY. That dress! What is it—what is it (*Seizes it.*)—that dress, those flowers—that hem—surely that is the hem that I kissed!

WIDOW DEENY. A nice broad hem it is, and well sewed.

HEADLEY. Get out of this, woman! Leave that alone! That is no thing for you to handle! (*Drives them out.*)

WIDOW DEENY (*at door*). A very unmannerly man! (*They go out.*)

HEADLEY (*pulling bodice down from chimney*). That silk—I am making no mistake—that ruff, that headpiece—What has happened—what does it mean—there is no delusion—that *is* the hem that I kissed.

CANAVAN (*who has sat down at table examining shoe*). It is the right shoe is mine. Then yours must be the left. It is the right should mean the most share of favour.

HEADLEY (*wildly*). What is it has happened? You were here—where is she? Where is the Queen's Majesty—did you see her leave the room in the Castle?

CANAVAN. What way would I see her? "Close your eyes and your ears," she said, and I put down my head in the bed. Would you think I would break the first order she laid upon me?

HEADLEY. But her dress is here—you must know something——

CANAVAN. When I rose my head and looked around, there was no sign of her at all, and I made my way home. But quick as I was, that lying rogue Antony was here before me.

HEADLEY. What was he doing?

CANAVAN. He was thrusting something up the chimney with the two hands of a tongs.

HEADLEY. The Saints of Heaven preserve us! What did he say?

CANAVAN. I asked him nothing, and he told me nothing, unless lies. It was well to get quit of him. He would be no sort of credit to a loyal man at all.

HEADLEY (*shaking him*). Don't you see what has happened?

CANAVAN. He has made off, and my joy be with him.

HEADLEY. You were his abettor!

CANAVAN. A very unkind thing for you to say.

HEADLEY. You are concealing his crime.

CANAVAN. Stop that, I will not be molested! I have the Queen's right shoe! I will not quail before any man!

HEADLEY. You miserable villain! Don't you see I have discovered that your fellow criminal has killed the Queen!

CANAVAN. Killed the Queen is it?

HEADLEY. You saw him hiding her dress in the chimney.

CANAVAN. I suppose that was it now.

HEADLEY. He had made an end of her first!

CANAVAN. You say he did that?

HEADLEY. He must have done it.

CANAVAN. Well now, that is a great overthrow!

HEADLEY. What can he have done with the body? He could not have carried it down the Castle stairs?

CANAVAN. There was a rope from the window.

HEADLEY. I saw it! A rope from the window, ribbons on it—it is certain he let down the body into the river!

CANAVAN. That was a good thought now.

HEADLEY. There is a strong current in the stream that would sweep it away.

CANAVAN. Out into the sea. So it would too. It's with mermaids she'll be doing her travelling from this out, grabbing well-looking men from the rocks.

HEADLEY. But her death will be heard of.

CANAVAN. It is certain it cannot be long hid.

HEADLEY. The murderer will be searched for.

CANAVAN. He is safe enough, never fear.

HEADLEY. Some one will be suspected. Essex will take revenge.

CANAVAN. He may not have the chance. It is not himself will be uppermost now, not having the support of the Queen.

HEADLEY. You will be questioned—they will put you on the rack.

CANAVAN. They need not, I will tell all before the torture will begin.

HEADLEY. They will say you did it. They will think you yourself have killed the Queen.

CANAVAN. What do you take me for? What an opinion you have of me! I would not take the credit from the man that deserves it, and that is my only brother, Antony Canavan!

HEADLEY. You confess it was he did it?

CANAVAN (*examining clothes*). I never thought now he would have the force to do a thing like that, and she so fine a woman and he no great hero of a man.

HEADLEY. Was it done with a sword?

CANAVAN. A sword would be the quickest, I would have heard a shot of a gun.

HEADLEY. A stroke from behind?

CANAVAN. No discredit if it was. It would be very hard to stand up and to face a woman of that sort.

HEADLEY. To do it so quick!

CANAVAN. Within three minutes, I suppose, of you yourself going out. Well, Antony Canavan, I never thought you would turn out so great a man!

HEADLEY. The black-hearted coward!

CANAVAN. Coward yourself! You yourself kneeled to the Queen, and humbled yourself, and cried for mercy. But my brother, without arms, or help of soldiers, or troops at his call, or meat in his stomach, it was he made an end of her. A great man, a great man, there can be no doubt at all of that!

HEADLEY. You make a boast of it?

CANAVAN. Why wouldn't I make a boast and he my own brother? Oh, he will leave a great name after him in history! "Queen Elizabeth was very strong," they will say, "she killed lords and priests and bishops; but poor Antony Canavan was stronger; it was he killed Queen Elizabeth!"

HEADLEY. Oh, stop, stop! (*Puts hands over ears.*)

CANAVAN. I will be going now to join him. The whole country will be up supporting him. Essex did you say? Neither Essex nor another will dare let a squeak out of himself, before the man that made an end of the Queen!

HEADLEY. You boasted of your loyalty!

CANAVAN. So I am loyal, to be sure. Loyal to the strongest, I always said I would be that. I have but one head only, and the place I will shelter it is under the strongest shelter to be had.

HEADLEY. A terrible thought has come to me. Suppose, after all, the danger may fall upon me? It may be known it was to see myself she came!

CANAVAN. Don't be affrighted. I will protect you. Sure I said before you are of our own blood, a Canavan, Henry Canavan. Who would be safe if the kindred of Antony Canavan would not be safe?

HEADLEY. Yes, yes, we are of one blood, but it would be better the crime not to be found out. I will destroy all the testimony. I will burn these clothes! (*Seizes dress.*)

CANAVAN (*stopping him*). Quiet now and easy. There will be two words to that.

HEADLEY. Her death cannot be hidden. But who can prove that she came to Scartana? Even Essex does not know that.

CANAVAN. Wait a while. I say these testimonies should be kept.

HEADLEY. She said she kept her coming a secret.

CANAVAN. Just so. And I, being Antony's brother, they might not accept my witness.

HEADLEY. They may think she was drowned crossing some stream.

CANAVAN. And the clergy would be taking the praise of it, saying they brought it about by their prayers.

HEADLEY. Let them think Essex himself made away with her.

CANAVAN. So help me, no Englishman will ever take that credit to himself.

HEADLEY. She had to pass many enemies.

CANAVAN. I wouldn't doubt O'Donnell to say he did it, or O'Neill to be claiming it for the North.

HEADLEY (*putting dress and ruff on hearth*). What can they accuse me of without evidence?

CANAVAN. It is I myself and Antony will carry the evidence through Munster! (*Takes dress off hearth,* HEADLEY *puts it back.*) I will frustrate that! Antony will have it for a banner through the whole of the five provinces!

HEADLEY. Give me the tinder-box. I will kindle the heap!

CANAVAN. Here is an answer to your kindling! (*Takes water-jug and empties it on hearth.*) Am I going to allow evidence to be made away with by fire? It seems to me you are forgetting that I am Mayor of Scartana.

(*Enter the* TWO WIDOWS.)

WIDOW GREELY. Take warning, Miller Canavan, your brother is coming against you with a pick.

WIDOW DEENY. To bring away your gold by force he is going, where you would not give it for his aid.

WIDOW GREELY. Bad as you treated us a while ago, we would be loth to see a neighbour to be robbed.

(ANTONY *comes in with a pick, goes to board near door, and begins to rip it up.*)

ANTONY. This is the board where the widows said it was hid—the second board from the door. It is no robbery I to get what I was promised, and what I am in need of for a way of living.

(WIDOWS *rush to stop him.*)

WIDOW GREELY. Let you quit robbing the miller, I tell you, or I'll have you scandalised through the town.

CANAVAN. Whisht your wordy mouth! Leave meddling with my brother!

HEADLEY. Oh, he is tearing up a board! It is under that board he has the body buried! He is going to bring it away! Oh, I will not see it! I will not look at those royal bloodstains on that pearl-white neck! Oh, it would haunt me, it would start me in a faint! No, no, I will not look! (*Turns away and hides his face in ruff.*)

ANTONY (*shaking off* CANAVAN). I got the promise, and I will bring away my share of money in spite of you!

CANAVAN. Oh, Antony, my dear brother, take it! Take all that I have!

ANTONY (*taking a bag from under board*). I'll get handsome work now! I'm thankful to you, Peter. It's a wonder you to have turned kind.

CANAVAN. Ah, why wouldn't I be kind after the kindness you have showed to the whole nation? Take my cloak now, and my chain to put around your neck!

ANTONY. It's not an hour hardly since I was a ragtail, and a fly-swarm, and a rebel, and a breaker of the laws!

CANAVAN. You can make new laws yourself now for the good of the whole nation!

ANTONY. You drove me out, where I would not swear to the Queen!

CANAVAN. What ailed you not telling me you had done better than to swear to her? Take it, take it, take all my treasure and my gold! You will want it, you will want it for the suit a general should wear! All that I have is yours! You are my only brother! I am proud of you, Antony Canavan, for the deed you have done this day! (*Hugs him.*)

HEADLEY. Is he gone? Has he the body carried away? No, but he is there still! Wretch! Monster! Traitor! Rebel! I will not leave you living. (*Draws sword and rushes at him.*)

WIDOW GREELY (*seizing him*). Whatever Antony Canavan may have done, I will not let a Queen's man attack him.

WIDOW DEENY. The Queen's army to make an attack on him, we are sure he has done some good thing!

CANAVAN. Bad cess to you, Henry Canavan! Let you quit making that assault. Tie him to the chair. I'll learn him manners! I'll learn him to attack my only brother! (*He and the* WIDOWS *overcome* HEADLEY *and tie him to chair.* CANAVAN *and* ANTONY *kneel down by board searching for more money.*)

HEADLEY. Send me back to Lord Essex! It is as well for me go confess all. "She is dead," I will say, "it is my fault, it was on my account she came here, on the head of my features and my face. Disfigure my face," I will say. "Destroy my beauty, strike off the hand that wrote the verses that brought the Queen to her death!"

WIDOW GREELY. Brought her to her death! Are you in earnest saying the Queen was brought to her death?

HEADLEY. It is true, it is true. But it was that traitor Antony that killed her, it was he struck that wicked blow.

ANTONY (*making ready to go*). I wonder, Peter, for what length of time should I be a miller before I'd get the name of a hare's heart like your own?

WIDOW GREELY. You to have a hare's heart! The heart of a roadside gander, and it defending its brood!

WIDOW DEENY. The heart of a horned heifer, its first calf being brought away!

CANAVAN. The candle of bravery and courage you are, the tower of the western world! Oh, my comely Antony, it is to you I will give the branch!

ANTONY. Have you a mind to destroy me and to shorten my days? Let ye stop, I say, from praising me and from putting up my name.

CANAVAN. Bashful he is, no way high in himself, as bashful and as humble as a child of two years! I tell you, Antony Canavan, it is you are the pride of your race!

WIDOW GREELY. Our blessing for ever on the man that put terror on the heart of the tyrant!

WIDOW DEENY. A shout on the three heights of Ireland for the mightiest hero of the Gael! (*They shout and with* CANAVAN *begin to dance slowly round him.*)

ANTONY. What at all are you doing? What at all have you against me? Is it to destroy me you would, putting a big name on me to lead me to my death? (*They shout* "Hi for Antony.") Is there no one at all in the whole country to shout for that you must go shouting for myself? You to have done that, I am a gone man. It is my grave every shout is digging in the clay, and it's boards for my burying you are readying with your dance. It would be as well for me to go out, and meet my death in some fight.

CANAVAN. To fight is it? There will be no fighting where you will be, and where myself will be! The enemy will run before us the same as long-tailed lambs! It is the sight of my brave Antony will set them flocking into the tide!

WIDOW DEENY (*looking out of door*). Oh, let you look! A troop of soldiers and Lord Essex at the head of them! They are passing down the road by the mill-stream!

ANTONY (*sits down beside* HEADLEY). So long as you are all joined in a league for to bring about my death, I will wait for it here and now. There is no use at all trying to escape a prophecy. Give me your hand, Henry Canavan, it is the one blow might put an end to the two of us.

HEADLEY (*clinging to him*). It is happy for the widows spinning wool and flax and tow, and that never went knocking about among the great ones of the earth. It would be best for the two of us, Antony, we never to have laid an eye at all on the Queen, as it is little she served us in the end.

WIDOW GREELY. Will you look at the pair of them trembling, as weak as water and as pale! It is you yourself, Miller Canavan, is the hardiest in the house at this time.

CANAVAN (*seizing gun*). Ha! Is that so? So it is too. Queen Elizabeth was strong, Antony Canavan was stronger—what is he now beside me? Wait now till I have my eye cocked to take aim at Lord Essex and his men. (*Takes aim out of door*.)

WIDOW DEENY. Do not be so daring, to destroy the whole army, and you without protection unless it is the thatch above your head.

CANAVAN. Little I care for them! I'm as venturesome as a robin in the snow! I would fire, and it to bring earthquakes! (*Fires off gun from door, and falls back from kick of gun*. WIDOWS *shriek as he fires, then look cautiously out*.)

WIDOW GREELY. We are as good as dead this time anyway.

WIDOW DEENY. No, but taking off his hat Lord Essex is, and saluting the miller as he goes.

ANTONY. A salute to himself he thought it to be, there being no bullet in the gun.

CANAVAN (*looking out of door*). To take off his hat he did! To bow and to bare his head he did! To bid his men hasten their horses he did, and to run before myself and my gun! (*Turns and holds out his arm over* HEADLEY *and* ANTONY.) Let you not be daunted! It is I will protect the whole of ye! Where is fear? It is banished from the world from this day! The strongest! Isn't it the fool I was wasting time—wasting the years—looking here and there for the strongest? I give you my word, it was not till this present minute that I knew the strongest to be myself!

Curtain.

THE WHITE COCKADE

THE WHITE COCKADE

PERSONS

    PATRICK SARSFIELD. *Earl of Lucan.*
    KING JAMES II.
    CARTER. *Secretary to King James.*
    A POOR LADY.
    MATT KELLEHER. *Owner of an inn at Duncannon.*
    MARY KELLEHER. *His wife.*
    OWEN KELLEHER. *His son.*
    FIRST SAILOR.
    SECOND SAILOR.
    FIRST WILLIAMITE.
    SECOND WILLIAMITE.
    A CAPTAIN AND OTHER WILLIAMITES.

ACT I

SCENE. *An Inn kitchen at Duncannon.* OWEN KELLEHER *lying on the hearth playing jackstones.* MRS. KELLEHER *rubbing a bit of meat. A barrel beside her.*

OWEN. One—and one—and five—that's scatters.

MRS. KELLEHER. Leave playing jackstones, Owen, and give me a hand salting the meat.

OWEN. Two—and two—and one—that's doubles. There is time enough. Sure it's not to-day it's wanted.

MRS. KELLEHER. What's put off till harvest is put off for ever. It's best to catch the pig by the leg when you get her. The French ship might be going before we have the barrels ready, and some other might get the profit.

OWEN. The ship didn't get orders yet from King James. The sailors were not sure was it to Dublin he would bid them go, or to some other place. It is time for us to be hearing news of him. I have a mind to go ask it.

MRS. KELLEHER. Come over and rub a bit of the meat, and leave thinking about King James. We hear enough talk of him, listening to poor Lady Dereen.

219

OWEN. You have not enough of salt to pack the meat till my father will bring it back from Ross.

MRS. KELLEHER. The lamb teaching its mother to bleat! If I have not itself, I have what serves for rubbing it. (*She pushes back dresser from before a side door.*) Be moving now, and come down to the cellar till we bring up another leg of the pork.

OWEN (*going on playing*). One—and one—and one—crow's nest.

MRS. KELLEHER (*going through door to cellar*). I give you my word it is as hard to make you stir as to make a hedgehog run.

(OWEN *whistles "The White Cockade."*)

MRS. KELLEHER (*coming back with another bit of meat*). It is yourself finds the hob a good harbourage!

OWEN. It is not worth my while to be bringing it up bit by bit— if it was to bring up the whole of it now——

MRS. KELLEHER. I suppose not! I wonder now what is worth your while if it is not to mind the place and the inn that will be coming to yourself some day. It is a poor hen that can't scratch for itself!

OWEN. There might be something worth doing outside this place.

MRS. KELLEHER (*scornfully*). There might! It's the hills far off that are green!

OWEN. It is beyond the hills I would like to be going. There is no stir at all in this place.

MRS. KELLEHER. What is it at all you are wanting or talking about?

OWEN. There is fighting going on through the country.

MRS. KELLEHER. And for all the profit it will bring ourselves it might be the fighting of the hornless cows! It is best for us to be minding our own business.

OWEN. There used to be great fighters in Ireland in the old times.

MRS. KELLEHER. If there were, they had no other trade! Every crane according to its thirst. Believe me, if they had found as good a way of living as what you have, they would not have asked to go rambling. I know well it is an excuse you are making, with your talk of fighting and your songs, not to be doing the work that is at your hand. You are as lazy as the tramp that will throw away his bag. You would have got the sluggard's prize from Aristotle of the books!

OWEN. Well, it's good to be best at something.

MRS. KELLEHER. If you saw a car and horse coming at you, you would not stir out of the rut! You would spend your night on the floor sooner than go up a ladder to the loft! Stir! You would not stir yourself to turn the crispy side of a potato if you had but the one bite only!

OWEN. One—and four—high castles.

MRS. KELLEHER. I tell you a day will come when you will grow to the ground the way you never will reach to heaven!

OWEN. It is time for you to leave off faulting me. There is some one coming to the door.

MRS. KELLEHER (*looking out of door*). It is the poor Lady. She wasn't here this good while. It is a pity she to have gone spending all for the King the way she did, and to go in beggary and misery ever after. (OWEN *sings*)

> The cuckoo has no word to say,
> Sharp grief has put us under rent,
> The heavy cloud is on the Gael,
> But comely James will bring content!

MRS. KELLEHER. I believe it is herself put the half of those songs in your head. (*Pulls dresser over door.*) It is best shut this door. There is no use too many eyes seeing it.

(OLD LADY *comes in. Her hand is over her eyes as if half blind. She wears ragged clothes that have once been handsome.*)

MRS. KELLEHER. You are welcome, my poor Lady Dereen.

LADY. I thank you, Mary Kelleher. I have always found a welcome in this house, and a shelter from the heat and the rain.

MRS. KELLEHER. Who should get a welcome here if you wouldn't get it, Lady? And I born and reared on your own estate before you lost it through the wars.

LADY. I have had great losses, but now I will have great gains. I lost all through Charles; I will get all back through James. My eyes are tired watching for the sun to rise in the east. The sun of our success is rising at last!

MRS. KELLEHER. It is time for success to come to yourself, Lady, indeed. I remember the time you had great riches.

LADY. I did not grudge anything, my lord did not grudge anything to Charles Stuart, our King. I shall be rich again now; I never lost my faith.

MRS. KELLEHER. Well, I would never have faith myself in the thing I wouldn't see.

LADY. I lost all through Charles; I will get all back through James!

MRS. KELLEHER. That you may, Lady. I would sooner you to have kept it when you had it. A wren in the fist is better than a crane on loan. It's hard getting butter out of a dog's mouth.

LADY. The Stuart has been under the mists of night. The sun is rising that will scatter them. The whole country is going out to help him. The young men are leaving the scythes in the meadows; the old men are leaving the stations and the blessed wells. Give me some white thing—some feathers—I have to make cockades for the King's men.

MRS. KELLEHER (*giving her feathers from the dresser*). Look at that now! These come as handy as a gimlet. I was plucking ducks yesterday for the captain of the French ship.

LADY (*taking feathers and beginning to fasten them together with shaking hands*). James, our own King, will bring prosperity to us all.

MRS. KELLEHER. So long as we get it, I wouldn't mind much what King brings it. One penny weighs as good as another, whatever King may have his head upon it. If you want to grow old, you must use hot and cold.

LADY. Is it nothing to you, Mary Kelleher, that the broken altars of the Faith will be built up again?

MRS. KELLEHER. God grant it! Though indeed, myself I am no great bigot. I would always like to go to a Protestant funeral. You would see so many well-dressed people at it.

LADY (*beginning to make another cockade*). I must be quick, very quick. There will be a hard battle fought. William, the Dutchman, has brought trained men from all the countries of Europe. James has gone out to meet him.

MRS. KELLEHER. Is it going to fight a battle he is? It is likely he will have sent orders to the French ship, so. It is to take his orders it was here. The dear knows where it might be tomorrow, and the pigs we have killed left on our hands! Only for you giving me no help the way you did, Owen, the meat would be nearer ready now than what it is. Look at him now, Lady; maybe he'll mind what you will say. Bid him leave lying on the floor at midday.

LADY. It is time you should get up, boy; there is plenty of work to do.

MRS. KELLEHER. That is what I am saying. Work for all hands.

LADY. Work for all, and no time to lose.

MRS. KELLEHER. That is what I am saying. What is put off till harvest——

LADY. It is not right for a young man with strong hands to be taking his ease. (OWEN *gets up and stands awkwardly.*)

MRS. KELLEHER. And his mother not sparing herself.

LADY. You lying there, while there is a friend out under the heat of the day fighting our battle.

MRS. KELLEHER. My poor man! So he is. Striving to bring the salt.

LADY (*giving* OWEN *a cockade*). Take that White Cockade. Go out, go northward. Join the King's army, go and fight for the King!

MRS. KELLEHER. To fight for the King, is it?

LADY. Hurry, hurry, you may be in time to strike a blow for him! (*Sings with a feeble voice*)

> Our heart's desire, our pleasant James,
> Our treasure and our only choice!

MRS. KELLEHER. Look here now, Lady, have sense. I have but the one son only, and is it sending him away from me you would be?

LADY. Our King has no son; he has false daughters. We must give our sons to the King!

MRS. KELLEHER. It is my opinion we must keep them to mind ourselves. What profit would he get joining the King's army? It is not the one thing to go to town and come from it.

LADY (*putting hand on her arm*). It would be a pity to disappoint so great a friend.

MRS. KELLEHER. That is true, but reason is reason. I have but the one son to help me; and it is what I say: you can't whistle and eat oatmeal; the gull can't attend the two strands; words won't feed the friars. How will Owen mind this place, and he maybe shot as full of holes as a riddle?

OWEN. When you have your minds made up if it's to go fighting I am, or to go rubbing the bacon I am, it will be time enough for me to stir myself.

LADY. Do you grudge your service? Will you betray the King as the English betrayed him? O my heart leaps up with my pleasant Stuart!

OWEN. I would like well to go serve the King; but I don't know how could I do it.

LADY. You say that because of idleness. It is through idleness you have come to have a coward's heart, the heart of a linnet, of a trader, a poor, weak spirit, a heart of rushes.

223

MRS. KELLEHER. You are too hard now, Lady, upon the boy. Leave him alone. There is no man knows which is best, hurry or delay. It's often it's not better to be first than last. Many a tattered colt makes a handsome horse. The first thread is not of the piece. It's not the big men cut all the harvest. When the times comes, the child comes. Every good comes by waiting.

LADY. King James in the country wanting all his helpers!

MRS. KELLEHER. Let every herring hang by its own tail.

LADY. It is for our comfort he has come.

MRS. KELLEHER. He might. It's to please itself the cat purrs.

LADY (putting hand on OWEN's shoulder). The Stuart in the field!

MRS. KELLEHER (seizing other shoulder). The meat in the cellar!

LADY. Our hero in danger!

MRS. KELLEHER. Our bacon in danger!

LADY. Our prince under mists!

MRS. KELLEHER. Our meat under mildew!

LADY. Oh! The great Stuart!

MRS. KELLEHER (striking it). The empty barrel!

(OWEN turns from one to the other, undecided. Voices are heard singing a French song.)

LADY. Is that the army of the King?

MRS. KELLEHER. It is what is worse. It's the French sailors coming for the meat and it not ready.

(TWO SAILORS come in singing)

> Madame, si vous voulez danser
> Vite je vous prie de commencer
> Avec l'air des Français,
> Avec l'air de la Cour.

FIRST SAILOR. We are come, Madame, for the pork and the bacon.

SECOND SAILOR. And de sau-sa-ges.

MRS. KELLEHER. I haven't them ready yet.

FIRST SAILOR. We must sail this night before morning.

MRS. KELLEHER. Did you get any orders from King James?

FIRST SAILOR. We did not get them. He is fighting in the north, at some river. We go to Dublin. If he succeed, we carry news to France. If he is beaten, he will want help from France. We sail at sunrise when the tide is high.

MRS. KELLEHER. Well, look now; I will have the meat for you before that.

FIRST SAILOR. All right. There is moon. We will come to the pier before sunrise, after the midnight.

MRS. KELLEHER. There is a quick way. Maybe you don't know the outer door to the cellar?

SECOND SAILOR. I do know it. I did put wine in there last week—no duty; no douane. (*Puts finger on nose.*)

    (MATT KELLEHER *comes bursting in. He throws a bag of salt on the floor.*)

MRS. KELLEHER. Here is himself, and he running like a hare before hounds. Give me here the salt.

MATT. Salt! salt! salt! Who would be talking of salt?

MRS. KELLEHER. The ship is going.

MATT. Where is the use of salt on such a day as this, unless it might be to make a man drouthy?

MRS. KELLEHER. I tell you I was as idle without it as a smith without bellows.

MATT. To make a man drouthy! To give him a good thirst, the way he will drink to the King.

MRS. KELLEHER. Indeed, if signs are signs, I think you yourself have been drinking to the King!

MATT. We will all drink to the King! Where are the glasses?

MRS. KELLEHER. Quiet yourself now. You are too good a customer to yourself; putting on the mill the straw of the kiln.

MATT. Would you begrudge me so much as one glass on a day like this?

MRS. KELLEHER. What has happened on this day more than any other day?

MATT. This day has brought news of the battle, I tell you—of the great battle at the Boyne!

FIRST SAILOR. The Boyne—that is it! That is the same story we heard.

MATT. Where would you hear your story? It was away in Ross I got mine. There was news brought to the barracks there.

MRS. KELLEHER. Tell me now, was the battle fought in earnest?

MATT. Fought is it? It is it that was fought! A great battle—the ground that was hard turning soft, and the ground that was soft turning hard, under the trampling of feet! The sea coming in on the land, and the land going out into the sea! Fire from the edges of every sword! The blood falling like a shower in harvest time!

The air black with ravens; the river reddened with blood; Sarsfield going through the field the same as fire through furze.

MRS. KELLEHER. What there is good comes out in the blood. Sure he is of the race of Conall Cearnach. What would an apple be like but an apple? What would the cat's son do but kill mice?

MATT. King James raging like a lion in every gap!

LADY. Oh! I knew it! I knew it! The brave Stuart!

MRS. KELLEHER. And who was it, will you tell me, that won in the fight?

MATT. Sure, amn't I telling you, if you would listen? The man has won that should win, great King James!

LADY. I knew the sun would rise at last for victory!

MATT. You will get your rights now, Lady. We'll all get our rights. (*Sings*)

> Three times the fairest of the Scots,
> The blossomed branch, the Phœnix rare,
> Our secret love, our only choice,
> The shining candle of the war!

LADY. My lord spent all upon Charles. James will pay all back again!

MATT. He will, he will! You will get your estates, Lady, and your white halls! We will drink the cellar dry the day you get your estates. There will be red wine of Spain running through your white halls!

LADY. I have his promise! I have the King's seal to his promise!
(*She takes a large seal and folded parchment from a bag hanging at her side and shows it.*)

MATT. It is a good seal—a grand seal. Drink a health, I say, to the King's seal! Let me go down to the cellar for spirits—no, but for wine!
(*He pushes back dresser.* MRS. KELLEHER *pulls him from the door.*)

MRS. KELLEHER. You will not go down. Thirst makes thirst!

MATT (*to* SAILORS). Go down there, I say. Bring up a bottle— two bottles—plenty of bottles! (*They go down.*)

LADY. I will go to Dublin. I will go to his Court. I will show him the promise and the seal.

MATT. You will, ma'am. He can't deny the seal.

LADY. I will put on my silks and my velvets. I will have jewels about my neck. I will bid my waiting-women to spread out my dress. (*Makes a gesture as if spreading out a train.*)

MATT. It is you will look well, Lady, as you did in the old times, with your silks and your jewels.

LADY. I will come to the door. The coach will stop—the young lords will hand me out of it—my own young kinsmen will be there.

MATT. I will go see you in the coach, Lady. It is I myself will open the door!

LADY. They will bring me to the throne-room. I will leave my cloak at the door. I will walk up to the throne! (*She walks a few steps.*)

MATT (*walking crookedly*). I will walk up myself. I would like well to see the King on his throne.

LADY (*curtsying*). A curtsy to the right to the Queen—a curtsy to the left to the princesses.

MATT (*curtsying*). That is it, that is it! We will curtsy to the princesses.

LADY. The King will smile at me. I will take out the King's seal. (*Touches it.*) I will kneel and kiss his hand.

MATT. I will kneel—no, I will not. (*Stumbles and kneels.*) There, I did now in spite of myself. Here, Mary, help me up again.

MRS. KELLEHER. Stop where you are, Kelleher, and be ashamed of yourself. When wine goes in, wit goes out.

OWEN (*helping* THE LADY *up*). All will go well with you now, Lady, since the King has gained the day.

MRS. KELLEHER. Maybe he was not the winner after all. It is often we heard news from Ross that wouldn't be true after.

MATT. Why wouldn't he win? He has the prayers of the people with him.

LADY. He has God with him.

OWEN. He has Sarsfield with him.

LADY. Oh! who will go to the King? Who will go for news of the King?

OWEN. I will go.

LADY. Yes, go, go! Here, take these to give to the King's men. (*She gives him cockades.*)

MRS. KELLEHER. Do not go until we are sure is the battle over. The last of a feast is better than the first of a fight.

OWEN. I will go now. I delayed long enough. I wish I had gone in time for the fighting.

MRS. KELLEHER. Well, since he is the winner—a friend in Court is better than a coin in the pocket—it might be for profit.

(OWEN *begins washing hands and face in a basin. Puts on coat.* SAILORS *bring up an armful of bottles from cellar.*)

227

MATT (*still on the floor, seizing a bottle*). Here's to the King's health, I say!

(*The* SAILORS *give him glasses; he opens bottle, fills them, and they hand them round.*)

LADY (*touching glass with her lips, and throwing it down*). The King and the King's right!

MRS. KELLEHER. The King and the Catholics in fashion!

OWEN. The King that fought the battle!

SAILORS. The King and France!

MATT. The King and wine without duty!

ALL TOGETHER. King James and Ireland!

ALL (*singing*)

O well-tuned harp of silver strings,
O strong green oak, O shining Mars,
Our hearts' desire, fair James our King,
Our great Cuchulain in the war!

Curtain.

ACT II

Scene I

SCENE. *A wood.* JAMES *sitting on a camp stool. He is richly dressed, and wears an Order.* CARTER *standing beside him.* SARSFIELD *pointing with sword to a map on the ground.*

SARSFIELD. If your Majesty will look at the plan I have marked on this map, you will see how we can make up for the defeat of the Boyne. The news we have had of William's march makes it very simple. He will be in our hands by morning. You know what we have to do to-night. To-morrow we shall be dictating terms from Limerick.

JAMES. Yes, yes, you told me all that. I wonder if this wood is quite safe. (*Looks round.*)

SARSFIELD. If our army had to fall back, it fell back in good order. We have guns, stores, horses. We have plenty of troops to strengthen Athlone. We can keep the mass of the enemy from passing the Shannon.

JAMES. I hope the bridge we crossed that last little river by has been broken so that no one can follow us.

SARSFIELD. Kilkenny must be strengthened too. Waterford is loyal. Munster and Connacht are safe. Our success will give us back Dublin. In half an hour our horses will be rested. We must be at Clonmel before midnight.

JAMES. But there is a troop of William's men somewhere about. We might fall into their hands.

SARSFIELD. They are in small divisions. We and our few men will be more than a match for them.

JAMES. Of course, of course; but we must not risk our lives.

CARTER. Not a doubt of it! The King's life must not be put in danger!

SARSFIELD. Danger! Who says that? Who said it at the Boyne? Was it you drove the King from the battle? Bad advisers! Bad advisers! He who says "danger" is a bad adviser.

CARTER. I did nothing—it was His Majesty's own doing.

JAMES. Yes, yes, of course. I am more than a soldier. I have the whole kingdom to think of.

CARTER. Not a doubt of it. But you and I, Sarsfield, have only ourselves to think of.

SARSFIELD. You and I—may be—this dust (*striking himself*)—that dust of yours—has the King's livery made us of the one baking? No, no; there is some leaven in this dough. (*To the King*) Rouse yourself, sir. Put your hand to the work.

JAMES. I suppose I must carry out this plan of a surprise.

SARSFIELD. That is right, sir. Carry it out and the Boyne will be forgotten.

JAMES. Is that some noise?   (*Starts.*)

SARSFIELD. It is but the trampling of our own horses.

JAMES. Just go, Sarsfield, and see to the breaking of that bridge. If we are caught here by those murderous Dutch, your plans will be ended with a rope or a scaffold.

SARSFIELD. I will send orders on to Clonmel. The Boyne will be forgotten! —forgotten!   (*Goes out.*)

JAMES. I hope Sarsfield knows what he is talking about.

CARTER. H'm—he may.

JAMES. If we are sure of winning——

CARTER. Just so.

JAMES. He says we are sure.

CARTER. He does.

JAMES. I hope there will be not much more fighting.

CARTER. Or any.

JAMES. That would be best; if they would give in without a fight.

CARTER. Best, indeed.

JAMES. But if there is danger——

CARTER. There is always danger.

JAMES. Of another battle——

CARTER. Or a surprise.

JAMES. I would prefer to be elsewhere. It is all very well for those who have a taste for fighting. I had it once myself—when I was a boy. But it has gone from me now with the taste for green apples.

CARTER. Not a doubt of it.

JAMES. A king's life does not belong to himself.

CARTER. He must not let it be taken.

JAMES. He must not let it be risked.

CARTER. That is what I meant.

JAMES. Now if we had come to the sea——

CARTER. We would be handy to it.

JAMES. If there were a French ship——

CARTER. And a fair wind.

JAMES. We might—what is that?

(OWEN's *voice heard singing* "*The White Cockade*.")

CARTER. It is a friend—he is singing "The White Cockade."

OWEN (*comes in singing*)

> The heavy cloud is on the Gael,
> But comely James will bring content.

JAMES. Where are you going, boy?

OWEN. I am going looking for news of King James. (*Sits down and wipes his face.*) I'm after wringing my shirt twice, with respects to you. I would not have walked so far for any one living but the King! And it is bad news of him I am after getting.

JAMES. Then the defeat is known. What did you hear?

OWEN. I heard a great clattering of horses, and then I heard a fife and drum—a tune they were playing like this.

(*Whistles* "*Lillibulero*.")

JAMES. The rebels are here! It is "Lillibulero"!

OWEN. Then I saw a troop of men and of horses.

JAMES. Were they Dutch?

OWEN. They were not. They were as good speakers as myself.

Men from the north they were, and they were giving out as they passed that William had gained the day, and that King James was running, and if they got him, they would give his legs rest for a while.

JAMES. Heavens! What a terrible threat!

CARTER. Terrible, indeed! Is there no place where we could be safe?

OWEN. If you belong to King James, you would be safe where I come from, and that is the inn at the harbour of Duncannon.

JAMES. The harbour! Do many ships come in there?

OWEN. There do not. But there is one in it presently.

JAMES. An English ship?

OWEN. It is not, but a ship from France. But if it is itself, it is not long it will be in it. It will be sailing at sunrise. There will be a boat coming from it after midnight, for the meat my mother has them promised.

JAMES. I must go to Duncannon! Look here, boy, would it be safe if I—if the King himself were to go there to-night?

OWEN. Now that he is down, I think there is not one in the place but would carry a hurt dog if it belonged to King James.

JAMES. But tell me—if—I only say *if* the King should come and should be seen by anyone—is there any chance he would be known?

OWEN. Every chance. Sure he is well known by the songs.

JAMES. By the songs?

OWEN (*singing*)

> Curled locks like Angus of the Sidhe,
> Friendly, brave, bright, loving, fair;
> High hawk that gains the mastery,
> Cupid in peace, a Mars in war!

JAMES (*to* CARTER). It will be safer not to go till after dark. We must go quite quietly—we must leave our men and horses at a distance.

CARTER. That will be best.

JAMES. You must keep the inn clear, boy. You must keep the French boat till I come—till the King comes. He will knock at the door before midnight.

OWEN. Believe me he will get a good welcome! If it was known he was coming there would be a candle lighted in every harbour.

JAMES. No, no candles.

OWEN. I may as well be going now to make all ready. (*Goes out singing*)

Three times the fairest of the Scots,
My prince and my heart-secret, James,
Our treasure and our only choice—
The darling Cæsar of the Gael!

JAMES. That was a good chance. We can go on board at once, and slip away to France. I have done with this detestable Ireland.
(*Kicks the ground.*)

CARTER. And I.

JAMES. It might be as well——

CARTER. Well?

JAMES. Not to mention anything——

CARTER. I won't.

JAMES. That is, nothing more than the sending of despatches to —here he is coming.
(*Puts his finger to his lips.* CARTER *nods.* SARSFIELD *comes in.*)

SARSFIELD. I have sent orders to Clonmel, sir. A thousand of our men will have gathered there to meet us at midnight.

JAMES. I have changed my mind. I have had messages. I knew France would not desert me. There is a ship at Duncannon. I have despatches to send to King Louis. I will go to Duncannon to-night, and not to Clonmel.

SARSFIELD. We cannot afford that delay, sir. We should lose the chance of surprising the Dutch troop.

JAMES. That is enough, General Sarsfield. You will obey orders.

SARFIELD. Are they, sir, what is best for Ireland?

JAMES. Yes, yes, of course. She is a very good rod to beat England with.

SARSFIELD. Whatever use you may put her to, sir, you are bound to do your best for her now.

JAMES. Yes, yes, of course.

SARSFIELD. The troops coming to us must not be left to scatter again. They believe yet in the King. They are sure he will not betray them again——

JAMES. I am not betraying them. I am getting them help from France. You need say no more. When I think well of fighting I will fight; when I think well of retreating I will retreat.
(*He walks to end of stage and looks at himself in a hand-mirror.*)

CARTER. Not a doubt of it! I hope General Sarsfield will loyally follow your Majesty's orders.

SARSFIELD. Obey them? And what about Ireland—the lasting cry? Am I listening to that?

CARTER. You have sworn to obey the King.

SARSFIELD. Just so, just so, we have sworn.—He is our King— we have taken the oath. Well, is not a feather in a hat as good a cry as another? A feather in a hat, a King in a song:

> The darling Cæsar of the Gael,
> The great Cuchulain of the War!

(*Fife and drum hear playing "Lillibulero."*)

JAMES (*rushing back*). That is Lillibulero! Oh, the rebels are coming!

SARSFIELD. It is that troop we knew of. They are not many. We have enough men to stand against them.

(*Music heard, right.*)

JAMES. They are coming very close!

CARTER. Here, sir let us hide in the wood!

(*They run left.*)

JAMES. They are coming this way!

(*They cross to right. Music follows.*)

CARTER. Is it an army or an echo?

(*They run left again.*)

JAMES (*clinging to* SARSFIELD). It is all around us!

SARSFIELD (*taking up cloak which* JAMES *has dropped*). I can offer your Majesty's ears the protection of this cloak. (*Holds out cloak over them, as music dies away.*)

SCENE II

SCENE: *Inn kitchen, much as before, but without the barrel; night-time, candles burning.* OWEN *standing as if just come in.* MATT *and* MRS. KELLEHER *with back to audience listening to him.* OLD LADY *sitting, her head in her hands, rocking herself.*

MRS. KELLEHER. The King beaten! Sure they said first he had won. Well, the bottom comes out of every riddle at the last!

MATT. I had it in my mind there was some great misfortune coming upon us. I was trying to hearten myself through the whole of the morning. I give you my word, now, I am as sorry as if there was one dead belonging to me!

OWEN. Did you hear me, Lady, what I was telling?

LADY (*sitting up*). If it was true, it was a dark story, a dark sorrowful story!

(*She gets up and looks out of door into the darkness.*)

OWEN. King James is beaten surely.

LADY. The King beaten, and the moon in the skies not darkened!

OWEN. Beaten and wandering.

LADY. The King beaten, and the fish not dead in the rivers!

OWEN. Beaten and wandering and hunted.

(MATT KELLEHER *gives a groan at the end of each sentence.*)

LADY. The King beaten, and the leaves on the trees not withered! (*She turns from the door.*) The sun is a liar that rose in the east for victory. What was the sun doing that day? Where was God? Where was Sarsfield?

(*She walks up and down, wringing her hands.*)

MRS. KELLEHER. It is what I was often saying, there is nought in this world but a mist.

LADY. Where were the people that were wise and learned? Where were the troop readying their spears? Where are they till they smooth out this knot for me? (*Takes* OWEN *by the shoulders.*) Why did not the hills fall upon the traitors? Why did not the rivers rise against them?

MRS. KELLEHER. Sit down now, Lady, for a while. It's no wonder you to be fretting, and your lands and your means gone like froth on the stream. Sure the law of borrowing, is the loan to be broken.

LADY. I will not sit under a roof and my King under clouds. It is not the keening of one plain I hear, but of every plain. The sea and the waves crying through the harbour! The people without a lord but the God of glory! Where is he? Where is my royal Stuart? I will go out crying after the King!

(*She goes out.*)

MRS. KELLEHER. But is it surely true, Owen, that the King is coming to this house?

OWEN. Sure and certain sure.

MRS. KELLEHER. If we had but known, to have killed a sheep or a kid itself! I declare I would think more of him now than when he had all at his command.

OWEN. It is likely, indeed, he found no good table in the wood.

MRS. KELLEHER. The man without dinner is two to supper. Well, the cakes are baked, and eggs we have in plenty, and pork if we had but the time to boil it, and a bit of corned beef. Indeed if I had twenty times as much, I wouldn't begrudge it to the King.

MATT (*looking at bottles*). There is good wine for him anyway. The Frenchmen knew the best corner.

MRS. KELLEHER. Mind yourself, now.

MATT (*indignantly*). Do you think I would take so much as one drop from what I have put on one side for the rightful King?

MRS. KELLEHER. Give me a hand to get down the best delft. It's well I had the barrels packed out of the way. It's getting on for midnight. He might be here any time.

> (*Trampling of horses heard, and fife and drum playing "Lillibulero."*)

MATT. What is that? Is it the King that is coming?

OWEN. It is not; but King William's men that are looking for the King.

MRS. KELLEHER. Keep them out of this! Foxes in the hencoop!

OWEN. It is here they are coming, sure enough.

> (*Music comes nearer.* MRS. KELLEHER *hurriedly puts food in cupboard and flings a sack over bottles. Door is opened; two men of William's army come in. They have fife and drum.*)

FIRST WILLIAMITE. That is good! I smell supper.

SECOND WILLIAMITE. We are lucky to find an inn so handy.

FIRST WILLIAMITE. I knew where the inn was. I told the Newry troop to come meet us here. (*Turns to door.*) Here, you lads, go and spread yourselves here and there through the town: don't go far; I will fire two shots when you are wanted. (*Voices outside.*) "All right." "We'll do that, sir."

SECOND WILLIAMITE. I don't think King James is in these parts at all.

FIRST WILLIAMITE. There is a French ship in the harbour. He might be making for her.

SECOND WILLIAMITE. We will stop here anyway. We have a good view of the pier in the moonlight.

MRS. KELLEHER. I am loath to disoblige you, gentlemen, but you can't stop here to-night.

FIRST WILLIAMITE. Why do you say that? Inns were made to stop in.

MRS. KELLEHER. This is not an inn now—not what you would rightly call an inn—we gave up business of late—we were stumbling under the weight of it, like two mice under a stack.

FIRST WILLIAMITE. I wouldn't think so small a place would be so great a burden.

MRS. KELLEHER. A hen itself is heavy if you carry it far. It's best to give up in time. A good run is better than a bad battle. We got no comfort for ourselves—who is nearest the church is not nearest the altar.

FIRST WILLIAMITE. Quiet this woman, some of you. Where is the man of the house? The hen doesn't crow when there is a cock in the yard—you see, ma'am, I have proverbs myself.

MRS. KELLEHER. (*to* MATT). We must keep them out some way. (*To* WILLIAMITES.) There are no beds for you to get. The beds are damp. Aren't they, Matt?

MATT. Damp, indeed—rotten with damp.

OWEN. Damp and soaked with the drip from the roof.

FIRST WILLIAMITE. Beds! Are we asking for beds? It is not often we feel a blanket over us, thanks to King James. These chairs will do us well.

MRS. KELLEHER. You don't know what lay on those chairs last night!

FIRST WILLIAMITE. What was that?

MRS. KELLEHER. A corpse—wasn't it, Matt?

MATT. It was—a dead corpse.

OWEN. Cold and dead.

FIRST WILLIAMITE (*contemptuously*). Corpses! I was own brother to a corpse in the last scrimmage. A knock I got on the head. Sit down.

MRS. KELLEHER. It is likely you don't know what sickness did this one die of. Of a smallpox—didn't it, Matt?

MATT. It did. Of a pitted smallpox.

OWEN. And it left lying there without a coffin.

FIRST WILLIAMITE. It would be worse news if it had got a wake that had left the house bare.

MRS. KELLEHER. Bare! This is the house that is bare! I have a bad husband, haven't I, Matt?

MATT. What's that you are saying?

MRS. KELLEHER. A while drunk, a while in fury, tearing the strings and going mad! (*Giving him a nudge.*) And a son that is a gambler. (OWEN *starts, but she nudges him.*) Two hands scattering and but one saving. They spent all we had. There is nothing for you to find in the house, I tell you. It's hard to start a hare out of an empty bush!

SECOND WILLIAMITE (*taking sack off bottles.*) Here is something that looks better than holy water. (*Takes up bottle and uncorks it.*)

FIRST WILLIAMITE (*opening cupboard*). I see the scut of a hare in this bush!

(*Takes out meat.*)

SECOND WILLIAMITE (*drinking*). Faith, you have a strong cellar. (*Hands on bottle and opens another.*) Here, inn-keeper, have a glass of your own still—drink now to the King.

MATT. I will not. I will not touch one drop from those bottles that are for——

SECOND WILLIAMITE. Drink, man; drink till you are in better humour.

MATT (*taking glass*). Well, if I do, I call all to witness that I was forced to it! Four against one, and forced! (*Drinks and holds glass out again.*) And anyway, if I do (*Drinks*), it's not to your master I am drinking, but to King James!

FIRST WILLIAMITE. Little I care! I'd drink to any of them myself, if I had no other way to get it. Dutch or Scotch, there's no great difference. If we had a King of our own, that would be another story.

SECOND WILLIAMITE. You have taken your job under William.

FIRST WILLIAMITE. And amn't I doing the job, drinking the wine of a Jacobite? To fight for William by day, and to drink King James's wine by night, isn't that doing double service?

OWEN (*to* MRS. KELLEHER). I will go and turn back those that were coming.

MRS. KELLEHER. Do, and God be with you.

(*He goes to door.*)

FIRST WILLIAMITE. Stop here, youngster, and drink to the King.

OWEN. I will not.

FIRST WILLIAMITE. Well, stop and drink against the King.

OWEN. I must go. (*Puts hand on latch.*)

FIRST WILLIAMITE (*holding him*). You have nothing to do that is so easy as this.

OWEN. I have colts that are astray to put back on the right road.

FIRST WILLIAMITE. A fine lad like you to be running after colts, and King William wanting soldiers! Come, join our troop, and we'll make a corporal of you.

OWEN. Leave me alone. I have my own business to mind.

SECOND WILLIAMITE. The drill would take that stoop out of your shoulders.

FIRST WILLIAMITE. It would, and straighten his back. Wait till I drill you! I'll give you your first lesson. I'll have you as straight as a thistle before morning. See here now: left, right; left, right;

right about face. (*He holds him while the other swings him round.*)

SECOND WILLIAMITE. Give him the balance-step first. Now, youngster, balance step without gaining ground. (*Crooks up* OWEN's *leg.*) See now, this way; stand straight or you will fall over like a sack of potatoes. I should get promotion now; I am training recruits for King William.

MATT (*who is by the window*). Let him go, let him go. There are some persons coming. I hear them. Who now would be coming here so late as midnight?

SECOND WILLIAMITE. Are these our men?

FIRST WILLIAMITE. They are not. Our men will be riding.

OWEN (*passionately*). Let me go.

SECOND WILLIAMITE. You are not through your drill yet. Here now—(*A knocking at the door.*)

MATT. Customers, maybe. Wait till I open the door.

OWEN (*to* MRS. KELLEHER). Don't let him open it!

MRS. KELLEHER (*seizing him*). Leave opening the door, Matt Kelleher!

MATT. Let me alone! I will open it. It's my business to open the door.

(*He breaks from her.*)

MRS. KELLEHER. Stop, I tell you! What are you doing? (*Whispers.*) Don't you know that it might be King James.

MATT. King James! The King outside in the night and we not opening the door! Leave the doorway clear! A welcome, a great welcome to King James!

(WILLIAMITES *start up and seize muskets.* KELLEHER *flings the door open.* JAMES *comes in, followed by* CARTER *and* SARSFIELD.)

OWEN (*shouting*). Are you come, strangers, to join King William's men?

FIRST WILLIAMITE. They are wearing the white cockade!

SECOND WILLIAMITE. They belong to James, sure enough.

MATT (*seizing James's hand*). My thousand welcomes to you! And tell me, now, which of you is King James?

JAMES (*going back a step*). This is a trap!

CARTER. Not a doubt of it!

FIRST WILLIAMITE. Fire, fire quick! Bring back our troop!

(*They raise their muskets.* SARFIELD *rushes past* JAMES, *seizes the muskets which they are raising so that they are pointed at his own body.*)

238

SARSFIELD. Fire! Yes, here I am! Call back your comrades to bury the King!

MATT. Shame! Shame! Would you kill the King?

FIRST WILLIAMITE. We have orders to take him, alive or dead.

SARSFIELD. Back, back, put down your muskets! Damn you! Are these Dutch manners?

FIRST WILLIAMITE. You are our prisoner. We must call our troop.

SARSFIELD (*pushing them back angrily*). Dutch manners! I swear I will not go to prison on an empty stomach! Supper, host, supper! Is a man to be sent empty to his death, even if he be a King?

FIRST WILLIAMITE. We have orders. We are King William's men.

SARSFIELD. Whoever you are, I will sup here to-night. Hurry, host, hurry. What have you there? Here is a follower of mine who is always hungry. (*Pointing at* CARTER.) What have you here? Beef—good—and bread.

(WILLIAMITES *go and stand at door with muskets ready.*)

MATT (*bewildered*). I have, indeed—that is, I had. I had all ready. These traitors came— it failed me to get them out.

MRS. KELLEHER. Leave talking. You have done enough of harm for this night. With your wine-muddled wits you have brought your King to his death.

(*She puts plates on table.*)

SARSFIELD (*to* CARTER). Give me a chair. Here (*To* JAMES) are my gloves. (*He sits down.*) You may sit there. (*They sit down,* JAMES *keeping his face in shadow, and muffled in cloak. They begin eating. To* CARTER.) You, I know, are ready for your supper.

CARTER. Not a doubt of it! (*He eats greedily.*)

MATT (*falling on his knees*). O forgive me, forgive! To betray my King! Oh! oh! oh! It's the drink that did it.

SARSFIELD. That will do. I forgive, I forgive.

MATT. Take my life! O take my life! I to have brought destruction on my King!

SARSFIELD. Get up, old fool. Here, ma'am, those bottles.

MATT (*getting up*). I wish I had died of thirst before I had touched a drop, so I do. The curse of drowning be upon drink, I say!

SARSFIELD (*to* FIRST WILLIAMITE). I am in better humour now. War and hunger make rough manners. Were you in the battle? If so, you are brave men.

239

FIRST WILLIAMITE. We were not in that battle. We were at the Lagan.

SARSFIELD. There were good fighters there too. I am sorry they were not on our side. I am sorry all the men of Ireland are not on the one side.

FIRST WILLIAMITE. It is best to be on the winning side.

SARSFIELD. The winning side—which is it? We think we know, but heaven and hell know better. Ups and downs as with this knife (*Balances it on his fingers*). Ups and downs. Winning and losing are in the course of nature, and there's no use in crying.

FIRST WILLIAMITE. Some one must be the winner.

SARSFIELD. Ups and downs, ups and downs; and we know nothing till all is over. He is surely the winner who gets a great tombstone, a figured monument, cherubs blowing trumpets, angels' tears in marble—or maybe he is the winner who has none of these, who but writes his name in the book of the people. I would like my name set in clean letters in the book of the people.

MRS. KELLEHER (*to* JAMES). Take another bit of the beef, sir; you are using nothing at all. You might have hungry days yet. Make hay while the sun shines. It isn't every day that Paddy kills a deer!

JAMES (*in a muffled voice*). I have eaten enough.

MRS. KELLEHER. It is well you came before these Northerners had all swept. It's a rogue of a cat would find anything after them.

JAMES (*impatiently*). I have had quite enough.

MRS. KELLEHER. Look now, don't be down hearted. Sure you must be sorry for the King being in danger; but things might change. It is they themselves might be dancing the back step yet. There's more music than the pipes. The darkest hour is before the dawn. Every spring morning has a black head. It's a good horse that never stumbles. The help of God is nearer than the door.

JAMES. Let me be. That is enough.

MRS. KELLEHER (*turning away*). I knew he hadn't enough ate. It's the hungry man does be fierce.

SARSFIELD (*to* FIRST WILLIAMITE). I am sorry not to be able to ask you, fellow-soldier, to sit down with us. But I know you would sooner let the bones show through your coat than lower that musket that is pointing at me.

FIRST WILLIAMITE. I hope you won't take it unkindly, your Majesty. I am but obeying orders.

SARSFIELD. You are right; you are very right in not sitting down.

Suppose now you were sitting here, and the door unguarded, and the King should make his escape——

FIRST WILLIAMITE. Your Majesty would not get very far—we have other men.

SARSFIELD. Who knows? There are ups and downs. A King is not as a common man—the moon has risen—there are horses not far off—he might gallop through the night.

FIRST WILLIAMITE. He would be overtaken.

SARSFIELD. He might gallop—and gallop—and a few friends would know the sound and would join him here and there. He might go on very fast away from the harbour, past the wood, his men gathering to him as he passed—to Clonmel——

SECOND WILLIAMITE. Clonmel is full of King James's men, sure enough.

SARSFIELD. And then, with all that gather to him there, he would go quietly, very quietly, very quickly to the Gap of the Oaks——

SECOND WILLIAMITE. Listen. That is where the convoy stops to-night.

SARSFIELD. A little camp—four hundred horses well saddled, two hundred waggons with powder enough to blow up the Rock of Cashel—and in the middle of all, the yolk of the egg—the kernel of the nut—the pip of the orange.

SECOND WILLIAMITE. He knows that, too. He knows King William is making that secret march.

SARSFIELD. A shout—the King! Sarsfield—Ireland! —before there is time to pull a trigger, we have carried off the prize—we have him to treat with *inside* the walls of Limerick. We send the Dutchman back to his country. Will you go with him to the mud-banks, comrades, or will you stop in Ireland with your own King?

FIRST WILLIAMITE. The King will win yet. I would never believe that he gave the word to run from the Boyne.

SARSFIELD. Now, if I were the King——

MATT. Sure you are King yet, for all I did to destroy you, God forgive me!

SARSFIELD. That is true—yes, yes. I am a King to-night, even though I may not be one to-morrow.

OWEN (*who has been listening eagerly*). It must be a wonderful thing to be a King!

SARSFIELD. Wonderful, indeed—if he have the heart of a King —to be the son and grandson and great-grandson of Kings, the chosen and anointed of God. To have that royal blood coming from far off, from some source so high that, like the water of his palace fountain, it keeps breaking, ever breaking away from the common earth, starting up as if to reach the skies. How else would those who are not noble know when they meet it what is royal blood?

FIRST WILLIAMITE. I would know in any place that this King has royal blood.

SECOND WILLIAMITE. It is easy to see among these three which of them is King.

SARSFIELD (*looking at* JAMES). A wonderful thing! If he have the high power of a King, or if he take the counsel that should be taken by a King. To be a King is to be a lover—a good lover of a beautiful sweetheart.

FIRST WILLIAMITE. I suppose he means the country, saying that.

SECOND WILLIAMITE. I am sure he must have a heart for Ireland.

SARSFIELD. He goes out so joyous, so high of heart, because it is never possible for him to do any deed for himself alone, but for her as well that is his dear lady. She is in his hands; he keeps them clean for her; it is for her he holds his head high; it is for her he shows courtesy to all, because he would not have rude voices raised about her.

SECOND WILLIAMITE. The Dutchman would not have those thoughts for Ireland.

MRS. KELLEHER. It's not from the wind he got it. Mouth of ivy and heart of holly. That is what you would look for in a King.

SARFIELD. If she is in trouble or under sorrow, this sweetheart who trusts him, that trouble, God forgive him, brings him a sort of joy! To go out, to call his men, to give out shouts because the time has come to show what her strong lover can do for her—to go hungry that she may be fed; to go tired that her dear feet may tread safely; to die, it may be, at the last for her with such glory that the name he leaves with her is better than any living love, because he has been faithful, faithful, faithful!

FIRST WILLIAMITE (*putting down musket*). I give up the Dutchman's pay. This man is the best.

SECOND WILLIAMITE. He is the best. It is as good to join him.

OWEN. I will follow him by every hard road and every rough road through the whole world.

MATT. I will never drink another drop till he has come to his rights! I would sooner shrivel up like a bunch of seaweed!

MRS. KELLEHER. It is what I was often saying, the desire of every heart is the rightful King.

FIRST WILLIAMITE. We will follow you! We will send our comrades away when they come, or we will turn them to you!

SECOND WILLIAMITE. We will fight for you five times better than ever we fought for the Dutchman. We will not let so much as a scratch on one belonging to you—even that lean-jawed little priest at the end of the table. (*Points at* JAMES.)

SARSFIELD (*rising*). That is right. I knew you were good Irishmen. Now, we must set out for Clonmel.

JAMES. No, no; we cannot go. We must wait for the men from the French ship.

SARSFIELD. Write your orders to them. Tell them to come round, and bring us help at Limerick.

JAMES. It would be best to see them.

SARSFIELD. No time to lose! This good woman will give the letter safely.

(CARTER *reluctantly gets out pen and paper.* JAMES *begins to write. The door opens and the old Lady appears.*)

OWEN. It is the poor Lady.

MATT (*to* SARSFIELD). The poor Lady Dereen, your Majesty, that lost all for the Stuarts.

OWEN. Come in, Lady, come; the King himself is here, King James.

LADY. The King! And safe! Then God has heard our prayers.

OWEN. Come now, Lady; tell your story to the King.

(*Leads her to* SARSFIELD.)

LADY. I lost all for Charles. I will get all back from James. Charles was great; James will be greater! See here I have the King's own seal.

SARSFIELD. That is the seal indeed. The King will honour it when he comes to his own.

LADY. No more beggary; no more wandering. My white halls again; my kinsmen and my friends!

SARSFIELD (*to* JAMES). Have we any token to give this poor distracted lady?

JAMES. Give her a promise. We have nothing else to part with.

SARSFIELD (*taking off his ring*). Here, Lady! here is a ring. Take this in pledge that the King will pay you what he owes.

LADY (*taking it*). Is it the sunrise? See how it shines! I knew the lucky sun would rise at last. I watched in the east for it every morning.

(*She childishly plays with the ring.*)

MATT. Wouldn't you thank the King now, Lady, for what he is after giving you?

LADY. I had forgotten. I forgot I was in the Court! I was dreaming, dreaming of hard, long roads and little houses—little dark houses. I forgot I was at Whitehall. I have not been to Whitehall for a long time to kiss the King's hand. (*She gives her stick to* OWEN, *and stands very tall and straight.*) I know the Court well. I remember well what to do. A curtsy to the right to the Queen (*curtsies*); a curtsy to the left to the princesses (*curtsies*). Now I kneel to kiss the King's hand. (*She sweeps her dress back as if it were a train and kneels.* SARSFIELD *gives her his hand; she puts her lips to it. She gets up uncertain and tottering, and cries out*)—You have befooled me! That is not the King's hand; that is no Stuart hand; that is a lucky hand—a strong, lucky hand!

SARSFIELD. You have forgotten, Lady. It was a long time ago.

LADY. That is no Stuart voice! (*Peers at him.*) That is no Stuart face! Who was it said the King is here? (*She looks into* CARTER'S *face.*) That is no King's face. (*Takes his hand.*) That is no royal hand. (*Going to* JAMES.) Let me look at your face. (*He turns away.*) Let me look at your hand.

JAMES. Do not touch me! Am I to be pestered by every beggar that comes in?

LADY (*in a shriek*). That is the voice! That is the voice! (*Seizes his hand.*) That is the hand! I know it—the smooth, white, unlucky Stuart hand!

JAMES *starts up angrily.* WILLIAMITES *have gone to listen at the door. "Lillibulero" is heard sung outside*)—

Dey all in France have taken a swear,
    Lillibulero bullen a la!
Dat dey will have no Protestant heir:
    Lillibulero bullen a la!
    Lero, lero, lero, lillibulero bullen a la!

Though by my shoul de English do prate,
    Lillibulero bullen a la!
De laws on dere side, and Christ knows what:
    Lillibulero bullen a la!
    Lero, lero, lero, lillibulero bullen a la!

FIRST WILLIAMITE. It is the Newry troop!

OWEN (*bolting door and putting his back to it*). They must not see the King!

SECOND WILLIAMITE. It is too late to escape. We will fight for you.

MATT (*going to door and putting his back to it*). Believe me I won't let them in this time.

SARSFIELD (*drawing sword and going before* JAMES). We will cut our way through them.

MRS. KELLEHER (*pushing back dressed and opening door*). It's a poor mouse that wouldn't have two doors to its hole! (*She pushes* JAMES *and* CARTER *in*. SARSFIELD *stands at it*.) Go in now. When all is quiet, you can get through to the pier.

Voice of WILLIAMITE CAPTAIN *outside* (*with a bang at door*). Open! I say!

MATT (*rattling at door while he keeps it fast*). Sure, I'm doing my best to open it—if I could but meet with the latch.

VOICE. Open, open!

MATT. I have an unsteady hand. I am after taking a little drop of a cordial—

(*Another bang at door.*)

OWEN. I'll quench the light!

(*Blows out candles.* SARSFIELD *has followed* JAMES. MRS. KELLEHER *is pushing dresser back to its place. The door is burst open.*)

CAPTAIN. Who is here?

MATT. Not a one in the world, Captain, but myself and herself, and the son I have, and a few men of King William's army.

FIRST WILLIAMITE. We are here, sir, according to orders.

CAPTAIN. Strike a light! (WILLIAMITE *strikes it and lights candle*.) What is going on here?

FIRST WILLIAMITE. We are watching the pier, sir.

CAPTAIN. Why are the lights out?

MATT. It was I myself, sir—I will confess all. It was not purposely I did it. I have an unsteady hand; it was to snuff them I was striving.

CAPTAIN. Have you any news of King James?

FIRST WILLIAMITE. Great news!

CAPTAIN. What is that?

FIRST WILLIAMITE. He was seen to the east—up in the wood.

CAPTAIN. We must follow him at once.

FIRST WILLIAMITE. It is said he is going north—on the road to Wexford!

Curtain.

Act III

SCENE: *The pier at Duncannon the same night.* JAMES *and* CARTER *talking together.*

JAMES. Upon my word, I am as glad to escape from that dark cellar as I was to get into it an hour ago.

CARTER. I wonder how long Sarsfield will be away gathering his men.

JAMES. It should take him a little time; but one never knows with him when he may appear. He makes me start up. He has no feeling for repose, for things at their proper time, for the delicate, leisurely life. He frets and goads me. He harries and hustles. I hear him now! (*Starts.*)

CARTER. It is only the French sailors taking away another barrel of their meat from the cellar.

(*French sailors enter from left, singing as before. They roll a barrel away to right.*)

JAMES. The long and the short of it is, it will not be my fault if I spend another night in this abominable island.

CARTER. That is good news indeed.

JAMES. The only difficulty is how to get away.

CARTER. Why, your Majesty has but to get into the ship.

JAMES. Ah, if I could once get into it! But the question is how am I to escape—from Sarsfield? Of course he is under my orders. I made him obey orders when we left the Boyne. But since then there is something about him—some danger in his eye, or in the toss of his head. Of course, I am in no way afraid of him.

CARTER. Of course not, indeed.

JAMES. But for all that, when he begins drawing maps with a flourish of his sword (*Mimics* SARSFIELD), or talking as if he were giving out the Holy Scriptures, there is something—a something—that takes away my strength, that leaves me bustled, marrowless, uncertain.

CARTER. Not a doubt of it.

JAMES. I am resolved I will strike a blow for myself. I will take my own way. I will be King again. I will be my own master! I am determined that here, this moment, before he has time to come back,

246

before I cool, before my blood goes down, I will make these sailors take me into their boat and row me out to the ship.

CARTER. Well said, indeed.

JAMES. When Sarsfield comes back to this pier, if he wants to preach to me again, he will have to swim for it!

CARTER. Ha, ha, very good! (*Enter sailors from right.*)

JAMES (*to sailors*). Here, my men. I must go to the ship at once. You must take me in your boat.

FIRST SAILOR. Boat not ready yet, sir. More meat, more pork, for sau-sa-ges.

JAMES. I must go at once. Here, I will give you money if you will take me at once.

SAILOR. Give it now, sir, and I will take you (JAMES *gives it*)— after one more barrel.

JAMES. At once!

SAILOR. At once, sir. Only *one* more barrel. I will not be two, three minutes. You go, sir, wait in the boat. We will follow you very quick. (*They go left.*)

JAMES. Come to the boat at once, Carter. We shall be safe there. Oh, once at sea I shall be King again!

CARTER. Not a doubt of it!

JAMES. Come, come, no time to lose!

(*They turn right. Music is heard from right, "Lillibulero" suddenly turning into "White Cockade." The two WIL-LIAMITES appear playing fife and drum, OWEN with them.*)

FIRST WILLIAMITE. That is right! We are changing the tune well now. We had to keep up the old one so long as our Newry comrades were within hearing. That they may have a quick journey to Wexford! Now for the white cockade!

(OWEN *gives them each one, and they put them in their hats.*)

OWEN. You did well, getting leave to come back and to watch the pier.

SECOND WILLIAMITE. So we will watch it well.

JAMES. Let me pass if you please.

FIRST WILLIAMITE. Where are you going, my little priest?

JAMES. I am going on my own business. Let me pass.

FIRST WILLIAMITE. I don't know about that. I have orders to watch the pier. Double orders. Orders from King William to let no one leave it, and orders to let no one come near it, from King James.

JAMES. I tell you I am going on King James's business.

FIRST WILLIAMITE. He will be here in a minute. He is gathering men and horses below to the west of the town. Wait till he comes.

JAMES. No, no, I cannot wait. (*Tries to get through.*)

FIRST WILLIAMITE. You will have to wait. No hurry! The Mass can't begin without you!

JAMES. I can make you let me go with one word.

SECOND WILLIAMITE (*catching hold of him*). Faith, I can hold you without any word at all.

JAMES (*wrenching himself free*). Back, fool, back. I am the King!

BOTH THE WILLIAMITES. Ha, ha, ha! Ho, ho, ho!

SECOND WILLIAMITE. O the liar!

CARTER. You must believe His Majesty.

FIRST WILLIAMITE. I do, as much as I believe you yourself to be Patrick Sarsfield.

OWEN. *That* Patrick Sarsfield!

CARTER. How dare you doubt that this is the King?

FIRST WILLIAMITE. I don't. I have no doubt at all upon the matter. I wouldn't believe it from Moses on the mountain.

JAMES. You common people cannot recognise high blood. I say I am the King. You would know it quickly enough if you could see me in my right place!

FIRST WILLIAMITE. We might. Your reverence would look well upon the throne. Here, boys, make a throne for His Majesty. (*They cross hands and put him up as if on a throne.*) Hurrah! This is the third King we have shouted for within the last six hours!

JAMES. Let me down, I say!

FIRST WILLIAMITE. Throw out gold and silver to the crowd! Every King throws out gold and silver when he comes to the throne!

SECOND WILLIAMITE. Give us our fee! Give us an estate! I would like mine in the County Meath.

FIRST WILLIAMITE. Can you touch for the evil? Here is a boy that has the evil! We'll know you are a King if you can cure the evil!

ALL. Ha, ha, ha! Ho, ho, ho!

JAMES. Let me down, traitors!

(*A sound of keening heard.*)

OWEN. Here is the poor Lady.

(*She comes in keening. They put down the King.*)

JAMES. Here is a witness for me. She knew me last night.

CARTER. She knew the true King's hand.

JAMES. Lady Dereen, you knew me last night. Tell these fools what they will not believe from me, that I am the King.

248

(*She begins keening again.*)

JAMES (*touching her arm*). Look at me. Am I not a Stuart?
Touch my hand. Am I not the King?

(*He holds out his hand; she takes it, looks vacantly at it, drops
it, and is silent for a minute.*)

LADY (*crying out*). The King! There is no King! The King is
dead; he died in the night! Did you not hear me keening him? My
lord is dead, and my kinsmen are dead, and my heart is dead; and
now my King is dead! He gave his father a bad burying; we will
give him a good burying—deep, deep, deep. Dig under the rivers,
put the mountains over him; he will never rise again. He is dead,
he is dead! (*She sits down rocking herself and sings.*)

> Ochone, ochone, my pleasant Stuart;
> Ochone, heart-secret of the Gael!

(SARSFIELD *comes in hurriedly, motions them all back. Speaks
to* JAMES.)

SARSFIELD. All is well, sir. Our men are coming in fast. There
are two hundred of them to the west of the harbour. We are late
for the surprise—that chance is gone; but we can bring good help
to hearten Limerick. The King's presence will bring out the white
cockade like rush-cotton over the bogs.

JAMES. Yes, yes; very good, very good.

SARSFIELD. Are you ready, sir?

JAMES. Oh, yes, ready, very ready—to leave this place.

SARSFIELD. This way, sir, this way!

JAMES. I know the way; but I have left my papers—papers of
importance—in that cellar. I must go back and get them.

SARSFIELD. Now William's troop has left, I will have the horses
brought to the very edge of the pier—all is safe now.

JAMES. Yes, yes, I am sure there is no danger. Yes, go for the
horses; take care they are well saddled.

(*He goes out left;* SARSFIELD *right.* MATT *and* MRS. KEL-
LEHER *come on from left.*)

MRS. KELLEHER. And is it true, Owen, my son, that you are
going following after the King?

OWEN. It is true, surely.

MRS. KELLEHER. You that would never stir from the hearth to
be taking to such hardship! Well, I wouldn't like to be begrudging
you to the King's service. What goes out at the ebb comes in on
the flood. It might be for profit.

MATT. Here is the belt your grandfather owned, and he fighting at Ross; pistols there are in it. Do your best now for the King. I'll drink—no I swore I would never drink another drop till such time——

MRS. KELLEHER. There is my own good cloak for you—there is something in the pocket you will find no load. (OWEN *puts on cloak and belt.*) And here's cakes for the journey—faith, you'll be as proud now as a cat with a straddle!

OWEN. You will hear no story of me but a story you would like to be listening to. Believe me, I will fight well for the King.

(SAILORS *come from left, rolling a very large barrel; they are singing their song.* CARTER *is walking after it.*)

MATT. Stop there! What is that barrel you are bringing away?

SAILOR. It is one bacon-barrel.

MATT. It is not. It is one of my big wine barrels.

SAILOR. Oh, ah! I assure you there is meat in it.

MATT (*putting his hand on it*). Do you think I would not know the size of one of my own barrels if I met with it rolling through the stars? That is a barrel that came from France, and it full of wine.

CARTER (*to sailors*). Go on with the barrel.

MATT. I will not let it go! Why would I let my good wine go out of the country, even if I can have no more than the smell of it myself? Bring it back to the cellar, I say, and go get your meat.

CARTER. It must be taken to the ship. It is the King's wish.

MATT. The King's wish? If that is so—where is the King, till I ask him? (*Looks around.*)

CARTER. I tell you it must go. I will pay you for it—here is the money. What is its worth?

MATT. Well, if you pay fair, I have nothing to say. If it was to the King himself it was going, I would take nothing at all. He would be welcome.

CARTER (*giving money*). Here, here. (*To sailors.*) Go on, now; hurry! Be careful!

FIRST WILLIAMITE. It is a pity now, to see good wine leaving the country, and a great drouth on the King's good soldiers.

SECOND WILLIAMITE. He should not begrudge us a glass, indeed. It will strengthen us for all we will have to do at Limerick. (*Puts his hand on barrel.*)

CARTER. This belongs to me! This is my property. If you commit robbery, you must account to the King!!

MATT. Look here, I have still-whiskey in a jar. I brought it out to give you a drop to put courage into you before you would go. That is what will serve you as well.

FIRST WILLIAMITE. We will let the barrel go, so.

SECOND WILLIAMITE. We could bring away the jar with us. I would sooner have wine now to drink the King's health.

LADY (*standing up, suddenly, and coming in front of barrel*). Wine, wine, for the King's wake!

SECOND WILLIAMITE. Listen to her! That is a good thought. We will drink to the King living, and she will drink to him dead.

LADY (*to* MATT). Wine, wine, red wine! Do you grudge it for the King's wake? White candles in the skies, red wine for the King's pall-bearers! (*She lifts up her hands.*)

FIRST WILLIAMITE. She is right, she is right. (*To* MATT.) Since you yourself turned sober, you are begrudging wine for the King! Here!

(*Tilts up barrel. A muffled groan is heard from inside.*)

SECOND WILLIAMITE. That is a queer sort of a gurgling the French wine has—there is ferment in it yet. Give me an awl till I make a hole. (*Another stifled groan.*)

CARTER. Oh, oh, oh, oh!

(*Puts his cloak over his ears, and retires to back.*)

FIRST WILLIAMITE (*taking out bayonet*). Here, let me at it!

(*Knocks head off barrel;* CARTER *giving short groans at every stroke.*)

CARTER. Oh! be gentle.

FIRST WILLIAMITE. Never fear. I have no mind to spill it. (*Takes off top.*)

(THE KING *stands up, pale and shaking, His cloak has fallen off, and chain and Order are displayed.*)

FIRST WILLIAMITE. It is the little priest!

SECOND WILLIAMITE. Is he King yet? Or fairy?

MATT (*looking in*). Would any one, now, believe that he has drunk the barrel dry!

FIRST WILLIAMITE. I wish I had been in his place.

MRS. KELLEHER. It is trying to desert he was. That's as clear as a whistle.

OWEN. The traitor! Wanting to desert the King!

MATT. But will any one tell me now, what in the wide world did he do with all the wine?

LADY. Is not that a very strange coffin, a very strange coffin to have put about a King?

MRS. KELLEHER. Here is King James!

(*They all turn to right.* SARSFIELD *comes in. He stands still.*)

OWEN. Deserting your Majesty, he was!

MATT. Making away in my barrel!

FIRST WILLIAMITE. Having drunk all the wine!

MRS. KELLEHER. Let a goat cross the threshold, and he'll make for the altar!

SARSFIELD (*taking off his hat*). Your Majesty!

JAMES. I wish, General Sarsfield, you would control this dangerous rabble.

ALL. Sarsfield!

MRS. KELLEHER. Who are you at all?

SARSFIELD. I am Patrick Sarsfield, a poor soldier of King James.

MRS. KELLEHER. And where, in the name of mercy, is King James?

SARSFIELD. You are in His Majesty's presence. (*He goes to help*
    JAMES *out of barrel.*)

ALL TOGETHER. *That* His Majesty!

MRS. KELLEHER. It seems to me we have a wisp in place of a broom.

OWEN. Misfortune on the fools that helped him!

FIRST WILLIAMITE. Is it for him we gave up William?

MATT. And that I myself gave up drink!

SARSFIELD (*who has helped the* KING *out of the barrel, takes him by the hand*). Any roughness that was done to the King was done, I am sure, unknowingly. But now, if there are any little whisperings, any hidden twitterings, as to what His Majesty has thought fit to do, it is I myself who will give a large answer! (*He unsheaths sword.*)

JAMES. I have business in France. You may stay here, General Sarsfield, if you will. But I will lead you no longer; I will fight no more for these cowardly Irish. You must shift for yourselves; I will shift for myself.

CARTER. Not a doubt of it!

JAMES (*going off, stops and turns*). When I come back as a conqueror, with my armies and my judges, there are some I may pardon—my servants who deserted me, my daughters who turned against me. But there are some I will never forgive, some I will remember now and ever, now and for ever—those of you who stopped the barrel, those who tilted it up, and those who opened it!

(*He goes out right followed by* SARSFIELD *and sailors.* OWEN,
    *throwing off cloak and belt, and tearing cockade from his
    hat, throws himself down and begins to play jackstones as
    in First Act.*)

LADY (*turning to face other way*). Where is the sun? I am tired of looking for it in the east. The sun is tired of rising in the east; it may be in the west it will rise to-morrow!

MRS. KELLEHER. Gone is he? My joy be with him, and glass legs under him! Well, an empty house is better than a bad tenant. It might be for profit.

MATT (*taking up jar*). Well, I am free from my pledge, as the King says, now and ever, now and for ever! (*Drinks from jar.*) No more pledges! It's as well to be free. (*He sits down beside* OWEN.)

FIRST WILLIAMITE. Which King are we best with; the one we left or the one that left us?

SECOND WILLIAMITE. Little I care. Toss for it. (*Tosses a penny.*) Heads, William; harps, James!

FIRST WILLIAMITE (*picking it up*). Heads it is. (*Taking cockade from his hat.*) There's good-bye to the white cockade.

> (*He and the others throw cockades on the ground, and walk off.*)

MRS. KELLEHER (*to* OWEN). And what will you be doing, Owen? You will hardly go fighting now.

OWEN. What business would I have fighting? I have done with kings and makings of kings. (*Throws up jackstones and catches all.*) Good, that's buttermilk!

MRS. KELLEHER. You are right; you are right. It's bad changing horses in the middle of a ford. (*She takes back her cloak.*) Is all safe in the pocket? It's long before I'll part with it again—once bit, twice shy. It might all be for profit.

> (SARSFIELD *comes back. Stands still a minute, holding hat in his hand. Lets sword drop on the ground.*)

SARSFIELD. Gone, gone; he is gone—he betrayed me—he called me from the battle—he lost me my great name—he betrayed Ireland. Who is he? What is he? A King or what? (*He pulls feathers one by one from cockade.*) King or knave—soldier—sailor —tinker—tailor—beggarman—thief! (*Pulls out last feather.*) Thief, that is it,—thief. He has stolen away; he has stolen our good name; he has stolen our faith; he has stolen the pin that held loyalty to royalty! A thief, a fox—a fox of trickery! (*He sits down trembling.*)

MRS. KELLEHER (*coming to him*). So you have thrown away the white cockade, Sarsfield, the same as Owen.

SARSFIELD (*bewildered*). The same as Owen?

MRS. KELLEHER. Owen threw away the King's cockade the same as yourself.

SARSFIELD. Threw it away! What have I thrown away? Have I thrown away the white cockade?

MRS. KELLEHER. You did, and scattered it. (SARSFIELD *lifts his hat and looks at it.*)

MRS. KELLEHER. If you want another, they are here on the ground as plenty as blackberries in harvest. (*Takes up a cockade.*)

SARSFIELD. Give it here to me. (*He begins putting it in his hat, his hand still trembling.*)

MATT. You will go no more fighting for King James! You are free of your pledge! We are all free of our pledge!

SARSFIELD. Where is my sword?

(MRS. KELLEHER *gives it. He put it in sheath.*)

MRS. KELLEHER. Look, now, the skin is nearer than the shirt. One bit of a rabbit is worth two of a cat. It's no use to go looking for wool on a goat. It's best for you to fight from this out for your own hand and for Ireland. Why would you go spending yourself for the like of *that* of a king?

SARSFIELD (*buckling on his sword-belt*). Why, why? Who can say? What is holding me? Habit, custom. What is it the priests say?—the cloud of witnesses. Maybe the call of some old angry father of mine, that fought two thousand years ago for a bad master! (*He stands up.*) Well, good-bye, good-bye. (*To* MRS. KELLEHER, *who is holding out cakes*). Yes, I will take these cakes. (*Takes them.*) It is likely I will find empty plates in Limerick.   (*Goes off.*)

LADY (*to* MRS. KELLEHER). Is not that a very foolish man to go on fighting for a dead king?

MRS. KELLEHER (*tapping her forehead*). Indeed, I think there's rats in the loft!

LADY (*tapping her forehead*). That is it, that is it— we wise ones know it. Fighting for a dead king!—ha! ha! ha! Poor Patrick Sarsfield is very, very mad!

Curtain.

THE DELIVERER

THE DELIVERER

PERSONS
  ARD
  DAN
  MALACHI
  ARD'S WIFE
  DAN'S WIFE
  MALACHI'S WIFE
  THE KING'S NURSELING
  A STEWARD
  AN OFFICER
  ONE OR MORE SOLDIERS

SCENE: *Steps of a palace at the Inver of the Nile. At bottom of steps* ARD, DAN, *and* MALACHI *are mixing mortar and carrying stones. Music and laughter heard from window of palace above. Banners with Pharaoh's ensigns, hawk, globe, and sun. The men are in poor clothes and look tired.*

DAN. It is time for the women to be bringing the dinner. I'm near starved with hunger.

ARD. Here they are now bringing it. Where would be the use them coming, and the bell not to have rung?

(*Bell rings. They all fling down what is in their hands and throw themselves on the ground.*)

MALACHI. I am racked with raising stones and bearing them to their place. That is work I never was reared to.

DAN. What call had our old fathers bringing us away out of our own place?

MALACHI. It was the time of the great hunger drove them away, the time the palmers on the leaves had the crops entirely destroyed.

ARD. We would be better off there in hungry times itself, than the way we are in this place, with the over-government taking the hens off the floor and the plates from the dresser, and the bed itself from under us with their taxes and with their rates.

MALACHI. The time I was rising we were treated fair enough.

257

But the nice stock is all done away with now, and buried and gone to the grave.

DAN. It is a bad story for us they to be wore away.

MALACHI. There is nothing left in it at this time but tyrants and schemers.

DAN. We to be back in our own country we could knock a living out of it. It is only an odd time the hunger makes headway. It is often my father told me he had two horses belonging to him, and they drawing loads for eight of his first cousins.

ARD. If it is law it is bad law that keeps us labouring out under the mad sun. A King of Foreign to be getting his own profit through our sweat, and we to be getting poor and getting miserable.

DAN. If we had but the means to shape these boards into some sort of a curragh, and to put pins in it and to settle it with oars like, we might go steer towards our own harbour.

MALACHI. You have not the means to do it. Sure at the time of the Flood they were a hundred years making a bark. And if it took but three ships or four to bring the twelve families to this place, three times three would hardly be enough to hold us at this time, and every third man or so bringing a wife along with him.

DAN. There is a troop of ships out in the Inver at this time, and scraping against the quay. Speckled sails they were putting up and pulling down a while ago.

ARD. It is the King's heir is after being put in command of those ships, and he being come to sensible years. There is talk of a young queen is looking out from her window for him, in Spain or Armenia or some place of the sort. I was picking news out of a man of the Egyptians a while ago. It is more than *that* he was telling me. (*The women come in.*)

DAN. What is it you have for me, astore, within in the fold of your shawl?

DAN'S WIFE. It is but a bit of cold stirabout.

DAN. It is made but of yellow meal. I'm in dread I might heave it up again. You wouldn't have e'er a drop of milk?

DAN'S WIFE. I thought to make kitchen with an eel I chanced in the mud of the river, and I filling a tin can at the brink. But there came a cat of the King's cats into the house, and snapped it off of the plate. I was afeard to lay a hand on him, and he coming from the place he did.

MALACHI. You did well to lay no hand on him. Those cats are a class in themselves. To claw you they would, and bite you, and put

258

poison in your veins the same as a serpent, as maybe they might be in the early time of the world.

MALACHI'S WIFE. That's right. I'd sooner the mice to be running in and out like chickens than to bring one of them in on the floor.

ARD. To gather here at the steps at the fall of night they do, and to fight and to bawl for the bits are thrown from the King's house.

ARD'S WIFE. To come into my own little street a one of them did, and left me with nothing but one bare duck.

ARD. It is made too much of they are entirely. One of them to die at any time, to cry and to keen him the owners will, the same as they would a child or a human.

DAN. To meet with one of them in the moonlight I did a while ago. I am not the better of it yet. It went into some sort of a hump, and said it had to walk its seven acres. I give you my word you would say it to be as big as an elephant.

ARD'S WIFE. I wouldn't doubt it, and all they get thrown out from that kitchen. Sure the rinsings of the plates in the servants' hall would grease cabbage for the whole province. Every day is Christmas in that house.

ARD. There is a grand supper to be in it now that the King is come, and his big men and his friends.

MALACHI'S WIFE. Sure the world knows that. It is likely it will be a feast will last through a year and a day.

ARD. It will not but till to-morrow sometime, when the King's nurseling will make his start in the ships.

ARD'S WIFE. A hundred cooks that are in it, boiling and roasting and mixing cakes, with currants and with caraway seeds. Sure the bacon they have dressed in frying pans, you would smell it through the seven parishes.

DAN. And ourselves dragging with hunger. Nothing to eat or to fall back on.

ARD'S WIFE. It is the poor know all the troubles of the world.

MALACHI. To be a stranger and an exile, that is the worst thing at all. The feet bending under me, and no one belonging to me but God.

ARD. If it is law it is wrong law some to get their seven times enough, and ourselves never to get our half enough.

DAN. We to be without a peck hardly upon our bones, and that King to be nourished with sweets and fooleries, and his stomach as big as that you wouldn't know what to make of it.

MALACHI. They would not leave us on the face of the earth if it wasn't that we do their heavy work.

DAN. Is there another crumb of meal in the handkerchief?

DAN'S WIFE. There is not, and no earthly thing in the house itself, unless it might be a few young nettles I put down to boil in the pot.

DAN. An ass that would go forage on the highway would get better provision, or the dogs that go preying for themselves.

MALACHI'S WIFE. There is no nature in them at all.

ARD. It is not right and it is not justice, riches to be coming in to them, and they asleep in the bed.

MALACHI. I would ask no riches at all besides being in a little village of houses among my own people, that would have a wish for my bones.

DAN. That I may never sin, but I am getting a smell I never felt since my grandfather's time, the smell of a roasted goose!

ARD. It is a smell of wine I am getting, that is giving me a twist-like in the heart.

MALACHI'S WIFE. You would know there to be wine in it, and the laughing is among them, and the stir.

ARD'S WIFE. There is one of them facing the window—throw your eye on him now—a holy circus for grandeur he is, and having a gold chain about his neck.

DAN'S WIFE. He is very comely surely and gay. A lovely dotey young man.

ARD. It is easy be comely and be light-hearted, and want or trouble not to have ever come anear you.

MALACHI'S WIFE. Who is he now? Is it he himself is the King's son?

DAN'S WIFE. He should be that, and he so well-shaped, and curls on every side of his poll, the same as a ridge of peas.

DAN. Sure they all do have curls of that sort in the King's house. I am told it is hair grew on horses' necks, or maybe on the head of a corp. To shape it into rings-like they do, with a bar-like would be reddened in among the coals.

MALACHI'S WIFE. There is not a tailor or a dressmaker in the district slept a wink these seven nights, and all the grand suits were ordered for this big day.

DAN'S WIFE. There is no one can become his suit better than that King's son with the laugh on his mouth. He should make joy for his lady of a mother, and she to be looking on him this day.

DAN. You think yourself very wise now, to be giving out judgments about kings' sons.

DAN'S WIFE. Hasn't he the lovely face? His head held up so lofty and so high, and he having a hurl in his hand, and a crown of posies on his brow.

MALACHI'S WIFE. The world has flowed upon him. There are some born having luck through the stars and through the strength of the moon.

DAN'S WIFE. Why wouldn't he have luck, and he to be born in the King's own palace?

ARD. That is what he would wish you to be thinking.

DAN'S WIFE. Why wouldn't we think it? He's as nice as you'd ask. I see no flaw in him at all.

ARD. You are thinking him to be far above myself I suppose?

ARD'S WIFE. Sure there must be some difference in station and in blood. It was the Almighty Himself put that in the world.

ARD. What would you say hearing he is not far in blood from ourselves?

DAN. That is what we are after being told, whether or no it is true. Of our own race and of our tribe.

MALACHI. To one of the twelve families he belongs. To the one breed with myself, but that the generations are scattered.

ARD. I heard that, and that his father gave in to the hardship.

MALACHI. He did so. In heaven he is now, and on earth he was driving cattle.

DAN. And his mother a girl of the Kohaths, threw him out from her on the rising flood.

MALACHI. The King's daughter that took notice of him in the flag-flowers, and she washing herself at the time the flood began to slacken down.

ARD. To rear him up as her own she did, and on her death-bed she willed him her father's heir.

DAN. It is on this day he is to be put beyond all the rest nearly of Pharaoh's people.

MALACHI. The curse of his own people be on him, he to be frolicking where he is, and treading the stones were quarried through our labour.

ARD. Going here and forth, spending what would buy an estate, sparkling abroad in the fields. Following foxes with huntsmen and hounds, or fowling after snipe and teal. That the whole of them may turn against him, and put their beaks through his guts, or their claws or whatever disagreeable weapon-like the Lord may have given them for their own protection and their aid!

(*Bell heard ringing.*)

DAN. Mind yourselves, boys, there is the boss at the bell.

ARD. It is his own bones I would wish to see leaping and swinging up there in the place the bell is!

DAN. Where's the use talking. (*Sings.*)

> Trouble I ne'er did find
> > Till I joined the work with the cruel Turk
> At the Inver of the Nile.

ARD. Let ye all draw to silence. It is the Nutcrackers is in it. He is the worst tyrant of them all.

DAN. He wouldn't as much as give leave to rise your back or look around you. There would be no labourer alone with him, but would be in dread he would kill him.

MALACHI. That's the way with those low quality stewards that belong to the middling class.

ARD. The dirty savage! He'd think no more of a person's life than he would of a crow.

DAN. Whist your tongue. I would say he has drink taken. It is out of the parlour he is come.

STEWARD (*coming rather unsteadily down steps.*) Get back now to your work, you scheming michers! Bring over mortar there, it is wanting beyond. These steps had a right to be readied and finished before the King coming here at all. Go bring mortar, I say.

DAN. We will, your honour, the very minute it will be ready.

STEWARD. It should be ready by this, and you not to be sleeping and idle and playing odd and even with bits of stones.

MALACHI. It failed us to mix it, the lime being all used and spent.

STEWARD. How well you didn't go look for more, you crippled jackass.

DAN. Sure we went seeking it, and there was no lime in it, and no stones broken, and no fire kindled in the kilns.

MALACHI. The men had charge of them were brought away to be blowing the bellows for the ovens were put up for the King's big dinner.

STEWARD. It is too much gab you have! It is well able you are to make up stories and lies. If it was beef and cabbage you were sent seeking, you would track it out swift enough!

MALACHI. We are telling no lies. There is no lime to be got.

STEWARD. Let ye mix the mortar, so, without lime.

MALACHI. There is no one, tradesman or college bred man, could mix it without lime.

(*King's Nurseling appears at top of steps and stands behind a pillar*.)

STEWARD. Let you do it so with your enchantments. You that have the name of being an old prophecy, let you rise up and make it from that bit of a board. Sure, you are able to change yourself into an eel, the same as the King's Druids.

MALACHI. There is no reason in what you are saying.

STEWARD. No, but let you change yourself and your two comrades into the shape of three hares till I'll go coursing. I'll engage I'll come up with you! I'll put my teeth in you! (*Cracks whip*.) If you can't do no other thing you can make sport for us!

MALACHI. Any work I have to do, I will do it fair and honest. There is no justice asking me to do more than that.

STEWARD. I'll show you justice! All the justice you have to look for in this place is in my own cat-o'-nine-tails! (*Cracks it*.)

MALACHI. Is it to strike me with your lash you would?

STEWARD. It is, and to strip the hide off of you, to make tacklings will yoke your brood and your litter to the plough. (*Lifts whip*.)

DAN. Ah, now your honour, you will not lay the whip on Malachi! Old he is and failing from the world. He is delicate, he cannot stand.

ARD. He is no way deserving of cruelty. An honester man never followed a beast. There is not the weight of that on his character.

STEWARD. There will be the weight of this upon his back! (*Flourishes whip*.)

MALACHI. Take care but I will stop your hand!

STEWARD. Is it to your devils you are calling now, and to the witches of the air? It is not to flog you I will be satisfied. You'll be making provision for the crows to-night if there's a rope to be found in Egypt!

MALACHI. I will call for help to the King's nurseling. Let him say am I to be abused.

STEWARD. The King's nurseling! Ha, ha, ha! Is it that you are thinking that one will come to your help?

MALACHI. It is certain he would be able to save a man from the foot of the gallows.

STEWARD. Is it the like of ye he would stretch out to, and the whole shoal of ye to be dying like fish? Didn't you hear the trumpets braying for him since morning? This is his big day. Sure, myself and the rest of the bailiffs and the stewards are after drinking to his good health!

MALACHI. He is of our race.

STEWARD. If he wasn't you might have some chance. He'd as soon confess himself to be a pig of a herd of pigs. He that was reared to the army, and is apt to be made king in the finish.

MALACHI. We are as good as him, but that we are drowned under trouble.

STEWARD. Ye are, and under dirt and filth. He wouldn't come anear you or within three perches of you unless it might be to be picking fun out of you. Ye that use neither head bath or body bath.

MALACHI. There was one of his family joined with my own family in marriage, two hundred years ago.

STEWARD. You to say that in his hearing, he'd knock the wits out of you, as quick as the blast of a pipe.

MALACHI. I tell you it is as true as that God's sunlight is shining upon us.

STEWARD. So it is, and as true as that there's a tail on Pharaoh's cat. Why wouldn't it be true, and he the very dead spit and modelling of yourselves? He should know that every time he would look in a body glass. (*King's Nurseling moves as if startled.*) But to let on that it is true, he'd sooner drown himself on the race course, that is at this time under flood.

MALACHI. He to know the whole truth he will help us.

STEWARD. He will not. Very high up in himself he is. He would think you to be no credit to him. Very proud and stiff;—and if it wasn't for the King's kindness, and the King's daughter that picked him from the gutter, it is squealing under the lash he would be at this minute the same as yourselves. The King's nurseling! A scamp that is ignorant of his mother and of his father along with that!

KING'S NURSELING (*coming before them suddenly*). What are you saying?

STEWARD. Oh, sir, your honour, I said nothing, nothing at all worth while!

KING'S NURSELING. I heard what you said.

STEWARD. Sure, you never thought it was of your honour I was speaking. I would never do a thing like that. I was talking of—of a mermaid's son my grandmother used to be telling me about, and she enticing me to stop beside the hearth.

KING'S NURSELING. You said I was one of these common men.

STEWARD. Oh, sir, what are you saying? What trade or what consanguinity could there be between the like of you that was reared in golden cradles, and these slaves, these paupers, these tricksters, rebels, liars, herds, sheepstealers, worms of the earth, rogues of the highway, thieves, informers?

MALACHI. Stop your lies! We had some in our generations that never knew the power of death. We had saints and angels visiting our old fathers, before ever there was a Pharoah on the Nile!

STEWARD. Listen, sir, to that! That's rebellion! That's treason-felony! That word will have you hanged! Call out now your soldiers, sir! (*He seizes* MALACHI *and strikes him.*)

KING'S NURSELING. Leave your hold. (*Strikes* STEWARD *with his hurl. He reels and falls back out of sight over the steps.*)

MALACHI. He is dead!

ARD. He has his neck broke.

DAN. That was a good blow and no mistake.

ARD. He has him killed with one blow of the hurl.

KING'S NURSELING. Throw the carrion in a hole of water! (DAN *and* ARD *bear him away. The women have gone aside.*)

MALACHI. You stood up well to him. It took you to tackle him. You behaved well doing that. But I'm in dread it will bring you under trouble. The punishment for murder is death.

KING'S NURSELING. I am under trouble from this out, surely.

MALACHI. It might not be found out, and you going back quick into the King's house.

KING'S NURSELING. I would have been long out of that house, if I knew it was not from my own mother and father I had a claim to it.

MALACHI. Is that the way with you?

KING'S NURSELING. Yesterday I was son to the King's daughter, and to-day I do not know, east or west, to what tribe or family I belong.

MALACHI. Be satisfied. You are a good man's son.

KING'S NURSELING. And is it to yourselves I belong by my birth? (MALACHI *nods.*) The world knows I never knew that!

MALACHI. It is not with ourselves you will stop. We are in danger now to be flogged and tortured and hanged.

KING'S NURSELING. What way could I have an easy mind in it, and my own people being under cruelty and torment? It is along with you I will stop.

MALACHI. Take care now, dear. It would be a pity you to die in your young age.

KING'S NURSELING. They did a great wrong putting a bad name

on my mother's race, and rearing myself to shun and to mock at you, thinking myself a better breed.

ARD (*who has come back with* DAN). Is it that you will take our part?

KING'S NURSELING. I will not eat bread or take my sleep again in that house. I will banish it from me for ever.

DAN. You do not know well what you are doing, and we being a crushed miserable race.

KING'S NURSELING. It is not to a crushed miserable race I have a mind to belong.

DAN. Stretch out so to help us, and to bring us away out of this.

ARD. Let you strive to put the fear of God on the King, the way he will let us go free.

DAN. You not to be able to ready the road and to make a path before us, it can be done by no other one.

ARD. They have put great cruelty upon us. It is you are the most likely one might get it taken off.

DAN. There is no one but yourself to look to. Every person in this place is very combined against us.

MALACHI. It was dreamed to me it was one from the King's house would take in hand our escape.

KING'S NURSELING. I will do all I can do.

DAN. Do that, and you will get the blessing of the people.

KING'S NURSELING. I will bring you out from this disgrace.

MALACHI. So he will. That is in the prophecy. I saw it in the clouds of heaven of a winter night. He will win in the end, but he will not pass within the mering of the Land of Promise.

KING'S NURSELING. Come up with me to a place will have no ears. I have my plans to make. I have commands to give you I am thinking I see a road.

(ARD *and* DAN *follow him.* MALACHI *tries to but fails and sits down.*)

MALACHI. I have no bend in the leg. I cannot get up the steps.

KING'S NURSELING. Stop where you are for a while and take your rest while you can. When this moon will be over and the next moon begun, we will be back in the place our fathers owned. (*Walks up steps. The women come and kneel on steps blessing him.*)

ARD'S WIFE. God love you! My thousand blessings on my two knees to you!

DAN'S WIFE. That the world may wonder at the luck you'll have!

MALACHI'S WIFE. That my blessing may comfort you, and make you that you'll never be broken up!

DAN'S WIFE. May God increase you!

ARD'S WIFE. The Lord have mercy on every one belonging to you!

DAN'S WIFE. And on every one ever went from you!

MALACHI'S WIFE. And on yourself at the latter end.

ARD'S WIFE. The laugh that is in his eye should be sunshine to ripen the barley, and bleach the flax in the field!

DAN'S WIFE. The kindest man that ever broke the world's bread!

MALACHI'S WIFE. That he may have the bed of heaven whoever will be left out!

(KING'S NURSELING, DAN, *and* ARD *have gone off*.)

MALACHI. The Lord be praised it is in my own country my bones will be coffined at the last !

MALACHI'S WIFE. There is a hundred years come into your life with that great news.

DAN'S WIFE. Is that country I wonder as good as what they say?

MALACHI. It is good and kind. The best for meadows and for fair water. Everything a farmer would wish to have around his house he will have it.

ARD'S WIFE. It is estated people we will be that time. Hay and oats in the haggards, a stack upon every small patch.

MALACHI'S WIFE. Sure the vessels will not hold the milk there, it is down on the ground it must fall. There is honey on the tops of the grass.

MALACHI. I to be a beggar on the roads there beyond, I would have neither cark nor care. Keening done away with and treachery. It is a blessed place. There will no snakes live in it. They must perish at the touch of its earth. The sea does be full of all sorts of fish.

DAN'S WIFE. I heard that. Quality fish it would be easy to be eating. The bones of them will melt away in the fire. The smiths do be forging gold the same as iron.

ARD'S WIFE. The next young son that will be born to me, it is not as a slave he will be reared.

MALACHI'S WIFE. Here is Dan coming. He will say are we in a vision or in a dream!

DAN'S WIFE. What did the King's Nurseling say to you? Is it in earnest at all he is?

DAN. He is, surely. He wanted but the wind of the word. Believe me that one has a good head for plans!

MALACHI. What way at all will he get us out of this?

267

DAN. By the miracles of God, and the virtue of those ships beyond at the quay.

MALACHI'S WIFE. The ships did you say! That is a great thought. They should be very answerable.

ARD'S WIFE. What time will we make our start?

DAN. It is on board of those ships the whole of us are to go tonight. There are orders sent to the rest of the twelve families in secret. Believe me, there is a good headpiece on that young boy.

DAN'S WIFE. And is it to our own country they will bring us?

DAN. To go voyage with his left hand to the shore the King thinks he will, and his right hand to the wideness of the sea. He to be out of the harbour, it is not that way he will go, but his left hand to be facing the sea. At the flight of night he will be facing towards a safe harbour near the borders of our own country, and that is free from Pharaoh's rule.

MALACHI. He will send his armies after us there.

DAN. It is what the youngster was saying, we to be out of his hand, every enemy has any complaint against Pharaoh will be on our own side. Believe me, he is great for plans.

MALACHI'S WIFE. Ah, it is only foolishness. It is impossible to steal away unknown.

DAN. It is far out in the night we will go, the way they will feel no noise. The choice captains at the supper till morning, the guard will not be without every sort of beer and of wine. The lad has the Heads of Police sent watching higher up the river, putting in their mind that the place being deserted there will be wild lads spearing the King's fish. He is sending provision to the ships; food for eating, gold for bestowing, arms for to banish enemies. For every five pounds of meal he is sending twenty pound of lead. Bags and bags of money he has, gold and notes to the world's end. I wish I didn't wipe the mortar from me awhile ago. There might some of the riches have stuck to my feet.

MALACHI'S WIFE. Let us be going from this ugly place. It will seem to be the length of a year till I will set out.

ARD'S WIFE. Where now is my man? I would wish to put a white shirt on him before we'd set out, and to round the corners of his head.

DAN. He was sent to forewarn the neighbours to make ready, and to strengthen themselves for the start. To go borrow the makings of a cake he will bid them, and to boil the soup of a hen.

DAN'S WIFE. I should go ready the children. I should wish them to put on a good appearance going back to their own country. It is well I have a bleach of clothes out drying on the bush.

ARD'S WIFE. I got the lend of a little skillet-like from a cook of the King's under-cooks. Copper it is. Would it be any harm I wonder to bring it away in my box?

MALACHI'S WIFE. I'll make no delay and bring no load with me but to put my apron about my head and to walk out of this. Look at what came to me from my father and he dying. The key of the housedoor in my own village. It is here in the bosom of my dress. I have but to turn it going in, and to sit down beside the hearth.

ARD'S WIFE. It is likely it is a tribe of grabbers you will find on the hearth before you.

MALACHI. If there are grabbers there before us we will know a way to make them quit.

ARD'S WIFE. We'll be plentiful from this out surely.

DAN'S WIFE. There'll be currant cakes on the table next Shrove!

MALACHI. No strangers to be meddling with us, and leave to keep the feast days and to gather to prayers.

DAN'S WIFE. Let you shout out now for the King's whiteheaded boy!

MALACHI. He is good and he looks good. He is the best we ever met!

ARD'S WIFE. As simple as if he wasn't worth a shilling, and he dealing out money in sacks.

DAN'S WIFE. A real blood he is!

DAN. Ah, he is no great family man. Just a clean family, that's all.

MALACHI. A man that ignorance was hid from. He should know the seven languages!

ARD'S WIFE. We should knock great comfort out of him. He is no way flighty but good.

DAN'S WIFE. The skin of his face showed out as fair as a sovereign. He has seven colours in his clothes!

DAN. I'm not too bad-looking myself, and I to have good means and a good way and not to be poor and badly clad.

DAN'S WIFE. The sweet eyes and the smile of him! He is a dear loughy man!

DAN. That is enough of gab about himself and his looks. Let you stop your clatter and your talk! (ARD comes in.)

ARD'S WIFE. The sea and the hills would go bail for him! Sure that one would have no harm in him no more than a child.

DAN'S WIFE. We will lift him up on our shoulders passing every bad spot on the road! We'll have a terrible illumination for him the day we will come to our own!

ARD'S WIFE. We will, and put out shouts for him through the whole of the seven parishes! His name will be more lasting than the cry of the plover on the bog!

ARD. You are very ready to give praises and to give trust to one you never cast an eye on till this day.

ARD'S WIFE. Sure any one would think more of a stranger than of a person they would know.

MALACHI'S WIFE. We have good dependence on him. He is kind hearted and willing hearted.

ARD'S WIFE. What could he be but good, and he after making every gap easy before us?

DAN. The women are that cracked after him. You would say they never got a sight of any man besides a cripple or a deformed person before this day.

ARD. That is the way with women and fools. All that is new is beautiful. There'll be another telling by and by.

MALACHI'S WIFE. I would say him to be a nice man and a good man for the world.

ARD. Wait a while till we'll see what way will he turn out. He didn't give us our travelling charges yet.

DAN. I wouldn't begrudge him praise, and I being certain he deserved it.

ARD. He didn't behave too decent not leaving us so much as a red halfpenny to drink his health. What way can we be sure this voyage will not be more for killing than for profit?

DAN. That is true for you. Has he skill to bring us ploughing over the hills and hollows and the rough headed rocks of the sea? The narrow sea or the wide?

MALACHI. He to have said he will rise us up out of our trouble, he will do it.

ARD. It would be a pity going so far, and black sails maybe to be put up for us before we would come to land. Well, drowning is laid down to be an easy death.

ARD'S WIFE. It is often I heard my grandmother saying there are great baulks and great dangers on the road, and a red stream that does be boiling with the heat.

DAN'S WIFE. It might be he has flying ships—or that the whole of the stream and of the ocean would open before him, he being blessed.

ARD'S WIFE. The blazing mountain she used to be talking of, and the mountain of needles.

DAN'S WIFE. It is likely he has enough of a charm to change the points of the needles to green rushes, and to bring us through the fire shivering.

ARD. I'm in dread it is to put a good mouth on himself he made big promises, and to leave us in worse case after.

ARD'S WIFE. I am thinking myself it will fail us to make our escape.

DAN'S WIFE. He to put a sleeping-pin through Pharaoh's plaits, it will keep him in the feathers through the length of nine days and nine nights.

ARD'S WIFE. Where would be the use, and the King having three times fifty beagles and three hundred soldiers at every cross road and every open road? There couldn't so much as a rib of hair go pass athrough them unbeknownst.

DAN'S WIFE. To put a mist-like about them he might, the way they would go astray and be striking and hitting at one another and at themselves.

DAN. I'm in dread whatever way it is, we will have a queer long road to travel.

ARD. That is true for you. I met with a priest of the King's priests, and I coming out over the threshold of the youngster's office. To stop and to talk with me he did. A very friendly man; and shook hands with me and gave me the hand out.

DAN. Is it that he will help us to make our escape?

ARD. It is likely he made a guess I had some notion of the sort in my mind. He was bidding me go quiet and easy, and the King would be apt to come around, and to let us go free in the heel.

MALACHI. I would have no trade with him or the like of him. The Egyptians, you never can get at the root of them.

ARD. I, now, to draw up a petition, he was saying——

MALACHI. You won't get the breadth of the black of your nail that way. They will give us what we will take ourselves, that is what they will do.

ARD. There might be some of themselves would speak for us to the over-Government.

MALACHI. Ah, what way would we wrench it out of the Government? To say that we will is only vanity!

ARD. It is what the priest was saying, the lad is proud and he is giddy. He is no way religious, he was saying, on the one or the other side.

MALACHI'S WIFE. It would be a pity surely if he would not be stiff in his religion.

ARD. He to have broke out of their creed, and not to have joined in our own, he would not be a fitting leader for ourselves. According to what I am told, he's a real regular Pagan.

ARD'S WIFE. I would be sorry to think he would be ignorant and not able to say off the Catechism.

MALACHI. Whatever he might be, we would be better off with him than with them we are under at this time.

ARD. It's hard know. Some are terrible wicked, but some are fair enough.

MALACHI. I would make no complaint, getting bad treatment from a person would be natural, and of our own tribe, besides the foreign troop. It is going trafficking with the Egyptians has you sapped and destroyed.

MALACHI'S WIFE. A priest of the Egyptians to be mistrustful of him, it is likely our own priests would not wish us to have dealings with them.

ARD'S WIFE. You may be certain of that.

MALACHI. So you may be too. Hit one and you hit all. That's the way with clergy rule.

ARD. He to be picking knowledge out of ourselves, he might maybe get through all the dangers and into the good country. It is himself would take the credit then, and be maybe craving to make our laws.

MALACHI. I was thinking before this it was jealousy rose up in your head, and that gave you a spleen against him.

ARD'S WIFE. Look at him! Is it himself at all is in it?

(KING'S NURSELING *walks across at back. He is wearing poor clothes like their own.*)

MALACHI'S WIFE. Take care has he the evil eye put upon us. He gave us no blessing as he passed.

ARD'S WIFE. He is no great gaff, and not having the grand clothes that he had, and the top-knot and the fringes.

MALACHI'S WIFE. He has put on poor clothes like our own for a mockery.

DAN'S WIFE. Take care might it be spying on us he is come.

ARD'S WIFE. To come as a spy and an informer, that is a foul thing to do.

MALACHI'S WIFE. I am a very bad lover of deceit and of treachery.

DAN'S WIFE. It was a queer story his mother to go cast him out of her hand, and leave him to be reared by strangers.

ARD'S WIFE. Ah, how do we know was she wed at all at that time?

MALACHI'S WIFE. That he may never come back alive or dead! I never will give in to a Pagan. I have promised God and the priest.

MALACHI. Is it going against him ye are, and turning from praising to dispraising and abuse?

MALACHI'S WIFE. Why would you go taking his side, and the whole of the rest of us being against him?

MALACHI. I was acquainted with his grandfather. It is a bad day I would see him wanting a friend.

MALACHI'S WIFE. You to be peaceable to this frog of the ditches, I will not be peaceable to yourself.

MALACHI. I tell you there is no other one can bring us out of this.

ARD. Take care but there might be.

MALACHI. There will not be any other one.

ARD. I would not be sure of that. I never heard that lad to have said two words upon a platform.

MALACHI. It is easy be handy in talk, and be supple. Is it that you yourself is thinking to free us?

ARD. The ships are ready. We have the password. Anyone could do the job now.

DAN. I'm as great a story as yourself any day. If any one of us is to take the lead, I have a mind to take it myself.

ARD. I won't give in to that, or to you putting out challenges of the sort.

MALACHI. Let you leave it to the man at the plough to drive the furrow to the end.

DAN. What I will not do is give Ard scope to be tricking, the way he will put himself on top. It's a mean thing to trick. I never would be trickish if I was to die with hunger.

ARD. Is it a man of your sort any person would take commands from?

DAN. You to be arguing like a consequential! A chap that couldn't put a jackdaw on a farm of land!

ARD. I'm able to put a name on you, that you are not more like doing a good deed than a deed of treachery.

MALACHI. Stop your chat! The noise you are making would bring upon us the whole army of police.

273

DAN. Why would I stop? He'd eat the head off me, and I'm not to eat him!

ARD. The latter end of the world to be tomorrow, I'd tell him he is not fit so much as to put fetters on a sheep!

DAN. Have a care now, or I'll whitewash the steps with your bones!

ARD. I don't wish you any harm, but God is unjust if you die a natural death!

DAN. The curse of my heart on you!

ARD. A short course to you!

DAN. You cur, you disgrace, you!

ARD. Keep your tongue off me, you rags! That bad luck may follow you! You that are a rogue since the first day you were born!

MALACHI (seizing DAN). Put the malice out of your heart or we are all destroyed!

DAN. Leave me alone! I am well able to best him!

ARD. You may set your coffin making, for I'll beat you to the ground!

DAN. It wasn't to-day or yesterday I learned to know your tricks!

DAN'S WIFE. Leave go of one another!

ARD. I will not till I squeeze the breath out of him!

ARD'S WIFE. Leave your hold!

MALACHI'S WIFE. Let some person drag them asunder!

DAN'S WIFE. They to get in an argument, it is hard part them from one another!

ARD'S WIFE. Oh, they are in flows of blood!

DAN. I've a grip of you now, you mean little tinker!

ARD. I'll knock the head of you, you shameful pauper!

DAN. Wait till I'll hit him a kick!

ARD. You common rascal!

DAN. You rap! You vagabone!

ALL. Oh, let you stop! They'll kill one another!

> (KING'S NURSELING comes out, parts them quickly, throws down ARD, holds DAN.)

KING'S NURSELING. Are you fools? Damning and blasting and cursing and shouting and beating one another! You will bring out the whole of the palace!

ARD. I done nothing. He drew a blow at me. I gave him but one box.

DAN. He did, and a pelt of a stone and a slap of the left hand on the jaw.

KING'S NURSELING. You are on the brink of your escape! Keep your uproar till you are out of this! (*Shoves down* ARD *who tries to rise.*)

ARD. Leave knocking me. Have you a mind to make an end of me with a blow of a hurl the same as the Nutcracker a while ago?

ARD'S WIFE. Let you leave meddling with my man!

DAN'S WIFE. Take off your hand! It is not in a bunch of rushes my own man was reared!

MALACHI'S WIFE. Take care will he call to the soldiers for to have us all destroyed.

ARD'S WIFE. We are in great danger that he will. It would be right gag his mouth.

DAN'S WIFE. It's best make an end of him.

ARD'S WIFE. It would be no harm to quiet him, giving him a prod of a knife.

MALACHI'S WIFE. A real idolator he is. That is what the King's priest said.

MALACHI. Is it at the bidding of the Egyptians you will give up the man of your own race?

ARD. He will betray us to the King's men.

KING'S NURSELING. I have broken with that troop altogether.

ARD. You will fail us yet, and the King to speak out stiff to you!

KING'S NURSELING. I tell you he to hinder us, I will redden that tide beyond, and twist a bit of crape on every house-door in Egypt.

MALACHI. That is right, that is right! That is the clean drop stirring in him!

DAN'S WIFE. It is misleading us he is.

MALACHI'S WIFE. A man to do that it would disgust you.

ARD'S WIFE. That my curse may follow him!

DAN'S WIFE. That his path may be as slippery as the ditch where he was born, if he did kill the King's steward.

MALACHI'S WIFE. A long trembling to you!

MALACHI. They are set on mischief. The very most people he did good to.

KING'S NURSELING. If you all turn against me, I will fight on with my back to the wall.

ARD. We will give no place to spies!

DAN. We will leave you no time to be an informer!

MALACHI. Ye are doing a great wrong! Give him a show and a hearing!

ARD. It's best make an end of him!

DAN. He can lodge no complaint that time!

MALACHI. Ye are mad, raging mad!

(ARD *pushes* KING'S NURSELING *down on step.*)

MALACHI'S WIFE (*throwing a stone*). Frog spawn!

ARD'S WIFE (*throwing a stone*). Foundling!

DAN'S WIFE (*throwing a stone*). By child!

ARD'S WIFE (*throwing a stone*). Drownded whelp!

(*All throw stones.* KING'S NURSELING *sinks back.*)

OFFICER (*appearing from palace, striking gong*). Where is the King's Nurseling!

(*All shrink back leaving* KING'S NURSELING *on step.*)

OFFICER (*loud*). The pipes and the flutes are ready! The boiled is ready and the roast! (*Sees* KING'S NURSELING.) Rise up, you drowsy vagabone, and say did you see the King's Nurseling in any place?

KING'S NURSELING. The King's Nurseling?

OFFICER. The supper ready and no leave to begin till he will come that is at the head of all. (*Strikes gong.*) I wish I never lost sight of him.

KING'S NURSELING. He will not go back to the supper. He is facing towards the wilderness of the marsh.

OFFICER. It is blind drunk you are and little you know about him.

(*Kicks* KING'S NURSELING *and goes away sounding gong.* KING'S NURSELING'S *head droops. He sinks back on the ground. The others come back cautiously.*)

ARD. There is no one to take notice of us. We can make our escape to the ships.

DAN (*looking at* KING'S NURSELING). There is no stir in him. I thought the life would not have left him so quick.

ARD. Leave him there where he is.

DAN. Take care would they find him and know his features, and follow after us to get revenge for his death.

(*A loud mewing and screaming heard.*)

DAN'S WIFE. What is that screeching?

MALACHI'S WIFE. It is the King's cats calling for their food.

ARD. Shove him over the steps to them.

MALACHI. Will you throw him to the King's cats?

DAN'S WIFE. A good thought. No one will recognise him. They'll have the face ate off him ere morning.

ARD'S WIFE. Throw him to the King's cats!

(*They screech again. Their shadow is seen on steps.* KING'S

NURSELING *is dragged into darkness. A louder screech heard.*)

OFFICER (*coming back*). What is this uproar of cats? Or is it the yelping of yourselves that are curs. It is the whole of this troop that is drunk and howling. (*Takes up whip and shakes it.*) Stop your ugly noise!

(A SOLDIER *appears.*)

OFFICER. Send out a squad of the guard to lodge these bawling blackguards in the black hole. Here, put on the handcuffs. (SOLDIER *comes and handcuffs them leaving them crouching on the steps.*)

OFFICER. Sound out a loud call. I didn't find him yet.

(*He goes up to door. A loud blast of trumpets is heard.*)

MALACHI. I'm on the seventy since last July. It is old bones I will leave in the gaol.

ARD. We were never destroyed out and out till now. It is in bad case we are this time surely.

DAN. It is you yourself was the first to overthrow and to banish him.

MALACH (*laughing to himself*). They were said to give him learning and it is bad learning they gave him. That young man to have read history he would not have come to our help.

MALACHI'S WIFE. Well, the story is done now, and let you leave it to God.

MALACHI. It is sorrow you will sleep with from this out. You will not find the like of him from the rising to the setting sun.

DAN'S WIFE. Look! He is living yet. He is passing!

(KING'S NURSELING *passes slowly at foot of steps towards right. His clothes are torn and blood-stained and he walks with difficulty.*)

DAN. It is but his ghost. He is vanished from us.

DAN'S WIFE. I wish I didn't turn against him. I am thinking he might be an angel.

DAN (*to* MALACHI). Will he ever come back to us?

MALACHI. I won't tell you what I don't know. Wandering, wandering I see, through a score and through two score years. Boggy places will be in it and stony places and splashes—and no man will see the body is put in the grave. A strange thing to get the goal, and the lad of the goal being dead. (*Another screech of the cats. He laughs.*) I wouldn't wonder at all he to bring back cross money to shoot the cats. He will get satisfaction on the cats.

Curtain.

NOTES AND MUSIC

NOTES AND MUSIC

Tragedies:

The Gaol Gate

I was told a story some one had heard, of a man who had gone to welcome his brother coming out of gaol, and heard he had died there before the gates had been opened for him.

Caione.

Tempo, ad lib.

What way will I be the Sun - day

And I go - ing up the hill to the

Mass, Ev' - ry wo - man with her own com - rade

And Ma - ry Cush - in to be walk - ing her lone;

Spoken. *Sings.*

What way—drive the furrow? The

sheaf to be scat-tered be - fore spring-time that

I was going to Galway, and at the Gort station I met two cloaked and shawled countrywomen from the slopes of Slieve Echtge, who were obliged to go and see some law official in Galway because of some money left them by a kinsman in Australia. They had never been in a train or to any place farther than a few miles from their own village, and they felt astray and terrified "like blind beasts in a bog" they said, and I took care of them through the day.

An agent was fired at on the road from Athenry, and some men were taken up on suspicion. One of them was a young carpenter from my old home, and in a little time a rumour was put about that he had informed against the others in Galway gaol. When the prisoners were taken across the bridge to the court-house he was hooted by the crowd. But at the trial it was found that he had not informed, that no evidence had been given at all; and bonfires were lighted for him as he went home.

These three incidents coming within a few months wove themselves into this little play, and within three days it had written itself, or been written. I like it better than any in the volume, and I have never changed a word of it.

Grania

I think I turned to Grania because so many have written about sad, lovely Deirdre, who when overtaken by sorrow made no good battle at the last. Grania had more power of will, and for good or evil twice took the shaping of her life into her own hands. The riddle she asks us through the ages is, "Why did I, having left great grey-haired Finn for comely Diarmuid, turn back to Finn in the end, when he had consented to Diarmuid's death?" And a question tempts one more than the beaten path of authorised history. If I have held but lightly to the legend, it is not because I do not know it, for in *Gods and Fighting Men* I have put together and rejected many versions. For the present play I have taken but enough of the fable on which to set, as on a sod of grass, the three lovers, one of whom had to die. I suppose it is that "fascination of things difficult" that has tempted me to write a three-act play with only three characters. Yet where Love itself, with its shadow Jealousy, is the true protagonist I could not feel that more were needed. When I told Mr. Yeats I had but these three persons in the play, he said incredulously, "They must have a great deal to talk about." And so they have, for the talk of lovers is inexhaustible, being of themselves and one another.

As to the Fianna, the Fenians, I have heard their story many a time from my neighbours, old men who have drifted into workhouses, seaweed gatherers on the Burren Coast, turf-cutters on Slieve Echtge, and the like. For though the tales that have gathered around that mysterious race are thought by many to come from the earliest days, even before the coming of the Aryan Celt, the people of the West have a very long memory. And these tales are far better remembered than those of the Red Branch, and this, it is suggested, is part proof of their having belonged to the aboriginal race. Cuchulain's bravery, and Deirdre's beauty "that brought the Sons of Usnach to their death" find their way, indeed, into the folk-poetry of all the provinces; but the characters of the Fianna, Grania's fickleness, and Conan's bitter tongue, and Oisin's gentleness to his friends and his keen wit in the arguments with St. Patrick, and Goll's strength, and Osgar's high bravery, and Finn's wisdom, that was beyond that of earth, are as well known as the characteristics of any noticeable man of modern times.

An old man I talked with on the beach beyond Kinvara told me, "They were very strong in those days, and six or seven feet high. I was digging the potato garden one day about forty years ago, and down in the dyke the spade struck against something, and it was the bones of a man's foot, and it was three feet long. I brought away one bone of it myself, and the man that was along with me, but we buried it after. It was the foot of one of those men. They had every one six or seven dogs, and first they would set two of the dogs to fight, and then they'd fight themselves. And they'd go to all countries in curraghs that were as strong as steamers; to Spain they went in their curraghs. They went across from this hill of Burren to Connemara one time, and the sea opened to let them pass. There are no men like them now; the Connemara men are the best, but even with them, if there was a crowd of them together, and you to throw a stick over their heads, it would hardly hit one, they are mostly all the one height, and no one a few inches taller than another."

Another man says, "They were all strong men in those times; and one time Finn and his men went over to Granagh to fight the men there, and it was the time of the harvest, and what they fought with was sheaves, and every one that got a blow of a sheaf got his death. There is one of them buried now in Fardy Whelan's hill, and there's two headstones, and my father often measured the grave, and he said it is seven yards long."

On Slieve Echtge I was told, "Oisin and Finn took the lead for strength, and Samson, too, he had great strength." "I would rather hear about the Irish strong men," said I. "Well, and Samson was of the Irish race, all the world was Irish in those times, and he killed the Philistines, and the eyes were picked out of him after. He was said to be the strongest, but I think myself Finn MacCumhail was tronger." And again, "It was before the flood those strong men lived here, Finn and Oisin and the others, and they lived longer than people do now, three or four hundred years.

284

"Giants they were; Conan was twelve feet high, and he was the smallest. But ever since, people are getting smaller and smaller, and will till they come to the end; but they are wittier and more crafty than they were in the old days, for the giants were innocent though they were so strong."

I hear sometimes of "a small race and dark, and that carried the bag," and that was probably the aboriginal one. "There was a low-sized race came, that worked the land of Ireland a long time; they had their time like the others." And, "Finn was the last of the giants, the tall strong men. It was after that the Lochlannachs came to the country. They were very small, but they were more crafty than the giants, and they used to be humbugging them. One time they got a sack and filled it with sand, and gave it to one of the Fianna to put on his back to try him. But he lifted it up, and all he said was, 'It is grain sowed in February it is.' " Another says, "An old man that was mending the wall of the house used to be telling stories about the strong men of the old time; very small they were, about three feet high, but they were very strong for all that."

Grania is often spoken of as belonging to that small race, as if her story had come from a very early time. "She was very small, only four feet. She was the heiress of the princes of Ireland, and that is why they were after her." "They say Diarmuid and Grania were very small. They made the big cromlechs, there's a slab on the one near Crusheen, sixteen men couldn't lift, but they had *their own way* of doing it." And again, "Diarmuid and Grania were very small and very thick." Another says, "Grania was low-sized; and people now are handsomer than the people of the old time, but they haven't such good talk."

I do not know if it is because of Grania's breach of faith, that I never hear her spoken of with sympathy, and her name does not come into the songs as Deirdre's does. A blind piper told me, "Some say Grania was handsome, and some say she was ugly, there's a saying in Irish for that." And an old basket-maker was scornful and said, "Many would tell you Grania slept under the cromlechs, but I don't believe that, and she a king's daughter. And I don't believe she was handsome either. If she was, why would she have run away?"

An old woman says, "Finn had more wisdom than all the men in the world, but he wasn't wise enough to put a bar on Grania. It was huts with big stones Grania made, that are called cromlechs now; they made them when they went away into the wilderness."

And again I was told at Moycullen, near Lough Corrib, "As they were passing a stream, the water splashed on Grania, and she said 'Diarmuid was never so near to me as that.' "

Kincora

Kincora was the first historical play I wrote, and it gave me a great deal of trouble and I wrote many versions, for I had not enough of skill to wrestle with the mass of material, and I think I kept too closely to history. It was produced at the Abbey Theatre in 1905 in the old printed version. This new version was produced in 1909.

I hoped then and still hope that we may give a week or more in every year to a sequence of history plays, or perhaps play them at schools, that schoolboys and schoolgirls may have their imagination stirred about the people who made history, instead of knowing them but as names. But Brian's greatness lives always in the memory of the people, and Kincora is remembered in the song translated by Mangan from the Irish of one of Brian's own household:

> Oh, where, Kincora, is Brian the great? And where is the
> beauty that once was thine?
> Oh, where are the princes and nobles that sat at the feast in
> thy halls and drank the red wine?
>
> I am MacLiag and my home is on the lake; thither often to
> that palace whose beauty is dead
> Came Brian to ask me and I went for his sake. Oh my grief!
> that I should live and Brian be dead!

The summary given by modern histories is as follows:

"Two Kings gained lasting renown during the contests with the Norsemen, Malachi the Great, who became High King in 980, and Brian, King of the province of Munster. Brian in a battle fought in 968 at Sulcoit, north of the Galtee Mountains, defeated the Norsemen and put them to flight. This was the first of a series of victories against the raiders who from this time forward are generally spoken of as Danes, though they came from Norway as well as Denmark.

"Malachi, the High King, was at the same time making attacks on the invaders' settlements in Dublin and as far north as the Boyne. He took Dublin in 996, winning there among other spoils the golden ring of the Danish chief. Two such strong personalities as Malachi and Brian, rulers of provinces which had long been rivals, could hardly be expected to live in brotherly union and concord. We find them constantly at strife, even when both were fighting against the common foe. They finally agreed to divide Ireland between them, Malachi taking the northern part and handing over the southern to Brian. This arrangement was made in 998, and not unnaturally gave great offence to the King of Leinster whose territory lay in the region assigned by Malachi to Brian. The King of Leinster made an alliance with the Danes of Dublin and determined to resist Brian's authority. Brian and Malachi immediately gathered an army and met and defeated the united armies of the King of Leinster and the Danes in one of the valleys of the Wicklow hills, Glenmama.

"Brian married Gormleith (Gormley), sister of the King of Leinster and widow of a former chief of the Danes, whose son Sitric was now their acknowledged leader. This alliance won over to Brian's side both the King of Leinster and the Danes of Dublin, and Brian presently felt strong enough to lead an army northward towards Tara to try conclusions with Malachi for the High Kingship of Ireland. Malachi recognised that his opponent was too strong for him and made his submission. This took place in the year 1002, and for the next twelve years, until he was slain at the battle of Clontarf, Brian was recognised as the High King of Ireland."

That is what the histories tell, and they tell also of the woman who walked all Ireland with a gold ring in her hand; though I have changed the rich clothes of the legend for rags, thinking them nearer to the inner meaning of the parable. As to the quarrel between Brian and the King of Leinster, the books say:

"As part of his tribute the Leinster King was bringing to Kincora three pine trees for ships' masts, and among the carriers some dispute arose as to who was to be in the first place. To end the dispute the King himself took the first place, and in his exertions in carrying the tree, one of the silver buttons of his tunic had been torn off. At Kincora he handed the tunic to his sister Gormleith, asking her to sew on the displaced button; but the lady, instead, heaped reproaches on him for being a mere vassal, and angrily flung the tunic into the fire. Her taunting words irritated Maelmora, and his irritation was soon shown. Looking on at a game of chess which was being played between Murrough and his cousin Conaing, Maelmora suggested a move which ended in Murrough losing the game. Murrough angrily remarked, 'That was like the advice you gave the Danes which lost them Glenmama.' Maelmora with equal anger replied, 'I will now give them advice and they shall not be defeated.' 'Then' said Murrough, 'you had better remind them to have a yew tree ready for your reception.' For Maelmora had hidden in a yew tree after his defeat at Glenmama. In bitterness of heart and in secret Maelmora left Kincora. He decided to revolt and was joined by the Dublin Danes. The Battle of Clontarf was the result. Brian was killed there, and Maelmora, but the Danes were driven from Ireland for ever.

"In bringing together the Danes for Clontarf nobody had been more active than Gormleith. Since Maelmora's visit to Kincora she had been repudiated by Brian and had become so 'grim' against him that she wished him dead. She had sent her son Sitric to the Danish leaders to beg their assistance. The two best known of these leaders were Brodar, Earl of Man, and Sigurd, Earl of Orkney. Both made it a condition to be acknowledged King of Ireland if Brian were defeated and slain, and also to get Gormleith in marriage . . . though the latter was now old, and it is unlikely that they were attracted by her doubtful virtue or coveted her faded charms."

So far the histories, founded, one must think, on the legends of the people. Around Kincora such legends still linger. One is shown where Brian's palace was, and where the fish were caught for his use and told of all his cellars and strong-rooms and passages, some of them underground. And a man in armour is seen now and again on the roads near the green mound where the palace stood, who is, it may be, the walking shadow of the High King.

When *Kincora* was first produced in Dublin, an old farmer came all the way from Killaloe near Kincora to see it, and he went away sad because as he said "Brian ought not to have married that woman, but to have been content with a nice quiet girl from his own district."

As to the Danes, the people tell me, "The reason of the wisps and the fires on Saint John's Eve is that one time long ago the Danes came and took the country and conquered it, and they put a soldier to mind every house through the whole country. And at last the people made up their minds that on one night they would kill the soldiers. So they did as they said, and there wasn't one left, and that is why they light the wisps ever since. It was Brian Boroihme (Boru) was the first to light them. There was not much of an army left to the Danes that time, for he made a great scatter of them. A great man he was, and his own son was as good, that is Murrough. It was the wife brought him to his end, Gormleith. She was for war, and he was all for peace. And he got to be very pious, too pious, and old, and she got tired of that." And I am told of the last battle. "Clontarf was on the head of a game of chess. The generals of the Danes were beaten at it, and they were vexed. It was Brodar, that the Brodericks are descended from, that put a dagger through Brian's heart, and he attending to his prayers. What the Danes left in Ireland were hens and weasels. And when the cock crows in the morning the country people will always say, 'It is for Denmark they are crowing; crowing they are to be back in Denmark!'"

But the Danes are often mixed up with the Tuatha de Danaan, the old gods, the invisible inhabitants of the forths, as in a story I have been told of the battle of Aughrim. "The Danes were dancing in the forths around Aughrim the night after the Battle. Their ancestors were driven out of Ireland before; and they were glad when they saw those that had put them out put out themselves, and every one of them skivered."

The small size of our stage and our small number of players forced me to do away with what our people call "the middling class," and I have used but servants and kings. As to their language, I have, to the grief of my printers, used the dialect spoken by many of my neighbours, who are though it may be by long descent, belonging to the families of kings.

Dervorgilla

Dervorgilla, daughter of the King of Meath, wife of O'Rourke, King of Breffny, was taken away, willingly or unwillingly by Diarmuid MacMurrough, King of Leinster, in the year 1152. O'Rourke and his friends invaded Leinster in revenge, and in the wars which

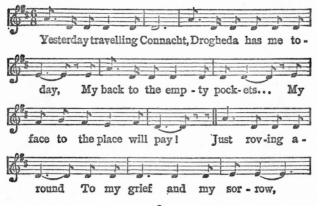

Yesterday travelling Connacht, Drogheda has me to-
day, My back to the emp-ty pock-ets... My
face to the place will pay! Just rov-ing a-
round To my grief and my sor-row,

Un - der a rock to - daý, Un - der a bush to -
mor - row... Sy - rup - y sweet to - day,
Sour as sloes to - mor - row ; Sweet to the lads that
pay, Sour to the lads that bor - row !

1. I am after being given two grand steppers
2. It's the roads of the world would be proud to see them,

Matching one another like two swallows on the wind,
It's a great ornament they will be, far and near ;

Made from the skin of the Brown Bull of Cuailgne, Or the
She that gave them never learned to be a niggard, Tho' the

cow Ar - gus - mind - ed, ... he that was not blind.
Gall are a - mong us this four and twenty year !

followed, Diarmuid, driven from Ireland, appealed for help to
Henry II of England, and was given an army under Strongbow, to
whom Diarmuid promised Leinster as reward. It is so the English
were first brought into Ireland. Dervorgilla, having outlived
O'Rourke and Diarmuid and Henry and Strongbow, is said to have
died at the Abbey of Mellifont, near Drogheda, in the year 1193,
aged 85.

That is how the story is told in the histories. And I have heard

It is pit - i - ful and sharp to-day are the
wounds of Ire - land, From Gal - way of white
flag-gy stones to Cork of the white strand; The
branch - es that were full of leaves and
hon - ey on the leaves Are torn and stripped and
short - ened by the stranger to our grief. It is
long, O Royal Ire - land, you were manner - ly and
kind, A nurs-ing mo - ther to your sons, fair,
hos - pi - ta - ble, wise; Now you are wine spilled
from a cup be-neath the stran-gers' feet, The
English-speaking troop to-day have trod-den down our wheat.

in Kiltartan: "Dervorgilla was a red-haired woman, and it was
she put the great curse on Ireland, bringing in the English through
MacMurrough, that she went to from O'Rourke. It was to Henry

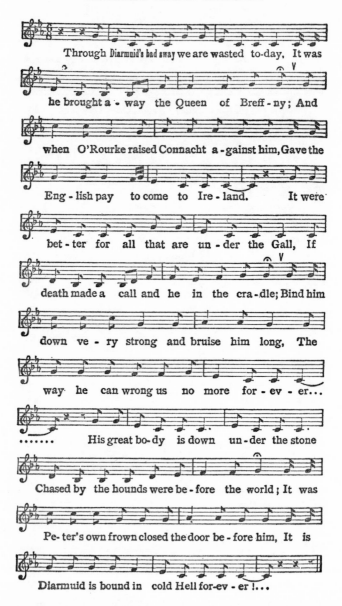

the Second MacMurrough went, and he sent Strongbow, and they
stopped in Ireland ever since. But who knows but another race

might be worse, such as the Spaniards that were scattered along the whole coast of Connacht at the time of the Armada? And the laws are good enough. I heard it said the English will be dug out of their graves one day for the sake of their law. As to Dervorgilla, she

queer for a Queen to be kind in her mind, To the

trai - tor she join-ed, to the fox of Lein-ster.

The rat in the lar-der, the fire in the thatch; The

guest to be fattening, and the chil - dren famished; My

curse up - on all that brought in the Gall, Up-on

Di - ar- muid's call, and in Der - vor - gil - la!

was not brought away by force, she went to MacMurrough herself. For there are men in the world that have a coaxing way, and sometimes women are weak."

McDonough's Wife

In my childhood there was every year at my old home, Roxborough, or, as it is called in Irish, Cregroostha, a great sheep-shearing that lasted many days. On the last evening there was always a dance for the shearers and their helpers, and two pipers used to sit on chairs placed on a corn-bin to make music for the dance. One of them was always McDonough. He was the best of all the wandering pipers who went about from house to house. When, at my marriage, I moved from the barony of Dunkellin to the neighbouring barony of Kiltartan, he came and played at the dance given to the tenants in my honour, and he came and played also at my son's coming of age. Not long after that he died. The last time I saw him he came to ask for a loan of money to take the train to Ennis, where there was some fair or gathering of people going on, and I would not lend to so old a friend, but gave him a half-sovereign, and we parted with kindly words. He was so great a piper that in the few years since his death myths have already begun to gather around him. I have been told that his father was taken into a hill of the Danes, the Tuatha de Danaan, the ancient invisible race, and they had taught him all their tunes and so bewitched his pipes, that they would play of themselves if he threw them up on the rafters. McDonough's pipes, they say, had not that gift, but he himself could play those inspired tunes. Lately I was told the story I have used in this play about his taking away fifty sovereigns from the shearing at Cregroostha and spending them at a village near. "I said to him," said the old man who told me this, "that it would be better for him to have bought a good kitchen of bacon; but he said, 'Ah, when I want more, I have but to squeeze the pipes.' " The story of his wife's death and burial as I give it has been told to me here and there. That is my fable, and the emotion disclosed by the story is, I think, the lasting pride of the artist of all ages:

> "We are the music makers
> And we are the dreamers of dreams . . . .
> We in the ages lying
> In the buried past of the earth
> Built Nineveh with our sighing,
> And Babel itself with our mirth."

I wrote the little play while crossing the Atlantic in the *Cymric* last September. Since it was written I have been told at Kinvara that "McDonough was a proud man; he never would go to a wedding unasked, and he never would play through a town." So he had laid down pride for pride's sake, at that time of the burying of his wife.

In Galway this summer one who was with him at the end told me he had a happy death, "But he died poor; for what he would make in the long nights he would spend through the summer days." And then she said, "Himself and Reilly and three other fine pipers died within that year. There was surely a feast of music going on in some other place."

[When Lady Gregory gave the manuscript of this play to John Quinn, she attached a note which read: "I began to write this little play, McDaragh's Wife, on board the Cymric, first making my scenario on a Menu, and then writing in pencil as I lay down in my cabin, quiet and undisturbed. Then I added to it and typed it out in Boston, and then 'The Outlook' asked for it and printed it—so here it is in its several states; and being still new to me I think it worth offering to you, dear John Quinn, but you shall have a better one if a better one should come—tho' this will be all the more valuable if it should be my last. I don't suppose anyhow you will be able to read a word of it. Augusta Gregory." The title was later changed to McDonough's Wife.]

Tragic-Comedies

The Image:

To a Certain Editor—"When the 'Image' was produced at the Abbey, I put on the programme a quotation, 'Secretum meum Mihi,' 'My Secret to Myself,' which I had for a while thought of taking as its name. I think from a note in your paper you and some others believed that the secret I wanted to keep was my own, whereas I had but given a 'heart-secret' into the keeping of each of the persons of the play.

"One of the old stories known in the cottages is of a beautiful lady loved by a king's son, who follows her to a garden where they love and are happy. She has laid on him one condition only: 'You must never wonder at me, or say anything about me at all.' But one day she passed by him in the garden, and when he saw her so beautiful, he turned and said to the gardener: 'There was never a lady so beautiful as mine in the whole world.' 'There never was,' said the gardener, 'and you will be without her now,' he said. And so it happened, and he lost her from that day because he had put his thought about her into common words.

"So it fell out with my old people. Brian Hosty's 'Image' was his native, passionately loved province of Connacht; but he boasted of it to some who could see its thorns and thistles with passionless eyes, looking over the mering wall. Mrs. Coppinger had her mind set upon America as a place where the joy of life would reach its summit, but that hope is clouded by the derision of one who has been there, and seen but the ugliness about him. Costello thought of an earth all peace, but when he spoke of peace 'they made themselves ready to war'. Thomas Coppinger dreamed of the great monument he would make to some great man, and old Peggy of one made beautiful through long memory and death; and Malachi of one who was beyond and above earthly life. And each of these images crumbled at the touch of reality, like a wick that has escaped the flame, and is touched by common air. And the more ecstatic the vision the more impossible its realisation until that time when, after the shadows of earth, the seer shall 'awake and be satisfied.'

296

"You are certainly proud of what your paper has done to bring back respect for the work of Irish hands. But I wonder if it is all you intended it to be when you wrote in a little book I edited ten years ago of a 'new Ireland rising up out of the foundations of the old, with love and not hate as its inspiration?' For you also have been an Image-maker. The Directors of our Theatre are beginning to get some applause, even in Dublin, for its success, but only they know how far it still is from the idea with which they set out. And so with my sisters' sons, to whom I have dedicated this play. One brought together the Conference that did so much towards the peaceable and friendly changing of land ownership. The other has made Dublin the Orient of all—artists or learners or critics, who value the great modern school of French painting. Yet I fancy it was a dream beyond possible realisation that gave each of them the hard patience needed by those who build, and the courage needed by the "Disturber" who does not often escape some knocks and buffetings. But if the dreamer had never tried to tell the dream that had come across him, even though to 'betray his secret to the multitude' must shatter his own perfect vision, the world would grow clogged and dull with the weight of flesh and of clay. And so we must say 'God love you' to the Image-makers, for do we not live by the shining of those scattered fragments of their dream?

"I do not know if I should have written this 'apology' at the first playing of 'the Image,' or if I ought to leave it unwritten now. For after all, those enjoy it most who say in what I think is your own formula—'this is what Lady Gregory calls a comedy, but everybody else calls a farce.' "

I owe an acknowledgment as well as many thanks to A.E., who gave me the use of an idea that had come to him for a play, which he had no thought of carrying out. It was about a man who collected money in a country town for a monument to one Michael M'Carthy Ward, I forget on what grounds. The money is collected, the collector disappears, and then only it is found that Michael M'Carthy Ward had never existed at all. I meant to carry this out in the manner of "Spreading the News" or "The Jackdaw," but the "Image" took the matter into its own hands, and whether for good or ill-luck, the three-act play has grown. I think I have not quite failed, yet it also is not what I set out to do.

It was after the play had been written that an old man strolling out from Gort one Sunday talked of O'Connell. "There is a nice monument put up to him in Ennis," he said. "In a corner it is of the middle of the street, and himself high upon it, holding a book. It was a poor shoemaker set that going. I saw him in Gort one time; a coat of O'Connell's he had that he chanced in some place. Only for him there would be no monument; it was he gathered money for it, and there was none would refuse him." And still later, this spring, I went to see the Hill of Tara, and I was told that the statue of Saint Patrick on it "was made by a mason—a common mason. If it wasn't that he had made it, and had it ready, and was a poor man, it would not have been put up." So the ambitions of Malachi Naughton and Thomas Coppinger have not been without ancestry.

The Canavans

This play is founded more directly upon folklore and less upon written history than the others, so far as the tradition of the Virgin Queen goes in Ireland. But the epithets given her by her courtiers are taken from the writings of the time. The desire possessing Peter Canavan to be on the safe side, on the side of the strongest, is not bounded by any century or kept within the borders of any country, though it jumps to light more aggressively in one which, like Ireland, has been tilted between two loyalties through so many generations. The play seems (to me now) somewhat remote, inexplicable, as if written less by logical plan than in one of those moments of light-heartedness that come, as I think, as an inheritance from my French great-grandmother, Frances Aigoin; a moment of that "sudden Glory, the Passion which maketh those Grimaces called Laughter." It plays merrily, and there are some who like it best of my comedies.

As to traditions of the Tudors, this is what I am told in Kiltartan:

"Henry the Eighth was crying and roaring and leaping out of the bed for three days and nights before his death. And he died cursing his children, and he that had eight millions when he came to the throne, coining leather money at the end.

"Queen Elizabeth was awful. Beyond everything she was. When she came to the turn she dyed her hair red, and whatever man she had to do with, she sent him to the block in the morning, that he would be able to tell nothing. She had an awful temper. She would throw a knife from the table at the waiting ladies, and if anything vexed her she would maybe work upon the floor. A thousand dresses she left after her. Very superstitious she was. Sure after her death they found a card, the ace of hearts, nailed to her chair under the seat. She thought she would never die while she had it there.

And she bought a bracelet from an old woman out in Wales that was over a hundred years. It was superstition made her do that, and they found it after her death, tied about her neck.

"It was a town called Calais brought her to her death, and she lay chained on the floor three days and three nights. The Arch-

Ye trai-tors all that do de-vise To plague our. Par-a-gon, And in your hearts in treach'rous wish Let such vain thoughts run on. Con-sid-er what your end will be Be-fore you far-ther go;..... The Crown of Li-lies joy-ful-ly Will hang you in a row!

bishop was trying to urge her to eat, but she said: 'You would not ask me to do it if you knew the way I am,' for nobody could see the chains. After her death they waked her for six days in Whitehall, and there were six ladies sitting beside the body every night. Three coffins were about it, the one nearest the body of lead, and then a wooden one, and a leaden one of the outside. And every night there came from them a great bellow. And the last night there came a bellow that broke the three coffins open, and tore the velvet, and there came out a stench that killed the most of the ladies and a million of the people of London with the plague. Queen Victoria was more honourable than that. It would be hard to beat Queen Elizabeth."

From *The Arrow* No. 2, 24 November, 1906. When I wrote "The White Cockade" I did not explain as perhaps I should have done, that I took my historical atmosphere less from history books than from the tradition of the people, who have not been taught English history in the schools, and so have learned it through tradition or the songs of wandering poets like Raftery, or another. Sarsfield—the people's hero—is "a man with God," and gets a hundred thousand welcomes in many songs. James is the man who ran from the Boyne, "didn't go into the thick of the battle, but made off to Dublin, bringing the best of the troops with him." It is not only in Connacht this feeling is alive, for when "The White Cockade" was in rehearsal I went into a little Dublin leather shop to buy a belt or strap for the play and told the owner what it was wanted for, and he said, "I hope, ma'am, you won't let King James off too easily."

When I was writing "The Canavans," I read in an Essay on Spenser and his poetry and his "expedient emotions," this passage "The queen was over sixty years old and ugly, and it is thought, selfish; but in his poetry she is 'fair Cynthia,' 'a crown of lilies,' 'the image of the heavens,' 'without mortal blemish,' and has an 'angelic face,' where 'the red rose has meddled with the white.' 'Phoebus thrusts out his golden head' but to look upon her, and 'blushes to find himself outshone.' 'She is a fourth Grace,' 'a queen of love,' 'a sacred saint,' and 'above all her sex that ever yet has been.' In the midst of the praise of his own sweetheart he stops to remember that Elizabeth is more beautiful, and an old man in 'Daphnaida,' although he has been brought to death's door by the death of a beautiful daughter, remembers that though his daughter seemed of angelic race, she was yet but the primrose to the rose beside Elizabeth. Then a poor basketmaker at the door told me many traditional things about Elizabeth's life, beginning with "Queen Elizabeth was awful". And of her death he told me, "She lay chained on the floor through three days and nights. The Archbishop was trying to urge her to eat, but she said, "you would not ask me to do it if you knew the way I am," for nobody could see the chains on her. After her death they waked her for six days in Whitehall, and there were six ladies sitting beside the body every night. Three coffins were about it—the one nearest the body of lead, and then a wooden one, and a leaden one on the outside. And every night there came from them a great bellow; and the last night there came a bellow that broke the three coffins open, and tore the velvet, and there came out a stench that killed the most of the ladies and a million of the people of London with the plague.' "

I have given in my play the two views of Queen Elizabeth's life, but I have not ventured upon the death scene.

The White Cockade

Some time ago I was looking through some poems taken down in Irish from the country people, and a line of one of them seemed strange to me "Prebaim mo chroidhe le mo Stuart glegeal"—"My heart leaps up with my bright Stuart"; for I had not heard any songs of this sort in Galway and I remembered that our Connacht Raftery, whose poems are still teaching history, dealt very shortly with the Royal Stuarts. "James," he says, "he was the worst man for habits, he laid chains on our bogs and mountains. The father wasn't worse than the son Charles, that left sharp scourges on Ireland. When God and the people thought it time the story to be done, he lost his head. The next James—sharp blame to him— gave his daughter to William as woman and wife; made the Irish English and the English Irish, like wheat and oats in the month of harvest. And it was at Aughrim on a Monday many a son of Ireland found sorrow without speaking of all that died."

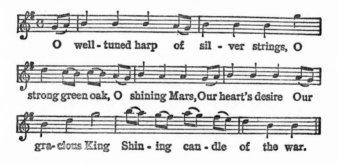

O well-tuned harp of silver strings, O strong green oak, O shining Mars, Our heart's desire Our gracious King Shining candle of the war.

So I went to ask some of the wise old neighbours who sit in wide chimney nooks by turf fires, and to whom I go to look for knowledge of many things, if they knew of any songs in praise of the Stuarts. But they were scornful. "No indeed," one said, "there are no songs about them and no praises in the West, whatever there may be in the South. Why would there, and they running away and leaving the country the way they did? And what good did they ever do it? James the Second was a coward. Why didn't he go into the thick of the battle like the Prince of Orange? He stopped on a hill three miles away, and rode off to Dublin, bringing the best of his troops with him. There was a lady walking in the street at Dublin when he got there, and he told her the battle was lost and she said: 'Faith you made good haste; you made no delay on the road.' So he said no more after that. The people liked James well enough before he ran; they didn't like him after that."

And another said: 'Seumas Salach, Dirty James, it is he brought all down. At the time of the battle there was one of his men said, 'I have my eye cocked, and all the nations will be done away with,' and he pointing his cannon. 'Oh!' said James, 'Don't make a widow of my daughter.' If he didn't say that, the English would have been beat. It was a very poor thing for him to do."

And one who lives on the border of Munster said: "I used to hear them singing 'The White Cockade' through the country; King James was beaten and all his well-wishers; my grief, my boy that went with them! But I don't think the people had ever much opinion of the Stuarts, but in those days they were all prone to versify." And another old man said: "When I was a young chap knocking about in Connemara, I often heard songs about the Stuarts, and talk of them and of the blackbird coming over the water. But they found it hard to get over James making off after the battle of the Boyne." And when I looked through the lately gathered bundle of songs again, and through some old collections of favourite songs in Irish, I found they almost all belonged to Munster. And if they are still sung there, it is not, as I think, for the sake of the Kings, but for the sake of the poets who wrote them. And in these songs of sorrow for Ireland and the indictment of England, the Stuart himself is often forgotten, or when he appears, he is but a faint and unreal image; a saint by whose name a heavy oath is sworn.

It is different with Patrick Sarsfield, Earl of Lucan, a "great general and killed thousands of the English"; the brave, handsome, fighting man, the descendant of Conall Cearnach, the man who, after the Boyne, offered to "change Kings and fight the battle again." The songs about him are personal enough. Here is one I have put into English:

"O Patrick Sarsfield, health be to you, since you went to France and your camps were loosened; making your sighs along with the

King, and you left poor Ireland and the Gael defeated—Och Ochone!

"O Patrick Sarsfield, it is a man with God you are, and blessed is the earth you ever walked on. The blessing of the bright sun and the moon upon you since you took the day from the hands of King William—Och Ochone!

"O Patrick Sarsfield, the prayer of every person with you; my own prayer and the prayer of the Son of Mary with you, since you took the narrow ford going through Biorra, and since in Cuilenn O'Cuanac you won Limerick—Och Ochone!

"They put the first breaking on us at the Bridge of the Boyne; the second breaking at the Bridge of Slaney; the third breaking in Aughrim of O'Kelly; and O sweet Ireland, my five hundred healths to you—Och Ochone!

"O'Kelly has manuring for his land, that is not sand or dung, but ready soldiers doing bravery with pikes, that were left in Aughrim stretched in ridges—Och, Ochone!

"Who is that beyond on the hill Beinn Edar? I, a poor soldier with King James. I was last year in arms and in dress, but this year I am asking alms—Och, Ochone!"

As to the poor Lady, she was not the only one to wander miserably, having spent all for the Stuarts.

The attempted escape of King James in the barrel had already been used by Dr. Hyde in a little play written in Irish. In these days, when so much of the printed history we were taught as children is being cast out by scholars, we must refill the vessel by calling in tradition, or if need be our own imaginings. When my *White Cockade* was first produced I was pleased to hear that J. M. Synge had said my method had made the writing of historical drama again possible.

The Deliverer

I used to say in defence of friends of mine, who were attacked for wild acts, and Mr. Yeats borrowed my saying, that Moses was of no use to his people until he had killed an Egyptian. Then I began to say in relation to a "gran rifiuto" of later days that some who had turned upon their leader would have their forty years of walking the sand. More lately in Kiltartan, I was told by one who had been present at the last meeting held by that deserted leader, how those who had crowded to him before had left him by order, and how fiery his words were and how white was his face. And, it was said "The ancient Jews turned against Moses in the same way."

303

I was at a Feis, a Festival, at Spiddal on Galway Bay in honour of the Irish language about ten years ago, and after it I wrote:

"In the evening there were people waiting round the door to hear the songs and the pipes again. An old man among them was speaking with many gestures, his voice rising, and a crowd gathering about him. 'Tha se beo, tha se beo'—'he is living, he is living,' I heard him say over and over again. I asked what he was saying and was told: 'He says that Parnell is alive yet.' I was pushed away from him by the crowd to where a policeman was looking on. 'He says that Parnell is alive still,' I said. 'There are many say that,' he answered. 'And after all no one ever saw the body that was buried.'"

I remember a visit of M. Paul Bourget to Coole and his being so excited and moved by the tragic wasted face of one of the last photographs of Mr. Parnell, that he could not leave it but carried it about the house. I had already written on the back of that portrait this verse from an old ballad:

> Oh, I have dreamed a dreary dream
> Beyond the isle of Skye,
> I saw a dead man win a fight
> And I think that man was I!

FIRST PERFORMANCES AT THE
ABBEY THEATRE

FIRST PERFORMANCES AT THE ABBEY THEATRE

The following plays in this Volume have been performed at the Abbey Theatre and the casts and the date of the first productions are given below:

Tragedies

The Gaol Gate
20th October 1906

Mary Cahel	Sara Allgood
Mary Cushin	Maire O'Neill
The Gatekeeper	F. J. Fay

Grania has not yet been produced.

Kincora (final version)
11th February 1909

Brian	Arthur Sinclair
Maelmora	Sydney J. Morgan
Malachi	Ambrose Power
Sitric	U. Wright
Murrough	Fred O'Donovan
Brennain	J. M. Kerrigan
Rury	J. H. Dunne
Phelan	J. A. O'Rourke
Gormleith	Sara Allgood
Beggar	Maire O'Neill

Dervorgilla
31st October 1907

Dervorgilla	Sara Allgood
Mona	Maire O'Neill
Mamie	Brigit O'Dempsey
Flann	F. J. Fay

Songmaker	W. G. Fay
A Boy	Arthur Sinclair
Another	J. M. Kerrigan
Another	J. A. O'Rourke

McDonough's Wife (first performed as *MacDaragh's Wife*)
11th January 1912

First Hag	Mary Roberts
Second Hag	Helena Moloney
McDonough	Philip Guiry

Sheepshearers: Messrs. Conniffe, George St. John, Farrell Pelly, Patrick Murphy, A. P. Wilson, J. R. Burke

Tragic-Comedies

The Image
11th November 1909

Thomas Coppinger, a stone cutter . .	Arthur Sinclair
Mary Coppinger, his wife	Sara Allgood
Malachi Naughton, a Mountainy Man . .	Fred O'Donovan
Brian Hosty, a small farmer . . .	Sydney J. Morgan
Darby Costello, a seaweed-gatherer . .	J. M. Kerrigan
Peggy Mahon, an old midwife . . .	Maire O'Neill
Peter Mannion, a carrier	J. A. O'Rourke

The Canavans
8th December 1906

Peter Canavan	W. G. Fay
Antony	J. A. O'Rourke
Widow Greely	Maire O'Neill
Widow Deeny	Brigit O'Dempsey
Captain Headley	Arthur Sinclair

The White Cockade
9th December 1905

Matt Kelleher	W. G. Fay
Owen Kelleher	F. Walker
King James	Arthur Sinclair
Sarsfield	F. J. Fay
Carter	J. Dunne

Mrs. Kelleher	Sara Allgood
Old Lady	Maire Ni Shiublaigh
Williamite Soldier	Ambrose Power
Another	U. Wright
Another	J. Magee
French Sailor	
Another	

The Deliverer
12th January 1911

Ard	Fred O'Donovan
Malachi	J. A. O'Rourke
Dan	Arthur Sinclair
King's Nurseling	J. M. Kerrigan
Steward	Sydney J. Morgan
Officer	B. Macnamara
Ard's Wife	Maire Ni Shiublaigh
Malachi's Wife	Sara Allgood
Dan's Wife	Maire O'Neill

Appendix

Kincora (first version)
25th March 1905

Brian of the Tributes, King of Munster, afterwards High King	F. J. Fay
Murrough, his son	George Roberts
Malachi, High King of Ireland	A. Power
Gormleith, his wife, afterwards wife of Brian	Maire Ni Shiublaigh
Sitric, her son by Olaf of the Danes .	P. MacShiubhlaigh
Maelmora, her brother, King of Leinster	Seamus O'Sullivan
Brian's servants:	
Brennain	Arthur Sinclair
Derrick	W. G. Fay
Rury, Malachi's servant	J. H. Dunne
Maire, Brennain's daughter . .	Maire Ni Gharbhaigh
Aoibhell, a woman of the Sidhe . . .	Sara Allgood
Brodar	R. Nash
A Dane	U. Wright

309

The Old Woman Remembers
31st December 1923

Spoken by Sara Allgood

Appendices

APPENDIX I: KINCORA (THE FIRST VERSION)

KINCORA

PERSONS
  BRIAN. *King of Munster.*
  MALACHI. *High King of Ireland.*
  MAELMORA. *King of Leinster.*
  GORMLEITH. *Wife to the High King, sister of Maelmora, mother of Sitric.*
  MURROUGH. *Brian's son.*
  SITRIC. *Leader of the Danes.*
  BRENNAIN ⎫
  DERRICK ⎭ *Servants to Brian*
  RURY. *Servant to Malachi.*
  PHELAN. *Servant to Maelmora.*
  MAIRE. *Daughter to Brennain.*
  BRODAR.
  A DANE.
  AOIBHELL. *A spirit.*

PROLOGUE

SCENE. *A wood.* BRIAN *seen lying asleep on the ground. Enter two men with swords, their cloaks wrapped round their heads.*

FIRST MAN. Are you here, Brian? Here he is sleeping. We should waken him now, but he has the look of being very tired.

SECOND MAN. Tired and worn out, and no wonder—a young lad that was used to lie on the pillars of a king's house, to be laying his head on the hard knotty roots of trees.

FIRST MAN. Fighting with the Danes through the daytime and resting on the ground by night; or fighting through the night time when he failed to harm them in the day. And not one of his own with him to give him a hand. It is a lonesome life he has.

SECOND MAN. He will be more lonesome again after a while, when the whole of us are killed. What way can a score of men drive a whole army out of Ireland?

315

FIRST MAN. If anyone can do it he will do it. Leave him there; we need not waken him till the rising of the sun. He will be tired enough before the day is over.

(*They go out.* AOIBHELL *appears.*)

AOIBHELL. Awake, young Brian! Brian, son of Cennedigh, awake!

BRIAN. Who is calling me? Are the enemy coming? Is it time for the fight?

AOIBHELL. I do not call you to battle, but to peace.

BRIAN. Who are you? Where do you come from?

AOIBHELL. I am Aoibhell of the Grey Rock, the helper of your race. I am come to bid you give up the sweetheart you have chosen, that hard sweetheart, Ireland. Come to me in place of her and I will bring you into the hidden houses of the hills. I will give you love; age will never fall on you as it has fallen upon me.

BRIAN. I will not go with you; I will not give up Ireland. For it is a habit of my race to fight and to die, but it never was their habit to see shame or oppression put on their country by any man on earth.

AOIBHELL. Those that serve Ireland take for their lot lasting battles, lasting quarrels. They are building and ever building, and ever and always ruin comes upon them before the house is built. Those that should be most their friends turn to be most their enemies, till the heart grows dry with bitterness, dry as the heads of the mountains under the summer heat. Come to me and leave her, Brian, young Brian.

BRIAN. Go from me, Aoibhell! Go back to your hidden house! I will never break my faith with the sweetheart I have chosen nor turn from her service till she can lift up her head in the sight of the whole world!

Curtain.

KINCORA

[Before Glenmama]

ACT I

SCENE. *A hall in* BRIAN'S *house at Kincora.* MALACHI *and* MAELMORA *at a table; their servants standing behind their chairs.* BRIAN'S SERVANTS *behind his empty chair.* BRIAN *at the window, looking out, with back to audience.* MURROUGH *looking on.* MAIRE *working at an embroidery frame.*

MAELMORA (*giving a paper to* MALACHI). See, I have written it all here, High King. (*Reads*) Submission made by Sitric, head of the Danes, for himself and the whole of his army——

MALACHI. I know, I know; let him read it himself when he comes. It is time for him to be here to put his name to it.

MAELMORA. He will be here before the fall of day.

MALACHI. This is a great work we have done this day; and though I am High King, it is the man in the window that has done it. The Danes binding themselves to quit the country, and Brian and myself and yourself, Maelmora, at peace with one another.

MAELMORA. It was time, indeed, for peace. The whole of my own province of Leinster is wracked and destroyed with the war.

MALACHI. The rest of Ireland is no better. Fighting against the Gall from morning to night, and from night to morning making attacks on one another.

BRIAN (*coming to the table and laying his hand on it*). I do not see Sitric coming. I am impatient for this submission to be signed.

MALACHI. He cannot be far off now, Brian.

BRIAN. I cannot be sure, until he has put his name to it, that peace has come at last.

MALACHI. No one would think that so good a fighter as you, Brian, had his mind so much set on peace.

BRIAN. My fathers were fighters, and I have followed their trade; Lugaidh, son of Aengus; Cathal, son of Aedh; Corc, son of Anluan; Lorcan, son of Luchta; Cennedigh, son of Lorcan; they lived and died fighting in defence of their own home and of Munster. It is time now for the race of Lugaidh to turn from war to peace.

MALACHI. You can do as you will. No man that ever saw you in battle will say you turned from war through any fear or slackness, for fear is a thing that never came into the one house with you.

BRIAN. I fought for Ireland when young boys of my age were at the hurling. I have done for her all that war can do. It is peace she is in want of now, to see her young men at the sickle in place of girls, and her strong men breaking the wild ground for seed. Fighting, fighting from Samhain to harvest—no time, no time for any other thing. I would have time now to forgive my enemies, and to make my peace with God.

MALACHI. There was a good saint spoiled in you, Brian, when you took to the sword instead of the crozier.

MURROUGH. It might have been better for yourself, Malachi, if my father had never meddled with a sword.

MALACHI. Listen to the crowing of the young cock! We are done with all that now, Murrough. Springtime is come; and the daws are mated to-day that were pecking at one another yesterday.

BRIAN (*turning towards the window*). My mind will not be at rest till Sitric comes.

MAELMORA. I have answered for my nephew Sitric. He gives in altogether.

MALACHI. He was forced to give in when you took away the help of Leinster from him.

MAELMORA. I will go out by the Hill of the Grey Rock to meet him if he is coming by that road. I promised him a good welcome from you, Brian.

BRIAN. You were right in that. Go, Murrough, with Maelmora. I myself will go towards the weir; he may be coming from the south.

MALACHI. I will go with you, Brian. We can be looking at the colts in the river-meadows as we go.

BRIAN (*to* SERVANTS). Make the table ready, Brennain. When Sitric comes, we have but to sign the peace and to sit down to supper.

(BRIAN *and* MURROUGH *go out.* MALACHI *is following them, when* MAELMORA *stops him.*)

MAELMORA. Where is my sister Gormleith?

MALACHI. She is far enough away, at home.

MAELMORA. Did you ask her to come with you?

MALACHI. Did I ask a swarm of bees to come into the house to help to make the peace?

MAELMORA. She might like this peace for her son Sitric's sake.

MALACHI. Believe me, we are best without her.

MAELMORA. That may be. She has a wild heart yet.

(*He and* MALACHI *go out.* SERVANTS *come forward.* MAIRE *goes to the window and stands looking after the kings.*)

DERRICK. Malachi the High King, king of the whole North! Brian, king of the whole South! Meddling with one another no more than the white and the yolk of an egg! Peace as sound and as round as the eggshell itself! Peace forever in Ireland and in Kincora!

BRENNAIN. If you were not a poet, Derrick, I would say you were a fool.

PHELAN. Why would you call Derrick a fool?

BRENNAIN. For thinking, Phelan, that words can stop an eggshell from being cracked or a peace from being broken. If truces and agreements are eggs, it is my belief there is some clucking hen, some mother of mischief, always at roost overhead in Ireland that will pitch on them and hatch them till they are pecked to pieces by their own young ones from within. Here, Maire, give me the plates. (*She gives them and he begins putting them on the table.*) Peaces and treaties! I would make no treaty with the Gall, but to strike their head off!

DERRICK (*taking parchment, ink, etc., from table*). You are always ready to put ridicule on what I say, Brennain. But I know well, whatever may have happened at other times, this peace will never be broken. Who is there to break it?

RURY. The Danes will not break it, anyway, and they as they are, not daring to let a squeak out of them. Keeping their heads under water they are, like a hunted otter in a stream.

PHELAN. Whoever breaks the peace it will not be my own master, Maelmora. Now the Danes are beaten, he has no mind to be beaten along with them, and in my opinion he is right.

RURY. Whoever may break it, it will not be my master, Malachi. He has fought through the whole of his life. He should have time now to train his three-year-olds, and to mind Gormleith, his wife.

DERRICK. Whoever starts a new war, it will not be Brian.

RURY. I suppose not. It is time for him to make his soul, after fighting like Malachi through the whole of his lifetime.

DERRICK. The whole country will shine out now, the path of white angels to the western world! (*Sings*)

Golden bridles, silver bridles,
Coming up along the strand;
Keening's not used or treachery
In the tilled familiar land!

MAIRE (*from the window*). Quiet, Derrick; leave off singing. There is a boat come to the shore—there is some queen-woman stepping out of it.

BRENNAIN. What sort is she?

MAIRE. She is tall, and has rich clothing, and there is some shining thing on her head.

RURY (*going to window*). The Lord be between us and harm! It is Queen Gormleith!

DERRICK (*coming to window*). The High King's wife!

BRENNAIN. What does she want coming into Munster?

MAIRE (*shivering*). I hope she will bring no harm on our king!

PHELAN. Malachi thought she would stop at home, keeping her maids to their needles. It is time for him to have got better sense.

BRENNAIN. What did he want marrying her? I would never like to meddle with a woman that had been married to a Dane.

(GORMLEITH *comes in and looks round. All the* SERVANTS *come forward and bow obsequiously.*)

DERRICK (*pulling forward a chair*). Welcome to Kincora, Queen Gormleith!

GORMLEITH (*sitting down*). I thank you. I thought to find all the kings here. Is the business finished that brought them together? Is not that Phelan, my brother's servant? And there is Rury, my husband's servant. Have the High King and the King of Leinster put their names to this peace?

RURY. The peace is made, Queen, but the names are not put to it yet. Malachi and Brian are kings of the North and of the South. But Malachi has the High Kingship yet.

GORMLEITH. That is a fine peace! What has delayed the signing of it?

PHELAN. They are waiting for Sitric. They are gone out to meet him. Maelmora brought his submission; he is coming to put his name to the treaty. If he does not come soon, the supper will be spoiled.

GORMLEITH. So my son Sitric has submitted! He never told me. He would not tell it to me. Sitric under Brian and under Malachi! (BRENNAIN *goes to the door.*) You are going to call in the kings?

BRENNAIN. I am, Queen. I will bring them in to welcome you.

GORMLEITH. Do not hurry them for my sake. I am well content to rest for a while in this beautiful Kincora, that is folded between the river and the hills.

BRENNAIN. It is fair enough, fair enough. We have not the hill of Tara or of Almhuin.

GORMLEITH. Brian has the great river to carry his orders. He has bound it to his service as far as the wide sea. And you have what is better than hills or rivers; you have the most plentiful house in all Ireland, your king is the best served, his people have the greatest name for bravery.

DERRICK. It is true. MacLiagh, the king's poet, has made a song about that.

GORMLEITH. The best songs in all Ireland are made in Kincora.

RURY. Derrick himself is a good songmaker.

DERRICK. Just middling. But I will make a song about your coming, Queen, will be remembered to the end of life and time. It will have in it the stir of a battle, the fighting of the sun against the cold, and of the stars against the dark.

GORMLEITH. It will be a good poem. The High King has no one at his court able to make a poem like that.

PHELAN. We have poets at the court of the King of Leinster— and feasts.

GORMLEITH. That court is like my own, being my brother's. You would not have me praise my own cradle. But I have often praised my brother's faithful servant. (*Gives him her hand. He kisses it.*)

BRENNAIN (*to* MAIRE, *aside*). Go, Maire, and see are the kings coming. This queen has too much of bee's honey in her mouth. (MAIRE *goes out*.)

GORMLEITH. I have stopped your work. Go on making the table ready.

BRENNAIN. All is ready, Queen. We have but to put the seats and to bring in the dishes.

GORMLEITH. You are standing idle, Rury. Is there no work for you to do?

RURY. I can be putting the chair ready for the High King. (*Pulls a chair forward.*)

GORMLEITH. Do not put that for him. That is King Brian's chair.

RURY. It is the custom to give the best chair to the High King of Ireland.

GORMLEITH. It was the custom. But remember the High King

is not above King Brian now. He is but his equal. They are the kings of the North and South.

RURY. I would never give in to putting Malachi below any other man.

PHELAN. Where should I put the King of Leinster's chair?

BRENNAIN. Put it there—to King Brian's left hand. That is it. A little farther down.

GORMLEITH. You were putting it too close, Phelan. King Brian is such a great man now, there must be the length of a sword left between him and any other king of a province.

PHELAN. My master is good enough to sit close up to any of the kings of the world.

GORMLEITH (*to* BRENNAIN). You must make these forgetful men remember that their masters have a master themselves now in King Brian.

BRENNAIN. So they have, so they have! Kincora will be the capital of Ireland.

MAIRE (*coming in*). I see Sitric and the King of Leinster coming over the hill.

BRENNAIN. It is best for us to be putting the food on the table. Go, Maire, for the dishes. (*She goes out.*) Sitric will sign his name with the less delay if he sees the fat of the mutton hardening.

GORMLEITH (*who has gone to window, turning from it*). They are a long way off. You have time. Be sure that the best dish is set before the greatest of the kings! (*She turns again to window.*)

MAIRE (*coming in*). Here is the king's dish, the round of the beef.

BRENNAIN. I will put it here before King Brian.

RURY. It is before Malachi it should be put. The best dish should be put before the High King.

BRENNAIN. You heard what Queen Gormleith herself said, that Brian is as good now as Malachi.

(GORMLEITH *turns and leans against side of window, listening with enjoyment.*)

RURY. He is not as good as the King of Tara; and he never will be as good. Put the beef here.

MAIRE. Here is as good a dish—a roasted quarter of a boar.

RURY. We have plenty of pigs in the North. A pig is no great dish for a king. The beef is the more honourable dish.

BRENNAIN. If it is, it is to the most honourable man it is going.

RURY. How do you make that out? The High King is the most honourable man!

BRENNAIN. The High King! Where would he be but for Brian!

RURY. What are you talking about?

BRENNAIN. I tell you, if it was not for Brian taking the Danes in hand the way he did, it is hares of the wilderness Malachi might be milking to-day in place of cows!

RURY. Brian! Where was Brian the day Malachi took the golden collar from the big Dane? Answer me that!

BRENNAIN. That Malachi may be choked with that same collar before the size of my nail of this beef will go down his throat until he has asked it of Brian first!

(GORMLEITH *claps her hands.*)

RURY. Asked it of Brian!

BRENNAIN. Asked it and begged it, the way a queen's lapdog begs at the table.

DERRICK. Put the beef before Queen Gormleith's chair, and everyone will be satisfied.

PHELAN. It is not I will be satisfied till I know what share of the meat the King of Leinster is to get! It is another round of the beef should be put before him!

BRENNAIN. The next time the King of Leinster comes here he will find his fill of beef before him—his own cattle that will be coming from now till then as tribute from the traitors of Leinster.

PHELAN. Holy Saint Bridgit! Listen what they are saying of your own province!

RURY. Brennain is right. Tripe and cowheels and pigs' crubeens are good enough for that troop, and too good!

PHELAN. O let me out of this! Tripe and crubeens and all this plenty in the house! I will call to all the poets of Leinster to put a curse upon Kincora!

DERRICK. My grief that I have not time to sharpen this knife. (*Seizes one.*) No matter! It is on your own bones I will sharpen it! (*All seize knives and threaten each other.* GORMLEITH *laughs and claps her hands.*)

MAIRE. Quiet, quiet. Here is the King of Leinster. Here are Murrough and Sitric!

(*They enter.* GORMLEITH *comes down and puts an arm round* SITRIC *and* MAELMORA.)

MURROUGH. What is this kennel of fighting hounds? Brennain, what is the meaning of this uproar?

BRENNAIN. It is these others made an attack on me. I am for quiet and for getting ready the table!

PHELAN. Taking the best beef he was! Leaving my master to the last!

DERRICK. Rury wanted the best of the chairs for Malachi!

RURY. Keep your chair! Malachi is master wherever he sits!

MURROUGH. Malachi master here! That is news, indeed!

GORMLEITH (*to* MAELMORA). Some say he is uppermost, and some say Brian; but the King of Leinster is put in the lowest place of all!

MAELMORA (*to* MURROUGH). Do you think me so much below Brian because I have consented to make peace with him?

MURROUGH. You have consented to send tribute. It is not the one who is uppermost that sends tribute.

MAELMORA. If Brian had spoken like that I would not have consented to send it. I have a mind to keep it back even now.

MURROUGH. As you will, King. If we send our men to look for it, you yourself will have forced it on us.

MAELMORA. I can hold my province against the men of Kincora! Let them fish and shiver like cranes in frost before they will see one head of cattle coming from Leinster.

SITRIC (*to* MAELMORA). I thought it was to make a peace you brought me here. It seems now you are making yourself ready for a battle.

GORMLEITH. That should be good news. You are young to give in to peace like a monk or a bishop.

SITRIC. They have deceived me, calling this a treaty. It is a bad day that brought me to Kincora without my hand on the sword.

MURROUGH. If you had come with your hand on the sword it is likely you would have got a welcome that would have kept you in Kincora to the day of judgment!

SITRIC. It is a pity we did not smoke out this den long ago!

MURROUGH. It is you yourself are smoked out of your den to-day and out of the hole where you were hiding!

GORMLEITH (*to* MAELMORA). It was you who brought Sitric here.

MAELMORA. Keep a quiet tongue, Murrough. Sitric will not take from you what he might take from Brian.

SITRIC. I will take no high words from Brian or any other man, whatever you yourself may be in the habit of taking from him.

MAELMORA. I will take nothing from him and he will get nothing from me. I swear I will send no tribute to Brian! I would sooner die! (*Draws sword.*)

MURROUGH. Many a man has died who set himself up against King Brian! (*Draws sword.*)

BRENNAIN. That is good talk! Brian has a long hand!

324

DERRICK. Murrough and Brian are the two hawks of battle of the Gael!

PHELAN. We will turn you into jackdaws! We will change your note for you!

RURY. Malachi and the Hill of Tara!

DERRICK. Munster and the Dalcassians!

PHELAN. No tribute! Hold the cattle!

RURY. Tara for victory!

DERRICK. Brian and Murrough! ⎫

PHELAN. Down with Kincora! ⎬ (ALL *together*.)

BRENNAIN. Drive out the traitors! ⎭

(BRIAN *and* MALACHI *come in*.)

MAIRE. The King! (SERVANTS *fall back*.)

BRIAN. (*sternly*). Swords out in this house! (*To* SITRIC *and* MAELMORA) I ask your pardon. My son is young and hot. He should be back in the schools.

MURROUGH (*sullenly, putting sword in sheath*). It was their fault. They roused me with their words. They said they were above you. They said—I forget now what they said.

BRIAN. Shut your ears, Murrough, when sharp words are spoken within your own walls. It is best not to hear what you must not answer.

(GORMLEITH *comes forward*.)

MALACHI. Queen Gormleith!

GORMLEITH. It is a surprise to you to see me?

MALACHI. No great surprise. I have not often known a battle, Queen, where you were not looking on from some perch or another.

BRIAN. Is this Queen Gormleith? (*Takes her hand and kisses it*.)

MALACHI. It is herself. Queen Gormleith that I brought back from the Danes, thinking to make a good Irishwoman of her again.

BRIAN. You did well for Ireland doing that. I am sorry, indeed, Queen, you have had so rough a welcome in my house.

GORMLEITH. I have had the best of welcomes. This is no sleepy place. I have found the stir and the high hearts I looked for in a king's house.

MALACHI. I would not wonder, Queen, if it was your breath helped me to blow this wisp alight. You will do some day, with your lightness and laughter, what will bring great trouble into the houses of kings.

BRIAN. There could be no unkind thought beneath such high beauty.

GORMLEITH. I thank you, King.

BRIAN. My people are rough. There has been no queen in this house since my own poor Connacht wife, Murrough's mother, died from me. A house without a queen grows to be like a windy hillside after the hunting, where orders are loud-voiced, and service is rough, and hounds are unloosed and snatching.

GORMLETH. I think that rough service well befits a king's house.

BRIAN. A queen's voice would turn it all to gentleness. It is seldom we hear a woman's voice in this hall, unless it may be in the keening, when the men of our race are brought back cold and dumb from their victories.

GORMLEITH. I think you have indeed the right house for a king.

MALACHI. Let us waste no more time. Here now is Sitric. Let him put his name to the peace, and the supper will turn the whole company to better humour. Good meat and good drink are the best peacemakers.

BRIAN. My welcome to you, Sitric. Here is the parchment. Maelmora, your uncle wrote down the terms of submission you had agreed to. You have but to put your name. The hostages can be sent to-morrow.

(SITRIC *is silent.*)

BRIAN. Will you read it? Or will you be content with what Maelmora has written?

MALACHI. He put in the writing that you and your army would agree to quit Ireland, or to live in it without arms, under tribute to myself and to Brian.

SITRIC. I will not sign it.

BRIAN. Not sign it! Why is this?

MALACHI. It was you yourself sent in your submission. Why should you draw back now?

SITRIC. Hot words have been said to me that I am not used to put up with.

BRIAN. This is Murrough's folly. I ask your pardon for it, and he will ask your pardon.

SITRIC. He need not do that. I have made up my mind. I will agree to no submission.

MALACHI. What is it you have against it?

SITRIC. I will not give in to Brian. I will not leave the country at Brian's bidding. I will not bid my men to give up their arms. I will bid them to go on fighting to the last.

BRIAN. This is folly, Sitric. You could not stand against us alone through the length of a winter day.

MAELMORA. He will not be alone. I give up my share in the

peace. I would sooner be with the Danes than with Brian of the Tributes!

MALACHI (*in a tone of vexation*). How hot you are for fighting, young men! Hot blood, hot blood, and all our trouble gone to loss! If Brian was of my mind, he would have let the hot blood out of you when he saw you weakening; and he might have got some ease and comfort for himself and for me. (*To* BRIAN) Let us offer something—let them do what they like with Leinster if they do not meddle with us. A war would be a heavy business. You were saying a while ago what a great thing peace would be for Ireland.

BRIAN. Entire peace is a great thing, but a half peace is no better worth winning than the half of the living child the Jewish mothers were fighting for.

MALACHI. It is my opinion you will not see entire peace and the end of war in Ireland, till the worms have been made an end of by the thrushes, or the clouds by the wind, or the nights by the long days.

BRIAN. I tell you I will make no settlement that leaves any one of the provinces a nest and a breeding ground for the enemies and the ill-wishers of the rest of Ireland. It is certain that Ireland must be as free as God made her before she can be as happy as He saw her in the making. Sitric must sign this (*holds out parchment*) or make himself ready to fight.

SITRIC (*takes parchment, looks at it a moment, then cuts it in two with his sword, and throws down the pieces violently*). There is an end of your peace!

BRIAN (*drawing his sword*). Come out then, old comrade! I thought to let you sleep for a while, but the day's work is not over yet. (*Unbuckles sheath.*) But this is what I will never make use of again so long as there is so much as a threat of trouble or treachery in any one of the provinces of Ireland. (*Throws away sheath.*)

SITRIC (*flinging down sheath*). There is mine, till I come to look for it again!

MAELMORA. And mine! (*Flings down sheath. He and* SITRIC *go to the door.*)

GORMLEITH. The sword in the hand and the sheath on the floor! That is a good sight in a king's house! (*To* BRIAN) War is best! War is best! When the swords of kings grow rusty in the sheath, the height of the noontide will be over for the world!

Curtain.

327

ACT II

[After Glenmama]

SCENE. *The same hall at Kincora. Heap of spoils on the floor.* BRENNAIN *has just come in with* PHELAN, *who is bound.* DERRICK *and* MAIRE *at window, waving branches.*

DERRICK. A welcome to the army of the Dalcassians! A welcome to the army that put down the Danes! A welcome to Brian! The branch to King Brian! (*Throws it. Turns to* MAIRE.) Come to the door. The King is coming. (*He and* MAIRE *step down and see* BRENNAIN.)

BRENNAIN. The branch to myself. What do you say to me, taking this prisoner in the battle? I drove him before me all the way from Glenmama. It's the Leinster men that can run well!

MAIRE. The King of Leinster's servant!

BRENNAIN (*pushing* PHELAN). Come on here. Jackdaws are we? You'll change our note for us? Give me a wisp of lighted straw till I make him shout for King Brian!

DERRICK. That's right! That's right! That's the way we're bringing back traitors to Kincora that went boasting out of it.

PHELAN. If I did boast, you needn't put the blame on me. When the dog smells a bone, the dog's tail must wag. I do but wag as my master pleases.

BRENNAIN. It is we ourselves are gnawing the bone now. Look at these spoils. Coming in since morning they are; the whole of the court is full of them. Did ever anyone see such riches? Robbed by the Danes they were from every dun in Ireland, and from the hidden houses of the Sidhe.

(*Enter* BRIAN *with shield; he wears a helmet.*)

MAIRE. My hundred welcomes to you, Brian of the victories!

BRIAN. I thank you, Maire.

DERRICK. My thousand welcomes to yourself and your whole army. I am making a song for you, King, about the great victory of Glenmama. A song with as many verses in it as my fingers and toes, and a great deed in every verse.

BRIAN. Let it be a good one, Derrick; for if I have my way, it will be the last battle song ever made in my lifetime.

DERRRICK. Good is it? The words will come as fast as the running of the Danes before you—galloping, gander-winged, grasshopping. Making for the sea they were, the same as gulls. I will put the screaming gulls in my poem—sky-sailing, sad-sounding, sea-searching.

BRIAN. That is enough. I have had my fill of battles. (*He sits down and takes off helmet.*)

MAIRE. Let me put away your sword, King.

BRIAN (*takes arm-ring from the heap of spoils*). Take that ring from the spoils, Maire. This war is over; but all Ireland is not at peace. I must not put away my sword till a girl like you can travel through the whole country wearing a ring like that, and no one lay a hand on her or on it.

MAIRE. It is too much for me, King.

BRENNAIN. Murrough sent to ask when you would judge the prisoners.

BRIAN. Not yet. I will wait for Malachi. He is on his way.

BRENNAIN. What will I do with the spoils?

BRIAN. Make three shares of them. A share for the High King, and a share for the men of learning, and a share for Kincora.

BRENNAIN. I will; I will keep the best for ourselves.

BRIAN. The best must go to the High King.

BRENNAIN. It is yourself should be High King, Brian, after this great victory. All Ireland is saying it.

BRIAN. The whole world may say it before it will make me break my peace with Malachi.

BRENNAIN. Malachi is all for ease. It is not Malachi that will master the five provinces, tearing and spitting at one another the way they are.

DERRICK. Take the High Kingship, Brian, and they will be like the five fingers of the one hand, the five features of the King's face, the five white leaves of an apple blossom!

BRENNAIN. It is what they are now, five wild cats struggling in a bag, and four times five claws on every one of them.

(*A clattering of horses is heard.*)

BRENNAIN. That is the sound of the High King's horses.

BRIAN. He is come to judge the prisoners of Glenmama. Let them be brought here now.

(*Exeunt* SERVANTS. *Enter* MALACHI.)

MALACHI. I was delayed in coming. Your Munster roads are good innkeepers. They were not willing to let the wheels of my chariot go from them.

BRIAN. You are in time, High King. I have given no judgment yet. I have sent for the prisoners.

MALACHI. We will show the Danes their leader will get the same reward from us as common men.

(*Enter* BRENNAIN *and* DERRICK.)

BRENNAIN. Here are the prisoners, King. (*Enter* MURROUGH *with* SITRIC *and* MAELMORA *in bonds.*)

MALACHI. Is Maelmora taken? That is good news. They said he could not be found. I thought he had escaped from the battle.

BRENNAIN. It was Murrough took him, High King! Hiding he was in a yew tree. Murrough dragged him out of it the same as a wren's nest.

BRIAN. Enough. We do not boast in time of victory.

DERRICK (*to* BRENNAIN). Mind yourself. It is not mannerly for you to be talking about that yew tree before the King of Leinster.

MURROUGH. The men of my army are waiting outside to bring these men to their punishment.

BRIAN. What punishment would you give them?

MURROUGH. How did the Danes treat their prisoners? How did the King of Leinster treat his rebels?

BRIAN. Have they any excuse to make for themselves?

MURROUGH. They have made none to me.

MALACHI. They have none to make.

BRIAN. What have you to say in your own defence?

MURROUGH. You hear, Maelmora and Sitric, what the King is asking?

SITRIC. I will say nothing. I fought, and I have lost.

MAELMORA. I will say nothing. Nothing I could say would change your mind.

BRIAN. What do you say, Brennain? You have seen many prisoners brought into Kincora.

BRENNAIN. I say a dead wolf will worry no sheep, and a dead fox will kill no lambs.

MALACHI. That is so. Take them to their death. They can make no complaint.

BRIAN. Wait. These are not all. Murrough, bring in the last prisoner that was taken.

MALACHI. What other is there high enough to be judged with kings?

(BRIAN *lifts his hand for silence.* MURROUGH *brings in* GORM-LEITH, *bound.* BRIAN *stands up.*)

330

BRIAN. Put a chair for Queen Gormleith. (*Chair placed.* GORM-LEITH *stands, taking no notice.*)

MALACHI. Have you been brought down, Crow of Battle?

MURROUGH. The queen was taken in the fight among Sitric's men. This broken spear was the last of her weapons.

MALACHI. Whatever punishment and whatever judgment may fall on Sitric and on Maelmora, a heavier judgment must surely fall on this woman, who left a woman's work, and was the very seed and root of the war.

GORMLEITH. Is it Malachi, and not Brian, that gives judgment in this hall of Kincora?

BRIAN. It is not for me, Queen, to judge the High King's wife.

GORMLEITH. Am I the High King's wife? Is not that story at an end, and that treaty broken?

MALACHI. It is broken, surely. When I knew you had gone out of my house to take the side of my enemies, my gates were shut against you. You were shut out of my house and my kingdom.

GORMLEITH. I made no secret war. Did you think I would creep back to ask for shelter?

MALACHI. My men had orders not to spare you. No one in Ireland would have dared to give you shelter if you had escaped from the battle. But you have not escaped. You have come to your death, and you have brought your son and your brother to their death.

MURROUGH. I have other witnesses that saw her fighting in the battle.

GORMLEITH. You need not bring them. I was there. I fought beside my son against Malachi and the men of Meath.

BRIAN (*to* MALACHI). What was it turned the Queen to be your enemy?

MALACHI. I know of no cause, unless she had some lover.

GORMLEITH. Some lover! The Danes could tell you I would rather lay my lips to a blue breast-plate than to the whitest skin in the world.

MALACHI. That may be so. It is hard to know with such a woman when there is a kiss behind her schemes, or a scheme behind her kisses. I am done with you now and forever.

GORMLEITH. I had no lover, Brian. I never came yet to the man I could give my love to—the man that could bind me to peace.

MALACHI. I think, indeed, that man is still unborn.

GORMLEITH. There may be such a man. A man that has sent his name out like the shout of a great army; that could quiet my hands with his strong hand; that could quiet my heart, filling it with pride of him, and my mouth, filling it with praise of him.

BRIAN. The High King of Ireland should be such a man.

GORMLEITH. His time is over. He is for ease; I would have no time for rest. He is for the jesters; I am for the proud songs of heroes. He is for the fatness of the barley in the ear; I am for the redness and the ferment of the ale.

BRIAN. That need not have driven a wife to battle.

GORMLEITH. Would you have me sit at home, and use false words, and wish for his death? That is not the lesson I learned from the Danes.

MALACHI. I will send her to her death. There will be no peace or ease in the country till then.

GORMLEITH. You are my judge, King Brian! I am sister of a king. I was a queen among the Danes.

BRIAN. You have lost the rights of a queen, taking arms like any fighting man.

GORMLEITH. There were high-hearted kings, and high-hearted queens in the old days, that went side by side into the battle. It is from such kings and such queens that you and I are come.

BRIAN. The old days are gone by. The sign of the Cross is upon us. We must bring the world to peace.

GORMLEITH. What is this peace you talk of? Is it so great a thing? There are some beyond the world that know better. In peace the little men grow many, and the great men lessen, and the high heart beats slowly, and the trader holds the sway. When the world is changed like that it will be no place for high-hearted men, no place for yourself, Brian.

MALACHI. Have done listening to words, Brian, and give your judgment, or I myself will give it.

BRIAN. Have you anything to ask, Queen, or to plead?

GORMLEITH. I will ask for no mercy for myself, or my son, or my brother. We fought and we are beaten. The men of our race know how to die—yet—it was my doing—Sitric is young—if it were Murrough——

MAELMORA. We are not children. We can answer for ourselves. We ask no mercy.

SITRIC. I will not shelter behind a woman. Keep silence, Queen.

MALACHI. Brian will give a right judgment. He has never spared the enemies of Ireland.

BRIAN (*standing up*). That is a true word. I have never spared them.

MALACHI. Ireland can have no worse enemies than these.

BRIAN. You hear, Queen, what the High King says. Ireland has had no worse enemies than these. My people have called them wolves and foxes; and they have earned that name, for they have torn and reddened the white fleece of Ireland. It was my heart's desire to mend that torn fleece; to gather up that ragged wool; to weave it into a border fit for the cloak of the King of Heaven. I made a peace. I thought to fill Ireland with joy; to make of her a brimming cup at the feast of the angels. That cup was overturned; that heavenly cloak was torn; that peace was broken. It was broken by you. The keening and the treachery were brought back again.

MURROUGH. I will bring in my men to take them away. Let them be buried in the place of traitors where the sun will not shine on their grave.

BRIAN. Stop! I have given no judgment yet. Maelmora, King of Leinster, is guilty of treachery to me, and to the High King, and to Ireland. Sitric the Gall is guilty of the great robbery and oppression he and his people have done upon Ireland. Queen Gormleith claims her share in the war—and yet—I will leave them their life and their freedom.

MURROUGH. You will let them go?

MALACHI. If Brian had not said that, I would say a fool had said it.

BRIAN. I will take hostages; but I will let them go. I have shed blood all through my life; I will shed no more of it.

MALACHI. If you let these men go, there will be shedding of blood again.

BRIAN. They have learned their lesson. They know their master. I am not willing to put a sod on the mouth or a clod in the hand of any man that may be on my side yet against the enemies of Ireland.

MURROUGH. Sitric is no Irishman.

BRIAN. His mother is of the blood of the kings of Leinster.

MURROUGH. His mother! This is her work. If you let them go, the army of the Dalcassians will not let them go.

BRIAN. Do you think to force me, my boy, with this threat of an army?

MALACHI. It is you yourself that are forcing a peace.

BRIAN. If I force peace now, I have the right to do it, for I forced on war often enough. It was I myself avenged my brother Mahon. My fathers avenged themselves on their enemies; and the sons of those enemies avenged themselves on the men of our race, death answering to death from side to side like words sung by the clerks at the Mass. But I will put an end to that. I have never been strong enough to spare life until now. I have only been strong enough to take life. I have had only the strength of my sword. Now I have the strength of my great name and my will. I will make an end of quarrels. I will cut these bonds. (*Takes sword from table and cuts rope that binds* GORMLEITH.)

MALACHI (*starting up*). I will not have them loosed.

BRIAN. The Queen is free. Murrough, cut those other bonds. Leave them to me.

MALACHI (*seizing* MURROUGH, *who is reluctantly drawing sword*). Leave them to me; leave them to me. It is not for you to free them.

GORMLEITH (*taking* BRIAN'S *sword from the table and quickly cutting their bonds*). You left the judgment to Brian! We took the first King of the world for our judge!

MALACHI. I have all Ireland in my care. I will not let these traitors go. (*Moves towards them.*)

BRIAN. Stay, King! I will not give them up! They are in my house. I have given them my word. There are no saplings in a walled garden safer than these two men. There is no blossom on the highest branch of the woods safer from rough hands than this Queen.

MALACHI. The right to free them is with those that took them. The heads of armies who fought as well as you, have the right over prisoners taken in battle. These are not Kings now, but shamed and beaten men.

BRIAN. I say they are Kings. Maelmora, I give you back your own Kingdom of Leinster. Sitric, I give you back your own town of Ath Cliath to keep in stewardship for me and for Ireland. Murrough, give them back their arms. (MURROUGH *gives them their swords and shields*.)

MALACHI. Then I use my right that is higher than yours—my right as High King of all Ireland to take these men, Kings though they may be, and this Queen, into my own hands, and to send them for judgment to the council of Tara.

MURROUGH. King Brian's is the greater right. All Ireland knows he has the power, if he would use it, to put you out of Tara to-day. It is only by his will and his kindness you are wearing the High King's crown.

MALACHI. Do you yourself say that, Brian, son of Cennedigh, or is it this hot boy that says it?

BRIAN. I do say it. I say the time has come when there can be but one master in Ireland.

MALACHI. That is true. Whoever has Tara is master.

BRIAN. Where the greatest strength is, the Hill of Tara is. My strength has dragged Tara westward.

MALACHI. This is war then, and the breaking of peace.

BRIAN. It is rather the beginning of peace.

MALACHI. I will raise Connacht against you, I will call to my kinsmen in the North.

GORMLEITH. Send to Connacht, and the men of Connacht will say they would rather have Brian over them than yourself! Send to the North, and your kinsmen in the North will say as they said before that if Tara was their own they would defend it; but as it is yours you may defend it for yourself, and that is a thing you know you cannot do. You will get no help from the North or any other place against Brian!

MALACHI. That will be known soon enough.

BRIAN. If you think you can keep the High Kingship by force, I will give you a truce of a week or a month or a quarter to bring your men together.

MALACHI. A month will be enough. I will lose no minute. The North and the West will be against you. (*Goes out.*)

BRIAN. War again. Well, I am ready.

GORMLEITH. He will get no help. No one will come against you. His own poet has said it in a song. He went East and West, North and South, and he got the same story everywhere. There was no man in all Ireland would raise a hand against King Brian.

BRIAN. His own poet has said that? Then the sap of power has turned from him to me. The Son of Mary is giving Ireland into my charge. His right hand is stretched over the North, His left hand southward towards the sun, His face is towards the West. His angels have set their ladder upon Usna, Victor angel of Patrick, Axel angel of Columcille, Michael leader of armies. It is a great thing they are doing for me, giving me the help of their sword. Ireland—Ireland, I see you free and prospering; wheat in every tilled field; beautiful vessels in the houses of kings; beautiful children, well nourished in every house. No meddling of strangers within our borders! No outcry of Gael against Gael! (*Stops a moment.*) It is not so. Malachi will get help. Why am I taking the words of a woman, of a song? I have not done with war.

(*Enter* MALACHI.)

BRIAN. If you have come to ask more time, I will give you a truce of a year.

MALACHI. A year would be the same to me as a month.

BRIAN. Do you ask a longer time yet?

MALACHI. I have a hard thing to say. I will not bring destruction on my people. I take back my boasting words. My luck has turned against me. I have no help to get. Queen Gormleith has spoken the truth.

BRIAN. You will not fight against me?

MALACHI. I will keep my sword edge sharp, but it will be against the Gall.

BRIAN. You would give up the crown?

MALACHI. I would not, but I must. (*Lays crown on table.*)

BRIAN. God has given me the power. I am answerable to God. It is for the peace of Ireland I take it.

MAIRE (*softly*). It is Brian that will bring the great peace!

MALACHI. That is enough of words. (*Pushes over crown.*) Take it and the weight of it. Yet it was in the prophecy that I should be King after you in Tara!

BRIAN (*takes crown*). I take it in my hand that is stronger than your hand. I have been chosen to do the work of God. I will bring all Ireland under the one strong rule.

GORMLEITH (*kisses his hand*). Long live Brian, High King of Ireland!

ALL (*raising their hands*). Long live the High King!

MALACHI. I have another word to say. I have another gift for you. The Queen of Tara must not lose the crown of Tara. She must go with it. Take her, Brian. She is cast out of my house. I have no more to do with her. You boast of forcing peace. Can you force a peace on her? Quiet her and I will believe you can master all the wild blood of Ireland.

GORMLEITH. You offer me in the market. Give me your help, Brian. Is he to say words of insult to me? I was not treated like this among the Danes.

BRIAN. I will have no word of insult said to a Queen within these walls.

MALACHI. She is no Queen now. Let her go out and let her find her place among the witches of the air.

(*He draws his sword and takes a step towards her.*)

BRIAN (*lifting crown over her*)—I give her the shelter of this crown. I give her the shelter of this roof. I take her as I take Ireland, under the power of my name. Brennain, you need not divide these

336

spoils. I offer them all as my first bride-gift to Queen Gormleith.

GORMLEITH. I thank you, great King.

BRIAN. See here, Queen, it is no bride-gift of a clown I offer you
—the great cauldron made by smiths of Murias; the sword of
Tethra; the crown of Buan from the well of Cruachan; the brooch
of the King of Britain's daughter and her little silver harp; the
shining candlestick of Ethne of the Sidhe.

(*All turn to look at spoils except* MALACHI.)

RURY (*coming to* MALACHI). The chariot is at the door yet, King.
Have you a mind to come away from this, or to stop for the wedding
feast?

MALACHI. I will go; I have been long enough in this little place.

RURY. Come out then, High King. The horses are rested.

MALACHI (*turns towards door*). A little place, a little place. We
have been in it long enough. It is too small a place for so much buying and selling. Great gains! Great losses! The crown for Brian!
The High Kingship for Brian! The spoils of Glenmama for Gormleith! (*Turns from door.*) Who has the worst of it? Brian has that
Crow of Battle. (*Exit.*)

Curtain.

ACT III

Scene I

SCENE: *The same hall at Kincora,* GORMLEITH *and* SITRIC
sitting at table; MAELMORA *standing.*

MAELMORA (*holding out his cloak*). Have you a clasp, Gormleith,
to sew on this cloak? The old one is gone from it.

GORMLEITH. I will do that. How was the old one lost?

MAELMORA. It was on the journey this morning. My people and
the people of the Desi were bringing our tribute of fir-trees; and a
dispute arose who should take the lead; and I was not willing there
should be any delay, and I put my own shoulder under one of the
trees.

GORMLEITH. You, my brother, carried a load?

MAELMORA. There was no dispute after that who was to take

the lead. But a branch of the tree caught in the clasp, and dragged it off, and it was lost.

GORMLEITH. You carried King Brian's loan into Kincora! I will sew no clasp upon the cloak.

MAELMORA. I saw no shame in doing that for Brian. He gave me my life, and my kingdom.

GORMLEITH. I see great shame in it! I see you all bowing down to Brian's law. There is not a hound of yours dares so much as follow a hare beyond the mearing, without leave from judges or priests. It is not the man that strikes a brave blow that is honoured now, but the man that shows obedience; that brings tribute——

MAELMORA. Quiet yourself, Gormleith. My mind is not set like yours, on swords and armies. You were wild and restless long ago, dragging me after you from the teachers and the nurses. You have had the tormenting of three husbands since then; leave your brother alone. I am going to the chess-players. Take the cloak, and have the clasp on it when I come again.

(*He gives her the cloak and goes out.*)

GORMLEITH. I will sew on no clasp! (*Flings it away.*) The fire is the right place for this livery of a hired man!

SITRIC. I told you this was no place for you; it is with the Danes you should be. The salmon that is used to the salt sea grows sick out there in the still river. You are tangled in the weeds of the river. Break away from them——

GORMLEITH. I told you I would not give you my help. I have done with the Danes.

SITRIC. They are coming; they will soon be landing; their plans are made. I have all ready for them at Clontarf; I trusted to you to help. If Maelmora has no power, what power have I? Am I, your son, and Olaf's son, to be a steward and caretaker to the day of my death? Am I to quarry stones for the churches, and shut myself in the schools to read books? I will break from it all. I am no traitor; I was born under the raven.

GORMLEITH. Go your own way; fight for your own hand. What do you want of me? I am but one woman; there is nothing I can do——

SITRIC (*taking out letters*). This is what you can do. Look at that letter from Sigurd, Earl of Orkney, and that from Brodar, of the Isle of Man. See what they ask—they will not come without a call from you, without a promise——

GORMLEITH. I know what they ask. I will not give a promise to either of them.

SITRIC. I was sure you would help me—you are nearer to me, your son, than to any other.

GORMLEITH. That is true. Brian is ageing; his strength is going; he is giving up the sword for the mass-book——

SITRIC. Brodar and Sigurd sent us messengers—they will send for help for us from Alban——

BRENNAIN (*coming in*). King Brian is wanting you, Queen, in the inner court, to give a welcome to King Malachi, that is after coming back at last in friendship to Kincora. (*Goes out.*)

GORMLEITH. Malachi! Is he here again? I have no great mind to see him. But I must go; he will treat me with honour now; he dare not say a word against King Brian's wife.

SITRIC. I told Brodar I would send him your promise. Give it to me now.

GORMLEITH. I will give no promise, child; I will not go against you, but I will give you no help against Brian. I am glad if I was a traitor to Malachi; I will never betray Brian. Go to the chess-players. I will go to the Kings.

(*She goes towards door.*)

SITRIC (*putting his hand on her arm*). Stay—listen——

GORMLEITH. Leave me; I will not listen. I have taken my own way. I belong to Brian; I will be faithful; I am bound to Kincora.

(*They go out.*)

(*Enter* BRENNAIN, DERRICK, RURY *and* PHELAN.)

BRENNAIN. Put the chairs here, for the Kings to rest for a while. (*They set chairs.*) They will be going out then to see the army do its feats, where it is gathered on the green to do honour to King Malachi.

RURY. What way is Queen Gormleith? Does Brian curb her better than Malachi?

BRENNAIN. What way would he curb her, having, as he has, his head in the skies, and his hand in very good work? No matter; no matter; we have more that the bitting of mares to attend to here. Tribute coming from every side, from the Gael and from the Gall! Wine, and cattle, and riches! Painted books and golden vessels from the King of Alban, and the King of Lochlann, and all the kings of the western world! We will have to widen our walls to store the whole of it.

RURY. You will; and if you have your way, Brennain, you will have to widen Ireland to hold Kincora; and to widen the whole world to hold Ireland. Age makes you as full of pride as a tree is of branches.

339

DERRICK. Golden birds among the branches
       And another in the hand;
       Keenings not used, or treachery
       In the tilled familiar land.

PHELAN. Whatever wits poor Derrick ever had they are gone from him in his age.

DERRICK. The King praised that song a while ago. He said it had worked itself into his dreams. He had a dream last night——

RURY. I wonder a man that has done such great deeds as Brian would give any heed to dreams.

DERRICK. Don't you know that every noticeable thing a man does is but the certain sign of the going and coming of dreams? Wrack thrown upon the rocks by the high tide—leaves heaped together in a hollow by the wind.

RURY. It is a wisp of withered leaves your own thoughts are, Derrick; and if you have any noticeable thing to do, you had best make no delay, or it is your ghost that will be doing it in the churchyard, knocking a start out of men and beasts.

BRENNAIN. I hear some voices outside, and shouting. It should be more tribute coming.

PHELAN. More likely it is your own daughter Maire. I passed her upon the road a while ago, and a crowd following her and talking with her.

BRENNAIN (*starting up*). My daughter Maire!

PHELAN. Your daughter Maire. What great wonder is there in that? I did not say it was the King of Greece I saw, or St. Martin of France in a cloud of heaven.

RURY (*to* PHELAN). Did you never hear his daughter Maire has been lost to him this long time?

(MAIRE *appears in the doorway.*)

MAIRE. I am come back to you, father.

BRENNAIN (*hobbling across to meet her*). Keep back there! I will not let you into the King's hall till I know where you spent the time!

MAIRE. It was well spent. I went a long way——

BRENNAIN. How do I know are you fit to come into the King's house at all? Wearing all your jewels that would buy half the cows in Kerry—dressed out like the rag-bush of a blessed well!

MAIRE. You will give me a good welcome if you will but listen—

BRENNAIN. I am thinking it is stuck in the mud of the river you were, or drifting out with the tide, and the beasts of the sea picking at you——

MAIRE. Listen, till I tell you——

BRENNAIN. Leaving me without one to will my little riches to! I have a mind to turn you out in earnest.

MAIRE. You will be proud. Did you hear the people shouting to make much of me?

BRENNAIN. The people! What do I care for the shouting of that troop? They would shout to see a river-rat crossing the highway! It is what the king thinks, and what I myself think, that matters.

MAIRE. Let me tell what I have to tell——

DERRICK. Here are the kings.

(BRIAN, MALACHI *and* GORMLEITH *come in.*)

BRIAN. What is all this?

DERRICK. It is Brennain's daughter come back to him.

BRIAN. Is Maire come back?

MAIRE. My father will not let me in, High King. He will not listen to my story.

BRIAN. Tell your story to me and to the Queen. Sit here beside me, Malachi.

(*They sit down.* BRIAN *puts* MALACHI *at his right hand.* GORMLEITH *sits left of* BRIAN.)

BRENNAIN. That is too much honour for her.

MAIRE (*coming forward*). It was on your own business and to bear witness for you I went, High King.

GORMLEITH (*scornfully*). How could you bear witness for the High King?

MAIRE. There used to be talk among strangers coming here about King Brian and his rule and his great sway, that had put down every bad thing.

MALACHI. The Danes are well put down anyway. There is no one in all Ireland will stoop the back to till the ground or grind a quern, but all putting a man or a woman of the Danes to do the work in their place.

BRIAN. I wish I could be sure the provinces have as little stir in them as the Danes. There were some stories of robbery——

MAIRE. That is what they said, High King. They said it was not true you had brought all Ireland to freedom and to peace; and I said it was true.

GORMLEITH. What has this talk to do with your journey?

MAIRE. They dared me, then, to travel through the whole country. And so I set out and went through the five provinces—to Toraigh in the North, and from that again to Cliodhna's Wave in the South, alone, and having this great treasure with me. (*She holds up arm-ring.*)

BRIAN. Did no one meddle with you?

MAIRE. No one at all. When I was passing through Connacht, there were young men riding on horses, and they came as if to take me. But then they said: 'We will leave her free, seeing we ourselves are free, and all Ireland is free.'

BRENNAIN. That is good. That is good. If Connacht is quiet, all Ireland is quiet.

MAIRE. When I came into Ulster, I saw a troop of rough men, and one of them said; 'It is no harm to rob this girl that is of the province of Munster.' But another man of them said: 'Do not, for it is not to the north or the south we belong now, but to the whole of Ireland.' And so I came safely through all, and for that, King Brian, I thank God and you!

BRIAN (*rising*). That is a great thing you have done, and a great story you have brought me. Many a woman has sat beside a king through her lifetime and has done less than this to be remembered by. (*He takes her hand and leads her to* GORMLEITH.) What great reward, Queen, should be given to this messenger of peace?

GORMLEITH. I have rewarded too many who came back from your battles to have any words now. Ask those who keep the King's treasure and his riches.

MAIRE. High King, I give you back your ring. It was for your own service I wore it.

BRIAN. I will give you your choice of rings and jewels in its place, but I will keep this one. I will bid the goldsmiths set it in a shield as a sign of unbroken peace, of all Ireland at one. Show it to the goldsmith, Maire, that he may make a pattern for the shield. (MAIRE *takes it, and goes out.*) See, at last, at last, I can put away my sword. (*Hangs up sword on the rack and sits down again.*) This great new peace was made for me beyond the world. I saw it all in a dream last night. I saw in my dream a woman coming to me that was Aoibhell of the Grey Rock. She came, and she called to me, and swept the darkness away, and showed me the whole country, shining and beautiful, an image of the face of God in the smooth sea. All bad things had gone from it like plover to the north at the strengthening of the sun. The rowan-berries upon Slieve Echtge were the lasting fruits of heaven; I could hear the joyful singing of the birds of the Land of Promise. The Gael had grown to be fitting comrades for the white angels.

MALACHI. That was a good vision. It must have some meaning.

BRIAN. It went from me then, and I cried out after it; but Aoib-hell said, 'It is only at Clontarf you will come again to that vision and to that lasting peace.'

MALACHI. Why did she say Clontarf, I wonder?

BRIAN. It is often dreams have not a straight meaning, or waking breaks it. It is here at Kincora I have had a witness to the perfect peace, and not at Clontarf. (*He turns to* GORMLEITH.) Now we can do great things for Ireland——

MALACHI. You have done that already. Bridges over every river, roads through every bog, churches the best in the whole world.

BRIAN. The churches I make now will shine like the candles of a king's house. The whole of Ireland will be a silver-walled dun of the angels.

BRENNAIN (*who has gone to the window*). The men of the army are gathered on the green yet.

BRIAN (*rises*). Come, Malachi, they are there to welcome you. This is the last time they may be gathered there. The old fighting men or those that have business to mind or children to rear may go home—there is no more work for them; I will break up the army.

(MALACHI, *followed by* BRENNAIN *and* DERRICK, *goes out right.* GORMLEITH *keeps back* BRIAN.)

GORMLEITH. You are not going to break up the army?

BRIAN. There is no work for them in Ireland. They are all free to put roofs on their houses again, and turn back the wild fields to apple-gardens.

GORMLEITH. That is no work for you to put your hand to! I came here to see you make your name the greatest in the world—the greatest that ever was in the world.

BRIAN. I thought to do that once, but age has come upon me. I am satisfied to do the wide, lasting works of age.

GORMLEITH. We of the high race need never give in to age! Our fathers mated with the gods, and took immortal wives! Do not give in to it, Brian; age is ugly and miserable, withering the hand that has given up the sword! Come out looking for strong men holding walled islands—islands with strange laughing armies—armies of tall, unconquered men. (BRIAN *shakes his head, and puts her from him.*) Bring out, then, the Cross you boast of! Carry it to the gardens of the east of the world! Strike at the people of the old gods. Try its strength against those you call the false gods. I will go with you. I will be obedient to you—my pride will be in you—do not keep me in the narrow roads!

BRIAN (*taking her hand from his arm, and touching her hair with his other hand*). Have I and time not quieted this whirling heart? Make yourself ready for the feast by-and-by; put on your silks and your jewels; your eyes are shining—you will shine out at the feast.

(GORMLEITH *lets him go, and turns away. He goes out.* MAIRE *comes back and lays ring on table.*)

GORMLEITH. I tried to waken him, but he is in his sleep. The sleep of age has come upon him. I have done with Kincora! The people of Ireland have surely lost their wits.—My brother carrying wood! Brian breaking up his army, building churches and bell-towers, sending his ships searching for books and parchments! You, Maire, leaving the feasts and the songs, and the troops of fighting-men, to go wandering like a strayed heifer, hurrying from road to road, through the whole country—wasting your young days in foolishness.

MAIRE. The king praised me for bringing news of peace. I am well satisfied to have made the journey for King Brian.

GORMLEITH. Satisfied! It is a strange thing to get satisfaction from a journey like that. When I was your age I would have thought it a shameful journey to have made! I would have thought it a poor, and a weak, and a shameful country that I could ride through without leaving fire in the hearts of those that met me, and red steel in their hands, and the seed of a war in every province.

MAIRE. O Queen, that is a terrible thing to say!

GORMLEITH. The heart is gone out from the young men of Ireland, and the blood from their bodies, and the daring from their lips, with their talk of peace and of learning. There is no praise now but for foolish messengers, and for monks and for saints—old, white-haired saints, with psalms and with fasting. I am sick of this country of bells and churches—little walled-in churches. My churches are the hill-tops, blazing at the coming of the sun, the plains flaming with fire through the night-time. I am for the gods that head great armies! (SITRIC *and* MAELMORA *come in.*) Go, girl, and serve the King of Leinster's woodcutters, as is the fashion! Take down the spears that are rusting in the racks! Put up the saws and the hatchets in their places! (MAIRE *goes out frightened.*) Are you back again, Maelmora? Why are you not splitting wood with the kitchen clowns?

MAELMORA. This is a good welcome I am getting in Kincora. Insults from you, and insults from Murrough.

GORMLEITH. What did you do to anger your master's son?

SITRIC. He was watching Murrough at the chess, and he gave an

344

advice, and Murrough took it, and lost the game, and that angered him.

MAELMORA. I would not stop to listen to what he said. He had no right to say words of insult.

GORMLEITH. No wonder he said them. Age is coming on you— age and sleep, and a coward's heart. It is certain you and Ireland were never under bonds till now.

SITRIC. I think you will sign these letters now, Queen, that you would not sign a while ago.

GORMLEITH. Give them here to me! I will put my name to them. (*Takes letters.*)

MAELMORA. What is it you are doing, Gormleith?

GORMLEITH. I will tell you that. I am breaking away from Brian. I am breaking Brian's peace.

MAELMORA. You would not do that—you, his wife!

GORMLEITH. It was to a great fighting man I came as a wife— not to a builder of bell-towers and altars.

SITRIC. Here is the pen.

GORMLEITH. No, no; I cannot sign. Brian is the bravest of the men I came to. A while ago, when I saw him here with Malachi— Malachi, that is to him as clay to crystal—I thought to waken him; to save him from sleep; to keep the armies; to give him the head-ship of the world. I might do it yet—

SITRIC. Sign the letters; there is no time to lose.

MAELMORA. This is treachery. I will go and call to Brian!

GORMLEITH. Call him if you will. He will not forgive us. Does it matter? Death is an easy thing.

SITRIC (*taking up ring*). Are you, too, bound in this ring of peace?

GORMLEITH. That ring! I was forgetting it! I will sign the letters—and here. (*Signs the letters.* SITRIC *takes them up.*) Brian is old! All the people of Kincora are old, or rusting, or in their sleep. Let them make much of the linnet in the cage; the hawk will leave them for the free air! I will not stay in this place of saints and of traders. (*She gets up.*)

MAELMORA. Where are you going?

GORMLEITH. I am going to Clontarf, to give my help to the armies of the Gall that are on the sea now, coming to Ireland!

MAELMORA. You will not do that! I will hold you here! I will never let my sister be a traitor in the King's house!

GORMLEITH. Be a king, Maelmora, and no man's servant! You, yourself, and Sitric would keep Ireland against the whole world.

345

(MAELMORA *breaks away*.) Go, then, and humble yourself before Brian, and before his son—let the son of the Connacht woman put loads on your son.

(MURROUGH *comes in*. SITRIC *goes quickly out, hiding the letters*.)

MURROUGH. Are you giving advice to the Queen, Maelmora, as you gave it to me a while ago? I am ashamed that you vexed me then, but she seems twenty time more vexed.

MAELMORA. It is the Queen that is giving advice to me—it may be better for you if I do not take it.

MURROUGH. I have no skill in riddles—but if there is some threat in your voice, I will answer it.

MAELMORA. Take care what you say. Your father's name will not save you, as it did when you spoke a while ago.

GORMLEITH (*to* MURROUGH). What was it you said?

MURROUGH. I said the King of Leinster was well able to give advice. I said it was good advice he gave his comrades, the Danes, the day they ran from us like scared sheep at Glenmama!

MAELMORA (*to* MURROUGH). It may happen to us yet to meet in another battle, where it is not my men, but your own men that will run like scared sheep!

MURROUGH. When that battle is coming, King, see there is a good yew tree near the battlefield, where you can hide yourself while your army is running, as you hid yourself at Glenmama!

MAELMORA (*half drawing sword*). I will not shed blood here— my answer will be in the battle.

MURROUGH. That battle will not be sooner than I wish it!

MAELMORA. It will be sooner than you think! I am going to it now. (*He goes towards door*.)

MURROUGH. That is great news! But it is not true. Our enemies only plot and plan now; they do not come into open fight.

MAELMORA. You cannot say that again. They are coming out now into open fight.

MURROUGH. From their hiding-places? No, they will be afraid.

MAELMORA. Those that are coming against you now will not run from you! The great armies of the Gall are coming against you this time. They will sweep you and your house out of Ireland before them! They are on the sea now, coming to Clontarf!

MURROUGH. That is idle talk. They would have a rough landing. Sitric would bring his men from Ath Cliath—Sitric! He has gone out! Brian should have struck the head off that sullen Dane.

GORMLEITH. Sitric is young; he has not lost his courage with age, or with idleness. His heart is the highest—he will master you; he will master Ireland! It is to help him I have called in the Gall. The old have had their time; it is for you and Sitric now to play the game.

MAELMORA. This is no place for us now. It is time for us to be gone.

(*Turns to door, and holds out his hand to* GORMLEITH.)

MURROUGH (*darwing his sword, and putting his arm across door*). Treachery! Treachery to the King! Here to me, friends of the King!

GORMLEITH. There is no need of your sword. I would not leave this house secretly.

(BRIAN, MALACHI *and servants come in.*)

BRIAN. What is this cry of treachery in my house?

MURROUGH. The armies of the Gall are on their way to Ireland. There are rebels to welcome them. Sitric is rising up against you. It is from your own house the word has been sent.

BRIAN. I would take no man's word for that.

MURROUGH. The traitors are here, before you.

BRIAN (*to* MAELMORA). Have you taken part in this treachery? (MAELMORA *is silent.*)

MURROUGH. Maelmora is in it—but—this is a hard thing for you to hear. It is your own wife that has stirred it up.

BRIAN. Let me hear no word of wife or kindred. You are speaking to the High King of Ireland.

MURROUGH. Give them the wages of their work. My work is to make ready to meet the Dane. (*He goes out.*)

BRIAN. Queen Gormleith, you hear what he has said. Give your answer.

GORMLEITH. What have I to say? Murrough has said it.

BRIAN. It is not true. You are trying to screen Sitric—

GORMLEITH. What Murrough has told you is true. Is it all my fault? You could have stopped me—I bade you go out and conquer the world. You would not—you have listened to the monks too long for that—it was a pity. Here, you may save your peace yet; the armies may be turned back. I hold out my hands to you—I bid you bind them; call for your men—let them bind me and put me to death!

BRIAN. Go! I do not make war upon women, but upon armies.

GORMLEITH. You do not understand—there are great hosts coming, the hosts of the Black Lochlannachs and of the White Lochlannachs, the men of Leodus and of Skye, and the trading men

347

of the Bretons, and a thousand of the best fighters of the Black Danes—they look to me to welcome them—they may turn back if I am not there—

BRIAN. It is folly to think your life or death could change the course of such a host!

MALACHI. Great God of heaven! Ireland has never faced such a danger!

GORMLEITH. Listen to him, Brian! He will tell you how to deal with me.

MALACHI. King, take her at her word; put her to death. I no longer speak in anger. I do not know who this woman is, whether she is of mortal birth, or outside the race of men—but this I do know, that while she is living there can be no peace in the world.

(BRIAN *points to the door.*)

GORMLEITH. If it is some affection for me that keeps you from taking my life, put it out of your heart. You will not take me at my word, High King? I will tell you all the truth. Brodar, of Mananaan's Island, would not come against you unless I promised him my love, and I promised it. Sigurd, Earl of Orkney, asked the same promise, and I gave it (*laughs*). I will not stay and die. I will go out to meet them. I would not for the wealth of the world miss being there when Brodar finds out—when Sigurd finds out—that I have promised myself to each of them. Ah! how their eyes will glitter! How their hands will clutch at the sword hilt. (*Puts hand on his shoulder.*) King, am I not a right wife to show mercy to! A right wife! Yet it is for me men break the peace of the world. (*He turns away.*) You were asleep; I tried to waken you. You chose to stay in your sleep. (*She goes to door; signs to* MAELMORA *to go out.*) You have chosen it, King. You have chosen it; not I, not I. It is you have chosen it. (*She goes out, and her voice is heard in a shriek.*) He has chosen it! He has chosen it!

BRIAN. It is I myself have betrayed my people. The blame is on me. (*He half kneels at table, covering his face with his hands.*) War, war, keening and treachery. Ireland red again. Red and stained through and through. Blood! blood! and war!

MALACHI. Have your orders ready for the army, Brian.

BRIAN. Is all ready for the Queen's journey? Give her the horses from Iar Connacht—

MALACHI. Listen to what I say. We must send messengers.

BRIAN. The speckled horses—she liked them best; and the carved chariot from the north.

MALACHI. Listen, Brian. (*Puts his hand on* BRIAN'S *shoulder.*)

348

BRIAN. But who was it—who was it that called in the Gall?

MALACHI. I cannot rouse him. No wonder. That treachery was too hard a blow.

(MURROUGH *comes in with standard in hand, and stands on threshold. Spears and banners appear at window. War march is played.*)

BRIAN. But what did she mean? What did Aoibhell of the Sidhe mean? She promised me lasting peace—lasting peace—lasting peace. She told it to me in my dream. (*He gets up, and walks up and down.*) What did she mean? Is there no truth? Is everyone treacherous? (*He comes face to face with* MURROUGH, *and stands still.*)

MURROUGH. The army is ready. We must lead it to Clontarf.

BRIAN (*standing very strong and straight.*) Clontarf! Now I know what Aoibhell meant! She said it was at Clontarf I should find peace. That is well. My place is ready in the long procession. Cathal, son of Aedh; Corc, son of Anluan; Lorcan, son of Luchta; Mahon, son of Cennedigh; all the race of Lugaidh reigned in this place, and went out of this door for the last time, and the traitors that betrayed them, and the women they loved. Give me my sword. (MALACHI *takes it down and gives it to him.*) It has another battle to win.

Scene II

SCENE: *A wood at Clontarf.* GORMLEITH, BRODAR, SITRIC, *and another Dane crossing to right as if in retreat.*

SITRIC. Come this way, Brodar. We must put courage into the men of Ath Cliath! The men of Connacht have driven them back from the ridge.

BRODAR. The heart has gone out of them since Maelmora was killed.

DANE. Murrough and his Dalcassians are close upon us. We cannot face them till we get the help of what are left of our own men.

SITRIC. Come, Queen, and call to the men of Leinster. It is for you to take Maelmora's place.

GORMLEITH. I will stay while I have a spear left to cast at some foolhardy enemy that is breaking through the wood. Go to his heart, swift messenger, beak of eagle, teeth of wolf. (*Throws a spear.*) Search out his secrets! Let out his rage! Sure love-token, bring him to my feet. (*Throws another.*) Darken his eyes! Whiten his face! Redden the grass!

BRODAR. Come on to our men. We may save the day yet.

SITRIC. The Danes will not fail us. They will gather to us. We will sweep away Murrough and his men.

GORMLEITH (*throwing another spear*). My grief! that is the last of my spears. Go, good messenger, do my bidding.

(*They go out. Enter* MURROUGH. *He staggers and sinks on one knee.*)

MURROUGH. Ah! these wounds! I did not know they had gone so deep! Come to me, men of Kincora! Have I outrun you all?

(*Sinks down, with head on elbow, and lies quiet for a moment.* AOIBHELL *appears.*)

AOIBHELL. I am come to your help, Murrough, son of Brian. I will give you healing from the well of healing that is in the hidden places of the Sidhe.

MURROUGH (*looks up*). Who is there? Who is speaking? Is that another of the enemies of the King?

AOIBHELL. No enemy, Murrough, but a friend to you and to your race. I am Aoibhell of the Grey Rock. It is long I have watched over Kincora. I have watched over you. I have come to befriend you.

MURROUGH. Call to my men. They will help me. I must get on to the battle. I must drive the Gall to the sea—into the sea. Brodar must not escape me. Brodar and his mate—(*Struggles to rise, but groans and falls again.*)

AOIBHELL. Quit the battle at my asking, Murrough, son of Brian, or your proud blood will be on the ground before tomorrow.

MURROUGH. I will not do that, Aoibhell of the Grey Rock; and I will tell you a little true story, that fear for my own life will never make me turn my face. And if I fall, the Gall will fall with me; and many a man will fall by my own hand, and their strong places will be divided by the Gael.

AOIBHELL. I, who know hidden things, know you must fall this day unless you come with me now to the happy country of all delight. And, indeed, Murrough, it is soon for you to die; and it is little time you have had for joy or for pleasure; your young youth worn away between the hard will of these great ones, the stirrings and strivings of the war-woman and the statecraft of the man of peace. Come with me now, and I will show you joys you have never known. I will give you the never-ending, never-lessening life.

MURROUGH. It is often before now I was offered that life and these gifts, in the hills and in houses of the Sidhe; but I never gave up for one night my country or my inheritance for them.

AOIBHELL. No wasting will come upon you. Sweet music, playing and drinking, beauty, riches, love and power; they are waiting for you in the Country of the Young.

MURROUGH. No wasting; no weakness; no withering of strength. There is weakness coming on me now.

AOIBHELL. You have had so little. Do not lose all for the sake of one hour; of a few blows in the battle.

MURROUGH. A few blows in the battle—a few blows (*rousing himself*); a few blows upon the enemies of Ireland! Ah! that is life. That is the life I want! Not the sluggish life; the feasting and the drinking; the love of soft hands and yellow hair; the sleepy songs and the pillows. (*Struggles to his knees, and holds up hilt of his sword.*) That is not the peace Brian fought for! That is not a life for a Christianed man! Go out! go out from me, tempter!

(AOIBHELL *disappears. Enter* BRENNAIN *and* RURY.)

BRENNAIN. The Dalcassians are at the edge of the wood. They have put down the Leinster men. The Danes are running to the sea like cattle in the heats of summer.

RURY. You would never think them to be fighting-men in the sharp wind of the Day of the Crucifixion.

BRENNAIN. The King sent word of you. Oh! you are wounded. (*Kneels and looks at wounds.*)

MURROUGH. Bind up the wounds. I must go to battle. A demon has been here in this place tempting me. Out with them! Out with them! It is time to have done with those witches of the air; some stirring up by their mischief the wars that should be the scourge of God; some calling us to the sluggish beds and the drinking-house! Out with you! Out with you all! (*Raises himself with* BRENNAIN's *help.*) And if I must die this day, I have not had my fill of fighting; and I pray God and St. Michael I may cast my spear yet at your vain whirling hosts from the ranks of the angels! (*A wail heard from where* AOIBHELL *has disappeared.*) Out with all heathen things in the world or out of it! Out I say, out I say with every heathen thing! (*Rushes out.*)

Scene III

SCENE: *Before* BRIAN's *tent.* BRIAN, BRENNAIN *and* MAIRE.

BRIAN (*coming out of tent*). Have the Danes made any stand, or are they still making for the sea?

BRENNAIN. There are none standing, unless those that have

reached the sea. They must stand, for the tide has taken their ships from them.

BRIAN. Is Malachi safe?

BRENNAIN. Safe and well. He has a strong ditch between him and the Gall. There is no fear for Malachi. He will outlast the battle.

BRIAN. He will outlast us all. That was in the prophecy. He will outlast us all.

BRENNAIN. O'Hynes and the men of Connacht are doing great deeds. There are no traitors among us but the men of Meath.

BRIAN. Can you see Murrough's banner?

MAIRE. I see it well. It has gone through the battle westward. It is standing yet; but the armies of the Danes, where it passed, are like a wood struck by the storm.

BRIAN. I think I see it. They are giving way before him on every side. The victory is won. The battle is won. Peace at last! I leave the sod of Ireland free of the Gall.

MAIRE. I will go with this milk to the wounded men. (*Exit.*)

BRIAN. Go, Brennain, and call to Murrough. Bid him to come back to me, now his work is done. I would speak with him again. I thought this day would have parted us; but it has been shown to me that we two will sleep in the one bed to-night. (BRENNAIN *goes out.*) I will give thanks to God. *Laus Deus.* (*He raises curtain of tent and goes in, letting it fall behind him. His voice heard repeating Latin psalm.*)

(*Enter* BRODAR *and a Dane.*)

DANE (*looking back*). Run, Brodar, run. The men of Connacht are close upon us. Let us get to the shelter of the wood.

BRODAR (*turning back as he goes*). There is some priest in this tent praying against us. I will silence him. (*Goes into tent. Comes out, wiping sword on curtain of tent.*) These priests that war with words must be answered with steel.

DANE. We have outrun the Queen.

BRODAR. She had best not wait for her son's burying. (*Enter* GORMLEITH.) Faster, Queen. There will be little mercy for you this time, if you are taken to Kincora.

GORMLEITH. Who is there?

BRODAR. Some prating bishop. I have made an end of his mutterings.

GORMLEITH. It is Brian's shield. (*Looks in.*) Oh! it is the king. You have killed King Brian.

DANE. That was a good chance. It makes up for great losses. (*Shouts heard.*)

BRODAR. They are gaining on us. Come, Queen.

GORMLEITH (*going into tent*). I will not leave him like that. (*Turns back.*) No! No! No traitor's hand must touch him. Brodar, you were his enemy, but you were not a traitor. Lay him straight. Set his feet together, as befits a king.

(BRODAR *and* DANE *go in, and come out, drawing back curtain.* BRIAN *is seen laid out on a bed.*)

GORMLEITH. You gave me a great bride-gift, Brian. Have I not given you a great gift for it? I have brought to every man I came to war and stirring of blood, but I brought this best gift to you. I did not leave you to die as a beast dies, sick and dumb in the darkness. I gave you the death of the great men in the high sounds of a battle.

(*Shouts heard nearer.*)

BRODAR (*seizing her*). Come! come! They are overtaking us.

GORMLEITH. Oh! I will come; I will come. From this time out I must go from country to country, driven by rough winds over rough seas; driven from place to place, with beaten men. (*They drag her away; she turns as she goes out.*) My thousand farewells to you, Brian of the victories!

(*As they go, a sound of keening is heard. Enter* MAIRE, BREN-NAIN, *and* DERRICK, *carrying* MURROUGH'S *shield and banner.*)

MAIRE. Oh! who is to tell King Brian that Murrough is cut down—the blossomed branch!

BRENNAIN. My grief! Whoever tells him that will have killed his peace forever.

(MAIRE *goes to tent; looks in; turns to them, crossing her hands on her breast.*)

MAIRE. Give great praise to God. The lasting peace of Brian is unbroken.

Curtain.

APPENDIX II: THE OLD WOMAN REMEMBERS

APPENDIX II: THE OLD WOMAN REMEMBERS

(Performed at the Abbey Theatre by Sara Allgood on 31 December 1923 and published in *The Irish Statesman*, 22 March 1924.)

An old woman is sitting in an almost dark room. She has placed seven candlesticks on the table. At the end of the first verse she lights a candle and puts it in a candlestick, and after that lights each one from the candle last lighted. She sits by the table and speaks to herself:

Seven hundred and a half of years
   Are gone since Strongbow took the sway,
Put Ireland under grief and tears,
   A ball struck here and there at play.
When the white cities turned to flames
   Who lived to hear the Masses said?
Now on the beads I'll tell out names,
   And light a candle for the dead.

When John mocked in his jibing youth
   Men had big names e'er he was born;
Laid on hard burdens, breaking truth,
   Donall O'Brien blew the horn.
It's Munster held the flail that day;
   The scattered scoffers ran for life;
They found that no great year for play,
   Eleven hundred eight-five.

(*She lights a candle.*)

Rebel and King, a Connacht lad
   Stood in the gap at Athenry;
Phelim O'Connor, proud and glad
   To shout the Connacht battle cry;
But in the losing fight he went
   The hard high way that rebels go;
And so his score of years was spent
   Five and six hundred years ago.

357

(*She lights a second candle.*)

When Art MacMurrough joined the rout
    And faced the King of England's sword
The cards were shuffled and showed out
    The trumps upon the Leinster board;
For Richard's credit ran to naught,
    His fortune's fatness ran to lean;
But Art MacMurrough reigned and fought
    Till fourteen hundred seventeen.

(*She lights the third candle.*)

O'Neill took Ulster in his hand
    In fifteen hundred fifty-one;
He'd have no meddlers on his land
    He kept their armies on the run;
Beat Sussex on the open plain—
    It's little but the Gael were free—
It was no man that put down Shane
    But Scottish treachery and the sea.

(*She lights the fourth candle.*)

Five hundred blessings on your head
    And blessings on the earth you trod,
It's well you earned the prayers are said,
    Sarsfield, that was a man with God.
When King and broken Treaty lied
    You brought your Wild Geese through the sea,
And out in foreign, conquering, died
    In sixteen hundred ninety-three.

(*She lights the fifth candle.*)

With five and five score years gone by
    Tone and Lord Edward struck the ball—
My grief such hurlers had to die
    And leave the goal to the Gall!
So each new age breaks each new hope,
    And so in eighteen-hundred-three,
Another twisting of the rope
    Set Robert Emmet's spirit free.

(*She lights the sixth candle.*)

In Easter Week the wisp was lit
    Waked Dublin from her drowsy years;
I mean the battle-anger; yet
    What did we ever win by tears?
The ballad singers long have cried
    The shining names of far away;
Now let them rhyme out those that died
    With the three colours, yesterday.

Aye and to-day.[1] That quick quenched flame,
    Thin rushlight in the dipper's hand,
Burnt out before his fullness came,
    His name a Saint's, with Saints to stand.
Or him the skillet and the mould
    Had rounded right to Nature's plan;
Terence, who waned, while moons grown old
    Thrice gazed on an unconquered man.

(*She lights the seventh candle.*)

(*Having lighted the seventh candle she stands up.*)

This is our rosary of praise
    For some whose names are sung or said
Through seven hundred years of days
    The silver beads upon the thread . . . .

(*She goes to the window as if startled and listens for a
moment, then comes back and stands beside the table.*)

My grief if ever they have heard
    The keen on every countryside
In our dark winter, or got word
    How brother by his brother died!

But[2] who forgives shall be forgiven.
    It's likely in the Shining land
Before that[3] company in Heaven
    From Cathal's hand and Michael's hand[4]

---

[1] And later yet .   [2] Yet . . .
[3] When near the . . .   [4] The wondering shadow-armies stand.

> The barren shadow-weapons fall,
>   The bitter battle-angers cease;
> And so God give to them and all
>   The blessing of His lasting peace!

I was staying at Kilteragh for a meeting of the Carnegie Committee on the 9th of July 1921 when the truce was proclaimed, and I wrote next day that "bonfires lighted on the hills for the peace were still blazing in the early morning". And that as I went through Dublin to the Broadstone though the English soldiers were still rattling their armoured cars through the streets, they were not carrying guns, and I wrote also that on the long journey to Galway the carriage was crowded and I was not in a mood for reading "and an old idea came to mind of making a poem about the rebellions from century to century, an old woman lighting a candle for the leader of each". And so in my corner I made a beginning, scribbling on the margin of the *New Republic* and on the back of a letter. But the first verse I wrote was not of a fighter of long ago, but of one who had worked with me in the Abbey Theatre for a while when our Company was in America and I was putting on some plays in their absence with what help I could find; for I had been grateful for his beautiful and distinguished work especially in the tragedy of *Kincora* and the comedy of *The Lord Mayor*. But that verse was not used in the end, for it did not seem fitting to give one name only among those who had lost their lives in those tragic Easter days. I had forgotten how the lines went, but have just now, in correcting the proofs, come across this scribbled half sheet:

> O branch that withered without age!
> Would we could see you where you're missed
> Step airy on the Abbey stage
> Play there The Revolutionist—
> Or fill with laughter pit and stalls
> With Bartley Fallon's croak and cry—
> What led you to those castle walls?
> We mourn you, Sean Connolly.

For as I was told he had been the first killed in the attack on Dublin Castle in that Rising of 1916. Terence MacSwiney's name is remembered even in England by the long hunger-strike he endured before his death in London. And that "quick-quenched flame" Kevin Barry, a lad of eighteen taken in an attack upon an armoured force in Dublin in 1920, was hanged in Mountjoy gaol.

Because of his youth and of rumours of his ill-treatment in prison and refusal to betray his friends, his name, that of the Saint who founded the Monastery at Glendalough, has been kept in memory through the country, even the Wrenboys at Christmas time putting it in their songs.

A.G.

The variant lines are from a version published in "Lady Gregory: A Literary Portrait" by Elizabeth Coxhead.

In yet another typescript dated September 4, 1921 (with the letters to Sally Allgood now in the possession of the Sligo County Library), there are a number of differences in the stage directions and in the ending. The sixteen lines given in the *Irish Statesman* are replaced by "The Binding".

> This is our Rosary of praise;
> God make us worthy all our days
> Of those who gave up life and ease
> To win us a long day of peace!